Debussy and the theatre

Debussy in June 1913 between the composition of *Jeux* and *La boîte à joujoux*. Charcoal
drawing by Ivan Thièle (Tretiakov Museum, Moscow)

Debussy and the theatre

ROBERT ORLEDGE

Cambridge University Press
Cambridge
London   New York   New Rochelle
Melbourne   Sydney

Published by the Press Syndicate of the University of Cambridge
The Pitt Building, Trumpington Street, Cambridge CB2 1RP
32 East 57th Street, New York, NY 10022, USA
296 Beaconsfield Parade, Middle Park, Melbourne 3206, Australia

First published 1982

Printed in Great Britain at the University Press, Cambridge

Library of Congress catalogue card number: 82-1348

British Library Cataloguing in Publication Data
Orledge, Robert
Debussy and the theatre.
1. Debussy, Claude – Dramaturgy
I. Title
780'.92'4   ML410.D28

ISBN 0 521 22807 7

Contents

Contents

List of illustrations

Preface

As its title suggests, the present study aims to give as full and varied a picture of Debussy's theatrical experiences as possible; it examines Debussy both as an uncompromising composer for the stage, trying to create works of the highest calibre which would survive the harshest treatment in rehearsal, performance and revival, and as a man of the theatre, responding to the multifarious characters and situations of its evanescent yet compulsive world. The story of this love–hate relationship is told, as far as it can be, in the composer's own words or from contemporary documents. Accounts of Debussy reacting to events in the theatre thus take precedence over such things as critical reviews of *Pelléas et Mélisande* or the popularity and frequency of its global revivals, because these relate to Debussy only at second-hand. Detailed formal analyses and complex manuscript studies make tedious reading and are indulged in only where they are of particular dramatic relevance. Much is made of what has been called Debussy's 'compulsive inachievement' (Holloway, p. 233), and reasons and excuses are assembled gradually chapter by chapter as to why he contemplated so many theatrical projects yet completed so few (and it should be remembered that in his view no two dramatic works were even remotely comparable). Finally, the reasons are separated from the excuses in Part V, which also attempts to place Debussy in a wider theatrical perspective.

Pelléas et Mélisande, as the turning-point in Debussy's career, naturally receives a substantial chapter; the climate in which it was created and Debussy's contemporary attitudes are explored in detail. Works are considered chronologically by genre, except in Chapter 6 where it is profitable to discuss Debussy's relationship with Diaghilev as a whole before dealing with *Jeux*, the only new ballet composed for the Russian company. Thus *Masques et bergamasques* is included here and not in Chapter 12, together with the *Prélude, interlude et paraphrase finale pour l'après-midi d'un faune*, which belongs generically in Chapter 11. The incomplete or unstarted projects are divided before and after the composition of *Pelléas* between Chapters 2 and 12, and

As you like it, which stretches from 1886 to 1917 in various formats — characteristically without a note of surviving music — is classed with the latter. The collaborations with René Peter and Gabriel Mourey are discussed as groups in Chapter 11.

Whilst much of the information and many of the extracts in this book can be found elsewhere, they have never before been collated in a single source. As the material has taken almost a decade to assemble and organise, it is hoped that the end result will make at least some worthwhile contribution to Debussy scholarship, even though it may reasonably be argued that a large proportion of it deals with the incomplete, the ephemeral or the non-existent. Summarised plots have been included for all important works except *Pelléas et Mélisande*, and for better or worse I have made my own English translation of almost all the original documents used. No discography is included because Margaret Cobb's excellent catalogue (1975) is available for records up to 1950. After that date it is best to consult current catalogues and select through personal preference, though one will be bound to lament the unavailability of the superb *Pelléas* recordings by Inghelbrecht and Désormière. For a fuller pictorial documentation I should like to draw readers' attention to François Lesure's *Iconographie musicale*, where Plates 58—85 comprehensively evoke the world of *Pelléas et Mélisande* and Plates 139—55 recreate at least some of the magic that once was the legendary Ballets Russes. I make no excuses for not contributing yet another life and works for the brimming bookshelves of Debussyophiles, and none for assuming a certain degree of specialist knowledge in my potential readers. Whilst only five per cent of French men and women had even *heard* of Debussy in a poll conducted by the magazine *Diapason* in 1979, I like to think that the percentage may be somewhat higher in England. Perhaps the present volume will even result in some conversions: I certainly hope so.

Robert Orledge
Liverpool, March 1981

Acknowledgments

I have received so much generous assistance from so many sources on both sides of the Atlantic during the preparation of this book that I hardly know where to begin my thanks. Indeed, one of the most impressive things about almost all the Debussy scholars whom it has been my privilege to know is the way they put their cause above personal motives in the unselfish spirit of research; I can only hope that this book meets with their approval and helps in part to repay my debt of gratitude to them. In England I think particularly of Dr Roy Howat, Dr Roger Nichols and Mr Richard Langham Smith; in France of MM. Jean-Michel Nectoux and François Lesure; and in America of Mrs Margaret G. Cobb, who has perhaps done more than anyone to further *le cas Debussy* in her own quiet way, and who kindly allowed me access to and permission to quote from her collection of autograph material.

In America too I should like to thank the staff of the Pierpont Morgan Library, New York, and especially J. Rigbie Turner. Also Elaine Dunlap and the staff at the Humanities Research Center at the University of Texas at Austin. Both libraries have sent me and allowed me to consult and quote from unpublished material in their collections. I should also like to thank for assistance of various kinds Mr James J. Fuld; Professor David Grayson; Dr Ralph Locke; Dr Marie Rolf; Dr William Weber; Professor Arthur Wenk; and the staff of the following libraries: the New England Conservatory of Music, Boston; the Music Division of the Library of Congress, Washington DC; the Houghton Library of Harvard University; the Lincoln Center for the Performing Arts in the New York Public Library; and the Los Angeles Public Library and County Law Library.

In France I should like to thank the publishing house of Durand et Cie and especially M. Guy Kaufmann and Mme Odette Vidal for making me so welcome when I consulted letters, contracts and manuscripts from the Durand archives on numerous occasions. I am also grateful for permission to quote from unpublished material in these archives and from published music by Debussy. For similar access to unpublished material in France, I should like to thank Mme Henry Goüin; M. Arthur Hoérée; M. Yves Koechlin; Mme Madeleine Li-Koechlin; Mme Gaston de Tinan; as well as the patient staff of the following libraries: the Département de la Musique of the Bibliothèque Nationale; the Paris Opéra; the Bibliothèque de l'Association des Régisseurs de Théâtre; the Archives Nationales, and the Centre de Documentation Claude Debussy at St Germain-en-Laye (now incorporated in the Département de la Musique of the Bibliothèque Nationale).

In England I should like to thank Dr Patrick Buckland; Mr H. Montgomery Hyde; Mr Michael Kettle; Mrs Doris Langley Moore; Mr Joseph Winter; and Mr Alexander Schouvaloff and the staff of the Victoria and Albert Theatre Museum for assistance with my Maud Allan problems. Also Mr Hugh Cobbe and the staffs of the British Library Music Department and the Sydney Jones Library of Liverpool University for help of various kinds; Dr Michael Talbot for help with German translation; Mr James Stammers and the Liverpool University Central Photographic Service for help with illustrations; Mr Brian Merrikin Hill for bringing the Saint-Pol-Roux project *La dame à la faulx* to my attention and for providing me with much relevant information on the subject; and Dr Michael de Cossart for invaluable advice and encouragement during the various stages of this book's preparation. I should also like to express my gratitude to Professor Hugh Macdonald and my hard-working editors Clare Davies-Jones, Rosemary Dooley and Rosemary Roberts who were responsible for my original Debussyan dreams becoming the reality of the present monograph.

Lastly, I owe an enormous debt to the University of Liverpool for granting me a sabbatical year in 1980-1 to write this book and for financial assistance from the Research and Senate Staff Travelling Expenses Funds with my research in France and America. Without this practical help and, of course, the constant support and very necessary encouragement of my head of department, Professor Basil Smallman, *Debussy and the theatre* might never have seen the light of day.

Abbreviations

General abbreviations

Cie	Compagnie
cond.	conducted by
Dos.	Dossier
facs.	facsimile
f., ff.	folio, folios
incl.	includes, including
M.	Monsieur
MS, MSS	manuscript, manuscripts
OS	orchestral score
prem.	première
R, red.	(piano) reduction
repr.	reprinted
Rés.	Reserve collection (*F-Pn, F-Po*)
rev.	revised
VS	vocal score

Other general abbreviations (including those for instrument names), used largely in the Appendix, are listed on pp. 303-4.

Bibliographical abbreviations

AMw	*Archiv für Musikwissenschaft*
CMc	*Current musicology*
FAM	*Fontes artis musicae*
Mf	*Die Musikforschung*
ML	*Music and letters*
MQ	*The musical quarterly*
MR	*The music review*
MT	*The musical times*
NZfM	*Neue Zeitschrift für Musik*
RBM	*Revue belge de musicologie*
RdM	*Revue de musicologie*
ReB	*La revue blanche*
ReM	*La revue musicale* (1920–)
SMz	*Schweizerische Musikzeitung/Revue musicale suisse*

Library sigla

CH: Switzerland
  B   Basle, private collection
  Gbodmer   Cologny-Geneva, Dr Martin Bodmer, private collection

F: France
  ASO   Asnières-sur-Oise, François Lang, private collection at the Abbaye de Royaumont (now the property of Mme Henry Goüin)
  Pan   Paris, Archives Nationales
  Pdavid   Paris, André David, private collection
  Pdurand   Paris, Archives of Durand et Cie
  Phoérée   Paris, Arthur Hoérée, private collection
  Pjobert   Paris, Mme Jobert-Georges, private collection
  Plifar   Paris, Serge Lifar, private collection
  Pmeyer   Paris, André Meyer, private collection
  Pn   Paris, Bibliothèque Nationale, Département de la Musique
  Po   Paris, Bibliothèque de l'Opéra
  Ppincherle Paris, Marc Pincherle, private collection
  Ppolignac Paris, Polignac family, private collection
  Pprunières Paris, Henry Prunières, private collection
  Ptinan   Paris, Mme Gaston de Tinan, private collection

GB: Great Britain
  Lbm   London, British Library, Reference Division (formerly British Museum)
  Lrussell   London, Sheridan Russell, private collection

US: United States of America
  AUS   Humanities Research Center, University of Texas at Austin
  Bc   Boston, New England Conservatory of Music
  NH   New Haven, Yale University, School of Music Library
  NYcobb   New York, Margaret G. Cobb, private collection
  NYhorowitz New York, Wanda Horowitz, private collection
  NYpm   New York, Pierpont Morgan Library
  R   University of Rochester, Eastman School of Music, Sibley Music Library
  STu   Stanford University, Division of Humanities and Social Sciences, Music Library
  Wc   Washington DC, Library of Congress, Music Division

Abbreviations for recurring sources

AND   Andrieux, G.: catalogue of sale (1 Dec 1933) at Hôtel Drouot, Paris, incl. the collection of Emma Debussy (MSS, pp. 34-9)

ANN   Tosi, Guy (ed.): *Debussy et d'Annunzio. Correspondance inédite* (Paris, Denoël, 1948)

BAR   Vallery-Radot, Pasteur (ed.): *Lettres de Claude Debussy à sa femme Emma* [formerly Bardac] (Paris, Flammarion, 1957)

CAP   Lockspeiser, Edward (ed.): *Lettres inédites à André Caplet (1908-1914)* (Monaco, Éditions du Rocher, 1957)

DUR   Durand, Jacques (ed.): *Lettres de Claude Debussy à son éditeur* (Paris, Durand, 1927)

GOD Jean-Aubry, Georges (ed.): *Lettres à deux amis. Soixante-dix-huit lettres inédites à Robert Godet et Georges Jean-Aubry* (Paris, Librairie José Corti, 1942)

LCat Lesure, François: *Catalogue de l'oeuvre de Claude Debussy* (Geneva, Éditions Minkoff, 1977)

LCr Lesure, François (ed.): *Monsieur Croche et autres écrits. Édition complète de son oeuvre critique* (Paris, Gallimard, 1971)

LL Lesure, François (ed.): *Claude Debussy: lettres 1884-1918* (Paris, Hermann, 1980)

LO Lockspeiser, Edward: *Debussy: his life and mind*, 2 vols. (London, Cassell, 1962, 1965; repr. Cambridge, Cambridge University Press, 1979)

LOU Borgeaud, Henri (ed.): *Correspondance de Claude Debussy et Pierre Louÿs (1893-1904)* (Paris, Librairie José Corti, 1945)

LPm Lesure, François (ed.): *Esquisses de 'Pelléas et Mélisande' (1893-1895)*, facs. with introduction by François Lesure (Geneva, Éditions Minkoff, 1977)

MES André-Messager, Jean (ed.): *L'enfance de Pelléas. Lettres de Claude Debussy à André Messager* (Paris, Dorbon-Aîné, 1938)

PET Peter, René: *Claude Debussy* (Paris, Gallimard, 1952) [rev. and expanded edn (incl. letters) of *Claude Debussy. Vues prises de son intimité* (Paris, Gallimard, 1944)]

POE Lockspeiser, Edward (ed.): *Debussy et Edgar Poe. Documents inédits* (Monaco, Éditions du Rocher, 1962)

RLS Smith, Richard Langham (ed. and trans.): *Debussy on music* (London, Secker and Warburg, 1977) [based on *Monsieur Croche et autres écrits*, ed. François Lesure (LCr above), but with extra items by Debussy and additional introductions]

SEG Joly-Segalen, Annie, and Schaeffner, André (eds.): *Segalen et Debussy* (Monaco, Éditions du Rocher, 1962)

TOU Martineau, Henri (ed.): *Correspondance de Claude Debussy et Paul-Jean Toulet* (Paris, Le Divan, 1929)

To Charles McFeeters

For a composer there is really only one route to follow to make a name for himself, and that is the theatre.

(Charles Gounod: *Mémoires d'un artiste* (Paris, Calmann Lévy, 1896), p. 175)

1   Introduction

This theatrical life repels me as much as it bewitches me.
(Debussy to Durand, 25 October 1903, during rehearsals for a
revival of *Pelléas et Mélisande*; DUR, p. 16)

During the third quarter of the nineteenth century there were no fewer than seventy-eight theatres of various types operating in Paris, nearly twice as many as in the previous two decades.[1] This corpus continued to expand and change its 'makeup' during the *fin-de-siècle* years when Debussy's career began; a career which, if not dominated by the actual production of music for the theatre, was certainly preoccupied with the artistic and commercial possibilities of this stimulating genre.

The complex causes of this state of affairs form the *raison d'être* of this book as much as does a discussion of the nature and importance of the few theatre scores Debussy managed to complete. Both beginning and finishing a work were the source of much agonising on Debussy's part; 'it is not without a certain amount of terror that I see the moment approaching when I shall positively have to write something', he admitted to Gabriele d'Annunzio in January 1911 (ANN, pp. 63-4); and sixteen years earlier he had confessed to Pierre Louÿs that the prospect of finishing *Pelléas* was 'like the death of a loved one' (LOU, p. 42). He was often filled with trepidation about his music's eventual fate at the hands of the various talents who would turn his dream into reality with varying degrees of success; the traumatic dress-rehearsal of *Pelléas* on 28 April 1902 left a scar that never properly healed. Perhaps all this is best placed in perspective by comparing the rarity of the occasions when Debussy spoke happily of the impression made by one of his dramatic compositions with the frequency of his acidulous criticisms of singers in revivals of *Pelléas*, or of the state of French opera in general.

But whatever the depth of his love–hate relationship with the theatre, Debussy, as Arnold Whittall rightly says, 'at his best, was always a dramatic composer' (p. 271). To put his dramatic music in any sort of perspective,

1

though, it is first necessary to look briefly at some aspects of French culture in the nineteenth century to see how their various developments relate to Debussy.

* * *

The manifesto, high-water-mark and death-knell of the Romantic movement can appropriately all be found in the theatre works of Victor Hugo. Although Debussy marginally preferred his plays to those of Alexandre Dumas *père*, he wisely never struggled to set Hugo's ill-suited verse to music as Fauré did at the outset of his career. Hugo was as prolific a writer for the theatre as Debussy was unproductive: some might say because Debussy put quality before quantity, although the truth is that there is inferior Debussy just as there is inferior Hugo. There is simply less of it, since Debussy never subjected himself to Hugo's regular creative schedules.

Hugo's Romantic manifesto can be found in the preface to *Cromwell* (1827); its plea for the 'liberty of art against the despotism of systems, codes and rules' finds direct echoes in Debussy telling Ernest Guiraud around 1890 that 'There is no theory . . . Pleasure is the law.' (LO, 1, p. 207) Hugo's views on the drama being a true representation of life are paralleled by Debussy's characters in *Pelléas et Mélisande* who 'try to sing like real people' (LCr, p. 62), and his views on beauty in art and critical objectivity would probably have found some favour with Debussy's *alter ego*, Monsieur Croche. René Peter tells us (PET, p. 131) that Debussy was not 'Romantic' in the sense of being extrovert and given to effusive speech, but he nonetheless found much of his inspiration in Nature as the Romantics did, and was a man of extreme sensitivity inclined to introspective melancholy and neurasthenia: Hamlet, a key figure for the Romantic movement, was a character with whom he often identified.

This is not to say that the Classical virtues of reason, clarity and good taste were not central to the aesthetic of 'Claude de France', as d'Annunzio christened Debussy, and in later life especially he saw himself as part of the French tradition, even to the extent of a little wartime chauvinism. To my mind the Classical and Romantic elements in Debussy's artistic makeup have almost as much bearing on his art as the Symbolist or Impressionist movements with which he is more readily associated. By his own admission he was, in the orchestral *Images*, 'attempting something different – in a sense *realities* . . . what idiots call "impressionism", a term which is as misused as it can possibly be' (DUR, p. 58). And the Symbolist case, that Debussy evoked rather than depicted, has I feel been overstressed, though there can be no doubt that he derived more inspiration from this literary movement than from anything connected with Impressionism.

To return to Victor Hugo: his enormous and unexpected success with *Hernani* in 1830 firmly established the Romantic movement through the theatre as a force to be reckoned with. And whilst René Peter considered 25 February 1830 to be as decisive a high-water-mark in dramatic history as the première of *Pelléas* in April 1902 (PET, p. 180), he elsewhere doubted (p. 131) whether Debussy would have been amongst those shouting for *Hernani* had he been alive at the time. In other words, Debussy was a far more retiring revolutionary than Berlioz, though both stormed the same artistic barricades of French operatic tradition and the pervasive academic influence of the Paris Conservatoire, whose coveted Prix de Rome ironically launched both their careers.

Debussy, René Peter tells us, respected the 'more elegant aspects' of Hugo's style, even if he found it rather showy and pompous overall. This would surely have been his opinion of Hugo's epic drama *Les burgraves*, whose failure in 1843 tolled the death-knell both of his theatrical career and of the Romantic movement as a whole. The latter was extinguished by the 1848 Revolution, actively supported by Baudelaire, and the political involvement of artists at this time can be seen both in the proclamation of the short-lived Second Republic that year by the poet Alphonse de Lamartine, and in the self-imposed exile of Hugo in the Channel Islands for the duration of the Second Empire (1852-70) after the *coup d'état* of the Prince-President Louis-Napoléon on 2 December 1851, whom Hugo had so vitriolically attacked in the national press. This political involvement by artists largely disappeared in the second half of the nineteenth century (and Debussy was typical of this trend), but the widening gap between the serious artist and the general public made life for the former increasingly difficult.

A particular thorn in the flesh, which affected Debussy with *Pelléas et Mélisande*, was official censorship of the press and theatre. An act of May 1819 prohibited the publication of books that constituted an 'outrage to public and religious morality', and under this both Flaubert and Baudelaire were brought ignominiously to trial in 1857, for *Madame Bovary* and *Les fleurs du mal* respectively. Debussy's future librettist, Catulle Mendès, was even sentenced to a month's imprisonment in July 1861 at the age of nineteen for publishing in his own *Revue fantaisiste* 'Le roman d'une nuit', a mildly bawdy verse narrative of a carnival night, which would have been better dismissed as an expression of youthful high spirits.

In the case of theatrical censorship, which had in the past plagued such classics as Molière's *Tartuffe* and Beaumarchais's *Le mariage de Figaro*, the dream of a socialist utopia in 1848 brought with it a temporary relaxation of official scrutiny. However, this new-found freedom was deemed unwise, and reactionaries such as Eugène Scribe, the veteran producer of opera librettos, whose 'well-made play' exerted a major influence in the second quarter of the nineteenth century, and the seasoned critic Jules Janin, actually wrote in favour of a return to the old censorship system, which was reinstated on 1 August 1850. One of the first to suffer was Alfred de Musset, whose play

Le chandelier was enjoying a revival at the Théâtre Français. Less lyrical and original dramatists in the Scribe tradition, like Émile Augier, also suffered, as did the leading dramatist of the Second Empire, Alexandre Dumas *fils*. Indeed, his difficulties in getting *La dame aux camélias* (1852) past the censors have become almost legendary, and Verdi and Piave who converted the play into *La traviata* the following year were no strangers to censorship battles either.

One happy result of all this, however, was the stimulation of private theatrical performances, and a direct descendant of the tradition that prompted Dumas's *Le verrou* for Jules de Castellane in 1856 can be seen in the *fin-de-siècle* entertainments of Madeleine Lemaire and the Comtesse Greffulhe with music by Fauré and others, and in the 'aesthetic pantomime' *Le chevalier d'or*, which Debussy planned in 1897 with the wife of the artist Jean-Louis Forain.

The second half of the century saw a move in the theatre away from the grandiose passionate dramas of the Romantics towards more intimate and compact plays which attempted to assess the effects of passion on the individual or on a small group of characters. They often included praise of domestic virtues, attacks on materialism, or pleas for social reform. Again examples are plentiful in the works of Dumas *fils*: *La question d'argent* (1857), or the *pièce à thèse*, *Les idées de Mme Aubray* (1867). But the predilection of the cosmopolitan Second Empire was for the novels of Ernest Feydeau, whose son Georges's powers of comic observation Debussy admired (PET, p. 147, n. 1), and for the frothy, inconsequential and witty *opéras bouffes* of Offenbach, whom Debussy in 1916 considered 'amusing because of the way in which he played around with his text, the music remaining willingly in the background' (LCr, p. 262). Like Victor Hugo, Offenbach was a 'workoholic', who died 'with a tune on the tip of his pen' as he had predicted.

The novel, with some influence from Gustave Courbet, provided the main vehicle for the Realist movement which succeeded Romanticism, and the concern for absolute sincerity and meticulous social observation is everywhere apparent in the works of Flaubert, the brothers Goncourt, and Balzac. The self-educated Debussy had an insatiable literary appetite and had devoured 'almost all' of Balzac and Dickens before he met René Peter in the late 1880s. He considered the story *La grande bretèche* from Balzac's *La comédie humaine* as a possible opera in 1895, and the fact that his favourite Dickens novel was *Bleak House* (PET, p. 133) is surely not unconnected with its superficial similarity to the desolate Usher residence, whose spectacular demise formed the climax of the Poe opera which obsessed Debussy's later life.

But whilst the shrewd Offenbach's newly invented operettas invariably made a handsome profit, grand opera (which was dominated during the Second Empire by the spectacular historical collaborations of Scribe and Meyerbeer) did not. Despite the continued popularity of the Romantic, Hugoesque *Robert le diable* (1831), which received its 500th performance on 1 March 1867, the vast expenses involved in mounting such lavish productions meant that the Paris Opéra had had to be a state-subsidised institution since July 1854. Hardly renowned for cultivating new talent, it virtually turned its back on Berlioz, provided the scene for one of Wagner's greatest disasters (the première of *Tannhäuser* on 13 March 1861), and gave Verdi endless nightmares with *Les vêpres siciliennes* in 1854-5 and *Don Carlos* in 1867.

Charles Garnier's palatial new opera house, inaugurated on 5 January 1875, did nothing to alter the situation. Most important new works from 1870 onwards were staged at the more progressive Opéra-Comique, from the 'realistic' *Carmen* in 1875 to Charpentier's *Louise* and, of course, *Pelléas et Mélisande*. Clearly there was nothing comic about any of these, and the distinction between 'opéra' and 'opéra comique' had disappeared by the close of the nineteenth century when the latter abandoned its traditional spoken dialogue.

In the 1880s Wagner became a cult figure in Paris, passing from one extreme to the other in popularity. Only a faithful few like Judith Gautier, Mendès, Baudelaire and Villiers de l'Isle-Adam had defended Wagner in the 1860s, and the climate following France's ignominious defeat by Germany in 1870 was hardly conducive to the spread of his musical ideas. But in 1876 the Bayreuth 'pilgrimages' began, and after Wagner's death the hostility predictably abated and numbers began to grow, including not only musicians like Debussy (who went in 1888-9) but also writers and members of high society. Curiously, the influence of Wagner on the development of French music was not particularly significant or long-lasting. Not, that is, on the surface, but Robin Holloway has demonstrated in *Debussy and Wagner* (p. 21) how, whilst 'Debussy could never be called the musical heir of Wagner . . . he must be recognised to be, within the limits of a subtle and specialised relationship, the most profoundly Wagnerian of all composers.'

A development from the Realist movement in the novel and drama, known as 'Naturalism', flourished in France between about 1865 and 1895. Both Realism and Naturalism owed much to the determinist philosophy of Hippolyte Taine which stressed the interdependence of physical and psychological factors in the formation of character, and sought to apply investigative scientific principles to art. The leader of the Naturalist movement, Émile Zola, brought precise documentation and the scientific approach to the fore, as well as specialising in the lowest and most brutal aspects of human nature. In this, he was also carrying to a logical extreme the Romantic conception of Victor Hugo that to be seen in its true perspective beauty also needs the ugly and grotesque.

Naturalism spread to the theatre in the 1880s through dramatisations of Zola and the brothers Goncourt and through the Théâtre Libre of André Antoine, which flourished intermittently between 1887 and 1896. The loosely constructed lyrical comedies of Musset had begun to liberate French drama from its Classical and Romantic conventions during the Second Empire, but it took the combined efforts of Zola, Henry Becque and the Théâtre Libre before the break with the Scribe tradition of solid construction was finally accepted by French critics. Debussy waged a similar war against rigid scholastic forms in music and must surely have been aware of the theatrical parallel.

As Samuel Waxman says (p. 64), Antoine 'stumbled into the creation of a theatre that was to revolutionise the dramatic art of France'. This came about through the recalcitrant attitudes of the organisers of the Cercle Gaulois in Montmartre, an amateur theatrical group with which Antoine (a self-educated clerk with the Paris gas company and an ex-member of the claque at the Comédie-Française) became involved in 1886. In his efforts to turn the group from their customary sentimental repertory, Antoine began to seek new works from young playwrights and by January 1887 had assembled four one-act plays, including a dramatisation of the Zola story *Jacques Damour* by Léon Hennique which had earlier been rejected by the Théâtre de l'Odéon. When the Cercle Gaulois refused Antoine permission to use both its name and its resources, he was forced to form his own company, raise money to pay for rehearsals, and find it somewhere to perform. After much procrastination, M. Krauss, the owner of the theatre where the Cercle Gaulois usually performed, allowed Antoine to rent it for one performance only at a cost of 100 francs. The name Théâtre Libre came from a suggestion by Arthur Byl, one of Antoine's less talented playwrights. Only the Zola adaptation was a success on the much publicised first night on 30 March 1887, and as a result was then requested by Paul Porel for the Odéon! As was often to be the case, Antoine made a financial loss though his acting was singled out for special praise.

Many of the Théâtre Libre's plays were of little more significance than the epithet 'slice of life' suggests, but it championed during its short career such authors as Becque, Porto-Riche, Ibsen and Strindberg. The height of its artistic success came in the 1892-3 season, contemporary with Lugné-Poë's first performance of *Pelléas et Mélisande*. Maeterlinck, however, was a dramatist whose plays Antoine never produced. The première of Ibsen's *Ghosts* had been given in 1890, and in May of that year, despite a deficit of 12,000 francs, Antoine produced a 200-page brochure setting out his vision of a new theatre. In his ideal dream everyone could see the stage rather than each other, and his theatre was designed in the modern funnel shape rather than the old circular model of Parisian theatres like the Comédie-Française. He appealed for a small, permanent and balanced repertory company in place of the 'star' system; for naturalness of delivery; for stage settings in conformity with contemporary life; and for an end to the exaggerated gestures of Romantic drama. Smaller, more significant and natural movements were to be encouraged; complex scenery was to be dispensed with; much more use was to be made of stage lighting; and the plays offered to subscribers were to be changed fortnightly regardless of their success or failure (though Antoine naturally was to choose, cast and direct them).

In putting many of these theories into practice, Antoine laid the foundations of the modern theatre. But his ideas were by no means all new; Zola himself had spoken out against wings, backdrops, artificial acting and lavish costumes. Similarly, Becque, whilst antipathetic to Zola's theories and scientific approach, nonetheless produced in 1882 a series of guide-lines for municipal officials, which read rather like a blueprint for Antoine's Théâtre Libre, though each play was to run for three weeks and the number of stage settings was to be reduced to four: a temple, a forest, a street and a drawing-room!

However, the Théâtre Libre was always a fighting theatre rather than a commercial enterprise and it began to founder seriously in 1894. In fact Antoine and his company found themselves stranded bankrupt in Rome that October on one of their 'money-making' tours. The theatre, now under the directorship of Paul Larochelle, was wound down during 1895-6 and in May 1896 Antoine was appointed co-director of the Odéon, though he quickly resigned due to disagreements with his fellow director, Paul Ginisty, who also effectively put paid to Debussy's incidental music for *Le pèlerin d'amour* in 1903 (see Chapter 12).

At the beginning of October 1897 Antoine renamed the Théâtre Menus-Plaisirs in the boulevard de Strasbourg the 'Théâtre Antoine'. In his souvenirs (1928) he vividly describes the ups and downs of his new venture, which lasted till May 1906 when he was appointed sole director of the Odéon. The climax of the Théâtre Antoine's achievements came in the 1904-5 season with his production of *King Lear*, planned initially with incidental music by Debussy. Somewhat to Antoine's surprise, *Lear* was a tremendous box-office success, though receipts were as usual absorbed by the production costs. When Antoine left for the Odéon he was replaced at the boulevard de Strasbourg site by the actor–producer Firmin Gémier, who in 1917 planned to produce *As you like it* in Toulet's translation, also with incidental music by Debussy. But the true successor to the small experimental theatres Libre and Antoine was the Vieux-Colombier, founded by Jacques Copeau, which flourished between 1913 and 1940.

The other principal artistic movement at the end of the last century, and one with which Debussy was more directly involved, was Symbolism, which began as early as the mid-1870s with Mallarmé's *L'après-midi d'un faune* and Verlaine's *Romances sans paroles* and gradually grew in influence through the 1880s in its reaction against theme, technique, and the 'exteriorisation' of the Parnassian poets such as Théophile Gautier and Leconte de Lisle. Baudelaire was an important precursor of the new movement, which soon allied itself with the prevailing Wagnerian cult. As F.W.J. Hemmings says (p. 225), 'it was above all Wagner's suggestive manipulation of mythology and allegory that appealed to the symbolist generation' who strove to transfer the properties and power of music to poetry. The publication of Maeterlinck's *Serres chaudes* in 1889 proved an important event in the acceptance of Symbolism as something more than an esoteric and vague phenomenon, and by the time of

Rimbaud's death in 1891 it had established itself as the foremost modern poetic movement.

In this year Symbolism was also transferred to the stage, through the efforts of the teenage manager of the Théâtre d'Art, Paul Fort. As Maeterlinck said about this time, 'the theatre is dying in the hands of the "vaudevillistes". It is the most backward of all the arts and the hour has come for its regeneration.' (Desonay, p. 81) To some extent the Théâtre d'Art was founded in direct opposition to Antoine's Théâtre Libre (which was then rehearsing Ibsen's *The wild duck*), but its first night fell far short of success. Fort's production of Pierre Quillard's poetic drama *La fille aux mains coupées* seems to have introduced the 'Symbolist' technique of a cast declaiming the text in slow, monotonous voices behind a muslin curtain, which subsequently plagued so many of Maeterlinck's plays. What followed was intended as a parody, but the banal naturalistic melodrama of a poor mother driven to prostitution to feed her starving children was one 'slice of life' which went down like the proverbial lattice-work canoe and acutely embarrassed Zola and Mallarmé who were in the audience.

A benefit performance for Verlaine and Gauguin at the Théâtre d'Art on 21 May 1891, however, proved more significant; not only was it the occasion of the première of Maeterlinck's *L'intruse*, but included in the company was a young actor who had initially trained with Antoine in 1888-90 and who soon became the foremost name in the Symbolist theatre, Aurélien Lugné-Poë. After a production of Maeterlinck's *Les aveugles* on 7 December 1891, the Théâtre d'Art closed. As Hemmings says (p. 239), 'Fort had given proof of enthusiasm and ingenuity but lacked experience and authority.' His experiments in Symbolist drama were carried through by Lugné-Poë, first with the Cercle des Escholiers and then with the company he founded in association with Fort, the Théâtre de l'Oeuvre. Here, between 1893 and 1929, Lugné-Poë proved himself even more of a champion of the young, the foreign and the unknown than Antoine, producing plays by Wilde, Péladan, Bjørnson, Jarry,[2] Claudel, Strindberg, and especially Ibsen whom he was really responsible for popularising in France. But the two works that contributed most significantly to the founding of the Théâtre de l'Oeuvre were both associated with Debussy: Villiers de l'Isle-Adam's *Axël* and Maeterlinck's *Pelléas et Mélisande*.

It was for a projected performance of *Axël* that Fort first invited Lugné-Poë to the Théâtre d'Art in early June 1891, where he was to play Commander Kaspar d'Auërsperg and assist with the *mise-en-scène*. But due to the eternal 'cash-flow problem', *Axël* (to be given in the 1890 edition by Mallarmé and Joris-Karl Huysmans) was postponed till September and finally abandoned after a legal battle with Rodolphe Darzens, the attorney of the heirs of Villiers de l'Isle-Adam who opposed the production. Nonetheless, Fort was still enthusiastic about *Axël* and, with financial backing from Mme Tola Dorian,[3] planned to reopen his Théâtre d'Art with it in 1893. *L'écho de Paris* of 21 January announced that the first performance would be at the end of February and the new premises, at 25 rue Turgot, soon became a Saturday meeting-place for poets like Charles Morice (later to collaborate with Debussy on *Crimen amoris*) and Camille Mauclair.

But as *Axël* went into rehearsal, some of the many current theatrical journals began to publish hostile accounts. Even Henri de Régnier, a staunch supporter of the play and its author, wrote in *Entretiens politiques et littéraires* on 10 February 1893 that 'to perform *Axël* seems to me rather like making sport with it. For does not this drama go beyond the bounds of the theatre as we know it?', and he suggested that the Théâtre d'Art abandon 'such an enterprise of untimely rashness'. As a result *L'écho de Paris* announced on 27 February that *Axël* would be replaced by the latest play of Maeterlinck, *Pelléas et Mélisande*, and the première was set for 10 March.[4] Tola Dorian claimed in *Mercure de France* that the substitution was her decision and was due to staging difficulties with *Axël*, but the idea of presenting *Pelléas et Mélisande* almost certainly came from Lugné-Poë, who finally directed it. For some reason, which remains unknown, the Théâtre d'Art never reopened its doors to the public.

Maeterlinck seems to have been suspicious of Paul Fort's plans for *Pelléas*; like Debussy he loathed rehearsals and was sceptical about any performance of his plays in the early days. But having worked with Lugné-Poë in *L'intruse* and *Les aveugles* he knew he had found an actor–director whom he could trust: whilst he never gave advice on staging or technical matters, he was extremely concerned about casting and costumes. Lugné-Poë also received much support from Camille Mauclair, a close friend of the author, who managed to extricate director and play from the Théâtre d'Art, and who also presented *Pelléas* to the public through an article (signed by Octave Mirbeau) in *L'écho de Paris* on 9 May 1893.

To find a venue for *Pelléas* Lugné-Poë first tried the Théâtre Montparnasse. Then, ironically, he approached the eventual producer of Debussy's opera, Albert Carré (then director of the Théâtre Vaudeville) who turned the play down! Finally, he managed to rent the Théâtre des Bouffes-Parisiens for a single afternoon on 17 May, and although the performance was not a great success, it proved extremely stimulating and influential for its distinguished audience.

The subscribers to the production present included Henri de Régnier, Tristan Bernard, Léon Blum, Robert de Rothschild, Jacques-Émile Blanche, Mallarmé, Whistler, the Comtesse Greffulhe and Claude Debussy, who apparently wrote to Lugné-Poë that 'he did not know the play or its author' and that 'the possibility of a musical composition had been suggested to him by [Camille] Mauclair' (Lugné-Poë, p. 229). In this connection it is interesting to consider that Maeterlinck told Jules Huret in an interview in *Le figaro* on the day of the première of *Pelléas* that 'a theatre piece should be above all a poem', and that amongst the reviews was one by Henry Céard (*L'événement*, 19 May 1893) which claimed prophetically that *Pelléas* 'resembles a fine opera scenario, but one that still awaits music; literary music and the instrumentation of words sought by the author not having the power to satisfy completely the listener's aspirations'. Otherwise the reviews were divided, as they were for Debussy's opera in 1902. Henri de Régnier (*L'art moderne*, 21 May) praised the scenery and Lugné-Poë's acting, whereas Alfred Vallette (*Mercure de France*, July 1893) thought that there were too many gestures. Others protested about the deliberate obscurity and over-frequent scene changes (eighteen in all), generally agreeing that Maeterlinck was better read than performed.

No one seemed to notice the setting of Mélisande's song in the third act (scene 2) by Gabriel Fabre. Quite rightly so, for his setting,[5] dated March 1893 in the vocal score, is repetitive and undistinguished. As Ex. 1 shows, Fabre curiously set 'Les trois soeurs aveugles', as published in the revised sixth edition (1898) onwards, and not 'Mes longs cheveux', found only in the original 1892 editions and in Debussy's score. This suggests that it was the impending stage performance that caused Maeterlinck to substitute the one for the other early in 1893, perhaps because Mélisande had already sung two lines from 'Mes longs cheveux' in Act 3 scene 1 ('Saint-Daniel et Saint-Michel/ Saint-Michel et Saint-Raphaël'). But as Debussy had already decided to cut this scene when he came to set Act 3 in 1894, the repetition was of no consequence to him and he retained Maeterlinck's original song in his opera. Fabre's three-bar phrasing in 'Les trois soeurs aveugles', which seems promisingly flexible at the outset (Ex. 1), unhappily persists unchanged until the rather murky coda (Ex. 2, bars 7-10). The material of Ex. 1 is varied only at intermediate cadences and at the end when earlier faint hints of modality are replaced with cloying sevenths (Ex. 2, bars 2-4). The awkwardness of Fabre's setting is best seen in his transition to F major (Ex. 1, bars 4-6), and in his prosody (Ex. 1, bar 10; Ex. 2, bar 4) which suggests that Maeterlinck's poem was forced to fit a preconceived melodic scheme of no great distinction. There was nothing here to influence Debussy or even give him cause for comment.

We know that Debussy owned a vellum-bound copy of the first edition of *Pelléas* because it survives in the collection of Mme Gaston de Tinan. Further evidence that he set directly from this edition is provided by its almost complete identity with the text of the opera and by Debussy's frequent reference to 'Pélléas' with the extra acute accent, which appears in the first edition only. The later, 1898, printing contains many textual emendations not found in the opera, chiefly concerning repeated words like 'oui' and 'non'. These may seem insignificant to us, but they were of primary importance to Maeterlinck in his creation of the symbolic dream-world of Allemonde. It is thus possible, de-

Ex. 1. Gabriel Fabre: *Chanson de Mélisande, F-Pn* Vm.[7] 54739 (3), bars 1-12

spite Lugné-Poë, that Debussy had read the play before he saw it produced, and that René Peter is correct when he says that Debussy bought a copy one 'evening in the magnificent summer of 1892' (PET, p. 162).[6] However, the earliest dated music for the opera comes from September 1893 which suggests that it was seeing the play that stimulated Debussy into creativity, though it was the first edition that then inspired his score.

Ex. 2. Gabriel Fabre: *Chanson de Mélisande*, *F-Pn* Vm.[7] 54739 (3), ending

Mars 1893

Pelléas et Mélisande also proved a catalyst for Lugné-Poë in that, whilst touring with it in Brussels in June 1893, he resolved to found his Théâtre de l'Oeuvre; and he made two tours of Belgium with *Pelléas* before opening his famous theatre in Paris that October. Lastly, I think few would deny that it is through Debussy's operatic setting of *Pelléas et Mélisande* that Maeterlinck is chiefly remembered today, and that its performance provided a turning-point both in Debussy's career and in the history of opera.

2 Before *Pelléas: Axël, Rodrigue et Chimène* and other early projects, including *Diane au bois*

> Why this unhealthy desire to write operas? . . . Spreading the
> dreadful misconception that it is necessary to 'write for the theatre',
> something that will never be compatible with 'writing music'.
>
> (Debussy as Monsieur Croche in *La revue blanche*
> (15 Nov 1901); LCr, p. 56)

The founding of the Société Nationale, with its motto 'Ars gallica', on 25 February 1871 did much 'to make known published or unpublished works of French composers', and can be said to have prompted a renaissance in non-operatic music in France in the last part of the nineteenth century. It assisted the careers of its founders Saint-Saëns, Fauré and d'Indy too and later served to introduce Debussy to the public with performances of *La damoiselle élue*, the String Quartet and *L'après-midi d'un faune* in 1893-4. But the production of operas still predictably continued unabated; even as great a champion of pure music as Fauré spent much of his time in these years trying to obtain a suitable opera libretto from such as Louis Gallet, Albert Samain and Verlaine (see Nectoux, 1976 and Fauré (ed. Nectoux)). Fauré even considered Catulle Mendès for a projected *Lavallière* in 1893 and Maeterlinck's *Soeur Béatrice* for an opera in 1899, and his score for *Pelléas et Mélisande* was, of course, the first to receive a public performance in 1898.

The main difference between Fauré and Debussy was the latter's ability to spot the operatic potential in *Pelléas* as it stood, and his good fortune in obtaining the author's consent to treat it as he wished. For Debussy was in reality no more motivated in theatrical terms than Fauré was, and as Jean-Michel Nectoux points out (Fauré (ed. Nectoux), p. 264), if *Pelléas et Mélisande* 'has become known to successive generations it is thanks to the dozen or so recordings from which it alone of contemporary operas has benefited'. Masterpieces like Dukas's *Ariane et Barbe-bleue*, Roussel's *Padmâvatî* or Fauré's *Pénélope* have never entered the repertoire despite their respective merits, though it must be added that none of them broke new ground in the way that *Pelléas* did, or came at so opportune a moment.

* * *

13

Axël (c1887-9)

Neither did Debussy get everything right at his first attempt. If Léon Vallas is to be believed (1958, p. 140), he set a scene from Villiers de l'Isle-Adam's *Axël*, the manuscript of which has now gone to ground in a private collection. Whether this was an operatic adaptation by Debussy or just incidental music is not known, but the choice of subject and author is crucial to Debussy's development and it is for this reason that I have elected to discuss it fully at this point.

Debussy's dramatic fragment must date from 1887-9 for it predates *Rodrigue et Chimène* and the revised play had only recently appeared in *La jeune France* (between November 1885 and June 1886). As Lockspeiser conjectures (LO, 1, p. 100), the score might well be fascinating for it is contemporary with Debussy's Bayreuth pilgrimages and, like *Parsifal, Axël* 'is a study of renunciation' which also had 'immense influence' in the artistic world. As Henri de Régnier observes (p. 30): 'No one employed a more solemn, momentous and subtle style . . . [Villiers] realised in the written word the divine power discovered by Edgar Poe; the power to create worlds.' And whilst, as André Dinar says (p. 56), it was the Symbolist movement that adhered to Villiers de l'Isle-Adam rather than vice versa, it is easy to see why it did so if his main influences after 1860 were Poe, Baudelaire and Wagner. Indeed, a study of Villiers's *Contes cruels* may have acclimatised Debussy for Poe, whom he first mentions in 1889, and it was Villiers who showed Maeterlinck what could be drawn from Poe's *Tales of mystery and imagination*. On the poet's own admission (p. 201), 'Princesse Maleine, Mélisande, Astolaine, Sélysette and the other phantoms which followed them awaited the atmosphere that Villiers had created in me to be born and finally to draw breath.' And if Mallarmé was the first French interpreter of Poe's poetry and aesthetic doctrines in France, then it was Villiers who led the way with the narrative works.

There are several other reasons why Debussy should have been drawn towards Villiers de l'Isle-Adam and to *Axël* in particular. First, the Wagnerian connections, for as Alan Raitt observes (1965, p. 131), both the *Ring* cycle and *Axël* share the theme of gold representing power and have adversaries battling for its possession. There are parallels between Maître Janus (who directs the destinies of Axël and Sara) and Wotan, just as the idealistic and non-materialistic hero himself has much in common with Siegfried in his obstinate courage and indifference to the wishes of others. Much is made of the mystical identities of love, death and night, as in *Tristan und Isolde*, though the 'Liebestod' in *Axël* culminates with the hero and heroine drinking poison together and being buried alive in a crypt, like the last act of *Aida* with a volunteer Radames! But the most important Wagnerian parallel is a stylistic one; the slow, hieratic actions and their symbolic significance make *Axël* seem at times like a Wagner libretto for which music was clearly intended.

This might have been the second feature which attracted Debussy, for Villiers himself was extremely musical and always had a piano with him during his nomadic existence.[1] However, he could not write down his music and on various occasions asked Augusta Holmès, Alexandre Georges and even Chabrier to do it for him. What he could do was improvise and there is an account of him conjuring up a Wagnerian 'Jupiter' Symphony at the keyboard. He also set two of the same poems as Debussy from Baudelaire's *Les fleurs du mal* (*La mort des amants* and *Recueillement*), and like Debussy gave solo performances at the piano of complete Wagner operas.[2]

Even though Villiers made *Axël* less and less performable as he expanded its static portions in 1885, he continued to view it in theatrical terms, as he had done when it was published in its original form in 1872 in the *Renaissance artistique et littéraire*. He envisaged it with incidental music rather than as a continuous music-drama along the lines of the Wagnerian *Gesamtkunstwerk*: whilst there are plenty of opportunities for organ and choral music in the first part ('Le monde religieux'), the only specific musical direction occurs when the heroine Sara starts to explain to Axël the symbol of the rose and, in a rather Satiean manner, 'harps repeating in the shadows the song of the Rose-Croix' are heard.[3] Either this fourth scene, from the end of the first section ('The proof through gold and through love') of Part 4, or the shorter following fifth scene with its male choruses of old military servants and woodcutters might have been the scene set by Debussy. And he probably did this before Villiers's death in 1889, not knowing that the author had discussed the music for *Axël* with his intended composer Alexandre Georges.

As we saw in Chapter 1, productions of *Axël* were planned by Paul Fort in 1891-3, though the première did not take place until 26 February 1894 when Paul Larochelle produced it to great acclaim at the Théâtre de la Gaîté with Georges's incidental music. Larochelle himself played the lead and the orchestra and chorus were conducted by Paul Viardot. Georges's score consisted of the following items from Villiers's play:[4]

Part 1 'Le monde religieux'	*Offertoire prélude* [start] including the *Chant des Rose-Croix* (Ex. 3) which is repeated at various points during the score modulating through different chains of keys. *Choeur des religieuses*: 'O virgo! mater alma!' [p. 32] A reprise of the opening prelude ends scene 4. Solo for the nun Sister Aloyse: 'Ego pro defuncta illa!' [scene 6, pp. 34-5] with 'choeur des religieuses'.

	Hymne des religieuses: 'Ecce inviolata Soror coelestis' [scene 6, p. 42]
Section 2 'La renonciatrice'	*Noël* for offstage double choir at start [pp. 47-8] Melodrama for the Archdeacon: 'In te Domine speravi' [end of scene 8, p. 56]
Part 2 'Le monde tragique'	*Scène du duel pendant l'orage* [melodrama at end of scene 13, pp. 172-84]
Part 3 'Le monde occulte'	No music
Part 4 'Le monde passionnel'	*Prélude*. Ex. 3 theme sets scene in burial vaults [pp. 219-20]. Melodrama passages for Axël and Sara towards the end of scene 4 further develop the Rose-Croix theme [pp. 247-51]. *Choeur des vieux serviteurs* [*militaires*] : 'Le maître s'en va du burg en décombres' [scene 5, pp. 257-8]
Section 2 'L'option surprême'	*Choeur des bûcherons*: 'En joie! En joie!' [p. 269] [*Aubade d'*] *Ukko*, sung from the wings by M. Rondeau: 'Sur le versant des monts fleuris' [p. 269] *Choeur des bûcherons*, reprise *Final*. Return of Ex. 3 plus wordless choir [pp. 270-1]

Ex. 3. Alexandre Georges: *Chant des Rose-Croix* from the *Offertoire prélude* to Act 1 of *Axël*, 1894, OS, p. 11

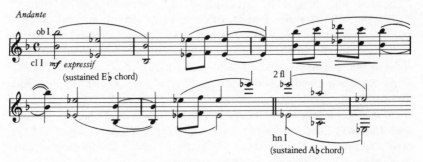

The length of the score for the duel scene and the fact that the *Choeur des vieux serviteurs* and the *Choeur des bûcherons* in Part 4 are continuous, suggest that fairly extensive cuts were made to Villiers's text for the première. Alexandre Georges was perhaps chosen to write the music for this because he had already written a score for the five-act drama *Le nouveau-monde*, first performed at the Théâtre des Nations on 19 February 1883, in which Villiers more explicitly aimed to integrate the musical and dramatic action, using *God Save the Queen* and *Hail Columbia!* played by a distant orchestra as part of a primitive Wagnerian leitmotif system.

According to Gustave Charpentier (p. 1), Debussy knew Georges well, and in 1890, after Charpentier's return from Rome, they sometimes met in the Brasserie Pousset in the rue de Châteaudun in a group which also included Mendès. Discovering the existence of Georges's plans for *Axël* around 1890 may be one reason why Debussy abandoned his own.

Debussy may also have been attracted to *Axël* because of its occult content, especially in Part 3 (Debussy's links with the hermetic movement will be discussed in more detail later). Villiers's interest in the occult was strongest in 1870 when he began *Axël*, though it had apparently waned when he revised the play in the 1880s; it is revealed chiefly in Maître Janus, though his double role as supernatural director of the action and as Axël's initiator confuses matters. In fact most of the occult content is borrowed from Éliphas Lévi's *Dogme et rituel de la haute magie*,[5] which Villiers had read in 1866 and which Debussy also apparently venerated, together with Catulle Mendès.[6]

In the end, however, Debussy probably did not get as far with his music for *Axël* as his contemporary Vincent d'Indy who, 'seduced by [the play's] beauty', worked on a score from shortly after *Axël* appeared in *La jeune France* until he heard about Georges's efforts whereupon he abandoned it to concentrate on his opera *Fervaal* (Jean-Aubry, 1938, p. 57).

* * *

Rodrigue et Chimène (1890-2)

It was probably through a mutual interest in the occult that Debussy met his first librettist, Catulle Mendès; the venue, as Victor-Émile Michelet recalls (p. 73), was Edmond Bailly's Librairie de l'Art Indépendant at 9 rue de la Chaussée d'Antin where Debussy 'arrived almost every day in the late afternoon, either alone, or with the faithful Erik Satie'. This could well have been in 1889, or even slightly earlier, as Michelet (p. 67) records the frequent visits of Villiers de l'Isle-Adam (who died in 1889) to Bailly's bookshop and says that his first project as an editor was to publish a collection of Villiers's writings entitled *Chez les passants*. Prince André Poniatowski also suggests that Debussy and Mendès met in 1889, but the story, told by Cortot (p. 13) and others,[7] that Debussy's father stood in for Georges Courteline one evening in Mendès' domino game at the Café Napolitain and spread the word about his son's Prix de Rome talents seems rather far-fetched: if there was an intermediary between composer and librettist, it was more probably Pierre Louÿs. In any event, Debussy and Mendès met regularly at the Brasserie Pousset in 1890 and Mendès offered help with the publication of Debussy's *Fantaisie* for piano and orchestra, perhaps as a result of being impressed by a private performance of the Wagnerian *Cinq poèmes de Baudelaire* in February 1890, when Mendès gave Debussy a copy of his *Méphistophela* with a dedication relating to the occasion (Dietschy, 1962, p. 83). All of this suggests that it was Mendès who tried to woo Debussy into accepting *Rodrigue et Chimène*, a conclusion which is corroborated by Robert Godet (p. 68) and by Michelet (p. 73), who reveals that 'Catulle Mendès had a system: to write opera librettos for all the young composers who showed promise. Amongst the number would surely be one that would have the same success as [Gounod's] *Faust!*'

However, whether Mendès was aware of it or not, there was even more pressure on Debussy from his parents to accept his offer. On his return to Paris from Rome in March 1887 Debussy had moved back into his parents' home at 27 rue de Berlin without any apparent means of self-support, and to make matters worse, his father was dismissed from his post as assistant book-keeper at the Compagnie de Fives-Lille a month later. Although Debussy spent as little time as he could at home in the succeeding years, he did not move away until some time in 1892 when he took rooms at 42 rue de Londres with Gaby Dupont; his letters to his patron Prince Poniatowski show how artistically desolate the period of *Rodrigue et Chimène* was. He admitted to him in February 1893 (Poniatowski, p. 307) that

> my family has been affected by several regrettable incidents in which I was automatically involved. They find me far too unproductive as a son, at least as far as fame is concerned, and have waged a niggling war against me, for reasons partly sentimental and partly spiteful. Moreover it is obvious that the castles in Spain that they had built out of my glorious future career have sadly collapsed!

Whilst Debussy was clearly using a figure of speech here, the extra edge given to his remark by the Spanish castles in *Rodrigue et Chimène* must surely have been at the back of his sharp, ironical mind.

Whatever serious reservations he may have had, Debussy accepted the libretto of *Rodrigue et Chimène* in April 1890, and between then and 1892 set the bulk of its three acts of music. After all, Mendès *was* an influential librettist, with Chabrier's *Gwendoline* to his credit and other prestigious, if overblown projects in the pipe-line. And Debussy *was* 'into Wagner' in 1890, though perhaps not so 'heavily' as his partner, who had written that 'the music-drama in France should be a work in which the inspiration, profoundly French, should be displayed according to laws borrowed from the Wagnerian system' (Inghelbrecht, p. 69).

With the *Cinq poèmes de Baudelaire*, *Rodrigue et Chimène* provided the means for Debussy to compose most of the superficial aspects of Wagnerism out of his system, but the process proved to be an agonising one. He told Gustave Charpentier (p. 1) that the opera was 'contrary to everything I wanted to express. The traditional aspects of this subject call for music which I cannot call my own.' He wrote to Robert Godet on 30 January 1892 (GOD, pp. 97-8) that

> My life is sadly unsettled because of this opera, where everything is
> against me . . . I am anxious for you to hear the two finished acts,
> for I am afraid to have won any victories over myself . . . Perhaps
> this will put an end to the intolerable feeling that I have now and
> then of living in a place of exile where nothing awaits me, and where
> I am condemned to a dreary little routine.

Nonetheless, the manuscript in New York (see Appendix) shows that
Debussy did complete a third act and that there was no falling off of inspiration after the first two. In fact the dramatic final pages suggest the reverse,
and the act as a whole has fewer and more comprehensible corrections than
the others. Contrary to previously expressed opinions, it is the first act of
Rodrigue et Chimène that remains unfinished and the most sketchy. All three,
however, begin as fairly advanced copies in Debussy's process of composition.
The second act even has advice to the engraver on p. 34 which suggests that
this is the final copy prepared for the printing of a vocal score. Roy Howat
has suggested to me that Act 2 was actually the first act to be written; this is
implied by the different type of manuscript paper used and the fact that this
act alone uses both sides of the paper and has clefs repeated for each new
system, both of which practices Debussy abandoned in Acts 1 and 3 and subsequently.

Debussy may have continued to work at *Rodrigue* past the final date of
1892 on the manuscript, for Paul Dukas wrote to d'Indy on 1 October 1893
(Dietschy, 1962, p. 85) that Debussy played and sang it to him, adding that he
was 'very surprised . . . at the dramatic breadth of certain scenes'. Perhaps it
was only the realisation of the operatic potential of *Pelléas et Mélisande* after
seeing it in May 1893 that caused Debussy to lay *Rodrigue et Chimène* aside
unorchestrated. The very untidy pencil corrections, chiefly to Acts 1 and 2,
suggest that Debussy was unhappy with the music as well as the plot, and the
similarity of these additions to the handwriting of the first sketches for *Pelléas*
in the Meyer collection (LPm, pp. 19-84) suggests that Debussy might still
have been tinkering with his first opera as he began his second. Certainly
Rodrigue provided him with valuable experience of what to avoid in the
future! But had Debussy had the prospect of a stage performance, the situation might well have been different; and in this context it should be remembered that he also left *Pelléas* unorchestrated for six years until after its
definite acceptance by Albert Carré for the Opéra-Comique in May 1901. If
Rodrigue was Debussy's 'purgatory' and a 'cartoon' for *Pelléas* (Dietschy,
1962, p. 85), then he had at least as many moments of self-doubt and artistic
anguish in bringing Pelléas and Mélisande alive in his only finished operatic
picture.

The chief difficulty with *Rodrigue et Chimène* is that Mendès' libretto *per se*
has not survived; this poses problems as to its original sources and the passages

in the manuscript that have been lost, or for which the text is incomplete. Michelet (pp. 73-4) maintains that Mendès based his opera on 'le *Cid* of Guilhen [Guillén] de Castro, which he considered superior to that of Corneille'; but most subsequent writers, largely I suspect from guesswork, favour the latter source, perhaps because they credit Mendès with better artistic judgment than Michelet does. Complications arise because Corneille's classical tragedy (whose first performance in January 1637 caused such controversy) was itself based on Castro's *Las mocedadas del Cid – comedia primera* (The youthful exploits of the Cid – Part 1), first published in 1618, which in turn was based on the first part of the *Romancero del Cid* (Ballad book of the Cid) collected by Juan de Escobar and published in 1612. The whole affair is rather like the apocryphal garbled message passed from mouth to mouth about the 'Germans advancing on the left flank', and the hero and heroine that Debussy found so unsympathetic when they put duty before love were actually very different from the characters whose exploits were recorded as fact at a distance of four literary stages and some 800 years.

The 1612 ballads chronicle the heroic deeds of the Castilian warrior Rodrigo Díaz born about 1043 in Vivar, just north of Burgos, and universally known as *El Cid Campeador* (the lord champion). His father, Diego Laínez, belonged to the lesser nobility, and Rodrigo's military career began in the service of Prince Sancho, the eldest son of Ferdinand the Great. Ferdinand's division of his kingdom between his five sons understandably caused jealousy, and the ensuing civil wars were initiated by Sancho when he became King of Castile in 1065. It was as successful commander against the heathen Moors that Rodrigo was christened 'Sidi' (my lord), and his career was only checked by Sancho's assassination in 1072. However, Sancho's brother Alfonso, who returned from exile as King of Castile and León, bestowed on Rodrigo the political honour of marriage to his cousin, Jimena Díaz, daughter of a powerful Asturian count, in 1074. But Rodrigo was not exactly of the temperament to be a subordinate vassal after his previous military glories, and for reasons unknown he found himself banished from Castile in 1081. The climax of his subsequent campaigns against the Moors was the capture of Valencia in 1094 and he died a ruler of considerable prestige in 1099.[8]

Thus the conflict between love and duty central to Castro, Corneille and Mendès does not feature in the original story. Here Rodrigo kills Jimena's father in a family quarrel where no questions of love or honour are involved. In these circumstances Jimena naturally demands vengeance, but whilst seeking justice she becomes attracted to Rodrigo. Understandably, the king will not punish his valuable army commander, and the situation is resolved by the marriage of Rodrigo and Jimena at the latter's suggestion. Rodrigo, in fact, is less than enthusiastic about this politically convenient alliance, and only consents when royally commanded to do so.

In Castro's account the exigencies of seventeenth-century Spanish drama cause the fighting qualities of Rodrigo to be tempered with the attributes of the perfect chivalrous courtier, constant in his love for Jimena, who obeys the complex Spanish code of honour to the letter and remains a model of unquestioning loyalty to king, Church and country. Jimena undergoes a similar transformation to become the faithful lover of Rodrigo, a refined lady who needs must avenge her father's death because of her noble upbringing.

Corneille was even more restricted than Castro, because of the unities of time and place which dominated the French theatre of his day; as a result he omits some of the characters and incidents to be found in Castro's more complex version. As William Watson puts it (p. 79): 'Corneille's contemporaries pointed out that the hero has to compress three years of action into twenty-four hours and has to work through the night in order to do so. These twenty-four hours have been called "probably the most crowded day in all recorded time".'

In his libretto Mendès used material found in Act 1 and the first part of Act 2 in Castro, and in Acts 1–3 of Corneille's five-act tragedy. Some aspects were taken from one source, some from the other, and some were added by Mendès himself. His decision to concentrate on the earlier parts of the epic story, which justified his change of title, may have been made in the light of *Der Cid* by Peter Cornelius,[9] produced in Weimar in May 1865, and more especially of the failure of Massenet's *Le Cid* at the Paris Opéra as recently as 30 November 1885.[10] In fact, after the latter event, choosing the subject at all seems strange.

At this stage, it will be profitable to give a list of the different characters in Mendès' sources and then the basic plot of his adaptation, both because it has a bearing on Debussy's setting and because it can only be deduced from the incomplete underlay in a single American library source.

Castro (1618)	Corneille (1637)	Mendès (1889-90)
El Rey Don Fernando	Don Fernand, premier roi de Castille	Le Roi Ferdinand de Castille
La Reina su mujer	–	–
El Príncipe Don Sancho		
La Infanta Doña Urraca	Doña Urraque, infante de Castille	–
Diego Laínez, padre del Cid	Don Diègue, père de Don Rodrigue	Don Diègue de Bivar, père de Don Rodrigue
Rodrigo [Díaz de Vivar], El Cid	Don Rodrigue, amant de Chimène	Don Rodrigue de Bivar
El Conde Lozano	Don Gomès, Comte de Gormas, père de Chimène	Don Gomez [Comte] de Gormaz, père de Chimène
Jimena Gómez, hija del Conde	Chimène, fille de Don Gomès	Chimène, fille de Don Gomez
Elvira, criada de Jimena Gómez	Elvire, gouvernante de Chimène	Inèz, servante de Chimène

Castro (1618)	Corneille (1637)	Mendès (1889-90)
Arias Gonzalo	Don Anas, gentilhomme castillan	? Don Juan d'Arcos
Peransules	–	–
Hernán Díaz, hermano del Cid	–	Don Hernán, frère du Cid
Bermudo Laín, hermano del Cid	–	Don Bermudo, frère du Cid
Don Martín Gonzales	Don Sanche, amoureux de Chimène	? Don Pedre de Terruel
		hommes de Gormaz et Bivar, filles de Bivar etc.

Rodrigue, the eldest son of a now elderly Castilian nobleman, Don Diègue de Bivar, is in love with and to be betrothed to Chimène, daughter of Don Gomez de Gormaz, a younger but arrogant count. After a prelude which represents the love of Rodrigue and Chimène, the former, accompanied by his brother Don Hernán, rides into the castle of Gormaz to pay a secret dawn call on Chimène before its inhabitants are up and about. The offstage trumpet calls somehow contrive to waken only Chimène in her turret boudoir and she descends with her servant Inèz.

In scene 2 Rodrigue and Chimène are left alone to declare their love in a lengthy duet ('Ô mon Rodrigue, je t'adore'), although Chimène is clairvoyantly apprehensive about their future together. The castle begins to waken, and finally Inèz and Don Hernán have to prise the lovers apart just before the men of Gormaz enter, topping up their alcohol levels somewhat early in the day in a rousing drinking-chorus ('Du vin! Du vin! Videz les caves!'). Meanwhile the girls of nearby Bivar are heard approaching and a lengthy stage direction[11] suggests that the inevitable is about to happen. The girls suddenly find themselves face to face with the lusty men of castle Gormaz who spring out of their hiding-places intent on something more than idle conversation. The girls are saved from a fate worse than embroidery only by the timely intervention of Don Diègue (scene 5) who gives the men a good dressing down. Unfortunately Don Gomez hears this and upbraids Don Diègue for criticising his men on his property. A heated argument ensues in which the old noble is insulted and humiliated in front of his servant girls by Don Gomez, who, it must be admitted, has had to tolerate Don Diègue's account of his glorious military past which he appears to be more than willing to relate. Before the score peters out on f. 51 of the Lehman manuscript, we learn that Don Diègue will be avenged by his sons, due to his advanced age.

Act 2 begins in the castle of Bivar where Rodrigue is deep in thought, oblivious of the chatter of his younger brothers Hernán and Bermudo as they play chess. The brothers see an old beggar outside, and taking pity, call him in. When he refuses food, drink and help, their curiosity is aroused, but when, Salome-like, he demands the 'head of the count' and raises his mantle, they are dumbfounded. It is Don Diègue, but a Don Diègue without name or honour. He tests Hernán and Bermudo with sudden pain, but their reactions show that they are too young (and effeminate) to avenge him. The obvious choice is Rodrigue, but when he discovers who must be killed to avenge his father, he is thunderstruck.

As he reflects on what this will mean to his relationship ('Ô mon amour! Chimène'), the music skilfully recalls his expression of love for her in Act 1, though as always with Debussy it is nowhere exactly the same. In his solo scene the conflict between love and duty, so dear to Verdi, is agonisingly resolved, though not without the intervention of the trusty men of Bivar who enter to offer Don Diègue their services in avenging his insult. Before the men can take the famous sword of the warrior Mudarra, which Don Diègue offers them, Rodrigue seizes it: he is now prepared for anything and will avenge his father himself. The men inform him that Don Gomez has left with his followers for Burgos where King Ferdinand is mustering his nobles to defeat the Moors; it is clear that Rodrigue must apprehend him *en route*.

The second tableau of Act 2 is set on the plain beside the River Duéro with a chain of mountains on the horizon. Rodrigue enters, armed, but with his visor lowered, and conceals himself behind some branches on a small hillock. The men of Gormaz are heard in the distance, singing to keep their spirits up on the long march. To Rodrigue's dismay, Chimène and her servants are there too. As Don Gomez passes, Rodrigue asks to speak alone with him and tells him that Don Diègue's wrong has now become his. The overbearing Don Gomez scorns the puny young champion who 'still has his nurse's milk on his lips'. The duel (missing in the manuscript, ff. 41-3) then presumably follows for, as the score restarts, Chimène is bending over her dying father, who with his last breath predictably demands vengeance, naming his assailant. A beautiful modal chorus in seven parts laments the passing of this 'Christian cavalier' with bell-like octaves on the orchestra punctuating the phrases.

Act 3 is set in the royal camp on a vast plain near Burgos and opens with yet another soldiers' chorus ('Boire aujourd'hui; tuer demain') which is silenced only by the trumpeting equerries of King Ferdinand. Severally, Don Juan d'Arcos, a group of men from a mountain district, 'strong as Asturian bears', a band of monks and Don Pedre de Terruel pledge their allegiance to Ferdinand in his fight for Castile against the Moors. Ironically the king singles out Don Gomez de Gormaz as the 'most trusted of heros on whom Spain relies', whereupon his men enter with the news that he is dead! Chimène and Don Diègue enter from the opposite side of the stage to try to explain the situation, each begging for justice in a dramatic duet (see Ex. 15), part of which (f. 9) is unfortunately missing. The body of Don Gomez is carried in and Chimène tells of his dying call for vengeance. Don Pedre de Terruel offers to fight as Chimène's champion, but Ferdinand proclaims that justice is his alone to administer. Don Diègue again reflects on his past prowess and his pride at being once more able to hold his head high thanks to the bravery of his son. But Ferdinand does not share his enthusiasm, maintaining that he is misled by paternal affection into praising the guilty. Ferdinand's equerries are ordered to locate and capture Rodrigue and he tells Chimène that her father shall be avenged, wielding his sword as a cross over Don Gomez' corpse.

An interlude leads to a scene between Chimène and Inèz, and an aria reveals that Chimène still loves Rodrigue as much as ever. As she remembers her betrothal, Debussy departs from the accompanying triplet quavers and masterfully recalls the music of the opening prelude (Act 1) in one of the only extensive revisions made during the copying of the manuscript (f. 17 v, see Fig. 1b). But after much anguish, Chimène decides that she must face up to her promise of vengeance. At this point, Rodrigue rushes in, having overheard the end of her resolve. She, Chimène, must kill him, he says, but they will be united in death. Human weakness in both parties is again countered with stern resolve and Rodrigue is about to yield without resistance to Chimène's sword when his father and brothers enter with a timely solution: Rodrigue is to return and serve King Ferdinand in command of 400 hidalgos. Both parties accept that destiny will take its course; should Rodrigue perish it will be in triumph for king and country.

Thus Mendès incorporated from Castro the brothers Hernán and Bermudo (omitted by Corneille) and their testing as worthy champions by Don Diègue. He took from Corneille the names of the characters plus the end of his third act as a *dénouement* (this comes in mid-act in Castro). He himself added Rodrigue's dawn call on Chimène, the chess game which begins the second act, and all the chorus material. This last represents perhaps his most skilful addition, for in both Castro and Corneille the quarrel between Dons Diègue and Gomez is over the right to be appointed tutor of King Ferdinand's son Prince Sancho, although the latter does not appear as a character in Corneille (whose Don Sanche is a champion of Chimène, rather like Don Pedre de Terruel in Mendès' libretto). Making the chorus a kingpin of the plot, indirectly responsible for the insult to Don Diègue (presumably the traditional Spanish slap in the face), was little short of a masterstroke. But at the same time this must be balanced against one of the main factors which would prohibit the performance of *Rodrigue et Chimène*, namely the continually changing role of the chorus. In the extreme case of the start of the third act, they are within the first six pages required to provide a double chorus of soldiers (six parts), four tenor equerries, six tenor mountaineers, six bass monks and then an eight-part double chorus, after which they remain silent for the rest of the opera!

Mendès wisely omits Doña Urraque (Chimène's rival for Rodrigue's affections) and Peransules (Don Gómez' friend), though he follows Castro in suggesting — as seems only sensible to modern audiences — that Gomez *apologise*

Fig. 1. *Rodrigue et Chimène* (*US-NYpm* Lehman deposit), Act 3: (a) f. 18 *r*, showing the original version of Chimène's aria (the revision to the passage here crossed out is shown in (b))

26

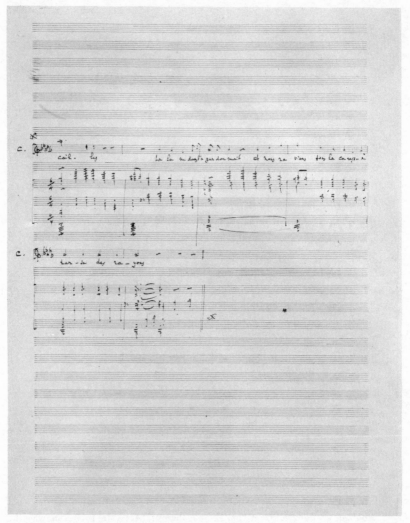

Fig. 1 (b). f. 17 *v*, showing the revised version of Chimène's aria, which recalls the music for the start of the opera to Don Diègue. Mendès also omits all the later exploits that earned Rodrigue the epithet 'El Cid' (which explains his different choice of title). This has the added advantage of bypassing all Chimène's vacillations between honour and love; the duel with her champion; and inevitably the final reconciliation, with a future marriage approved by King Ferdinand.

It is easy to see from a modern viewpoint what the hedonistic and amoral Debussy would have found uncongenial in this libretto, with its lovers labouring against impossible odds brought upon them by the ancestral pride and intransigent stupidity of their respective fathers. It offered passionate dramatic situations of a Romantic type rather than the subtle development and interaction of human characters towards which other literary genres were moving in the later nineteenth century. However well managed Mendès' libretto was, it was only so in terms of *conventional* historical opera. And by and large, Debussy's response to it resulted in conventional music. The contrast between *Rodrigue et Chimène* and *Pelléas et Mélisande* is between description and suggestion; between Germanic musical continuity and sensitive recitative; between the historical and the mythological past; and between stereotyped emotions and subtle psychology. If Mélisande can be as irritating as Chimène, it is for more acceptable reasons. If Maeterlinck's characters appear at first sight no more true to life than those of Mendès, then they are at least not cardboard cut-outs. And if *Pelléas* has faults, then it is at least an original play, and one of symbolic significance in which crossing the thresholds of time presents no problems.

Rodrigue et Chimène belongs to the tradition of the Wagnerian music-drama insofar as its foundation lies in a through-composed orchestral part of a symphonic nature. There are no self-contained set pieces, obvious cadences are eschewed, and the voice parts often appear to be appendages to the main musical argument, as in *Tristan und Isolde*. This is especially so in the first act choruses (ff. 25-41), where the vocal lines are often missing or incomplete while the orchestral reduction is present in full. However, the vocal parts overall are more lyrical, expansive and declamatory than in *Pelléas*, using wider intervals and more conventional melodic phrasing and climaxes.

On the question of leitmotifs, Debussy wrote to Ernest Guiraud during the early stages of *Rodrigue* in September 1890 (Hoérée, p. 33): 'What a bore these leitmotifs are! What everlasting war-horses! . . . The *Ring*, in which there are certain pages that astound me, is essentially a bundle of tricks; the very same tricks make my beloved *Tristan* seem faded, and it grieves me to feel that I am becoming detached from it.' Whilst Debussy made more extensive and obvious use of the 'Tristan' chord in *Rodrigue et Chimène* (see Exx. 12 and 13) than he did in *Pelléas et Mélisande*, an all-embracing system of motivic identification and metamorphosis is far less in evidence in his earlier opera. Rather, ideas are presented and developed within each particular scene and, if there are links between the acts, it is due more to textural, harmonic and rhythmic similarities than to anything resembling a leitmotif.

The nearest thing to a leitmotif is the playful idea associated with Don Hernán in Act 1 (Ex. 4), which features again in his chess game with Bermudo

Ex. 4. *Rodrigue et Chimène*, *US-NYpm* Lehman deposit, Act 1, f. 5, bar 2, entry of Don Hernán

at the start of the second act (pp. 1-10), where it is more extensively developed. And a theme which is first heard as a light appears at Chimène's tower window (Ex. 5), as well as crystallising from various individual 'Chimène' phrases heard in the prelude, could also be said to lead to the following passages: Ex. 6, the urgent accompaniment figure as Chimène appears with Inèz at the door of the tower and which continues on into and unifies the first part of scene 2 (pp. 9-12); Ex. 7 from Act 2, where the full impact of the implications of Don Diègue's insult finally dawns on Rodrigue (pp. 22-4); Ex. 8 (and see Fig. 1a) from Chimène's third act aria, as she dreams of the past happiness of moonlit nights with Rodrigue. This gloriously sensual passage, whose harmonies suggest that this act might be contemporary with *L'après-midi d'un faune*, incidentally follows the 'second thought' recall of the opening bars of the initial prelude where the plaintive F sharp minor theme is translated into glowing major chords in a piano reduction that could be by Rachmaninoff (see Fig. 1b). The last occurrence of the Ex. 5 theme comes (Ex. 9) in the middle of the third act duet between the lovers, at a point where Rodrigue dreams of being reunited with Chimène.

But whilst Debussy's unifying intentions are clear, his methods are subtler than Wagner's. No two statements are the same, and he creates a theme rather than a motif, which adapts itself to changing situations in the opera but can-

Ex. 5. *Rodrigue et Chimène*, *US-NYpm* Lehman deposit, Act 1, f. 6, bars 18-21

Ex. 6. *Rodrigue et Chimène, US-NYpm* Lehman deposit, Act 1, f. 8, bar 5

Ex. 7. *Rodrigue et Chimène, US-NYpm* Lehman deposit, Act 2, p. 22, bar 24 – p. 23, bar 1

Ex. 8. *Rodrigue et Chimène, US-NYpm* Lehman deposit, Act 3, f. 18, bars 14-18 (see Fig. 1a)

Ex. 9. *Rodrigue et Chimène, US-NYpm* Lehman deposit, Act 3, f. 24, bars 16-19

not be said to represent a specific person or a consistent emotion, as Ex.7 demonstrates. And is not the theme of the scene with Don Diègue disguised as a beggar in Act 2 (Ex. 10) simply a subtle variant of the same Ex. 5 idea? For the links between Exx. 5 and 10 are really no more tenuous than those between Ex. 5 and the theme that occurs later in the act as Chimène and her followers pass the concealed Rodrigue, who awaits his confrontation with Don Gomez (Ex. 11).

Ex. 10. *Rodrigue et Chimène, US-NYpm* Lehman deposit, Act 2, p. 12, bars 16-17

Ex. 11. *Rodrigue et Chimène, US-NYpm* Lehman deposit, Act 2, p. 37, bars 7-10

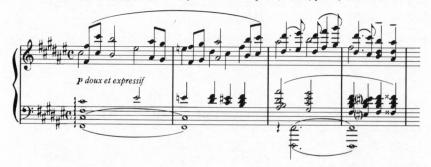

One curious aspect of the opera is the way that Debussy, perhaps subconsciously, links Rodrigue with Tristan. As Rodrigue springs from his hiding place to challenge Don Gomez, we hear Ex.12 in the orchestra. And as King Ferdinand first mentions Rodrigue in the final act and sends his equerries to search for him this is transformed into Ex. 13.

Ex. 12. *Rodrigue et Chimène*, *US-NYpm* Lehman deposit, Act 2, p. 39, bars 8-11

Ex. 13. *Rodrigue et Chimène*, *US-NYpm* Lehman deposit, Act 3, f. 14, bars 21-2

Unity through key is as important as thematic or harmonic unity in *Rodrigue* and this factor again sets it in marked contrast with *Pelléas*. The focal key in *Rodrigue* is E major (in which Acts 2 and 3 end), with F sharp major and minor associated with Chimène (it is suddenly established as she enters (see Ex. 11) after a long passage in a sort of modal D minor). Similarly, A major and hemiola rhythms are associated with the chorus (Act 1, ff. 28ff). If none of the acts begin in E major, then they soon establish it as the focal key. The first act opens in F sharp minor, but moves towards an ambivalent C sharp major/minor as Rodrigue enters, before finally settling in E for the love duet (f. 14). The chromatic opening of Act 2, which again features C sharp minor briefly in bar 5, establishes E major for the chess-playing scene on p. 2. The third act begins in G major, then wisely avoids E as a tonal centre, preferring its dominant (B) early on, D flat (C sharp) major at the midpoint (Ex. 8), and only definitely alighting on the home key in passing at the important point where Rodrigue tells Chimène that she will have to kill him herself to achieve vengeance (f. 22, line 2). E major recurs during Ex. 9 (f. 24), before returning in the last nineteen bars to close the opera (ff. 27-8). And it is surely not by chance that the characters controlling the destinies of the star-crossed lovers are associated with completely different, flat keys: F minor in the case of Don Diègue's solos in Act 1 (f. 45) and Act 2 (p. 29), and E flat major in the case of King Ferdinand (Act 3, f. 7).

Most of *Rodrigue et Chimène* is consistent harmonically with Debussy's other compositions of the later 1880s and it extensively uses augmented fifth chords, and minor and major sevenths rather than ninths. The desire for orchestral continuity makes the score unusually Germanic for Debussy, and, though sequences are used extensively, two-bar units are by no means the norm as they are after the watershed of *Pelléas et Mélisande*. Perhaps it was the uneven harmonic style which prompted Debussy to revise certain passages, for Wagnerian moments occur in close proximity to whole-tone passages, together with a liberal sprinkling of modality. Both the beautiful final chorus of Act 2 and the earlier duet for Hernán and Bermudo would not seem out of place in *La damoiselle élue*, and there is more than a touch of Russian influence in the lovely music of the duet (Ex. 14), though its source is Borodin

Ex. 14. *Rodrigue et Chimène, US-NYpm* Lehman deposit, Act 2, p. 11, bars 3-11

DON HERNÁN,
DON BERMUDO

Ve-nez! Ve-nez! Je vous le dis! En-trez, pour qu'on vous ré-con-for - te.

DON HERNÁN,
DON BERMUDO

Jé - sus   ou - vre son pa - ra-dis, À   qui   n'a pas fer-mé sa   por - te

rather than Mussorgsky. This is even more true of the music for the girls of Bivar in Act 1 (especially f. 32), which could come straight from the Polovtsian dances in *Prince Igor*.

But the climax of this scene before Don Diègue's entry (ff. 40–1) could be part of the contemporary second *Arabesque*, and f. 23 of Act 3 has distinct affinities with the 'Ballet' from the *Petite suite*. Overall, the third act is the surest and most consistent harmonically, but any passages which appear genuinely forward-looking usually turn out to be so because of missing clefs or accidentals, and Debussy had not yet mastered the technique of writing music that defined character in other than an obvious manner. It is difficult to see why many of the later pencil corrections were made, though some involve the smooth joining of bass pedal-points (as in Act 3, f. 7, bars 23-4), a harmonic device which was to assume far greater significance in *Pelléas et Mélisande*. Perhaps *Rodrigue* also explains why, beginning with *Pelléas*, Debussy wrote over three-quarters of his music with a dynamic of *piano* or lower, for in his first opera it is the frequent loud passages which are the most conventional and obvious.

Finally, there are two passages in particular which reveal Debussy's innate skills as a musical dramatist in *Rodrigue et Chimène*; predictably both come from the superior third act. The first occurs as Don Diègue and Chimène plead their respective cases before King Ferdinand in a tense duo (Ex. 15) and it is a great pity that the following page is the only one missing in the act. The second comes near the end of the opera as Hernán and Bermudo burst in upon Rodrigue with an urgent triplet passage (Ex. 16) which has some similarities to the end of *La chute de la Maison Usher*. As Don Diègue enters to announce the solution which will enable Rodrigue to live, the change of harmony to G flat major tells us at a stroke that all will be well; the sinister and tense suddenly becomes paternal and warm without rhythmic change.

Mendès curiously does not seem to have been put out when Debussy abandoned his opera, although perhaps Debussy avoided telling him definitely, or simply told him the truth about its being complete and pleaded difficulty in securing a performance for not taking matters further. Mendès even told Pierre Louÿs in February 1900 that he thought Debussy could provide an operatic equivalent to Charpentier's *Louise* after hearing it at its dress-rehearsal (LOU, p. 135). He also penned a quite favourable criticism after twice attending *Pelléas et Mélisande* (*Le journal*, 1 May 1902), though memories of *Rodrigue et Chimène* may have led him to voice the personal wish on leaving the Opéra-Comique both 'to hear the score without soloists in an orchestral concert . . . and to see Maeterlinck's charming lyric tale in the theatre without singers or instruments'.

* * *

Ex. 15. *Rodrigue et Chimène, US-NYpm* Lehman deposit, Act 3, f. 8, bars 19-26

Ex. 16. *Rodrigue et Chimène*, *US-NYpm* Lehman deposit, Act 3, f. 26, bars 19-24

The other projects up to 1892, including *Diane au bois*

It is not my purpose in this study to discuss choral and orchestral works which were not intended for theatrical performance, though the dividing line with the earlier cantatas and Prix de Rome *envois* is not always easy to draw, and *L'enfant prodigue* and *La damoiselle élue* have been included because they received stage performances in their revised orchestral forms after 1904. The early Banville projects, *Florise*, *Hymnis* and especially *Diane au bois*, merit more attention; in the case of *Diane* it is a vexed question whether Debussy intended the surviving score to be part of a full operatic treatment of Banville's two-act comedy, or whether he always meant to leave it in the form of a latter-day equivalent of a self-contained Handelian dramatic cantata. But as Richard Langham Smith says (RLS, p. 77), 'the theatrical projects of Debussy's earlier years . . . provide the key not only to the development of his musical ideas, but also to the literary ideas that attracted him'. In this respect *Diane au bois* comes into the first category, and Maeterlinck's *La Princesse Maleine* into the second. So the best solution seemed to include them all in a chronological list, with the exception of Shakespeare's *As you like it* which is better placed in Chapter 12.

Florise (*c*1882)

Raymond Bonheur (p. 4) says that Debussy planned to compose music for Théodore de Banville's four-act comedy, written and published in February–March 1870, in which 'the actress Florise sacrifices her domestic happiness for her art' (Souffrin, 1960, p. 206). Unfortunately, *Florise* remained only a project and no music has survived.

Hymnis (*c*1882)

Banville's lyric comedy *Hymnis* was first performed at the Théâtre Nouveau Lyrique in Paris on 14 November 1879 with incidental music by Jules Cressonnois. The text, in seven scenes, was published the following year, and rather conventional music for parts of scenes 1, 2 and 7 by Debussy (under the influence of Massenet) survives in private collections (see Appendix). The final scene is described as an 'Ode bacchique' for two voices and piano and its vocalises reflect the capabilities of Mme Vasnier to whom it is dedicated. Eileen Souffrin (1960, pp. 206-7) draws a parallel between her and the maternal, protective, but passionate Hymnis, seeing in her beloved Anacréon a reflection of Debussy himself. As Lockspeiser says (LO, 1, p. 70), Hymnis's line: 'Le plaisir est ma loi!' would have struck a sympathetic response in Debussy, who, when the registrar of the Conservatoire asked him what rule he followed, replied 'Mon plaisir!'.

Diane au bois (Paris 1883-4; Rome 1885-6)

This is by far the most important of the early Banville settings and the surviving New York manuscript consists of parts of scenes 3 and 4 from the second
act of Banville's comedy (first performed in 1863), for which Debussy sought
the poet's authorisation through Banville's godson, the painter Rochegrosse,
in 1886. The scenes in question, deriving from Ovid's *Metamorphoses*, concern
the conquest of Diana by Eros. While she loved Endymion, Diana had heart-
lessly expelled one of her nymphs for breaking her vows of chastity, and as a
punishment she is made to suffer the pangs of true love, succumbing in the
final seduction scene to Eros in the disguise of Endymion.

Debussy began *Diane au bois* in Ernest Guiraud's composition class at the
Conservatoire, prior to winning the Prix de Rome. The surviving scenes may
even date from this Paris period, for included on the back pages of the manuscript is a scribbled pencil copy of the variant of Alfred de Musset's poem
Les filles de Madrid[12] that Debussy used for his *Chanson espagnole* in 1883.
Debussy continued to work on *Diane au bois* during his stay in Rome, often
at the country home of Count Giuseppe Primoli at Fiumicino, and he may
have decided not to send it back to the Académie des Beaux-Arts either
because it meant too much to him or because it was incomplete. He almost
certainly sketched more music than has survived, for he frequently referred
to it in his letters to Eugène-Henry Vasnier. In 1886 he was planning to add
choruses, though these would still not necessarily have made it into an opera.

He chose the text, he told Vasnier on 4 June 1885 (Prunières, p. 29),
because 'it in no way recalls the poems usually chosen for *envois*' from Rome.
But by November of that year he was experiencing difficulty finding a phrase
of the correct 'beautiful coldness, not arousing any idea of passion – for love
does not come to Diana until much later' (p. 33). On 19 October 1886, he
revealed with remarkable self-awareness (p. 39) that

> I have undertaken a task which was perhaps beyond my powers.
> Not having any precedent, I find myself obliged to invent new
> forms. Wagner could be of use to me, but I have no need to tell you
> how ridiculous it would be even to try him. I could use his system in
> the succession of scenes, but I should want to retain the lyrical line
> without letting it be absorbed by the orchestra.

An extensive extract published by Lockspeiser (LO, 1, pp. 78-81) reveals
the sensuous and lyrical nature of *Diane au bois* with its frequent use of
parallel dominant sevenths and its orchestral short score accompaniment that,
unusually for Debussy, often employs close-spaced bass chords which give the
texture a Berliozian feel. Otherwise, apart from a relatively conventional final
duet with shifts to keys a third apart (pp. 25-6), the score is far more restrained, poetic and prophetic of what is to come than *Rodrigue et Chimène*.
Richard Langham Smith (RLS, p. 77) sees a foreshadowing of the orchestra-

tion and declamation of *Pelléas* here. The origins of *L'après-midi d'un faune* are also particularly obvious, both in Debussy's typically full stage direction: 'Eros sits on a large stone and plays on the flute of Silenus a dreamy and passionate song, to which distant horns reply, almost muted', and in the music which accompanies this (Ex. 17, and see Fig. 2). As Eros lies down to rest at nightfall, the moon rises to the accompaniment of beautiful ninth arpeggios, probably on the harp, followed a few bars later by a chord of the eleventh (Ex. 18), and here the two-bar units are already clearly visible.

Ex. 17. *Diane au bois*, *US-NYpm* Lehman deposit, p. 5, bars 7-12 (see Fig. 2)

Fig. 2. *Diane au bois* (*US-NYpm* Lehman deposit), p. 5, showing part of Act 2 scene 3, when Eros plays the flute of Silenus and is answered by distant muted horns

The Lisztian augmented fifths and tense whole-tone writing of *Rodrigue et Chimène* are foreign to *Diane au bois*. As Lockspeiser comments (LO, 1, p. 77), there is 'something of the character of the Forest of Arden in *As You Like It*' in Banville's play, and this enchanted atmosphere is most in evidence in the superior opening music for Eros. It was also at this time, coincidentally,

Ex. 18. *Diane au bois*, *US-NYpm* Lehman deposit, p. 6, bar 17 – p. 7, bar 5

EROS

(*Eros se couche sur le tertre, la nuit tombe tout à fait, la lune se lève*)

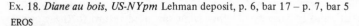

EROS

that Debussy first considered composing music for Shakespeare's comedy, a project which recurred intermittently throughout his life.

The last glimpse we catch of *Diane* is in a letter to Robert Godet in 1890 (GOD, p. 92) when, at 'a little reunion *chez* Mercier', Debussy heard two songs translated from Keats's *Endymion*. But here he found 'the landscapes rather humid, with a Diane who was very "stand-offish" at a point where others would persist', and in no way did this event inspire a return to the world of Banville's *Diane au bois*.

> *L'enfant prodigue* (24 May – 18 June 1884; orch rev. 1906-8 with André Caplet)

It was with this 'lyric scene' to words by Édouard Guinand that Debussy won the coveted Prix de Rome in 1884, when the committee commented on its 'marked poetic feeling, brilliant warm colours and lively dramatic music'. Although designed for concert performance (the first being at the Institut de France on 27 June 1884 when the young Wagnerian tenor Ernest Van Dyck created the role of the prodigal son, Azaël), its later revision prompted a series of stage performances.

Part of it was performed on 12 December 1907 at the Salle Gaveau, when the role of Azaël's mother, Lia, was taken by Charlotte Lormont, and the first complete stage version in French was actually given in London on 28 February 1910. Later that year, Debussy wrote jokingly to his publisher Durand that *L'enfant prodigue* would 'surpass *Pelléas* in popularity . . . and it is "prodigiously" comical'. Fig. 3 shows a rehearsal for an outdoor performance in September 1912 mounted by Jeanne Raunay, a disciple of Isadora Duncan. The first performance at the Théâtre de la Monnaie in Brussels on 9 December 1913 is discussed in detail by Albert van der Linden, who puts the work in a theatrical perspective when he says that it lasts thirty-five minutes and 'makes a pleasant concert rather than a drama'.

Salammbô (1886)

Flaubert's novel, set in Carthage and remarkable for its meticulously researched historical and archaeological background, inspired Debussy to plan a work that he may have intended to be an opera or a symphonic commentary. The plot revolves on the tragic love affair of the Libyan Mathô and Salammbô, the priestess daughter of the leader of the Carthaginians, Hamilcar. The only evidence of the project is to be found in a letter from Rome of 19 October 1886 to Eugène-Henry Vasnier, which suggests that it was to replace the abandoned symphonic ode *Zuleima*.[13] Debussy was, however, 'keeping it for Paris', having 'some notes which warrant further development' (Prunières, p. 39).

Printemps (February 1887)

Printemps was Debussy's second *envoi* from Rome; it is a symphonic suite for orchestra, piano and chorus, inspired by a painting by his fellow scholar Marcel Baschet, which was in turn inspired by Botticelli's *Primavera*. Its use as a ballet at the Alhambra Theatre, London, in its 1912 reorchestration by Henri Büsser is discussed in Chapter 8 (and see Figs. 20-2).

La damoiselle élue (1887-8; reorch 1902)

This work, a 'lyric poem' scored for two soprano soloists, female chorus and orchestra, is a setting of the poem by Dante Gabriel Rossetti as translated by Gabriel Sarrazin. Debussy, however, described it to Prince André Poniatowski (p. 306) on 9 September 1892 as 'a little oratorio which strikes a mystic and slightly pagan note'. The Académie des Beaux-Arts did not appreciate its modal and chastely religious Renaissance beauties, and it was not performed in public until April 1893 at the Société Nationale, when Julia Robert sang the role of Rossetti's Blessed Damozel. Debussy later told Catulle Mendès (*c*1897) quite curtly (Dietschy, 1962, p. 130, n. 9) that 'having [heard it] performed with orchestra', he was not prepared 'to run the risk of having it mangled by a performance with only piano accompaniment'.

Fig. 3. Rehearsal for *L'enfant prodigue* at the Théâtre en Plein Air des Tuileries at Saint-Cloud; choreography by Jeanne Raunay

In fact in 1902 Debussy even set about reorchestrating the work, and it seems to have been this, together with the *Pelléas* experience, that resulted in a theatrical performance. After the revised version was performed at the Concerts Colonne in December 1902 with Mary Garden as la damoiselle, she also gave the first (and only) performance of it at the Opéra-Comique on 4 February 1904, when the conductor was André Messager. Its next stage performance came after Debussy's death when Claire Croiza took the lead at the Théâtre Lyrique du Vaudeville on 10 December 1919. Here it shared the bill with the première of the children's ballet *La boîte à joujoux*, and Emma Debussy was forced to complain to the producer P.-B. Gheusi about the lighting (see Fig. 4).

An intermediate project by Gabriel Mourey to mount *La damoiselle élue* at the Théâtre des Arts met with little enthusiasm from Debussy, who told him on 22 January 1908 that the people associated with this theatre 'have a funny way of understanding a musical performance, of which – strictly between ourselves – I am extremely suspicious'.[14]

L'embarquement pour ailleurs (1890-1)

This was another of Gabriel Mourey's projects. As he recalls in his 'Memories of Claude Debussy' (p. 747):

> I was working then on a collection of prose poems, partly in dialogue, which I had named – and which is still named – "L'embarquement pour ailleurs", and it was arranged with Debussy, to whom I had shown the manuscript, that he should write, for the frontispiece, a tone-poem, which we termed a *glose symphonique*, as the other word seemed to us inadequate.

L'embarquement pour ailleurs with Debussy's symphonic commentary was advertised as being 'sous presse' on the second page of Mourey's play *Lawn-tennis* (a sort of overtly lesbian forerunner of *Jeux*) in the first edition published by Tresse and Stock in 1891. But as Mourey and Debussy met in 1889, and as it was the manuscript of *L'embarquement* that was concerned in their discussion, it is probable that Debussy's symphonic commentary was intended for the first edition (Paris, Albert Savine, 1890, 30 pp.), which consisted only of two playlets. In the second edition of 1893 (Paris, H. Simonis Empis, 182 pp.), almost as if to justify the existence of these two playlets, Mourey added the lengthy romantic, escapist, and probably autobiographical journal of the poet Damon, which would have made the project far too extensive for Debussy.

To return to the first edition: the first playlet (pp. 5-17), dedicated to the celebrated author of the 'decadent' novel *À rebours*, Joris-Karl Huysmans, relates the efforts of the wily Henriette to prompt the dreamy Damon into passionate action. When he finally responds he frightens Henriette with his ardour, and she promptly departs to Easter Mass, leaving him to contemplate the eternal truism that 'women are all the same'. The second playlet (pp. 18-30)

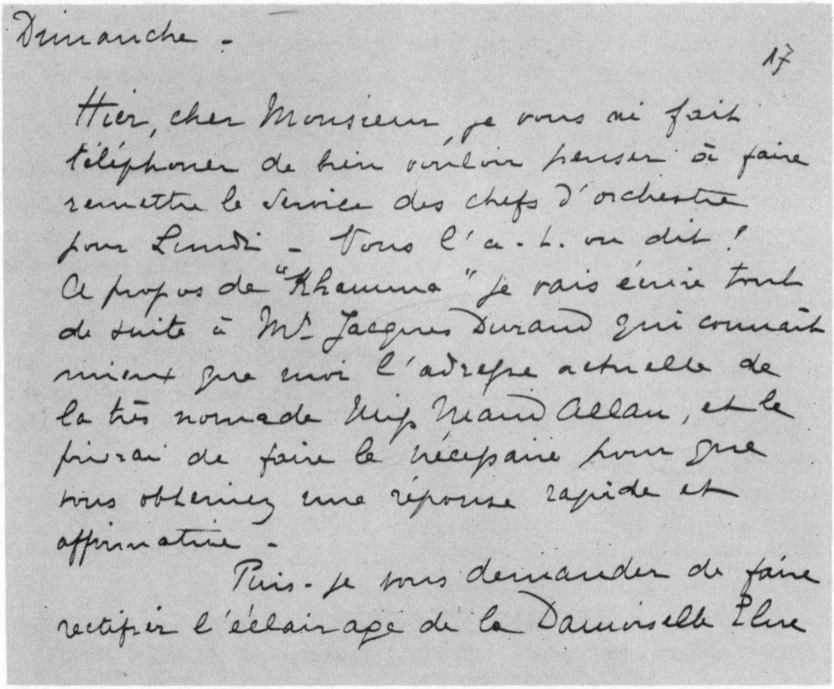

Dimanche – 17

Hier, cher Monsieur, je vous ai fait téléphoner de bien vouloir penser à faire remettre le service des chefs d'orchestre pour Lundi – Vous l'a-t-on dit !
A propos de "Khamma" je vais écrire tout de suite à Mr Jacques Durand qui connaît mieux que moi l'adresse actuelle de la très nomade Miss Maud Allan, et le prierai de faire le nécessaire pour que vous obteniez une réponse rapide et affirmative –
Puis-je vous demander de faire rectifier l'éclairage de la Damoiselle Elue

Fig. 4. Letter of ?21 December 1919 from Emma Debussy to P.-B. Gheusi concerning *Khamma*, the whereabouts of Maud Allan and the lighting for *La damoiselle élue* at the Théâtre Lyrique du Vaudeville (private collection of Robert Orledge)

is set amongst the prostitutes and sailors on an unspecified dockside. Damon asks a sailor where the ship is embarking for and receives the reply: 'Pour ailleurs, parbleu!' – hence the title of the book. After a few gins Damon too is tempted by the call of the unknown, and is only pulled back from his escapist fantasy by the timely arrival of Henriette and a vision of two lovers. Damon rather limply admits that he would prefer 'to cultivate tulips and have children', and the strange figure of the Abbé Constantin appears at the end to bless the pair and bid them 'be fruitful and multiply'.

It is easy to see how Debussy might have been attracted to some aspects of Mourey's rather Wildean dream-world inhabited by Damon, though he probably agreed to collaborate on the project rather to cement his new-found friendship than for artistic reasons. What is more difficult to imagine is how he would have reconciled his evocative symphonic commentary with the first of the two songs in Mourey's second playlet, which we are told in both editions had words and music by a certain S.P. Blundell. Although no music is given for this prostitute's song on the dockside, Mourey talks of 'shrill voices' and 'complex and fervent harmonies' (p. 20). S.P. Blundell may even have been a pseudonym for Mourey himself, for it is doubtful if he would have wanted to claim authorship for doggerel like the first of the prostitute's three verses:

> Quand les flots soulevés du vent
> Nous cachent ciel et terre,
> Jésus éprouve seulement,
> Il sait ce qu'il doit faire.

And I have no doubt Debussy was glad that S.P. Blundell had decided to set his own verse to music rather than rely on his talents!

La Princesse Maleine (1981)

Maeterlinck's first important play, published in Brussels in December 1889, may also have served as Debussy's introduction to the author's shadowy northern world. As Henri-René Lenormand says (p. 188), the kingdom of Thanatos shares the same atmosphere as Allemonde in *Pelléas*, that of 'Maeterlinck's native Flanders; a medieval world where the German forest stretches to the seacoast; where swamps, fogs and old crumbling castles still exist'. There are other similarities too between the plays: towers, forests, water and castles feature in the imagery used, and a sense of timelessness prevails in a mystical domain of the sort suggested to Maeterlinck by Novalis. Maleine, like Mélisande, meanders through the scenes, pale and white; her fiancé, Prince Hjalmar, like Pelléas, is passive and non-heroic, whilst his father, like King Lear, is an instrument of decline and destruction, though without the apparent wisdom of Arkel. It is the ruthless, amoral Queen Anne of Jutland who has no counterpart in *Pelléas et Mélisande*, though her son, Little Allan, is a sort of combination of Mélisande's child and Yniold in that he represents the renewal of life forces and relates most easily to Maleine.

La Princesse Maleine was published in France in February 1890, but it seems unlikely that Debussy read it at this stage, for he began work on the markedly different *Rodrigue et Chimène* two months later. Perhaps it was Octave Mirbeau's glowing review of the play in *Le figaro* on 24 August 1890 which awakened Debussy (and Paris) to the unknown Belgian author. Mirbeau described *La Princesse Maleine* as 'the most ingenious work of its time and the most extraordinary and naïve too, superior in beauty to the most beautiful of Shakespeare'. Maeterlinck tells us in his *Bulles bleues* (p. 207) that it was Mallarmé who sent Mirbeau his copy, and he replied humbly to the critic that he was not a great poet, but 'merely a groping child' who saw 'only the influence of Shakespeare, Poe and that of my friend Van Lerberghe' in his 'poor princess'.

Similarly, it may have been Erik Satie who introduced Debussy to *La Princesse Maleine* for, according to Jean Cocteau (*ReM*, 1 March 1924),

Debussy repeated to him phrases of Satie's which

> determined the aesthetic of *Pelléas*: 'There is no need for the or-
> chestra to pull faces when a character comes on stage. Take a look.
> Do the trees or the scenery grimace? What we have to create is a
> musical scenery, a musical atmosphere in which characters move and
> talk. No couplets. No leitmotifs. But we should aim to create the
> sort of atmosphere that suggests Puvis de Chavannes.'

This oft-repeated passage, supposedly dating from 1891, should be treated
with caution, as Cocteau, since *Le coq et l'arlequin* of 1918, had been intent
on establishing Satie's reputation and influence, largely at Debussy's expense.
Satie is also supposed to have told Debussy that he was considering setting *La
Princesse Maleine* but did not know how to obtain Maeterlinck's authorisation.
Whereupon Cocteau would have us believe that 'several days later, Debussy,
having obtained the authorisation of Maeterlinck, began work on *Pelléas et
Mélisande*'!

However, according to Vallas (1958, p. 143), Debussy did write to Maeterlinck, through the intermediacy of Jules Huret, critic of *L'écho de Paris*, to
obtain the necessary authorisation to set *La Princesse Maleine* as an opera.
Perhaps this was as a result of being inspired by Paul Fort's première of Maeterlinck's *L'intruse* at the Théâtre d'Art on 20 May 1891. But whatever the
reason, permission was refused on 23 June that year, as Maeterlinck had
already promised it to none other than Vincent d'Indy, a composer whose
dramatic tastes appear to have been far closer to Debussy's than one might
imagine, and who at the time was the more prominent figure.

Thus *La Princesse Maleine* may have planted a seed in Debussy's mind
which both encouraged dissatisfaction with *Rodrigue et Chimène* in 1891-2
and prepared the way for *Pelléas et Mélisande* in 1893.

Les noces de Sathan (1892)

Jules Bois's esoteric verse play in one act was first published in *La revue
indépendante* in April—June 1890, and Debussy's choice of it provides one of
the only positive pieces of evidence that he was linked with the thriving occult
movement of his time. His friends Michelet, Régnier and Mendès were all associated with the Ordre Kabbalistique de la Rose-Croix founded by Joséphin
Péladan and Stanislas de Guaita in 1888, which met on the first floor above
the Auberge du Clou. All the evidence points towards Debussy's at least
knowing what was going on, although it is difficult to ascertain whether he
was in fact Thirty-third Grand Master of the Prieuré de Sion (Ordre de la
Rose-Croix-Véritas) from 1885 to his death[15] as Henri Lobineau maintains in
his *Dossiers secrets* (p. 21).

But Jules Bois, despite books like *Le satanisme et la magie* (Paris, Léon
Chailley, 1895), was probably more of a fascinated journalist than a true

initiate into the occult, belonging to the rather dubious Ahathoor Temple, founded in Paris in 1890 as an off-shoot of S.L. MacGregor Mather's Order of the Golden Dawn. Bois also waged a complex press campaign against Guaita's order which climaxed in the celebrated duels in 1893 with both Guaita and his Rosicrucian colleague Papus, during which Bois claimed that both his pistol and carriage-horses had been bewitched! In fact everything points against Debussy having taken very seriously the work of a man whom Guaita's secretary Oswald Wirth described as 'a delinquent in magic as well as in art' (Billy, p. 91).

Les noces de Sathan, as revised for performance and publication in 1892, depicts Satan as a beautiful, androgynous youth 'whose crackling hair reflects the heavenly stars like a glistening sea'. Psyche, representing the forces of goodness, tries to appease Satan and convert him, but he only wants to be her 'horrible and charming lover'! Various other characters appear connected with the evil in the world: Adam and Eve, revelling elohims and incubuses etc. In the end, Psyche defeats Satan who then declares himself to be the 'Jesus of another age', to which Psyche replies that she is 'the feminine spirit of Calvary'. The voice of God blesses them as the play ends.

It is small wonder that Debussy got nowhere with such sacrilegious and effusive garbage, even though the play was announced with his incidental music for Paul Fort's Théâtre d'Art in *Le Saint-Graal* on 8 March 1892.[16] As a surviving letter to Bois makes clear, Debussy was having none of it, though the reason given was chiefly the impracticality of the musical provisions, as was to be the case with *Le pèlerin d'amour* and Antoine's *King Lear* in 1903-4.

> I have decided, my dear Bois [Debussy wrote], and whatever the cost to our friendship, I have not the necessary confidence to write the promised music for *Les noces de Sathan*. The orchestra, it seems to me, exists only on a scrap of paper; and as to knowing the names and addresses of the players, it is impossible, apart from a M. Burger who makes continual visits, but who cannot, however, do everything himself.
> Forgive me, and above all do not think that I bear you ill will. Only it would all be too much like a venture into the unknown, and a bit too much like 'bad news'! (Guichard, pp. 13-14)

In the end, two performances of *Les noces de Sathan* did take place on 28 and 30 March 1892 at the Théâtre d'Application, and with music by Henri Quittard, a pupil of César Franck and an archivist at the Paris Opéra. No trace or criticism of his score survives. Lugné-Poë played the role of Satan, and Bois went on to collaborate with Debussy's fellow Rosicrucian Erik Satie on *La porte héroïque du ciel* in 1894.

3   *Pelléas et Mélisande* (1893-5, 1901-2)

> The power of *Pelléas* lies not just in mysteriousness or delicacy, but
> in a great humanity. It offers a representation of its characters' inner
> life which is uniquely subtle in opera, and it does not do that in
> order to express an enfeebled excess of sensibility. Rather it offers a
> certain picture, a strong picture, of what in the inner life is most
> alive, and of what in the way of tenderness and imagination is
> needed to keep it alive.   (Bernard Williams, p. 390)

Aims, composition, productions and interpreters

So much literature and so many conflicting opinions exist about Debussy's
only completed opera that it is difficult to know where to begin. Some can
easily be discounted: like Cyril Scott's opinion that the opera fails because
Debussy tried to wed 'nature-spirit music to a drama of human jealousy'
(p. 137); or Camille Bellaigue's damaging contemporary criticism of the opera's
lack of vitality which 'tends towards the impairment and destruction of our
very existence' (p. 455). But at least Bellaigue's misconceptions about *Pelléas*'
'malevolent germs . . . of decadence and death' have provoked other writers,
notably Bernard Williams (quoted above), to probe for the profounder truths
about the opera's originality and implications.

From the mountains of verbiage which have threatened to envelop the frail
inhabitants of Allemonde, only a handful of writings have contributed substantially to our deeper understanding of the opera by penetrating deep into
its shadowy mythical recesses. The same is even more true of the numerous
analyses of *Pelléas*, like the bar-by-bar 'stylistic study' of Mary Jeanne van
Appeldorn,[1] or the numerical tables of Constantin Bugeanu relating to the
supposed use of bar-forms in Act 3 scene 4. Neither really leaves the reader
any the wiser about what makes *Pelléas et Mélisande* 'tick', and Bugeanu's
conclusions are, incidentally, undermined by his ignorance of a second
(thirteen-bar) cut near the end of the scene.[2]

As usual, careful study of Debussy's articles and letters can provide answers for many of the questions that arise. So, despite the risk of duplication, I should like first to trace the aims and genesis of *Pelléas et Mélisande*, using the composer's own words wherever possible.

First, there is the celebrated conversation of October 1889 with Ernest Guiraud as recorded by Maurice Emmanuel (pp. 35-6). Debussy had recently returned from the overwhelming experience of seeing *Parsifal, Die Meistersinger* and *Tristan* at Bayreuth and it is clear that the aesthetic directions in which he was moving at the time arose as a reaction *against* the Wagnerian conception of the *Gesamtkunstwerk*. It is, however, difficult to believe that he had not read at least something by Maeterlinck before he made the following definition of his operatic ideals:

Debussy: I am not tempted to imitate what I admire in Wagner: I visualise
  a quite different dramatic form. In it, music begins at the point
  where the word becomes powerless as an expressive force: music is
  made for the inexpressible. I should like her to appear to emerge
  from the shadows and at times to return there, and she should always
  be discreet.
Guiraud: What sort of poet could provide you with a suitable text?
Debussy: One who, only hinting at things, will allow me to graft my dream
  upon his; who will not despotically impose on me the 'scene to be
  set' and will leave me free, here and there, to show more artistry
  than him and to complete his work. But he need not be afraid! I shall
  not imitate the follies of the lyric theatre where music insolently
  predominates and where poetry is relegated to second place. In the
  opera house they sing *too much*. One should *sing* only when it is
  worthwhile and hold moving lyrical expression in reserve. There
  should be expressive variety, though. In places it is necessary to paint
  in cameo and to be content with greys . . . Nothing should impede
  the progress of the drama: all musical development not called for
  by the words is a mistake. Besides, musical development that is even
  a little protracted cannot match the mobility of the text. I dream of
  poetic texts which will not condemn me to long, heavy acts, but
  which will provide me with changing scenes, varied in place and mood,
  where the characters do not argue but submit to life and destiny.

These lines describe precisely what Debussy found in Maeterlinck's *Pelléas et Mélisande* just as the latter was creating *La Princesse Maleine*. With both parties firmly believing in the occult, it is tempting to speculate about some form of spiritual telepathy: even Charles Koechlin, when writing his own book on Debussy, needed some reassurance about this interview, which presupposes that Maurice Emmanuel was extremely adept at shorthand. So Emmanuel wrote back on 4 March 1927[3] confirming the early date and accuracy of his music examples, adding that Debussy was not given to 'hoaxing' or 'pontificating'.

Koechlin's unpublished study of *Pelléas et Mélisande*[4] gives the date of the first edition of the play as May 1892,[5] which means that Maeterlinck must have moved quickly after his visit from Charles Van Lerberghe on 30 March when the latter heard the author read the first three acts, the only ones then complete in manuscript. Van Lerberghe's published notes reveal first that Arkel was originally present in the final scene of the first act, though Mélisande was absent. Second, they show that there was no Act 2 scene 4 between Pelléas and Arkel (a scene which Debussy himself later omitted). Third, they reveal that Van Lerberghe thought of Poe's tale *The fall of the House of Usher* as he heard Maeterlinck read the scene from Act 3 where Golaud takes Pelléas into the sinister castle vaults.

Van Lerberghe's notes on Act 5 are dated '13 May' (p. 11), which is presumably the date on which he finished reading his (published) copy of the play. As four further reprints had appeared by the end of 1892, and as Debussy's own first edition copy, printed on Holland paper and bound in vellum, is dated 1892 (Auguste Martin, p. 40, no. 130), it seems very likely that he purchased it '*chez* Flammarion' in Paris from the limited edition available in the early summer of that year. Louis Laloy's 1909 biography, approved by Debussy, supports this, and the composer's close friend Robert Godet claims (pp. 77-8) that Debussy began sketching music after he had read the play, beginning with the horn theme which accompanies 'On dirait que ta voix a passé sur la mer au printemps' (OS, p. 333, fig. 44). This idea begins the music for this scene in the Meyer manuscript sketches (LPm, p. 53), which may thus represent the first notated ideas for the opera. However, this is by no means certain to be the case, as Godet also claims for 1892 Golaud's distinctive rhythm which is conspicuous by its absence in the newly recovered 'September-October [18]93' manuscript of Act 4 scene 4.[6]

In 'Pourquoi j'ai écrit "Pelléas"', penned early in April 1902 on the request of Georges Ricou, the manager of the Opéra-Comique,[7] Debussy would appear to settle all the arguments when he says: 'My acquaintance with *Pelléas* dates from 1893.' But his next sentence creates the usual doubts about the retrospective precision of French chronology. Although he maintains that 'despite the enthusiasm created by a first reading and perhaps a few secret ideas about possible music, I did not begin to think seriously about it until the end of this same year (1893)', we know that he already had a scene rewritten to his satisfaction by October 1893. In addition, his article ends by asserting that the whole *Pelléas* project 'represented pretty nearly twelve years of my life', which would take us through to 1905!

But of far greater importance are Debussy's subsequent 'reasons for choosing *Pelléas*'. As he explains:

> For a long while I had been seeking to write music for the theatre, but the form in which I wanted to create it was so unusual that, after several attempts, I had almost abandoned the idea. Earlier explorations in the field of pure music had led me to hate Classical development, whose beauty lies entirely in technique and can only interest the mandarins of our profession. I wanted music to have a

freedom that was perhaps more inherent than in any other art, as it is not restricted to a more or less exact reproduction of Nature, but rather to the mysterious links between Nature and the imagination.

After several years of passionate pilgrimages to Bayreuth, I began to have doubts about the Wagnerian formula; or rather it seemed to me that it could only serve Wagner's particular genius . . . One should therefore seek to be 'post (*après*) Wagner' rather than a Wagner imitator (*d'après Wagner*).

The drama of *Pelléas*, which despite its dream-like atmosphere contains much more humanity than so-called 'slice-of-life' plays, fitted in admirably with what I wanted to create. It has an evocative language whose sensibility can be extended in music and in the orchestral backcloth. I also tried to obey a law of beauty that seems to be singularly neglected when it comes to dramatic music: the characters of this opera try to sing like real people, not in an arbitrary language made up from worn-out clichés. From therein stems the criticism concerning my so-called predilection for monotonous declamation where nothing ever seems melodic . . . First of all, that is untrue. Further, the feelings of a character cannot always be expressed melodically. Lastly, dramatic melody should be something quite different from melody in general . . . This may appear incomprehensible, but one must not forget that a work of art, an attempt at true beauty, always seems to be taken as a personal insult by a great many people.

This is the nearest that one can get to Debussy's reactions from his seat in the orchestral stalls on 17 May 1893, for Henry Lerolle unfortunately does not mention his friend's opinion in the detailed letter he wrote to Ernest Chausson after the première of *Pelléas* (LPm, p. 7). Lerolle himself 'preferred Ibsen' (then newly fashionable) and complained that in *Pelléas* 'the curtain fell and the setting changed with each scene . . . [making it] too chopped up. And the mania for repeating the same word three times is exhausting. But despite everything, it is very attractive and well executed.' Little did Lerolle know that there were even more repetitions in the first edition which Maeterlinck had removed in the interim, but which Debussy was to retain.

Debussy probably kept quiet about his plans (and musical sketches) for *Pelléas* until after he had secured Maeterlinck's willing authorisation on 8 August. This was obtained through the intermediacy of the poet Henri de Régnier, who wrote to Maeterlinck in early August that his 'friend Achille Debussy, who is a musician of the most clever and delicate talent, has begun some charming music for *Pelléas et Mélisande* which deliciously garlands the text while scrupulously respecting it' (Leblanc, p. 168).

Maeterlinck's permission obtained, Debussy forged ahead with the climactic scene of love and murder at the end of the fourth act, which had perhaps been a major source of attraction for him. He told Chausson he was finishing this scene on 3 September 1893 and would like his opinion. The summer of 1893, which also saw the composition of the third and fourth of the *Proses lyriques* in June and July, was, however, one of frequent self-doubt and neurasthenic depression. On 26 August when Debussy must have been working on (or at least contemplating) Act 4 scene 4, he told Chausson he had spent a miserable evening with Raymond Bonheur and saw stretching ahead only 'a succession of long days, like an avenue of dead trees' (*ReM*, 1925, p. 116).[8] Some of his letters from this period read as desolately as those written during the serious financial crisis of 1910 or at the time of the onset of cancer in 1916.

Chausson's priorities were, however, very different as he wrestled with his own Wagnerian opera *Le Roi Arthus*. 'When I think I have finished a scene', he explained to Debussy on 4 (or 11) September (p. 119), 'I see after several months away from it that there are lots of things in the words that won't do. So I change them, and naturally I have to change the music too.' For Debussy and his sacrosanct text in which only omission was possible, the reason for abandoning his first efforts on 2 October concerned precisely what Chausson or Chabrier would have admired, that is 'the ghost of old Klingsor, alias R. Wagner' (p. 120). After a sleepless night on 1 October, Debussy admitted to Chausson that he had been 'too hasty in shouting victory over *Pelléas et Mélisande*' and that he had

> torn it all up and set out in search of my own little formula of more personal phrases, trying to be as much Pelléas as Mélisande. I have been looking for the music behind all the veils that she accumulates, even for her most ardent devotees! . . . I am using, quite spontaneously, the all-too-rare resource of silence as a means of expression (don't laugh) and as perhaps the only way to point the emotion of a phrase. (p. 120)

This could well refer to the previously mentioned Lehman manuscript, which has a different beginning (see Fig. 5) but a strikingly similar ending to Act 4 scene 4 when compared with the printed vocal score.[9] Pelléas' words 'Il faut que je la voie une dernière fois, jusqu'au fond de son coeur . . . Il faut que je lui dise tout ce que je n'ai pas dit' occur without orchestral accompaniment on p. 3 (VS, pp. 235-6), though the subsequent appearance of Mélisande *is* accompanied. The celebrated declaration of love (VS, p. 244) is sadly missing, but can be found in the Bréval manuscript (LPm, p. 101) of which the Lehman manuscript may once have been a part (see n. 6).

This earliest surviving neat draft would seem to have been completed by 19 October when Chausson told Debussy that Raymond Bonheur was 'quite enamoured by the scene from *Pelléas et Mélisandre* [*sic*]' (*RdM*, 1962, p. 57). Lerolle told Chausson on 21 October that it was 'surprising . . . and sent a shiver up by back' (LPm, p. 11), and both of these reports must have increased Chausson's curiosity about the opera. However, he resisted all temptation to hear Debussy's setting, due to the effect he feared it would have on his own *Le Roi Arthus*. Besides, Debussy kept referring to the dangers of Wagnerism in his letters to him,[10] and Chausson was probably not amongst

Fig. 5. *Pelléas et Mélisande*, Act 4 scene 4, first version dated 'Septembre – [19] Octobre [18] 93' (*US-NYpm* Lehman deposit), showing the use of the Pelléas motif at the start of the scene

those present at the dinner to which Henry Lerolle was invited on 27 October to 'see the gates closed' and hear 'les grandes chaînes' (LPm, p. 12), which symbolised the point of no return as much for Debussy as for Pelléas and Mélisande.

In November Debussy must have been considering the discrepancies in performance time between plays and operas, despite having none of the set pieces to worry about which slowed up the dramatic pace in conventional operas. Being ever economical as regards travel, he contrived to combine a visit to Brussels in late November (during which he played Ysaÿe his latest works and discussed the violinist's forthcoming performance of the String Quartet at the Société Nationale) with a visit to Maeterlinck at Ghent. Pierre Louÿs who was also present at the historic meeting, claimed in 1914 that both parties were so shy that *he* had to do all the talking,[11] but Debussy described the meeting to Chausson as follows (*ReM*, 1925, p. 124):

> I saw Maeterlinck, with whom I spent a day in Ghent. At first he assumed the behaviour of a young girl being introduced to her future husband. Then he thawed and became quite charming, and his talk of the theatre made him seem a truly remarkable man. He gave me *carte blanche* for the cuts in *Pelléas* and even suggested some very important and *very useful* ones himself! Now from the musical side, he says that he understands nothing: with a Beethoven symphony he is like a blind man in a museum. But really he is a very fine man who speaks of extraordinary things with an exquisite simplicity. When I thanked him for entrusting *Pelléas* to me, he insisted that it was he who ought to be grateful to me for wishing to set it to music! As my opinion was diametrically opposite, I had to employ what little diplomacy nature had endowed me with.

Debussy cut four of Maeterlinck's nineteen scenes altogether. First, Act 1 scene 1 in which, symbolically, the servants open the castle gates at dawn and scrub the threshold. Second, Act 2 scene 4 in which Arkel successfully persuades Pelléas to postpone his trip away from the castle as his friend Marcellus is now dead. Third, Act 3 scene 1 in which Mélisande is spinning in the castle in the company of Pelléas and Yniold, who is afraid that Mélisande will leave him. Golaud returns from hunting and his lamp reveals that Pelléas and Mélisande have both been crying. Lastly, Debussy cut Act 5 scene 1 with the frightened servants assembled below stairs discussing in hushed tones the events resulting from Act 4 scene 4. Golaud has returned with blood on his sword; Mélisande on her deathbed has given premature birth to a frail baby girl; and Pelléas has been found dead at the bottom of the fountain of the blind.

The third act omission is the most important for it is the only time that Pelléas, Mélisande and Yniold are together. It also includes the symbolic image of the swans fighting the dogs, which Yniold sees from the window, and it introduces part of the song that Mélisande sings in the following scene in the first edition. Mélisande's spinning scene also inspired the beautiful 'Fileuse' movement in Fauré's incidental music for *Pelléas et Mélisande* in 1898.

Broadly speaking, the cuts Debussy made (or Maeterlinck suggested) removed the more obviously symbolic passages, as well as those which slow up the dramatic action or which over-clarify external events or personal relationships in the shadowy, elusive world of Allemonde. On the practical side, the inhabitants of the castle of Allemonde ('all the world') cover four generations, a rare circumstance in opera, and whilst the plot is too well known to need repeating here, the complexity of the royal family tree justifies its inclusion. Pelléas, as can be seen, has the misfortune to fall in love with his older half-brother's second wife, and there are several subsidiary characters who remain unseen and unnamed so as not to detract from the tragic interaction of the main protagonists.

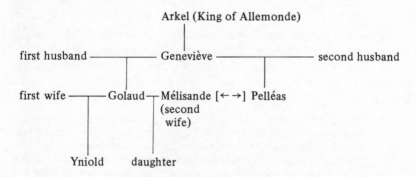

From the dating of the manuscripts and other documentary evidence, the following chronology can be established for the composition of the vocal score as it appears in the 1902 edition:

Act 1   December 1893 – February 1894
Act 2   scene 1: ? June 1895
        scenes 2 and 3: June–August 1895 and completed by 17 August
Act 3   scene 1: May–June 1894
        scene 2: July–August 1894
        scenes 3 and 4: August 1894
Act 4   scenes 1 and 2: ? early 1895
        scene 3: August 1894
        scene 4: August–October 1893 (second version late September – 19 October)
        Whole act revised and completed May 1895 with extra work carried out in January 1900 and May–September 1901 (scene 4).
Act 5   April–June 1895

Thus, after completing Act 4 scene 4 to his satisfaction and establishing precisely what textual cuts were to be made, Debussy went back to the beginning and more or less worked his way through, apart from the start of Act 4, and Act 2 (which he left until after he had completed Act 5). As he told Henry Lerolle on 17 August 1895 (the final date on Act 2 of the Boston manuscript), the completion had not been

> without certain infuriating moments, especially in the [second] scene between Golaud and Mélisande! It's there that one begins to stir up disaster as Mélisande begins to lie to Golaud, worthy fellow that he is, who demonstrates that he cannot be other than completely frank, even with little girls. I think that you will like the [third] scene outside the grotto: it tries to capture all that is mysterious in the night, where in the silence even a blade of grass disturbed from its slumbers makes a quite alarming noise. Then the distant sea pours out its troubles to the moon, and it is Pelléas and Mélisande who are slightly afraid to speak amid so much mystery. (Denis, p. 32)

Neither had the first act in 1894 been exactly plain sailing, and in January Debussy refused to play any of his opera to as respected a friend as Paul Dukas until he had 'an act or two complete', so as to avoid making a fragmentary impression (LL, p. 63). About this time he told Chausson[12] that it was all

> Mélisande's fault! . . . I have spent days in the pursuit of the mere 'nothing' of which she is made . . . Now it is Arkel who torments me; he is from *beyond the grave* and he has the disinterested and prophetic tenderness of those who are soon to leave this world. All this must be evoked with doh, ray, me, fah, soh, lah, te, doh!!! What a profession! (*ReM*, 1926, pp. 87-8)

But on 31 May 1894, Pierre Louÿs was busily inviting his friends Thadée Natanson (director of *La revue blanche*) and his young wife Misia,[13] the painter Paul Robert, and Léon Blum to a dinner to hear Act 1, Act 4 scene 4 and Act 3 scene 1 ('if it was completed') (LOU, p. 32). By 20 July Louÿs knew that Debussy was working on Act 3 scene 2, and this and the following scene were complete by 20 August. The scene in the castle vaults was 'full of covert terror and mysterious enough to make the most seasoned souls dizzy', Debussy told Lerolle on 28 August (Denis, p. 29). Whereas the marvellous emergence into the daylight he described as full of 'sunshine suffused by our good mother the sea', an image and source of natural inspiration to which Debussy often returned.

Before writing Act 3 scene 4, Debussy moved to Act 4 scene 3, the 'scène des petits moutons', which was also complete by 28 August 1894. Here, he told Lerolle, he had

> tried to put a little of the compassion of a child to whom a sheep at first represents the idea of a game in which he cannot take part, and also a sense of the pity which the aspiring bourgeoisie no longer have.

Now I am working on the scene between father and son [Act 3 scene 4], and I am afraid: I must say such profound and trustworthy things! There is a 'petit père' in it which gives me nightmares. I have also had an idea for the death of Mélisande, which is to put an orchestral group on stage . . . What do you say to this? (pp. 29-30)

Lerolle's reply must have been unfavourable, or Debussy later thought better of his original conception of a 'death full of sonority' for Mélisande. When he came to describe the composition of the end of the fifth act to Louÿs in April 1895 he confessed that he had been 'surprised by the death of Mélisande which made me uneasy: I trembled as I worked' (LOU, p. 50). He referred to Pelléas and Mélisande as his only companions,[14] though when he did emerge in public, Debussy seems to have feigned reluctance to demonstrate his latest progress on *Pelléas*: there is a long account by Lerolle in a letter to Chausson of 19 December 1894 which describes one gathering when d'Indy played the third act of *Fervaal* and then ended up turning pages for Debussy, 'grimacing with his moustache' as he did so (LPm, p. 15).

But as Debussy confessed to Lerolle in August 1895, once the music was finished his worries were really only just beginning (Denis, p. 32). Describing Allemonde from a distance and 'building up a scaffolding of dreams that would be cruelly dismantled by reality' had been difficult enough, but how would 'the world behave in the company of these two poor little beings? – How I hate crowds, universal suffrage and tricoloured phrases!' The death of Mélisande had hardly moved his editor, Georges Hartmann, and for most people in France

> every time a woman dies in the theatre it has to be as in *La dame aux camélias*. It is sufficient merely to replace the camellias with other flowers and the lady with a bazaar princess! People cannot admit that one departs discreetly, like someone who has had enough of this planet Earth and is going to where the flowers of tranquillity blossom!

But before the ordeal of public reaction had to be endured, Debussy faced the more practical task of securing a performance of his opera. He must have begun doing this immediately, for in *L'écho de Paris* on 12 October 1895 Paul Larochelle announced a performance of *Pelléas et Mélisande* with music by Debussy at the Théâtre Libre. Debussy must have had high hopes that this would take place for he contacted Maeterlinck, who replied agreeably on 17 October: 'As to *Pelléas*, it goes without saying that the matter rests entirely with you and that it can be performed wherever or whenever you like.' (Dietschy, 1962, p. 117)

From the first, however, Debussy rejected anything but a full theatrical performance of *Pelléas*. On 27 November 1895 (LOU, p. 65) Louÿs asked Debussy why he had turned down the offer to arrange a symphonic suite for a London performance of the play, probably, as Lockspeiser suggests (LO, 1,

p. 195), for Lugné-Poë's production at the Independent Theatre in the Strand. We also indirectly owe Fauré's incidental music of 1898 to Debussy, as Jean-Michel Nectoux has discovered (1979, p. 21). The celebrated actress Mrs Patrick Campbell, inspired by Lugné-Poë's London production to play the role of Mélisande herself, first commissioned Jack Mackail's English translation and then tried to elicit incidental music from Debussy through the writer Camille Mauclair. Debussy told his editor, Hartmann, on 9 August 1898 (Nectoux, 1979, p. 22) that he had refused because he had 'understood and envisaged this drama in an entirely musical setting [as a lyric drama], and could not undertake something which would have looked like a denegation of this'. Therefore Fauré was approached instead and the success of his score, first heard at the Prince of Wales' Theatre, London, on 21 June 1898, clearly made Debussy jealous, the more so because its more limited conception, relative conformity, and of course great beauty attracted Hartmann straight away.

As this was also the first music to be associated with *Pelléas et Mélisande* there was for Debussy a serious risk both of unfavourable comparison (if and when his opera was performed) and, at worst, of permanent identification in popular opinion between Maeterlinck's play and Fauré's music. The frequency with which the two were performed together in both England and France in the subsequent years must have raised doubts in Debussy's mind as to whether his opera, with its higher costs and risks, would ever reach the stage at all. In addition Hartmann's opinion mattered to Debussy, not least because he feared the withdrawal of vital financial support during the difficult years before his reputation was fully established. So when Hartmann wrote, praising the success of Fauré's *Pelléas*, Debussy was provoked into condemning his efforts, almost certainly without having heard his score, hypocritically citing the elevated social circles whence Fauré's patronage came to support his case. In the same letter of 9 August, Debussy continued:

> Your letter greatly annoyed me because of the importance you attach to a matter which seems to me to be purely anecdotal . . . Moreover, the impression this music makes must be confined to this production alone, and if I may be so vain, it appears to me impossible that there should be any grounds for confusion, unless it is over a question of substance.[15]
> But then Fauré is the music-case (*porte-musique*) of a band of snobs and fools who will never see anything in or do anything for the other *Pelléas*. The most vexing thing, once again, is that you were vividly moved by it. As for myself, I swear to you that nothing leaves me so utterly indifferent.

As Nectoux rightly concludes (1979, p. 23), the two versions of *Pelléas* are so different as to be incomparable, though 'it is precisely from *Pelléas* onwards that Debussy's aesthetic really forms itself, definitively leaving the paths which had brought it near to that of Fauré' around 1887-90. Fauré himself told Albert Carré early in May 1902, after seeing *Pelléas* twice at the latter's expense, that he remained 'rebellious to Debussy's [musical] processes'. But he thought Carré's production 'truly *miraculous*' (as Debussy did), and it is interesting that this same letter reveals that Fauré was considering setting Maeterlinck's *Soeur Béatrice* with Carré and the Opéra-Comique in mind (Nectoux, 1979, p. 24), although this unfortunately came to nothing.

So did Debussy's attempt to interest the Théâtre de la Monnaie (Brussels) in *Pelléas* through his friend Ysaÿe in 1896. But this may have been due to Debussy's repeated refusal to allow Ysaÿe to conduct extracts from his opera in the concert hall. On 13 October 1896, Debussy wrote firmly (Auguste Martin, p. 43, no. 151):

> If this work has any merit, it is above all in the connection between its scenic and musical movement. In concert performance this quality would disappear and no one could be reproached for seeing nothing in those eloquent silences which abound in the opera. Moreover, the simplicity of the means employed can only acquire its true significance on the stage and I should be immediately compared with Wagner in terms of lavishness, beside whom I should look like a poor fellow who couldn't afford to employ contrabass tubas.
>
> In my opinion, *Pelléas et Mélisande* must be performed as it is written. People can then either take it or leave it. If I have to fight for it, it will at least have been worth the effort.

But Ysaÿe did not give up easily with his concert plans for Brussels, and Debussy was forced on 17 November[16] to refuse outright to give him permission to conduct it, after he had announced that 'fragments' of *Pelléas* would be performed at one of his symphonic concerts.

The years 1897 to 1899 were largely occupied with work on the *Nocturnes* and Debussy told Hartmann on 16 September 1898, perhaps untruthfully to justify delays in their completion, that 'these three were giving him more trouble than the five acts of *Pelléas*' (*ReM*, 1964, p. 119). But this does not mean that he had given up hope of hearing his opera in the near future, as Dietschy suggests (1962, p. 125). *Pelléas* had been accepted 'in principle' by the Opéra-Comique in May 1898, thanks to Messager who had been appointed musical director there on 14 January. On 14 July Debussy was pressing Hartmann to try to secure a firm undertaking from Carré (the new director) for performance there the following winter. Perhaps mindful of the London success of Fauré's incidental music and anxious to capitalise on this, he told Hartmann (*ReM*, 1964, pp. 112-13) that 'lots of people have already spoken of *Pelléas* and it is vital not to lose or lessen the power of its artistic newness to arouse contemporary interest . . . We must not let too much "fluff" accumulate in the ears of our beloved dilettantes.' And to keep the subject fresh in Hartmann's mind, Debussy told him on 23 July (p. 113) that he had had 'the most amazing nightmares. I was present at a rehearsal of *Pelléas* where Golaud was suddenly transformed into a bailiff and carried out his business to the musical formulae which characterise his part.'

After the disappointment of Hartmann's preference for Fauré's *Pelléas*, Debussy nonetheless continued to give private solo performances of his opera at the piano to stimulate interest and support. On 2 February 1899 it was the turn of the family of Arthur Fontaine, and around that time he played it to Pierre Louÿs and Camille Mauclair at his flat in the rue Cardinet, where he told Mauclair that two performances were planned at Robert de Montesquiou's Pavillon des Muses.[17]

Apart from the date of January 1900 on the fourth act of the Boston manuscript, there is no direct evidence that Debussy worked on his opera between completing the vocal score in August 1895 and completing the orchestration after its definite acceptance for the Opéra-Comique on 3 May 1901. The announcement of *Pelléas* in *Le ménestrel* of 5 August 1900 for the following season was just another of the many theatrical false promises from which Debussy suffered throughout his career, and on 3 July 1899 he lamented to Hartmann (LL, p. 98) after reading Carré's choices for the 1900 season: 'But what will become of poor little Pelléas and Mélisande? M. A. Carré must have very little heart not to adopt two such gentle children at once.'

But after hearing the opera again in the rue Cardinet in April 1901 at Messager's request, Carré did finally 'adopt' them for 1902 and Debussy was suddenly faced with a period of intensive work in the company of his two demanding 'children'. According to a letter to Louis Laloy on 25 July 1907 (*RdM*, 1962, p. 26), he began in May 1901 by revising Act 4 scene 4,[18] most probably the opening section and the link with the previous scene. The final Act 4 date on the Boston manuscript is September 1901.

Precisely when Debussy orchestrated *Pelléas* is uncertain. When he told Louÿs in November 1901 that he had 'taken it into his head to reorchestrate' the opera (LOU, p. 167), this may mean that he had begun and abandoned the process earlier that year, probably in May. As usual, Debussy would have done much advance planning in his head before he wrote anything down, and on 2 September he told Louÿs (p. 165) that he had 'worked for a long time in the company of that little neurasthenic Mélisande, who cannot be accompanied by violins unless they are divided into eighteen parts'. As usual, also, Debussy had other theatrical matters in his mind that summer and a major item in the correspondence with Louÿs was his projected symphonic suite to accompany *Le voyage de Pausole* (see Chapter 12).

It is most unlikely that Debussy orchestrated *Pelléas* twice, even in part, for only one orchestral manuscript score exists (see Appendix) and he often claimed more progress on theatrical works than was actually the case. The orchestral textures involved in *Pelléas*, whilst extemely subtle, were in the main less complex than those in the contemporary orchestral works, and as orchestration was always something Debussy left to the last possible moment (or like Fauré assigned to someone else), the most likely hypothesis is that

Pelléas was orchestrated in one intensive burst between November 1901 and January 1902 when the first detailed rehearsals began. During this period in purdah, virtually everything was abandoned in favour of 'attending to the machinery of *Pelléas et Mélisande* . . . which consumes my days and nights' (LOU, p. 169).

In the meantime the celebrated row with Maeterlinck over the casting of Mélisande was brewing. Whether or not Debussy 'approved' of Georgette Leblanc's 'interpretation' in the four or five rehearsals she claimed they had together late in 1901 (p. 170), Mary Garden, the star of Charpentier's *Louise*, was announced for the role in *Le ménestrel* on 29 December. It is difficult to believe that this provided Maeterlinck's first inkling that his mistress had been dropped in favour of la Garden, and he must have known that his subsequent attacks on Debussy through the Société des Auteurs in February, through the famous letter to *Le figaro* of 13 April,[19] through the challenge to a duel, and even through the disparaging and parodistic programme placed on sale at the dress-rehearsal of *Pelléas* were doomed to failure, since Debussy had had his written authorisation to proceed since 17 October 1895.[20]

All this nonsense simply added to the overworked Debussy's problems. What came far closer to undermining the whole enterprise was the plethora of faults in the orchestral parts, copied (no doubt on the cheap) by an inexperienced neighbour of Debussy's in the rue Cardinet. These necessitated much last-minute correction by Debussy and the young chorus-master Henri Büsser to prevent Messager from postponing the whole project.

Then there was the question of lengthening the interludes to cover several of the complicated scene changes. The first sign of this came as late as the day before the first full rehearsal when Debussy told Paul-Jean Toulet that 'towards 10 p.m.' on 1 April Messager 'visited me to ask for a linking passage of seventy-five bars in the second act of *Pelléas* . . . Naturally it is needed at once!' (LL, p. 114) In the end, Debussy added fifty-two bars to Act 2 and composed and orchestrated 148 extra bars for Acts 1, 2 and 4 which proved the most expansive and obviously Wagnerian in the opera. However, a purist reversion to Debussy's more restrained original as printed in the Fromont score of 1902 would not, I feel, be in the opera's best interests, even though, with improved modern techniques and machinery or in a less complex production, the scene changes would now be possible in the time the original interludes allow. The musical losses would be as follows:

Act 1 scenes 1-2   Durand VS, p. 22, bar 8 – p. 25, bar 3 (cf Fromont VS, p. 22, bars 2-5; 33 bars added)

Act 1 scenes 2-3   Durand p. 37, bar 14 – end of p. 38 (cf Fromont p. 34, bars 7-8; 18 bars added)

Act 2 scenes 1-2   Durand p. 73, bar 3 – p. 75, bar 16 (cf Fromont p. 65, bars 3-6; 37 bars added)

Act 2 scenes 2-3   Durand p. 103 (cf Fromont p. 91, bars 3-4; 15 bars added)
Act 4 scenes 2-3   Durand p. 220, bar 10 – end of p. 222 (cf Fromont p. 199, bars 6-8; 45 bars added)

It was the omission of these passages from the Fromont edition, together with the testimony of Henri Büsser,[21] which gave rise to the misconception that the interludes were not expanded in time for the first performance on 30 April. But Debussy, like Manuel de Falla in the case of his last-minute additions to Le tricorne for Diaghilev's London première in 1919, could compose extremely fast when he had to, and several accounts of the première can help to clarify the situation. Messager (pp. 111-12) claims to have collected the interludes from Debussy page by page between rehearsals, a procedure prophetic of Le martyre de Saint Sébastien in 1911. He implies that all was ready by the time of the dress-rehearsal on 28 April.[22] On 10 May Paul Flat comments (p. 592) on the Wagnerian nature of the interludes separating the tableaux; on 15 May Calvocoressi specifically mentions (p. 157) the later expansions 'not in the score', as does Adolphe Jullien in Le théâtre (p. 14) in an article which also refers to the impression made in performance by the (now lost) song cycle Nuits blanches (p. 13). No review mentions any delays during the acts, and as the expanded interludes are present in the manuscript conducting score (F-Pn MSS 961-2, 964) it is reasonable to suppose that Messager rather than Büsser is telling the truth. Vallas (1958, p. 227) supports this hypothesis too. It is also significant that Büsser's earliest account was published over a quarter of a century later than Messager's.

As far as the rehearsals, première and revivals of Pelléas are concerned, I should like to concentrate mainly on the insight they offer into Debussy as a working theatre musician reacting to his singers and other thespian colleagues.[23] Although Debussy frequently went to the theatre throughout his life and never managed to dissociate himself from it, Pelléas et Mélisande provided his first real 'inside' experience of a production. The accounts of Georgette Leblanc and Mary Garden of rehearsals with Debussy are so often retouched from hindsight, to their authors' benefit, that they should not be taken too literally. But Leblanc (p. 170) does get over the point about Debussy's shyness when she says that 'while we worked, our understanding was perfect. But when we stopped to rest we found it difficult to talk.' Messager (p. 110) says of the early rehearsals at his house that Debussy inspired the artists with enthusiasm for his opera through his own solo performance at the piano, 'singing all the roles in that deep sepulchral voice which often necessitated transposition down an octave, but whose expression gradually became irresistible', particularly in the moving music for the death of Mélisande.

Mary Garden also recalls his sense of humour as they first tried through 'Mes longs cheveux' in Act 3 (1962, p. 9). After a long silence, the conversation ran as follows:

Debussy: Who are you? Where do you come from?
Garden: From Scotland.
Debussy (joyfully, almost ecstatically, like an urchin): From Scotland! From
Scotland! Oh! that's very good . . . I suppose my Mélisande *had*
to come from Scotland!

Rehearsals moved into the Opéra-Comique on 13 January 1902, but Debussy was already a frequent visitor there for he apologised to Robert Godet on 10 January (GOD, pp. 102-3) for being out when he called, as he 'was stupidly in a corridor of the Opéra-Comique awaiting M. Albert Carré on the subject of *Pelléas* . . . which I have, in truth, played rather too often of late!'

Debussy seems to have been present for all of the twenty-one ensemble rehearsals needed for his unconventional masterpiece. Mary Garden reveals how seriously he took them in that no one was permitted to move or talk while the changes to the interludes were being rehearsed (1952, p. 69). Much of the time after the orchestral rehearsals began on 21 March was occupied in sorting out mistakes in the parts: Büsser undertook the correction of the strings, whilst Debussy tried to find time to take care of the wind (22-5 March). Before the final panic we find Debussy on 4 March turning pages for Louis Landry as he supervised the soloists rehearsing in the Opéra-Comique library (Büsser, 1955, p. 109), and Debussy, as tongue-tied in public as he was articulate on paper, is mainly remembered during rehearsals for his repeated requests to the orchestra to play 'quietly, quietly; less loudly, I beg of you' (Büsser, 1952, p. 536). He was also furious when Jean Périer and Hector Dufranne were still singing 'at the tops of their voices' on 17 April in the operatic manner that they were used to.

Two other major problems faced Debussy during March 1902. The first was that his friend André Messager, whom he trusted implicitly to make his dream into a reality, was also musical director of Covent Garden. His commitments there meant that, with the delays to the dress-rehearsal of *Pelléas*, he could conduct only the first three performances. So, as early as 19 March, the inexperienced Büsser was approached with a view to assuming the role, which he did with great trepidation at the fourth performance on 8 May. Debussy informed Messager the following day (MES, p. 16) that poor Büsser appeared in the theatre 'looking like a man who was about to take a cold bath but did not relish the idea'. But with the encouragement of Debussy and the leader M. Forest, and despite the refusal of Mary Garden to look at him during the special extra dress-rehearsal on 7 May, Büsser succeeded in winning through by the fourth act, from which point neither he nor his career ever looked back.

Debussy's second problem, with which Büsser was also involved, arose from the search for a suitable Yniold. Dispatched to the *solfège* classes at the Conservatoire on 24 March, Büsser thought he had captured the ideal 'rare bird' (1966, p. 275) in Noël Gallon, later to become professor of fugue there. But his voice was the equivalent of a mezzo-soprano, and Debussy insisted on a lighter soprano voice. Eventually a young lad named Blondin (who later, in contrast, became a taxi-driver) was selected from the children's chorus of *Carmen*. But his inexperience as a soloist and the rather over-insistent repetitions of the phrase 'petit père' provoked hilarity amongst the opera's detractors at the dress-rehearsal and Debussy might have been wise to have accepted Gallon. However, the withdrawal for the initial series of performances of Yniold's scene with the sheep in the fourth act was probably more of a safety measure than a considered artistic decision on Debussy's part.[24]

The other source of amusement at the dress-rehearsal on 28 April was Mary Garden's French pronunciation, which still showed liberal traces of her Aberdeen origins, especially in such important lines as 'Je ne suis pas heureuse'. According to René Peter (who had to absent himself for some reason or other during Act 2 scene 1), the audience imitated her every word and had 'almost as much fun as in Feydeau' when Pelléas played with her golden hair in the third act (1942, p. 9). After Yniold's scene in Act 4, however, appreciation grew, for Mary Garden's vocal and acting talents were considerable.

Debussy remained backstage, closeted in Carré's office (Büsser says Messager's!) chain-smoking, as one would take refuge 'in a lighthouse during a tempest'. Afterwards he walked through the streets with René Peter resolutely changing the subject when *Pelléas* was mentioned, and the evening ended (perhaps drunkenly) in a sort of 'sleepy fog' before the two men and Lilly Debussy took a cab home. Mary Garden claims (1962, p. 8) to have found Debussy late that night 'at the Café Riche, melancholy in front of a beer glass and an ash-tray overflowing with half-smoked cigarettes'. This either forms the missing link in the chain of events or suggests that, unable to sleep, he went out again alone.

Carré blamed Maeterlinck's text for the disruptions at the dress-rehearsal, doubtless inflamed like the audience by his ridiculous synopsis which had been put on sale in programme form outside the theatre. Cuts were planned in conjunction with Debussy and Messager before the première, but it is difficult to tell whether any were carried out, or whether those mentioned in the Durand vocal score as being 'Opéra-Comique practice' were in fact made at this juncture. Unfortunately Carré's surviving *mise-en-scène*, prepared with the aid of the Fromont vocal score and dated 27 April 1902, does not help, for it contains all the passages in question as well as Act 4 scene 3.[25] Neither does it confirm anything about the interludes for it simply marks each new tableau with the words 'changement rapide'.

Compared with the dress-rehearsal, the evening première on 30 April was a huge success. As Peter says (1942, p. 9), the uproar changed to 'rumours', then to 'murmurs', and then to murmurs of admiration. The critic Paul Locard described the reactions of some of his distinguished neighbours in the audience as follows (p. 167): '[Alexandre] Guilmant dreams in admiration; the high priests of the Schola [Cantorum], [Vincent] d'Indy, [Pierre] de Bréville and [Charles] Bordes, approve of it; Charles Koechlin is thrilled; [Édouard] Colonne enjoys this "new theatre"; and on either side of me, a very interested [Léon] Jéhin picks up the happy smiles of Albert Diot.' Subsequent critical reactions were, however, divided, with those against (like Bellaigue and Arthur Pougin) making the greatest errors of judgment in retrospect and revealing more about their own musical prejudices than about Debussy's opera. Théodore Dubois, the reactionary director of the Conservatoire, actually forbade his students to attend the opera! As Roger Nichols so succinctly puts it (1980, p. 296):

> Accusations were largely of formlessness (no arias), melodic and rhythmic monotony (no dances), lack of noise (sparing use of trombones) and unintelligible harmonic progressions (few perfect cadences). Possibly these criticisms might have been tempered by a perusal of the vocal score but this did not appear in print until ten days after the première and by that time positions were entrenched.

In the end, it was the enthusiastic support of colleagues like Dukas, Pierné, Koechlin, Caplet and Ravel who bought gallery seats for performance after performance that helped secure *Pelléas et Mélisande* a place in the standard repertory of the Opéra-Comique. This was at least as effective as the favourable, and on the whole perceptive reviews of such as Henry Baüer (*Le figaro*) and Gaston Carraud (*La liberté*) which have been extensively quoted elsewhere and do not need repeating here.[26]

Where Debussy was during the première is not known, though it is likely that he was in the theatre for most of the initial series of performances. Mary Garden's claim (1952, p. 73) that he 'never came to a single performance' and told her 'I gave it to the public and now it doesn't interest me any longer' is surely as false as the story of his declaration of love to her in the park at Versailles in June 1904 (pp. 77-8); by then he had already decided to leave Lilly for Emma Bardac, a desertion which Mary Garden never forgave and which she allowed to colour her picture of the composer. However, her account of Debussy being infuriated by a performance of Maeterlinck's play in London on 18 July 1904, with Sarah Bernhardt as Pelléas and Mrs Patrick Campbell as Mélisande, may have more truth behind it (pp. 76-7). Garden whispered to a restless Debussy that the fifty-nine-year-old Sarah Bernhardt was 'trying to impersonate Robin Hood', and when Mrs Patrick Campbell let fall an 'avalanche of jet-black hair' in Act 3, Debussy apparently 'almost screamed' and asked his companion when the next train left for Paris. Thereupon they both escaped from the theatre and from London with their nerves completely shattered!

We know that Debussy was no W. S. Gilbert (who never saw his own operettas on stage) from his accounts of Büsser's conducting and the other observations forwarded to Messager at Covent Garden. Debussy was apparently very pleased with the première when Büsser visited him on 1 May (Büsser, 1955, p. 115), though he predictably refused to take curtain-calls after the third performance on 3 May. When he and Lilly dined with Büsser in the rue de Saint-Petersbourg on 5 (or 6) May, Debussy told him (p. 116) that he had 'tried to move his audience by the simplicity of my vocal parts and by the discretion of my orchestration. I have a horror of brutal effects, so much sought after by my predecessors', he added. But when Büsser first mounted the podium on 8 May, Debussy told Messager (MES, p. 16) that he did not 'trouble himself at all with the singers and threw their chords at their feet without the least care about their harmonic qualities'. Whilst he admitted that the evening had eventually proved successful, Debussy regretted the departure of his ideal conductor, who had known

> how to awaken the inner sound world of *Pelléas* with tender delicacy. It is no longer necessary to search for this to be able to find it again for it is most certain that the interior life of all music depends on who evokes it, as each word depends on the mouth which utters it. Thus such impression as *Pelléas* creates is doubled in the context of your own emotional discoveries in the opera, and through these it is put marvellously into its proper perspective.

Debussy must, however, have been tactful to Büsser in the theatre, and recognised that it was essential to encourage him if *Pelléas* was to succeed. But his real opinions as expressed to Messager still show that a certain amount of hypocrisy was involved, for at the seventh performance on 20 May (of which Büsser recorded that Paul Taffanel, now a conducting *colleague*, was 'bursting with enthusiasm' (1955, p. 118) about his interpretation), Debussy complained to Messager that the hand at the helm was not exercising as tight a grip as he would have liked, in that M. Martenot was adding *glissandi* on the first harp in a manner that 'appeared excessive' (MES, p. 19). In addition, Jean Périer had a cold and only Mary Garden and Hector Dufranne 'remained unchangeable'.

Problems with the cast were nothing new, for on 14 May (MES, p. 25, letter wrongly dated 18 June) Debussy had told Messager that Périer was voiceless and that the critic Willy (Henry Gauthier-Villars) had wickedly branded the performance 'l'après-midi d'aphone'! Even though, according to Büsser, Messager had heard and commended his eleventh performance on 2 June, Debussy had earlier lamented to Messager on 14 May that without him 'there was something rotten in the state of Allemonde!' – one of his many *Pelléas* allusions to *Hamlet*.

In the end, Périer was not re-engaged for the 1902-3 revival, and after seriously considering Mme Jeanne Raunay as a Pelléas *en travestie*,[27] Carré replaced him with the tenor Rigaux on 30 October 1902. But before this was decided, Debussy discussed the Raunay question frankly with Messager on 28 June (MES, p. 31), when he maintained that she confessed to an irregular love for Pelléas which, in our particular case, curiously resembles lyrical masturbation, or to be less medical, narcissism.

To sum up, Pelléas has none of the amorous manners of a Hussar and his tardy manly resolves are so abruptly guillotined by Golaud's sword that there would perhaps be no drawbacks to this substitution.

Once again it was musical considerations that finally influenced Debussy, for on 2 July he told Messager that Mme Raunay had 'sung him fragments of *Pelléas* with the voice of a passionate old man who was rather short of breath'!

Debussy's love of colourful irreverence and his absolute disregard of possible libel action shows up best in his letters to close friends like his publisher Jacques Durand,[28] where his true opinions of his interpreters are also to be found. These, as might be expected, come in stark contrast to the compliments offered to the singers themselves. For instance, Debussy wrote to the soprano Jane Bathori in April 1908 (LL, p. 171) that Maggie Teyte had 'a charming voice and a very apt perception of the character of Mélisande', whereas he told Durand on 8 June that year that she 'showed about as much emotion as a prison door [and was] a more-than-distant princess'! This was as a result of her performance as Mélisande during rehearsals for a revival at the Opéra-Comique on 12 June.

Similarly Debussy wrote to Gabriel Astruc on 6 December 1908 that Rose Féart (who created Mélisande at Covent Garden in 1909) had a 'voice and musicality [which] much pleased me' (Lesure, 1975, p. 88). But he told Durand on 18 May 1909 that she was 'unspeakably ugly, lacking in poetry' and that now he 'continually missed the graceful Miss Teyte'! From this it becomes clear that Debussy's scathing comments were immediate reactions to a particular performance or rehearsal, and that his Mélisandes had to face comparison with Mary Garden, about whom Debussy never wrote or said an unkind word.[29] His glowing tribute to her in *Musica* of January 1908 (LCr, pp. 195-6) recalls his delight as she brought Mélisande to life with the 'fragility and distant charm' that the music sought to convey, but without one false move during her crucial 'long silences' which could so easily have destroyed the image he wanted to create. Debussy no longer wished to describe in detail those memorable rehearsals which 'made up my best hours in the theatre. There it was that I came to know the inestimable devotion of truly great artists . . . I hardly ever had to say anything to her as the character of Mélisande gradually became visible.' The high-spot of the première, which Debussy awaited 'with a strange confidence mixed with curiosity' was Act 5: Mélisande's death (see Fig. 6) filled him with 'wonder and inexpressible emotion. It was the soft voice that I had heard only in secret, with that feeble tenderness, that captivating art whose existence I had previously not believed in.'

Debussy also thought highly of Hector Dufranne, calling him the 'most profoundly human Golaud one could wish to hear' on 23 December 1906 (Auguste Martin, p. 58, no. 273) after the fiftieth performance of *Pelléas* at

Fig. 6 *Pelléas et Mélisande*, Act 5, the death of Mélisande; design by Lucien Jusseaume

the Opéra-Comique, though he had also told Félix Vieuille (Arkel) on 6 April 1905 that he was the 'most profoundly human of grandfathers' (p. 58, no. 276)! On 26 October 1906 Debussy wrote to Dufranne to 'excuse my nervousness during rehearsals of *Pelléas* which makes me go farther than I would wish in my mode of speaking. You and Vieuille are almost alone in retaining an understanding of my artistic intentions in *Pelléas*.' (p. 58, no. 272) He asked Dufranne to exaggerate the 'sad and poignant tenderness' of Golaud in the final act, to 'put across strongly the impression of all that he regrets not having said or done, and of all the good fortune which is escaping him for ever'. It is this reticence, which as Roger Nichols says (1980, p. 307) 'is a concentration of feeling not a lack of it', that goes to the heart of what *Pelléas* is about. It also gives some idea of why the opera was so much misunderstood, as for those 'nurtured on Verdi, Wagner and Strauss, it was hard to appreciate that passion need not be measured in decibels'.

With Périer, however, Debussy was more guarded, simply sending 'my thanks for everything that *Pelléas* and its author owe you' after a performance on 6 April 1905 (Auguste Martin, p. 58, no. 268). He wickedly told Durand on 8 June 1908 that Périer 'mimed admirably to the music' and he attributed his growing popularity as Pelléas ten days later to the fact that 'he no longer sings my music at all'!

But Debussy's wit could be as often benevolent as bitingly ironical and the following extract from a letter of 8 April 1905[30] to Albert Vizentini, the stage manager of the Opéra-Comique, shows that his consideration extended to those backstage as well. Thanking Vizentini for all the theatrical experience he had 'so willingly put at the service of *Pelléas*', he added that this had enabled an exceptionally difficult work to 'run like a car fitted with Michelin tyres that can cope with any obstacle, according to the advertisement!'

* * *

The revivals of *Pelléas* are too numerous to list in detail,[31] but Debussy attended rehearsals for the first performances in Brussels and London, such was his interest in seeing his opera properly performed in its early years. Brussels in January 1907 he found particularly agonising, partly because he disliked both travel and the Belgian people. He told Durand on 3 January that Sylvain Dupuis was 'more like an ox than a conductor . . . [with a] special way of deforming the simplest of rhythms which I hope is exclusively his own'. For Debussy the orchestra of the Théâtre de la Monnaie lacked 'tact and taste' and the 'bizarre assortment' of singers included a M. Arthus with 'neither the voice nor the physique' to play Arkel, who 'smelt of wine like a removal man'. No doubt spoiled by the superb realistic décors by Jusseaume and Ronsin at the Opéra-Comique (see Figs. 6-8 and 31), Debussy was understandably alarmed not to see any at all at this late stage in Brussels, despite constant reassurance as to their sumptuousness. 'Besides', he observed, 'the Belgians talk and promise much and then extricate themselves with the most tranquil hypocrisy. Moreover, these little people resemble the insignificant in their inflated pretentiousness, which is generally ridiculous, but becomes dangerous where a work of art is concerned.'

By 7 January his frustration with the second-rate was obvious. He complained to Durand (DUR, p. 38) that in the final act

> the bell which should be in G . . . is in C! – and sounds rather like the castle dinner-gong. [There is] a fountain in white wood . . . and vaults of such a kind as to be impenetrable! Little Yniold is such a child that he still does not know the music, and it is the *dress-rehearsal* tomorrow . . . God help my friends the artists in this country!

However, either Debussy's wrath worked wonders (which is unlikely) or things were not as bad as he made out, for J. Brunet recorded that there were eight curtain-calls for the artists at the close of the enthusiastically received first performance on 9 January.[32] He described the performance with Mary Garden as Mélisande (the last time that she rehearsed the opera in Debussy's presence) as 'moving . . . and beautiful. It awakened sensations that this was something artistically new.' Brunet was aware of the familiar Parisian criticisms that Debussy had 'abolished melody, rhythm and the barline, and excluded tonality through a constant abuse of chromaticism' (p. 28), but would have no truck with such bigotry. He wrote perceptively about the opera's 'profound impression of unity' and had kind words for each of the artists, even Mlle Das as Yniold.

And true to form, Debussy thanked Sylvain Dupuis on 8 January (LL, p. 156) 'with all my heart, for the devotion and artistic loyalty that you have expended so liberally to the benefit of the performance of *Pelléas* . . . I shall certainly never forget the pleasure I have had in working with you.'

Debussy's references to the bell and his later tribute to Mary Garden show the special interest he took in Act 5. This interest also extended to the question of stage lighting, for during the delayed dress-rehearsal for *Pelléas* at Covent Garden on 20 May 1909, Debussy made various notes in a *carnet* which has fortunately survived (*F-Pn* W. 54 (2)). After a few observations that the end of Act 1 was 'not sombre enough' and that the lighting should suggest 'twilight' in scene 3, the rest of the notes concern Mélisande's final moments and death. On p. 20 he wrote: 'Sun too white. The sun should diminish in intensity whilst Mélisande [Rose Féart] sings: "Il descend lentement, alors c'est l'hiver qui commence".' (VS, p. 269/OS, p. 393) Then a note 'les pieds de Mélisande' suggests that her feet were showing on her deathbed! Also, the sea visible through the window was 'badly lit' and again there were problems with 'the bell!!!' (OS, pp. 405-9)

But in his letters to Durand from the Royal Palace Hotel, Kensington,

Debussy's main concern was the bareness of the production by Fernand Almanz, who, he added on 18 May, was 'from Marseilles', as if that explained a great deal. He asked Durand (DUR, p. 71) to picture 'the ceilings where there is nothing but emptiness, and to imagine a wonderful profusion of flowers on the props which are as bare as a blind man's stick . . . I have rarely had such an inclination to kill someone! I have to do the work of electrician and machinist myself: God knows where it will all end!' He was, however, pleased with the orchestra under Cléofonte Campanini and with the male singers. He especially liked Edmond Warnery as Pelléas, even though he noted that he 'entered too late' during the dress-rehearsal in Act 3 scene 2. The truth behind Debussy's complaints is perhaps best shown by his admission to Durand on 18 May: 'My only thought is of coming home . . . *the atmosphere of the theatre makes me ill.* For any goodwill that one brings into it there is always something mediocre to turn the scale towards the wretched side.'

In many ways Carré's perfect production of 1902 coloured the rest of Debussy's theatrical experience, especially where *Pelléas* was concerned. As time went on distance lent enchantment to the original performances and his criticisms of revivals outside Paris became harsher, particularly as he was inclined to be chauvinistic and because Emma encouraged his natural tendency to bourgeois recluseness. His misery away from home, as his most important creation faced yet another potentially hostile and philistine public, shows clearly in his letters of 1907 and 1909. But once again, the Covent Garden launching on 21 May 1909 was a triumph, and Debussy's tone changed as he reported to Durand that the audience were 'shouting for the composer for quarter of an hour' (DUR, p. 73). Without avail, however, for he 'was peacefully back at his hotel, having no care for any glory whatsoever', and he eschewed public speaking and curtain-calls like the plague. The victory was telephoned to him by Campanini that night and confirmed by his visit the following morning, but Debussy was still incredulous after the 'deplorable' dress-rehearsal and could only believe that at Covent Garden 'they saved all their efforts for the première'!

During this visit, Debussy established a strong friendship with Percy Pitt, then musical director at Covent Garden, whom he thanked for his 'valuable assistance and sincere support during rehearsals'.[33] But, as might have been predicted, Debussy also accused Pitt of the universal theatre practice of trying to cram into 'eight days the work of a month' (TOU, p. 50); this letter to Toulet also describes Campanini's 'most singular' baton technique as 'resembling the action of a hand-pump'! But these apparently hypocritical letters were doubtless intended both to amuse his friends and to provide a diversion for himself in times of artistic tension.

If Debussy attended in person only the first foreign productions of *Pelléas*, he was nonetheless concerned about casting and other details during subsequent revivals. On 18 March 1910 he recommended Louise Edvina to Pitt and the 'young [David] Devriès who sings the role of Pelléas delightfully. This he has at his fingertips, being due to sing it in New York.' (*GB-Lbm* Fr. Egerton 3304, f. 135) The two together would make a '*Pelléas* that the whole of Europe will envy!' he wrote on 2 April. Pitt took his advice and the prophecies came true, according to Debussy's letter of 18 June (f. 139), though he was upset to have to say after the Covent Garden performances that he had 'noted in his "tablettes" — as Hamlet Prince of Denmark formerly did — that not one of these admirable artists had deigned to write to him!' On 3 June 1913 Debussy told Pitt that he hoped to come and hear the revival of *Pelléas*, especially as André Caplet was coming to conduct it on his recommendation (f. 141). 'He knows *Pelléas* as well as I do', he admitted, 'you can have absolute confidence in him.'

The same, however, cannot always be said of Debussy's press interviews about *Pelléas* revivals. In *Excelsior* on 18 January 1911 (LCr, p. 296) he could tell Georges Delaquys 'nothing precise' on the subject of impending productions in foreign cities, despite the fact that Louise Edvina was due to revive it at Covent Garden with Campanini as conductor. 'My interest is no longer there', he lied, for 26 August 1911 found him busy deploring the quality of productions in Nice and Cannes (DUR, p. 101), whereas he was ecstatic about Henry Russell's Boston project in January 1912 (p. 107). If he could truthfully say in January 1911 that his interest lay rather in the music itself than in public reaction to it, then he still avidly soaked up news of foreign productions even during the war, and on 14 December 1916 he announced that he would be pleased to hear Mme Villemin sing when P.-B. Gheusi's proposed new *Pelléas* progressed beyond being a mere advertisement in the press (DUR, p. 171). And according to José Bruyr (p. 343), this revival (planned by Debussy and Gheusi for the Opéra-Comique in 1915)[34] was to use much simpler scenery, though this may have been a wartime expedient rather than a definite change in artistic preference on Debussy's part.

Whilst *Pelléas et Mélisande* summarised Debussy's career to date and established his reputation as the leading modern French composer of his day, it never proved to be the 'pot of gold' that would solve all his financial difficulties, as he had anticipated in 1896. Then, according to René Peter (PET, p. 38 n.), he used it as a surety to tempt the wealthy Catherine Stevens into accepting his proposal of marriage. She, however, was more practical and replied: 'When *Pelléas* has been performed, we will talk about the matter again.' Ironically, Debussy was prosecuted for non-payment of debts during the final rehearsals, and the detailed receipts at the Opéra-Comique for 1902 to 1923 (Emmanuel, pp. 64-8) show that although few performances made a loss, the 107 before the interruption of war would only have brought Debussy in a small, if steady income. The first time the box-office returns passed the 10,000 franc mark and began to take off was, predictably, after Debussy's death.[35]

If in 1911 Debussy referred to more lucrative productions outside Paris as 'indispensable cogs in the glory machine' (DUR, p. 101), he was nevertheless as pleased as punch to report the London success of *Pelléas* to his parents on 23 May 1909. And he did so in much the same terms as he reported it to Durand (Dietschy, 1962, p. 201; cf DUR, p. 73), for the approval of all of them mattered greatly to him. Now at last, *just* during his parents' lifetimes, he was a public success as they had hoped, and he was careful to maximise this by saying that 'this sort of acclaim is extremely rare in England, where the temperature of the public stays mostly below zero . . . Therefore, long live France! Long live French music! And above all music! For I am forced to occupy myself with scenery and lighting effects, without thinking about music' in the hard world of the professional theatre.

* * *

The manuscripts

The numerous manuscripts of *Pelléas et Mélisande* show its genesis to have been even more complex than its chronology and the patience of readers will not permit my tracing this in detail. Some conclusions can, however, be drawn from the detailed studies undertaken in America and elsewhere during the 1970s. The first, from James McKay, is that 'Debussy moved from a repetitive, symmetrical, hierarchical structure towards a supple, asymmetrical texture which was sensitive to the exigencies of text and drama' (1977, p. 12) and that this compositional process involved 'copying from one manuscript into another, correcting, changing and filling out details as he went' (p. 9). He would often, in fact, make improvements on several levels in a single revision, and the ends of the acts and the joins between scenes caused him particular difficulty. Exx. 19a-c from the Boston manuscript (p. 19, bars 8ff, dated 'June' and '17 August [18]95') show three attempts at the end of Act 2, of which the last is an almost exact reduction of the printed orchestral score (p. 150). Most of this material is present in the earliest Meyer manuscript sketch (LPm, pp. 50-1) though it is virtually impossible to trace Debussy's precise intentions for the continuity at this stage, other than the two versions of the final bars of the act (Exx. 19 d and e) which first ended in F major as opposed to A minor. The importance of the revisions lies in the ordering and placing of material (cf Exx. 19 a and c, bars 1-2), and the gradual process of concision can be seen elsewhere in the Boston manuscript, as, for instance, in Act 4 scene 3 where twenty-three bars are removed in all. This represents the final working stage on the music, for the pagination in the Bibliothèque Nationale manuscript orchestral score shows that it was prepared from the Boston short score.

The second conclusion, from Carolyn Abbate,[36] is that as well as being composed out of order, Act 4 scene 4 and Act 5 actually 'grew backwards by

Ex. 19 a-c. *Pelléas et Mélisande*, *US-Bc*, end of Act 2, p. 19, bars 8ff (the Boston manuscript is now on deposit in *US-NYpm*)

(a) first version

(b) second version

(c) third version

Ex. 19d. *Pelléas et Mélisande*, *F-Pmeyer*, Act 2 scene 3, p. 6, last 2 bars (LPm, p. 50)

Ex. 19e. *Pelléas et Mélisande, F-Pmeyer*, Act 2 scene 3, p. 7, last 2 bars (LPm, p. 51)

means of successive accretions to a small core of music', which suggests the possibility that *La chute de la Maison Usher* might also be complete since several sketches exist for the end of its final scene (see Appendix). Thus Debussy began work on *Pelléas et Mélisande* from areas of secure tonality, and his initial, relatively routine responses to the text were made ever more subtle as the stages of composition proceeded. During these stages, traced most fully in the manuscripts of Act 4 scene 4, the original tonal design (as seen in the Meyer manuscript), which sprang directly from the dramatic exigencies of the text, was made more expansive and varied:[37] traditional harmonic functions like the perfect cadence were obscured or removed as it passed through the Lehman–Bréval–Boston–Bibliothèque Nationale orchestral score stages. In the process the part of Pelléas was lowered in pitch and that of Mélisande was raised. The two were overlapped and finally brought together in duet during revisions in the Bréval manuscript, one of Debussy's only licences in the opera apart from textual cuts and the addition of an offstage sailors' chorus in Act 1 scene 3.

Exx. 20a–e show how the climax of the opera evolved, as the lovers kiss in ecstasy and 'Golaud falls upon them, sword in hand, and strikes down

Ex. 20. *Pelléas et Mélisande*, Act 4 scene 4, climax of the duet and murder of Pelléas

(a) *F-Pmeyer*, p. 5, line 4 (LPm, p. 57)

76

(b) *US-NYpm* Lehman deposit, f. 11 *r*, bars 20-9

(c) *F-Pn* MS 1206, Bréval manuscript, first version, p. 25, bar 27 – p. 26, bar 1 (LPm, pp. 119-20)

MÉLISANDE
*(Golaud se précipite sur eux, l'épée à la main, et frappe Pelléas, qui tombe
au bord de la fontaine. Mélisande fuit epouvantée.)*

(d) *F-Pn* MS 1206, Bréval manuscript, second version, p. 25, bar 27 – p. 26, bar 1, with
p. 24, line 3 (LPm, pp. 118-20)

[the next 4 bars of Ex. 20d are the
same as the last 4 bars of Ex. 20c]

78

(e) *F-Pn* MS 1206, Bréval manuscript, third version, p. 24, bars 3-14 (LPm, p. 118)

(f) *F-Pn* MS 1206, Bréval manuscript, p. 24, b. 11 (second version of upper instrumental line in (e))

(g) *US-Bc* (now in *US-NYpm*), p. 32, bar 30, and 3 bars which are added in the margins of p. 32 alongside systems 4-5

(h) Durand VS, p. 266, bar 5 – p. 267, bar 3 (OS, p. 361, bar 5 – p. 363, bar 2)

Pelléas who falls at the edge of the fountain' (VS, p 266, and see Fig. 7). 'Mélisande flees in terror' at the end of the example. Debussy seems to have been undecided as to the length and emotional intensity of this only passage of conventional 'realistic' action, and both aspects reach extremes in Ex. 20d. The idea of expansion, however, can be seen crossing Debussy's mind in Ex. 20c as he added and then crossed out the indication 'deux fois' in bars 5-6. The bass of bars 3-4 of Ex. 20d re-employs a rising figure from bars 5-6 of Ex. 20b in a different register, and there is a good deal of textural adaptation (see bars 1-6 in Exx. 20b–e, and 20h). But the real change comes between Exx. 20 d and e, the second and third revisions in the Bréval manuscript, which should be compared with p. 266, bar 5 – p. 267, bar 3 in the vocal score (Ex. 20h). The main difference is that Mélisande and Pelléas have their roles reversed in bars 1 and 2, and the afterthoughts Ex. 20f (in the Bréval manuscript) and Ex. 20g (added in the margin at the last minute in the Boston manuscript) reveal that what started out as Mélisande's orchestral sobs became in a flash of inspiration that most striking and aggressive use of the Golaud motif, which never fails to terrify in performance, as the four unison

Fig. 7. *Pelléas et Mélisande*, Act 4 scene 4, the death of Pelléas; design by Lucien Jusseaume

horns are crushed against the full string *tremolando* accompaniment *près du chevalet* (OS, p. 362).

The musical cuts Debussy made at various stages are also of particular interest in building up a picture of his intentions as a theatrical composer. They are as follows:

1 End of Act 3 scene 3	37 bars in the Boston MS (p. 19, bars 5-19a) replaced by 24 bars of interlude (Durand VS, p. 157, bar 4 – p. 158, bar 12). This does away with an interchange between Golaud and Pelléas, with the first reference to Yniold's sheep 'crying like lost children, as if they already had the butcher in mind', and an ecstatic climax as Golaud sings: 'Quelle belle journée! Quelle admirable journée pour la moisson!' This cut would have been particularly opportune for the first series of 1902 performances in which the 'scène des moutons' (Act 4 scene 3) was also omitted.
2 Act 3 scene 4	The reference to Pelléas and Mélisande being near the bed upset the censor and absurdly resulted in a fifteen-bar cut before the première (see Fromont VS, p. 164, bar 5 – p. 165, bar 7). The missing section should come between bars 3 and 4 of the Durand VS, p. 184, though the musical continuity is actually improved without it.
3 End of Act 3 scene 4	Thirteen bars and one line of text for Golaud cut between bars 4 and 5 of the Durand VS, p. 188 (see Fromont VS, p. 169, bars 1-13). This intensified the drama of the orchestral ending of Act 3.
4 Act 4 scene 4	See Exx. 21 a and b. Two lines for Pelléas removed in the Boston manuscript (p. 21; bars 1-3 of Ex. 21c were subsequently crossed out; Durand VS, p. 233, between bars 7 and 8); they refer to Pelléas' father, whom we never see but who is now 'out of danger'. Pelléas now no longer has any immediate obligations to prevent him fleeing the castle before Mélisande arrives and the inevitable tragedy ensues. The cutting of these lines reflects Debussy's policy of omitting material which clarifies personal relationships or events within Allemonde.
5 Act 4 scene 4	Twenty-four bars of music cut from the Lehman manuscript (f. 5, bar 8 – f. 6, bar 12), which prolong the scene between Pelléas and Mélisande just before the castle gates shut (Durand VS, p. 255, bar 2).

Besides speeding up the drama, Debussy's twelve-line cut in the text also makes Mélisande's final 'I am happy, but I am also sad' more elusive by leaving it in mid-air, and avoids further defining the emotional bond between the lovers. This must have been a difficult decision as some beautiful music and poetry were sacrificed to the benefit of the scene as a whole in terms of dramatic pace and proportion.

6 Act 4 scene 4

Three bars cut from the Lehman manuscript (f. 12, bars 7-9) before this passage was reworked in the Bréval manuscript (cf LPm, p. 117, line 3, and Durand VS, p. 263, bars 3-4). Here Debussy removed Pelléas' advice to Mélisande about Golaud – 'He will stay here as long as he believes that we don't see him' – which detracted from the breathless tension accumulated by Pelléas' other shorter commands and so had to go. In setting this line Debussy had also made one of only three tiny textual changes in this scene to Maeterlinck's first edition, substituting 'voyons' for 'savons' at the end of the line. Perhaps this was another reason for the omission.

The cuts in Act 3 scene 4, however skilfully Debussy turned them to his musical advantage, were nonetheless forced on him, as a recently discovered letter written to a critic after the première reveals:[38]

On the day of the dress-rehearsal M. Roujon [the Director of Fine Arts] called for M. Albert Carré to suppress the last scene in Act 3 of *Pelléas* altogether. This appeared to me to be so much of a surgical operation that I refused outright. All the same it proved necessary to consent to several cuts and to the alteration of certain expressions that I should certainly have asked M. Maeterlinck about if a rather ridiculous altercation had not so strained our relationship. You know better than I how much the atmosphere of a theatre is made up of contradictions and of unforeseen influences. And one does not submit easily to advice given through incomprehension. Please believe me that all this is beyond my independent control and let me finish by thanking you for having recognised my artistic sincerity with a refined understanding which has become so rare nowadays, when people pretend to be 'art critics' whilst forgetting, to be sure, all that this title means in terms of earnest honesty (*ardente loyauté*).

The remaining textual cuts, as far as is known, were made before Debussy began composing the relevant sections and mostly concern short passages which help clarify the character and actions of Mélisande (as with no. 5 above). Debussy makes her even more infuriating to Golaud than Maeterlinck does. 'Why should I not understand you?', he queries in Act 2 scene 2,[39] 'Tell me all and I shall understand all.' To which Mélisande replies: 'I don't know myself what the trouble is . . . If I could tell you, I would', the last admission being out of character with the elusive Mélisande Debussy sought to portray. Perhaps it is just another of Mélisande's lies, but Debussy does not want to run any risk of its being believed.

By far the longest cut is made to the scene in the castle vaults (Act 3 scene 2), where Golaud expounds at repetitive length on the deathly atmosphere. Information about Allemonde and its famine is minimised by Debussy and any references to additional characters are removed — like the strangers who visit the castle at the end of Act 4 scene 1 in Maeterlinck.

The fourth cut above merits further consideration for the flexibility it reveals in Debussy's compositional procedure and the scrupulous attention he devoted to the prosody. Ex. 21a gives the first neat version in the Lehman manuscript, with Ex. 21b showing the different setting of the phrases whose placing and accentuation so troubled Debussy: 'Il est tard; elle ne vient pas.' Here he saw the two phrases as coming closer together with a stronger accent on 'tard', the stress on *el-* rather than *-le* in 'elle', and a more interesting vocal line as Pelléas refers to Mélisande rather than the lateness of the hour. Bars 1–3 of Ex. 21a were then recopied into the Boston manuscript (p. 21, bar 11f) and Ex. 21c shows Debussy's first continuation, putting 'il' for the only time on a strong beat, with a two-quaver figure in the accompaniment, which can be seen as an addition in the Bréval manuscript (Ex. 21b, directly below the vocal line), but which was crossed out as being inferior. Then Debussy spotted his mistake and in pencil wrote Ex. 21d over the top of the copy of Ex. 21c, bars 1-2, making the important decision to keep the music in 6/4 time and to save the change to common time for the more exciting phrase beginning in the last two bars of Ex. 21a ('It would be better if I went away, without seeing her again', cf Ex. 21e). The two vocal settings above Ex. 21d show Debussy's persistent and minute concern with his two seemingly trivial phrases. First he ran them together (see the lower vocal line), hitting on the rising dominant seventh outline in the process and making the two phrases complementary whilst increasing their tension through their rising pitch. Then the longer 6/4 bar solved his problem and he kept 'Il est tard' where it was, but delayed 'elle ne vient pas', preserving the accentuation on *'el* le' but avoiding the unwanted strong accent on 'pas' because of the longer bar. The final result, which goes past in a flash but was nevertheless of great importance to Debussy, can be seen in Ex. 21e, which also restores the original accent on 'tard' in the first phrase, as in Ex. 21b.

This example may seem protracted, but it is typical of the care Debussy lavished on every phrase in his opera, however simple and natural each may appear. Another instance, showing the four bars previous to Exx. 21 b and e, can be found in McKay (1977, p. 13), who reveals Debussy in the second bar shifting the text along but keeping the same melodic line.

* * *

84

Ex. 21. The evolution of a passage near the start of Act 4 scene 4 of *Pelléas et Mélisande*

(a) *US-NYpm* Lehman deposit, f. 2, bars 2-8

(b) *F-Pn* MS 1206, Bréval manuscript, p. 3, bars 2-8 (LPm, p. 93)

PELLÉAS

Mon père est hors de dan - ger; et je n'ai plus de

PELLÉAS

quoi me men - tir à moi - mê - me... Il est tard;

PELLÉAS

el - le ne vient pas... Je fe - rais mieux de m'en al -

PELLÉAS

(c) *US-Bc* (now in *US-NYpm*), p. 21, bars 11-15

PELLÉAS

PELLÉAS

(d) *US-Bc* (now in *US-NYpm*), p. 21, bars 11-12, revisions

(e) Durand VS, p. 233, bar 8 – p. 234, bar 3

Other musical aspects and general conclusions

To return to more general musical aspects: the form of *Pelléas et Mélisande* has long vexed Debussy scholars: like so many of his theatrical works, it defies traditional analytical approaches. This is because, like *Jeux* and *Khamma*, it represents a direct musical response to a given scenario or dramatic text, almost in what might be termed cinematographic 'moment' form. It even resists proportional analysis using the principle of the 'golden section',[40] and the most satisfactory solution, as proposed by Arthur Wenk, is that Debussy's answer to the new operatic problems presented by Maeterlinck's play 'was a harmonic framework consisting of key areas associated with important events in the drama. Debussy extended these key areas by means of melodic embellishment and connected them by stepwise progressions of the bassline, weakening the bonds of individual chords to a tonic and allowing them to be used expressively rather than functionally.' (AMS *Abstracts*, 1978, p. 116)

This allowed Debussy to provide a musical parallel to Maeterlinck's play with its dream-like, fleeting milieu in which bass pedal-points play an important role and silence is a vital factor in defining musical sentences or paragraphs. On the harmonic side, modality and the whole-tone scale evoke an atmosphere of mystery and the distant past from the very start, and to a certain extent the opening prelude is a microcosm of the opera in that it presents the main motifs (see Exx. 22a-c) associated respectively with the forest and antiquity, Golaud and Mélisande. The last two combine, but with Golaud's motif persisting after Mélisande's peters out (bar 20). As Roger Nichols points out (1973, p. 37), 'the whole-tone chord is used for its negative qualities. As it negates tonal harmony, so it destroys confidence and casts the shadow of doubt over bland assertions. In many cases, it is associated with Golaud, whose jealousy, like Othello's, feeds on lack of proof', and the way Golaud's motif develops and changes to suit the psychological exigencies of

Ex. 22. *Pelléas et Mélisande*, motifs

(a) the forest/antiquity, VS, p. 1, bars 1-2 (OS, p. 1, bars 1-2)

(b) Golaud, VS, p. 1, bar 5 (OS, p. 1, bar 5)

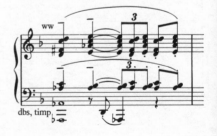

(c) Mélisande, VS, p. 1, bar 14 – p. 2, bar 1 (OS, p. 2, bar 7 – p. 3, bar 1)

(d) Pelléas, VS, p. 33, bars 10-11 (OS, p. 40, bars 1-2)

the drama is clearly laid out in this excellent study (pp. 43-4). So too are some of the very few perfect cadences in the opera (pp. 35-6), which, in contrast, present images of 'immediate presence or decisiveness, either mental or physical'. The most memorable is perhaps Golaud's biting irony as he builds into his first outburst of jealous rage in Act 4 scene 2 (Ex. 23). The mock-religious chords give Debussy the chance to use a favourite harmonic device of the pre-*Pelléas* years to great dramatic effect, and the irony is increased by putting bars 1–2 of Ex. 23 on soft, divided strings, surrounded by passages

Ex. 23. *Pelléas et Mélisande*, VS, p. 211, bar 6 – p. 212, bar 1 (OS, p. 283, bars 1-4)

on harsh, accented woodwind. Bar 3 shows Golaud in his true colours as oboe and cor anglais snap him discordantly back into angry denunciation.

One way of seeing *Pelléas et Mélisande* in broad terms is, as Roy Howat has suggested (private communication), by means of its tension and volume overall (see the graphs in Howat, 1983, Chapter 10). Acts 1 and 2 begin *pianissimo* and stay mainly on a level with only a few small undulations in the graph. In Act 3 the tension starts to mount, with the violent streaks first appearing in the second (castle vaults) scene and increasing towards Yniold's screams as Golaud forces him to keep eavesdropping on Pelléas and Mélisande through the turret window (VS, p. 187). The tension returns at the start of the fourth act, but then drops a little to mount again through Golaud's rage in scene 2 towards the high-point of the opera as the lovers kiss at the end of scene 4 and Golaud murders Pelléas. The contrast in the lighter third scene with Yniold and the sheep serves only to delay the tension and thus intensify the climax when it finally arrives. Then in Act 5 the tension falls off quickly after the high-spot well over four-fifths of the way through the opera.

The same broad graph holds true for other theatrical works. In *Jeux* the violent streaks first appear in a parallel position, around figs. 32-3, with the 'jealousy of the second young girl', and the main climax comes with the triple kiss at fig. 78, relatively near the end. The placing of this uniquely 'violent' climax is directly comparable to that of Khamma's death at the height of the gradual *crescendo* which intensifies during her final delirious dance. Similar patterns occur in orchestral, but no less dramatic compositions like 'Jeux de vagues' and *Gigues*. Indeed, it is perhaps the very absence of such patterns (or the scope for them) in *Rodrigue et Chimène* and *La chute de la Maison Usher* which caused Debussy to disown the first and be unable to complete the second.

On the vocal side, the continuous recitative in *Pelléas*, verging at times on lyrical arioso, has been seen as fulfilling the vision of Debussy's illustrious predecessor Jean-Jacques Rousseau, whose opera *Le devin du village* achieved similar immediate acclaim in 1752. Although Debussy wrote in the *Revue de la Société Internationale de Musique* of 1 November 1913 (RLS, p. 296) that France could 'certainly do without his naïve aesthetics', Rousseau's *Lettre sur la musique française*, after decrying current operatic practice, suggested that the kind of recitative best suited to the French language should 'wander between narrow intervals, and neither raise nor lower the voice very much. It should have little sustained sound, no noise, and no cries of any description — indeed, nothing that resembles singing, and little inequality in the duration and value of the notes, or in their intervals'. This could almost be a blueprint for Geneviève's reading of Golaud's letter in Act 1 scene 2, a passage that Debussy can never have intended to be so flat and lifeless as it often is in modern performances.

Whilst there are no self-contained arias as in conventional opera, all the male characters in *Pelléas* have their own set pieces within Act 4. Those of Arkel and Golaud are again a microcosm of the whole opera as regards tension, like the play within a play in *Hamlet*. First Arkel takes the stage in scene 2 (VS, pp. 198-204) with mounting climaxes in pitch and volume (bars 132, 151, 155). Then comes Golaud's jealousy 'aria' (VS, pp. 210-18), sparked off by Arkel's seeing only 'une grande innocence' in Mélisande's eyes; this has even greater vocal climaxes (bars 248, 264, 278, 289, 301, 311) before dying away relatively quickly after Arkel's interruption takes the wind out of the sails of Golaud's near-hysteria. Yniold has his chance in Act 4 scene 3, and Pelléas' soliloquy opens scene 4 (VS, pp. 232-6) before he is joined by Mélisande, who, as usual, has less to sing than the characters she is with – an imbalance only partly rectified by the final act.

Just how Wagnerian *Pelléas* is and in what ways has occasioned much discussion, notably in Chapters iv, vi and ix of Robin Holloway's excellent study *Debussy and Wagner*. Here many adroit musical parallels are drawn with *Tristan*, *Parsifal* and the *Ring* cycle, amongst which the most impressive are his Exx. 18 a and d (pp. 115-18) which demonstrate how Pelléas's ecstatic music at the first climax of the Act 4 love duet (VS, p. 258 bar 5 – end) is a 'compacted version of Brangäne's music in the *Tristan* love duet' (OS, pp. 614-18). In the interludes it would seem that Debussy, as in *Le martyre de Saint Sébastien*, turned most readily to Wagner when composing against the clock, re-using (often at the original pitch) 'Wagnerian *minutiae* that appeal to him both in themselves and for their context'. But as far as vocal passages and technique go, *Pelléas et Mélisande* usually *sounds* much closer to Mussorgsky, though Debussy complained to Pierre Lalo on 23 June 1908 (LL, p. 172), after seeing Lalo's article in *Le temps* comparing *Boris Godunov* with *Pelléas*, about the 'skill people are showing in order to discover – no matter where – a resemblance' between the two.[41] The innovations that Debussy admired in Mussorgsky and liked to be seen to benefit from in *Pelléas* were his 'spontaneous art, free from arid formulae', and his form, which was 'so varied that it is impossible to relate to established, or one might say official, forms, since it depends on and is made up from successive tiny touches linked by a mysterious line and by a gift of instinctive clairvoyance'.[42]

Replying to the critics of *Pelléas* in *Le figaro* in May 1902 (LCr, p. 271), Debussy told Robert de Flers that his 'composing method owed nothing to Wagner and consisted above all in dispensing with composing methods. In Wagner's case', he added, 'each character has . . . his "visiting-card", his photograph, his "leitmotif" which must always precede him. I find this procedure rather clumsy, I must confess.' But Debussy was often guilty of creating smoke-screens to obscure the truth, and in *Pelléas* he employed the Wagnerian system as a basis for want of a better, though not in Wagner's straightforward pictorial, referential or 'visiting-card' manners. Rather, as Robin Holloway says (pp. 136-7):

> it is precisely in his employment of Wagnerian leitmotifs in *Pelléas*
> that Debussy stands farthest from his original . . . In *Pelléas* every
> motif shares the same intervals with every other; they can be
> fragmented into accompaniment or ostinato; every ostinato or
> accompaniment can emerge as a motif; and the harmony everywhere
> consists of these same intervals superimposed into chords . . . The
> music in *Pelléas* actually *reacts* to the words rather than, as in
> Wagner, being the expression and embodiment of them.

Of course, as Jacques Dubois (p. 483) observes, the repetition of scenes, language and symbols plays an integral part in creating the closed world of Allemonde in Maeterlinck's play, so leitmotifs are built into the work before the music even gets to it. So it is thus perhaps not surprising that different writers see different numbers of motifs in *Pelléas*,[43] though far more important is the way that the main ideas (Ex. 22) are transformed and combined, and the way that secondary (or accompanimental) ideas like those in Ex. 24 assume a role of almost equal importance in a sort of pre-Proustian 'remembrance of things past'.

This last aspect seems to me more characteristic than the clear distinction Joseph Kerman draws in *Pelléas* between 'themes whose main function is to organise scenes' and 'leading motives essentially in the Wagnerian tradition' (p. 15), the former usually appearing in the interludes, which subtly change the mood and material between tableaux. But is not the 'solo violin' theme which 'organises' Act 1 scene 3 (Ex. 25) rather a return of Mélisande's motif (Ex. 22c) than a distinctly different sort of organising theme?[44] And is not

Ex. 24. *Pelléas et Mélisande*, secondary motifs

(a) VS, p. 25, bar 10 (OS, p. 30, bar 1)

(b) VS, p. 115, bar 6 (OS, p. 152, bar 1)

(c) VS, p. 309, bar 2 (OS, p. 408, bar 1)

Ex. 25. *Pelléas et Mélisande*, OS, p. 44, bars 2-6 (VS, p. 37, bars 8-12)

Ex. 26. *Pelléas et Mélisande*, VS, p. 104, bar 3 (OS, p. 130, bar 3)

Ex. 26, which might be said to 'organise' Act 2 scene 3 and which recurs several times (along with Mussorgskian chains of chords, such as those in VS, p. 111, bar 5 – p. 112, bar 2), also linked to Ex. 22? The shape of the motif is a variant of that of Pelléas (Ex. 22d), but the rhythm is Golaud's (Ex. 22b). Thus the two ideas are transformed and combined to introduce Pelléas, who ostensibly dominates the scene from his arrival with Mélisande to search for her lost ring in the grotto (Fig. 8). But Ex. 26 also reminds us that Golaud is the motivating force behind their futile quest and the real controller of the situation.

Debussy helps to confirm this hypothesis when he says in a review of Bruneau's opera *L'ouragan* (in which he discusses the Wagnerian leitmotif system) that 'music has a rhythm whose secret force controls development' (LCr, p. 41). Thus it is *rhythm*, first and foremost, that distinguishes a motif, and one of Debussy's favourite definitions, which he first jotted down in a notebook around 1907, was that 'music is not naturally a form: it is made up of colours and barred rhythms'.[45] On an extremely basic level, the Golaud motif (Ex. 22b) might even be seen as a rhythmic variant of that of the forest (Ex. 22a), which brings us back to Holloway's important observation that 'every motif shares the same intervals with every other'.

Kerman also refers to Ex. 24a, which frames Act 1 scene 2 (VS, pp. 25 and 37), as a motif that holds the scene together. But the importance of this seemingly insignificant idea, which buries itself in the listener's unconscious mind, reaches far beyond the single scene of its initial appearance. Its shape is fundamentally different from that of the main motifs of the opera and it is the source of all later semiquaver movement, notably that of the fountain scene (Act 2 scene 1), where its minor seventh chords recur unarpeggiated in a similar position in bars 3 and 4 on the harp (OS, p. 70). Likewise its appearances at the end of Act 3 scene 3 (VS, pp. 157-8) suggest that it frames this scene too, and thus gave rise at its outset to the beautiful music as Pelléas and Golaud emerge from the dark castle vaults into the fresh air above (VS,

Fig. 8. *Pelléas et Mélisande*, Act 2 scene 3, the grotto scene; design by Eugène Ronsin

pp. 147-9). Ex. 24a recurs in its original form on the harp during Arkel's 'aria' in Act 4 scene 2 (VS, pp. 200-1) and is heard in both its original and inverted forms in the earlier woodwind scoring (OS, p. 269, bars 3-4/VS, p. 201, bars 11-12). The opera also closes with its broken chord figuration turned, as elsewhere, into arpeggiated chords.

Some of these recurrences might be said to be asociated with water and light, but there is no common factor behind them all; so they cannot be said to have any more precise significance than Proust's madeleine dipped in tea in *Du côté de chez Swann*, though they are just as vital in illuminating and recalling whole stretches of past action. A similar instance is provided by Ex. 24b, which is again associated with the flute; it first appears as the main accompaniment idea which unifies the start of Act 3. Then it occurs near the end of Act 5 (OS, p. 408, bar 1) as Arkel comments that Mélisande looks like the 'elder sister of her child'; the flute figure is now extended from a three-into a four-quaver pattern (Ex. 24c), but the stimulation of involuntary memory is far more effective than another recall of Mélisande's motif would be.

This is primarily because Ex. 22c in particular has undergone so much transformation that it becomes difficult to remember exactly what the original was. In fact, Mélisande's motif becomes almost more eloquent than Mélisande herself, and recurs some eighty-five times in forty different variants, being perhaps best considered as the source of lyricism in the opera: soft, calm and slightly sad. We meet it in its most extended form at the start of Act 1 scene 3 (Ex. 27a), in which Pelléas meets Mélisande for the first time. As Jacques Chailley observes (p. 889), although '*nothing happens*, it is the most important scene in the drama'. Apart from the interlude between scenes 1 and 2 of the third act (VS, p. 141) and one final reappearance near the end of Act 5 (VS, p. 308, bars 7-8), Mélisande's theme does not recur in this its fullest form, though to my mind it is (appropriately) the parent of Maurice Emmanuel's theme XII, 'L'enfant' (Ex. 27b), in Act 5.[46] In this final and most beautiful act, Ex. 22c undergoes its most important and imaginative transformations. From the slow beginning (Ex. 27a) where it loses all its rhythmic character (just as Golaud's motif later loses its aggression), it passes through the sequential Ex. 27c to a vertical conversion into an unresolved major ninth chord (Ex. 27d),[47] where it symbolises the unresolved question about 'the truth' behind Mélisande's relationship with Pelléas. Then comes its final full appearance (VS, p. 308, as in Ex. 27a), from which we pass to its poignant statement on the trumpet in the last six bars when it is finally allowed to resolve logically for the first time onto its tonic (C sharp major).

Just as the Wagnerian elements in Debussy's music passed from the songs into the stage works at the time of *Pelléas*, when the former were no longer fully able to contain them, so some of the motifs found in the theatrical works came from non-theatrical sources. It was Robert Godet who first noticed that

Ex. 27. *Pelléas et Mélisande*, uses of the Mélisande motif

(a) VS, p. 39, bars 1-2 (OS, p. 46, bars 1-2)

(b) VS, p. 274, bars 4-5 (OS, p. 371, bars 7-8)

(c) VS, p. 276, bars 1-2 (OS, p. 373, bars 4-5)

(d) VS, p. 286, bars 12-14 (OS, p. 384, bars 2-4)

Mélisande's theme appeared in the first chords of the accompaniment to the Banville song *Nuit d'étoiles* of *c*1880 (LCat, p. 21). Likewise, the Mallarmé setting *Apparition*, dated 8 February 1884, provided the atmospheric start of the third act of *Pelléas*, and the cyclic theme of the String Quartet of 1893 recurs as the main theme of *La chute de la Maison Usher* in 1909 (cf Exx. 34 a and b).

Ex. 27d above is perhaps the best-known use of the unprepared and unresolved ninth chord in *Pelléas* because it moves here as a non-functional thickening of the melodic line. In reality the chord flexibly pervades the entire score, and especially Act 5, at different pitches and in different contexts. It is often associated with the expression of grief and anguish: from Golaud's 'Pourquoi pleures-tu?' (VS, p. 6, bar 3), through the climax of the grotto scene in Act 2 (VS, p. 111, bar 4), to Yniold's struggles with his heavy stone in Act 4 scene 3 (VS, pp. 223-4). The spacing is all-important and is usually as in Ex. 27d, with the ninth uppermost and a wide-spaced minor triad below.

This is by no means the only musical association in *Pelléas* between a technical aspect and a dramatic idea, and the frequency and subtlety of some of these show just how limited Wagner's leitmotif system was for Debussy's conception of opera. For instance, long bass pedal-points are associated with suggest the light which comes from the sea to alleviate the darkness (VS, pp. 103-4) or in Act 3 scene 3. The alternation of two pitches in a rhythmic ostinato suggests darkness and gloom, as in Act 1 scene 3 (VS, pp. 39-40) or Act 2 scene 3 (VS, pp. 105-6), though, depending on the pitch, it can also suggest the light which comes from the sea to alleviate the darkness (VS, p. 41, bars 4-5). Similarly, the symbolic imagery of light and water associated with Debussy's frail, blond and mysterious ideal woman, Mélisande (who is found by a well and arrives at Allemonde by sea), is often represented by the keys of F sharp or E major: light, as in Act 1 scene 3 (VS, p. 41) or in Act 3 scene 4 (VS, p. 176-7), where the light falls on Golaud and Yniold from Mélisande's window; and water, as in much of the fountain scene in the second act. C major might be considered to be associated with the sensations of seeing (VS, p. 11, bar 5) or touching (VS, pp. 223-4), but these analogies are by no means consistent and the tonality is rarely still for any length of time. A passage near the start of Act 3 scene 1 (VS, pp. 122-6) demonstrates the futility of this line of enquiry, for the passage is all about touching and establishes no key whatsoever amidst its modal allusions, sevenths and ninths.

As far as the orchestra is concerned, the associations are clearer. Many are established in the opening prelude: thick, low string spacing (bars 1-2) represents the shadowy forests of Allemonde; timpani rolls (bar 7) foretell impending doom; Mélisande and her poignant sadness are captured by the oboe (bars 14-20). To this can later be added the flute and harp (water, freshness and light in Act 2) and the trombone and tuba (violence and death in Act 4, or the cruelty of Golaud). It is also evident from the opening prelude that the horns and bassoons are to play a large part in the scheme of things, and that they and the woodwind will carry much of the thematic and developmental interest, with the strings assuming a supportive role as they were to do increasingly after *La mer*.

In many ways the orchestra is the main character in *Pelléas et Mélisande*: besides acting as a unifying force it creates the atmosphere and takes over what the voices are 'powerless to express'. What is fascinating about the orchestra, which 'supports the drama as impressively as the vocal line' (Kerman, p. 14), is the purity of its conception. Although, as Maurice Emmanuel observes (p. 141), it is the same size as that of Wagner's *Tristan* minus the bass clarinet, Debussy's restrained chamber conception and his deliberate contrast with Wagnerian practice emerges clearly from a conversation with Victor Segalen in December 1908 (SEG, p. 107).

> In *Pelléas* [Debussy maintained] the sixth violin is as necessary as
> the first. I try to use each timbre in its pure state; like Mozart for
> example. People have learnt to mix timbres too much; to cast them
> in relief through obscurity or the sheer weight of numbers, without
> allowing their true characteristics to show through in performance.
> Wagner departs very far from this ideal; he doubles up most of his
> instruments two by two or three by three. But the worst of all is
> [Richard] Strauss who has cast all discretion to the winds. He
> doubles the trombone with the flute: the flute gets lost and the
> trombone assumes a strange voice. I, on the contrary, strive to retain
> the purity of each timbre and to put it in its proper place.

And perhaps with *Pelléas* in mind, Debussy described his ideal orchestral
layout as follows (p. 108):

> The strings should make not a barrier in front of, but a circle *around*
> the other instruments. Scatter the woodwind: mix the bassoons with
> the cellos; the clarinets and oboes with the violins, so that their
> intervention is something other than a 'mayday' distress call (*la
> chute d'un paquet*).

The changes of orchestral colour in *Pelléas* are kaleidoscopic and Debussy
was especially forward-looking in blending solo timbres. Besides making the
chameleon bassoons serve as extra horns, he even contrived to make the oboe
(not the flute) sound like a distant trumpet (OS, p. 7, fig. 6), and to make the
horn merge perfectly with the flutes (OS, p. 47, bars 1-2) as well as with the
double bass (OS, p. 112, bars 1-2). He was forever retouching the orchestration in *Pelléas*, and the Royaumont annotated scores (see Appendix) reveal
the lively interest he retained in perfecting the *Nocturnes*, *Jeux* and *Pelléas* in
later life. He sought to make Act 3 scene 2 even more sinister by adding extra
timpani rolls (OS, p. 192, bars 1-4); he added full string support below the
harp chords in Act 5 (OS, p. 385, bars 1-2); and three trombones were introduced to add force to the orchestral climax before Golaud kills Pelléas
(OS, p. 362, fig. 58). But most of the changes between the manuscript score
in the Bibliothèque Nationale and the printed orchestral score, and between
the latter and the Royaumont corrected version, concern the minute adjust-
ment of the internal balance between wind and strings, the substitution of a
clarinet for a viola here, or a horn for a cor anglais there. By and large the
most dramatic moments or those with their own special colour (like the end
of Act 5) needed the fewest changes and Debussy's prime concerns seem to
have been clarity, clear contrast for new phrases or sections, some strengthening of climaxes (in the Royaumont score), and making his 'timbres variés'
even more so in his quest to convert sonority into a structural element.

* * *

Debussy complained to Victor-Émile Michelet in 1902 (Michelet, p. 74) that *Pelléas* had been 'swallowed but not digested'. This was still evident over half a century later if scholars like Kerman could write (p. 14) that 'the singer cannot go wrong; Debussy's vocal writing assures a many-sided characterisation', and René Leibowitz could in contrast (p. 30) talk of 'a total absence of dramatic characterisation . . . [and] uniform vocal writing' and declare that the true daring of *Pelléas* lies in its 'almost complete negation of all that constitutes the very essence of lyric art'! All of this is directly comparable to the critical reactions of 1902 when Camille Bellaigue (p. 452) maintained that there were 'no leitmotifs at all', whilst the more perceptive Jean Marnold (p. 808) saw Debussy employing 'all the resources of the leitmotif . . . short profoundly expressive themes connected with the sentiment or character in question which accompany the action of the drama step by step'. Surprisingly, however, both critics found one point of agreement in observing that harmonic originality lay at the centre of Debussy's style (cf Bellaigue, p. 452, and Marnold, p. 807), though they approached their similar conclusions from opposite directions.

Nor were established composers any more able to 'swallow' *Pelléas* than Bellaigue. Rimsky-Korsakov thoroughly disliked it, according to Oscar Thompson (p. 174), and found that 'the harmonic combinations were incomprehensible, the orchestra lacked body and firmness of texture, the whole was monotonous; and he could see no future for this "curious experiment"'. Puccini lamented its lack of variety and Richard Strauss its lack of spontaneity: 'cela manque de *Schwung*', he told Romain Rolland! (p. 162) And W.H. Auden later went so far as to call *Pelléas* 'anti-opera', which 'only succeeds because it flatters its audience' (Holloway, p. 205), proving that its 'digestion', even by the intelligentsia, was taking far longer than Debussy anticipated.

Annoyance with a set of indecisive characters, whom A.E.F. Dickinson (p. 163) aptly describes as 'waiting for Golaud', has led some scholars, perhaps misguidedly, to try to inject a sense of reality into the pervading remoteness of Allemonde. Thus, just as it helps to know that the action of James Joyce's *Ulysses* takes place within a single day, so audiences might perhaps be informed that the time-span of Debussy's apparently timeless opera is one year, beginning and ending at twilight on an autumn day. But it is Bernard Williams, once again, who best identifies the main problems facing contemporary audiences and producers, at the centre of which lie Golaud's unresolved questions to Mélisande. A balance must be maintained between the agonised reality of the obsessional jealousy which forces him to ask these questions, and the fact that they cannot be answered satisfactorily because Mélisande does not belong to his matter-of-fact, morally upright world. Moreover she does not love him. 'The difficulty', as Williams says (p. 394), lies in keeping the edge on Golaud's questions . . . Go one way, and one has a mysterious haze, with music indeed sensuous and marvellously structured, but losing human and dramatic interest: go the other, and one is left with the irritable feeling that there must *be* a truth there, and it is a tiresome and accidental limitation that we and Golaud do not know what it is.

Williams also warns of the dangers of being 'overimpressed by the theme of fate if one places the centre of the play's truth in the character of Arkel', whom he does not credit with the same 'exalted philosophical capacity' as Ferneuil did in 1902 (p. 340). In fact, Williams says (p. 392), Arkel 'gives us no insight into the events of the opera at all, but is rather shown up, ironically, as quite inadequate to them'. After Golaud has dragged Mélisande by the hair and thrown her to the ground in his jealous rage in Act 4, all Arkel can weakly suppose is that he is drunk. To Mélisande's tragic plea that he no longer loves her comes the famous reply: 'If I were God, I should have pity on the hearts of men' (VS, p. 219) which *appears* to be a profound reflection, lent weight by its religious allusion, but, as Williams observes, is in 'plain truth . . . utterly idiotic'. Unlike Golaud, however, Arkel does realise that some questions cannot be answered and that we can never completely understand our own actions or destinies. Pelléas knows this too and soon learns never to force an answer from the flirtatious and mercurial Mélisande, whose important words are heard in orchestral silence. It is only when the castle gates slam shut in Act 4 that the lovers' inner, childlike bond is confronted with reality and the world of positive action. Now it is Golaud who for once is silent, but the orchestra makes it clear that his child*ish*, uncomprehending silence is the most terrifying of all and can only be expiated in darkness and death.

* * *

If *Pelléas et Mélisande* had no direct successors then it has had numerous descendants[48] and its impact on twentieth-century music has been considerable. It served to accelerate the development of French music and establish Debussy's reputation at a level which he found almost embarrassing, whilst forming a unique 'impasse' in itself, as Ravel put it in 1925. Albert Carré in 1932 saw *Pelléas et Mélisande* as 'representing the genius of Claude Debussy standing erect in the face of the genius of Richard Wagner and liberating French music from foreign influence',[49] but such panegyrical appraisals too often get diverted from the truth in the flood of their own rhetoric, and modern writers are both more objective and more perceptive. Thus Roger Nichols sums up the Wagnerian situation nicely when he says (1973, p. 41) that 'in the complex love-hate relationship between Debussy and Wagner, *Pelléas* is an act of homage and partial exorcism.'

Space does not permit me to trace what composers as diverse as Bartók, Berg, Poulenc and Boulez have found of value in *Pelléas*, but its reputation has grown rather than diminished, and since 1902 the relationship between text, music and drama has been altogether different. It was also Debussy's opera that maintained Maeterlinck's reputation through the vagaries of his subsequent literary career.

At the same time, *Pelléas* owed much to the art of the past, and Vincent d'Indy (p. 379) was the first, but by no means the last, to compare Debussy's operatic achievements with those of Monteverdi. Unexpectedly, he was attracted to the opera straight away and was the first to discover the real reason for its survival in its overriding humanity. Has not the composer 'felt and expressed human sentiments and sufferings *humanely* . . . despite the exterior aspects of mystery and the dream which the characters assume?' he asked pointedly. If we are taken in by the latter, we miss the main message of the opera which is always there for those with ears to hear. 'I do not pretend to have discovered everything in *Pelléas*', Debussy wrote in *Le figaro* in April 1902 (LCr, p. 63), 'but I *have* tried to forge a path ahead that others will be able to follow, widening it with my own discoveries, which will perhaps extricate dramatic music from the heavy constraint under which it has lived for so long.'

But the main problem that Debussy then faced was the theatrical path that he himself would follow after having achieved so much in *Pelléas et Mélisande*, and it was a problem that was to concern him increasingly as he searched in vain for a second ideal poet and poem. He rightly realised, perhaps thinking of Massenet as he did so, that any theatrical composer worth his salt should not seek to recreate his past successes. If this began to happen he might as well give up composing to 'cultivate indoor pineapples' (1903; MES, p. 74) or 'go quietly away and tune pianos' (1910; RLS, p. 242). That Debussy never had to resort to either was largely thanks to Edgar Allan Poe and his *Tales of mystery and imagination*.

4 After *Pelléas*: the Poe operas (*Le diable dans le beffroi, La chute de la Maison Usher*)

> I beg Maeterlinck's pardon, but many needlessly aggravating 'events' have occurred . . . I have been spared nothing: illness; Chouchou sick; and to cap it all Mme [Lilly] Texier — another malady![1] People commit suicide for less, and if I did not feel anxious as much as duty-bound to finish the two little dramas based on E. Poe, this would already have taken place.
>
> (Debussy to Durand, 21 July 1916; *F-Pdurand*)

> It is possible that *The fall of the House of Usher* will also be the 'fall' of Claude Debussy. Destiny should allow me to finish it, for I shall not wish to rely entirely on *Pelléas* for the harsh judgment of future generations . . . a musician is no good to the dead!
>
> (Debussy to Dukas, 10 August 1916; from the catalogue for the sale at Hôtel Drouot, Paris, 20 June 1977, no. 102)

Debussy discovered the haunting visions of Poe's Gothic dream-world through Baudelaire's translations of the *Tales of mystery and imagination* (his *Nouvelles histoires extraordinaires*). Edgar Poe, as he became known in France, perhaps aided by the closeness of his surname to the word 'poète', 'became identified with the meaning and aspirations of poetry itself' (Beaver, p. 90); selections from his poems were published by Mallarmé in 1888 before a complete translation was undertaken by Debussy's friend Gabriel Mourey. But Poe's reputation began to be built in France even before his squalid death in Baltimore in 1849, and the Gallicisms and French names which abound in his tales assisted his adoption. A first tale appeared in the *Magasin pittoresque* in August 1845 (*La lettre volée/The purloined letter*) and was swiftly followed by others, including *Le chat noir* which Baudelaire avidly read in the winter of 1846. This was to spark off the translation of Poe's prose works which occupied him for seventeen years and made up half his published output.

Le diable dans le beffroi first appeared in *Le pays* on 20 September 1854 and *La chute de la Maison Usher* in the same source in February 1855. Both were included in the *Nouvelles histoires extraordinaires* of 1857,[2] in which Baudelaire translated out the stylistic faults and so-called incoherence which the Americans criticised in Poe. Poe's impulsive style, with his passion for obscure, atmospheric words, also fertilised Baudelaire's own writing, to the extent that he was accused of plagiarism. 'I found poems and stories which I had thought about', Baudelaire explained in defence (Beaver, p. 90), 'but in a confused, vague and disordered way, and which Poe had been able to organise and treat perfectly.' As Lockspeiser says (LO, 2, p. 140): 'None of the writers in the rich generation from Baudelaire to Paul Valéry, including Gide and Marcel Proust, escaped his fascination, and the aspect of Poe to which they were drawn was the rising to the surface of unconscious fantasies.' T.S. Eliot in his *Edgar Allan Poe and France* maintains that Poe's 'most vivid imaginative realisations are those of the dream', and that in Poe the Symbolists saw an expression of the new sensibility they were themselves seeking, and the emergence of the collective unconscious. Mallarmé learned English and visited London 'the better to read Poe' (Beaver, p. 91), and Maeterlinck was particularly attracted to *The fall of the House of Usher*, owing to Poe 'the birth in my work of a sense of mystery and the passion for the beyond' (Lockspeiser, *Opera news*, 1970, p. 11). Indeed, there are many links between the 'falls' of the houses of Usher and Allemonde, and a poem of 1844 called *Dream-land*[3] could equally well apply to the friend's journey to Roderick Usher as to Mélisande's coming to Allemonde:

> By a route obscure and lonely,
> Haunted by ill angels only . . .
> I have reached these lands but newly
> From an ultimate dim Thule –
> From a wild, weird clime that lieth, sublime,
> Out of SPACE – out of TIME.

Apart from the obvious Poe influence in the castle vaults scene in *Pelléas et Mélisande*, the links between Poe and Maeterlinck also show up in the characters they created: Pelléas and Roderick Usher are both indecisive, neurasthenic, hypersensitive and guilty of loving within their own families; Mélisande's fragile charm and mysterious death link her to Poe's Morella or Ligeia,[4] and even to the sickly Madeline Usher.

Despite Debussy's later claims that his Poe operas were fundamentally different from *Pelléas*, it is easy to see why he was naturally attracted to Poe, 'a story-teller who for ever seems on the very point of engagingly baring his psyche, while he disengages as narrator: who for ever holds out the promise of hidden truth, while contriving to offer forgeries, imitations, hoaxes' (Beaver, p. 91). The appeal to Debussy's fascination with the cryptic and occult is obvious, though he was not typical of other Frenchmen, who tended to substitute an emphasis on Poe's cerebral, logistic powers for a more psychological interpretation. That is to say, Debussy extended the idea of a parallel between the collapse of the House of Usher and Poe's own disintegration to encompass the breakdown of his own career through ill-health, as can be seen from the second of the introductory quotations to this chapter. And we know that Debussy had studied Poe's career in detail from an article in the *Revue de la Société Internationale de Musique* of 15 March 1913 (RLS, p. 284).

Whether Debussy discovered Poe's tales through the similarly extravagant and horrific *Contes cruels* of Villiers de l'Isle-Adam or *vice versa* is not known: the answer may emerge from future studies of Debussy's crucial Prix de Rome years. But at the same time as he was purportedly composing music for *Axël*, Debussy must also have been considering musical settings of Poe, for a letter from André Suarès to Romain Rolland of 14 January 1890 mentions a 'symphony on psychologically developed themes for which the idea comes from many a Poe tale, and in particular *The fall of the House of Usher*'.[5] His interest was perhaps temporarily distracted by *Rodrigue et Chimène*, but the discovery of Maeterlinck does not mean that the House of Usher had left his thoughts altogether. Compare the following two extracts (in which the italics are mine):

> I cannot manage to brighten the sadness of my surroundings; my journeys are *dull, dark, and soundless* like those of an Edgar Allan Poe hero.

> During the whole of a *dull, dark, and soundless* day in the autumn of the year . . . I had been passing alone . . . through a singularly dreary track of country, and at length found myself, as the shades of evening drew on, within view of the melancholy House of Usher.

The first comes from a letter to Ernest Chausson of 3 September 1893 (*ReM*, 1925, p. 117), just as Debussy was beginning work on *Pelléas et Mélisande*, and the second is the opening of *The fall of the House of Usher*.[6]

It is also possible that Debussy had in mind the quotation from Pierre-Jean de Béranger's poem *Le refus* (1831), which prefaces Poe's *House of Usher*, when he chose the extract from Sonnet 24 of the 'Willow-wood' sequence from Dante Gabriel Rossetti's *The house of life* to set in *La saulaie* around May 1896.[7] The Béranger reads:

> Son coeur est un luth suspendu;
> Sitôt qu'on le touche, il résonne.

Whereas the lines set by Debussy[8] (in Pierre Louÿs's translation) are:

> Mais il touchait son luth où j'entendais passer
> Des paroles mystérieuses.
> Nos yeux se rencontraient en silence
> [Dans le miroir de l'eau profonde.
> Et peu à peu le son de luth devint la voix]

* * *

Le diable dans le beffroi (June 1902 – ?1912)

The next news of the Poe operas comes little over a month after *Pelléas* had been performed. Debussy wrote to André Messager on 9 June 1902 (MES, p. 22):

> Meanwhile, I am working on *Le diable dans le beffroi*: to this end, I should like you to read (or reread) this story so that you can advise me. Something can be drawn from within it in which the real world would blend with the fantastic in harmonious proportions. One might also find there an ironical and cruel devil, much more of a devil than that sort of red-hot brimstoned clown which we illogically regard as traditional. I should also like to destroy the idea of the devil as the spirit of evil! He is more simply the spirit of contradiction and it is he perhaps who whispers to those who do not think like everybody else?

After completing the *Estampes* at Bichain in July 1903 Debussy turned in earnest to *Le diable*; the six pages of the scenario he wrote are dated 25 August at the head (see Appendix). On 28 August he assured his friend Paul-Jean Toulet that he still had his adaptation of Shakespeare's *As you like it* in mind (see Chapter 12), despite his present work on *Le diable*. In this letter (TOU, p. 21) Debussy's enthusiasm for theatre projects in the wake of the success of *Pelléas* is very much in evidence, as is his anxiety not to delay work on them any longer.

On 7 September he told Messager that he was still busy with his scenario and he announced on 12 September that work was finished as far as *Le diable* was concerned (MES, p. 74):

> The scenario is pretty nearly complete; the colour of the music I wish to use is more or less fixed. But there remain many sleepless nights . . . after all this.
>
> As to those who do me the kindness to hope that I shall never get away from *Pelléas*, they are deliberately blinding themselves to reality . . . the worst thing of all is to begin one's career all over again. Nevertheless, it is probable that these same people would find it shocking for me to have deserted the shadow of Mélisande for the ironic pirouette of the devil, and will accuse me once more of capriciousness.

But by now *La mer* was under way and it is unlikely that Debussy ever wrote down any more of his ideas for *Le diable dans le beffroi*, though he felt that work was sufficiently far advanced to sign a contract with his new editor Jacques Durand on 14 October 1903.[9] This describes the opera as a 'musical tale' in two acts and three tableaux, though it later officially shrank to one act when the question arose of making up a double-bill with *La chute de la Maison Usher* in 1908. From the complete scenario in two tableaux of 1903 it seems as though Debussy was deliberately exaggerating the dimensions

of his new project to secure a better financial deal. This included 6000 francs
‚to be paid after the 'first stage performance at the Paris Opéra-Comique'. Providing that the first act was delivered to Durand before 15 October 1904,
and the rest of the opera by 15 May 1905, Debussy was to receive 12,000
francs, to be paid in 500-franc instalments on the fifteenth of each month.
When it became clear that he was not going to deliver on time, a new contract
was drawn up on 31 March 1905[10] postponing Act 1 till 15 April 1906, and
the rest until 15 April 1907 'at the latest'. However, the wily Debussy managed
to secure another 9000 francs worth of monthly payments for his unfinished
opera on the strength of assigning to Durand all the remaining copies and
publishing rights to *Pelléas et Mélisande*.[11] He was beginning to realise how
much life cost with Emma Bardac, and it is possible that his experiences with
Durand and *Le diable* caused the rot to set in as far as theatrical works were
concerned when he discovered how easily he could obtain money by bluffing
about their state of completion. When one considers his later deals with Gatti-
Casazza and Maud Allan, it is obvious how royally Debussy disregarded contracts, for he also promised in 1903 to give Durand first refusal on 'all the
works he composed in the future'!

But all his devious contractual dealings concerning *Le diable* do not mean
that Debussy was not thinking about his project in the interim and trying to
solve the musico-dramatic problems it presented. He also once told Pasteur
Vallery-Radot (p. 117) that 'he destroyed everything which did not satisfy
him', though this being the case it is odd that *any* of the rough sketches for
the Poe operas have survived.

The next we hear of *Le diable* is on 7 July 1906 when Debussy told
Durand, perhaps prompted by a reminder that Durand had not received the
music for the first act, that 'I believe I have discovered a new way to treat
voices which has the double merit of being simple.' (DUR, p. 43) Unfortunately it was to be 'a secret' between the two of them, and so it remained
even after he had sold the first performance rights again to Giulio Gatti-
Casazza for the Metropolitan Opera House for 2000 francs[12] on 5 July 1908,
together with an option on *La légende* [*L'histoire*] *de Tristan* (see Chapter 12).
Le diable and *Usher* were both to be performed on the same evening and, to
be fair to Debussy, Gatti-Casazza apparently had to persuade him to sign the
contract. In the *New York times* on 15 March 1925 he recalled Debussy
saying: 'I must tell you honestly that of the three works there barely exists a
sketch of the librettos; and as to the music, I have written only some vague
ideas . . . Do not forget that I am a lazy composer and that I sometimes
require weeks to decide upon one harmonious chord in preference to another.'
Later, in his *Memories of the opera* (1977, p. 157), Gatti-Casazza remembered
that Debussy had prophetically remarked: 'It is a piece of bad business you
are doing . . . I do not believe that I will ever finish my part of all this. I write
for myself alone, and do not trouble myself about the impatience of others.'

This unusual honesty does not sound altogether like Debussy, and it is possible that Gatti-Casazza's memory played him false, as Debussy's reported words vary from one source to the other. But there is more than a grain of truth in it all, and a good case can be made for saying that Debussy was a lazy composer as far as actual production went, albeit one who always put quality above quantity. There can also be no doubt that his ever-pressing financial difficulties tempted him to take advantage of a *Pelléas* enthusiast who had recently been appointed manager of the Metropolitan and whom mild dissuasion seemed to make all the more eager (see n. 15).

Le diable is mentioned in conjunction with *Usher* in September 1909 (DUR, p. 81); then, in a letter to Godet on 6 February 1911 (GOD, pp. 126-7), Debussy again returns to its choral techniques. He confides that, because of *Khamma* and *Le martyre de Saint Sébastien*, the Poe operas have had to be

> postponed indefinitely! I can admit to you that I am not sorry, since there are many points of expression which still do not satisfy me. And the overall scheme is not sufficiently clear in my mind, notably for *Le diable dans le beffroi* in which I should like to arrive at an extremely simple, but nevertheless extremely supple sort of choral writing ... The placing of the chorus in *Boris* does not satisfy me, any more than the persistent counterpoint in the second act of *Meistersinger*. Something else needs to be discovered: an ingenious aural deception, for instance. It's the very devil! – without counting on that ridiculous practice of segregating the chorus by sex as if they were in the public baths!

According to Vallas, Debussy expanded on this idea to Pierre Lalo (trans. in LO, 2, pp. 145-6), maintaining that

> the people in *Boris* do not form a real crowd. Sometimes one group sings, sometimes another ... and generally they sing in unison. As for the crowd in *Meistersinger*, they are not a crowd either, they are an army solidly organised in the German manner, marching in rows. What I should like to achieve is something more scattered and split up, something both more nimble and intangible, something apparently inorganic, and yet with underlying control – a real human crowd in which each voice is free and in which all the voices combined nevertheless produce the impression of an ensemble.

On 31 March 1912, Debussy played Henri Büsser 'several very picturesque, amusing and atypical fragments on the piano' (1955, p. 185), and that is the last we hear of *Le diable dans le beffroi*. From nearly ten years' contemplation, all that emerged was a scenario and a forty-second piano piece, for late in 1904 Debussy supplied for a 'spot-the-composer' competition in the journal *Musica* a twenty-seven-bar offering, in which bars 1-8 and 19-22 come from the Meyer sketches for *Le diable*.[13] The Opéra-Comique nevertheless announced the Poe operas for their 1911-12 season and P.-B. Gheusi was still hopeful of a performance there when he sent his condolences to Emma Debussy on her husband's death.[14]

* * *

Debussy's scenario shows that Poe's lightweight tale (more of imagination than mystery) was to be very freely adapted. In the rather absurd original the only identifiable character is the devil, who in the Dutch village of Vondervotteimittis (which Baudelaire wisely left as it was and Debussy ignored) wickedly strikes the midday bell in the belfry thirteen times, thus undermining the sanity of the villagers who have sworn 'eternal fidelity to their clocks and cabbages' — the latter turn purple as all the village clocks go berserk at the end. In the chaos the devil remains astride the village bell-ringer, tolling the bell-rope with his teeth whilst playing Irish jigs on his violin.

Debussy's first tableau is also set in Holland and is practically adapted to the needs of the operatic stage, with musical reminders to himself and humorous explanations *en route*. For instance, the children singing and dancing at the start provide a 'pretext for elaborate counterpoint, showing that they will much later turn out to be good solid Dutch citizens'! The characters introduced are a bell-ringer (found fishing by the canal at the start), the mayor, and his daughter ('timid as a tulip'), with whom the bell-ringer's son innocently flirts. At midday the bell-ringer goes off to do his duty and the villagers prepare to check their watches. As thirteen strikes, the devil appears where the clock-face should be. He descends amongst the stupefied crowd and proceeds to tease and entertain them, being 'very jovial', unlike the traditional devil. The mayor says that as the devil dislikes the holy music of the bells, they should be rung again, and the bell-ringer's son runs the risk of obeying him. But the bells make strange cracked sounds which the devil proceeds to parody on his little dancing-master's violin, gradually transforming the rhythm and melody into a fantastic jig (in which 'the devil's violin battles with the trombones'). This has such rhythmic and sonorous power that the crowd begin to dance in a heavy, awkward manner. The jig continues without pity, forcing the villagers to follow the devil, pied-piper-like, towards the canal. When he jumps in, the crowd wants to follow, but he raises his bow, stopping them abruptly as he brings it down, 'like a good conductor cutting off the end of a piece'.

The second tableau set in an Italian village is pure Debussy, and all the characters have been transformed too. The men's hats are askew, the women's bodices are half undone, and the mayor's daughter has turned from 'timid tulip . . . to ostentatious peony' in this scene of wild abandon. The effect, Debussy says, is to be made by choral means, in contrast to the mainly orchestral first tableau. The girl's fiancé, Jean, remains outside the devil's influence through his love for her, but she disowns him and laughs in his face. When the devil prevents him from approaching her, Jean climbs the belfry and prays aloud. As the bells ring out, it is the devil's turn to shudder. He lays his hands on the villagers and they fall down one by one: the light fades, leaving only the devil visible, who vanishes in a red flash. Then everything returns slowly to normal, presumably as it was in the first tableau, for the 'raging river' becomes a canal again. The bells ring midday as usual: the villagers check their watches and are greatly relieved when they can stop counting at twelve. 'And thus the opera ends' without any sign of a third tableau or second act.

In the opera, whose scenario looks forward to Stravinsky's *The soldier's tale*, the devil was apparently to whistle throughout, and on the second page of the Meyer sketches can be found some curious bird-like indications (Ex. 28) which may be notation for this, or for the cimbalom which Debussy planned to include.

Ex. 28. *Le diable dans le beffroi, F-Pmeyer*, sketches, p. 2, line 4

* * *

La chute de la Maison Usher (June 1908 – 1917)

Poe, the inventor of the detective story, would surely have revelled in uncovering the intricate stages by which Debussy arrived at his final libretto for *La chute de la Maison Usher*; whereas Poe, the professional journalist, who considered the ideal literary work to be one that could be absorbed (or even written?) in a single sitting, would have been astounded that the libretto took Debussy so long. It is to the three stages of this libretto (? 1908[15] – June 1909; August 1909 – June 1910; October 1915 – September 1916: hereafter A, B and C) and to Roderick Usher's monologue in particular that most of the reasons why *Usher* remains 'Debussy's operatic might-have-been'[16] can be traced. Only when C was completed in 1916 was he able to make much headway with a continuous musical draft, but by then rectal cancer had been diagnosed and Debussy began increasingly to identify with Roderick Usher, whose mental breakdown Poe had identified with the crumbling House itself. He clearly intended to finish the opera and face the inevitable comparisons with *Pelléas et Mélisande*, even though completing it would have meant closing the doors forever on an obsessional inner world into which he loved to escape.

He may even have finished it, though this looks increasingly unlikely,[17] and quite why Debussy channelled his remaining creative energy in 1916-17 into the Violin Sonata and the *Ode à la France* can only be surmised. Perhaps he did not think his time would run out so soon, and doubtless he would have made the effort (or destroyed everything) had he known that his 'fragments of the *House of Usher*' would be engulfed in two equally unsympathetic stage productions in the later 1970s![18]

Losing sight of *Usher* in 1893, we next encounter it on 18 June 1908, when Debussy told Durand (DUR, pp. 61-2) that he had been working on it 'these last few days', probably since his last letter on 9 June when he had told Durand he was going to the final rehearsal for *Pelléas* at the Opéra-Comique (with Maggie Teyte), which he had specially requested for the previous day.[19] On 18 June he was finding Poe's tale 'an excellent way of strengthening the nerves against any sort of terror. All the same, there are moments when I lose contact with the ordinary things around me: if Roderick Usher's sister came into the room, I should not be particularly surprised.' Between then and 26 June 1909, when he had 'nearly finished a long mono-logue for poor Roderick sad enough to make the stones weep' (DUR, p. 76), it would appear that Debussy had written as much of *Usher* as he was ever going to. He had not worked only on the libretto (at this stage version A) but on the music too, for he was already thinking in orchestral terms, talking excitedly about a secret mixture of 'low oboe notes with violin harmonics'. And the first dated music for the opera, the late birthday gift for Emma of 11 June 1909[20] entitled 'Ce qui sera peut-être le prélude à *La chute de la maison Uscher* [*sic*]', seems to indicate that Debussy wrote the bulk of his opera in a concentrated sitting of just over a fortnight. This theory is, how-ever, demolished by the incontrovertible proof that Roderick's monologue is placed at the start of scene 2 in libretto C (it occurs at the start of scene 1 in libretto A), and that the *particell* in the Bibliothèque Nationale (MS 9885) is a setting of libretto C, which dates from 1916.

In transferring Poe's story to the operatic stage Debussy was faced with even greater problems than in *Le diable dans le beffroi* and his solutions were equally radical and original. *Usher* was, after all, quintessential serious Poe, with the author's autonomous imagination given its freest grisly rein. Whilst the recent Abbate/Kyr and Allende-Blin realisations of Debussy's sketches reveal moments of frenzied terror and an underlying atmosphere of mysteri-ous unrest, the music does not capture Poe's feeling of mounting tension. Roderick's monologue in particular is static, purposeless and fragmentary. As Andrew Porter puts it (p. 133), 'in refashioning Poe's tale for the stage, the composer destroyed its essential character, and on some level he may have realised this'. The extent of Debussy's unease manifests itself in the changing orders within his three librettos, which he tightened structurally from three scenes (A and B) into two (C). The aim was also to move the musical stumbling-block of Roderick's monologue away from the opening of the opera, so that in taking a run at it he could vault its artistic hurdles, so to speak. But in the years (1910-15) before he transferred the monologue to the start of scene 2 he often came up against a brick wall (being in the 'usines de néant' Debussy called it, referring to the poetry of Jules Laforgue). On 8 July 1910, just after he had finished libretto B for *Usher*, he was feeling particularly miserable and alone and lamented to Durand that

> an artist is, by definition, a man accustomed to dream, who lives among spectres. How can anyone expect that such a man can behave in everyday life in strict observance of the traditions, laws and other barriers put there by a hypocritical and base world?
> In short, I live in remembrance and regret[21] . . . two said companions! But they are more faithful than joy and good fortune!

Poe's tale is itself delivered as a dramatic monologue in the first person by Roderick Usher's friend. He himself has only one speech; Roderick has four and the mystic rhapsody *The haunted palace*, whilst the lady Madeline[22] just moans feebly in the distance as she wastes away from something akin to phthisis. There was therefore much transformation to be done, and in the process Debussy vastly expanded the role of the family physician, who in Poe is (like Madeline) mute and makes only a brief appearance. From Poe's statement that his 'countenance . . . wore a mingled expression of low cunning and perplexity', Debussy creates an evil monster (le médecin) who is a rival to Roderick's unnatural love for his sister, and who buries her alive without Roderick's knowledge whilst she is in one of her cataleptic trances. There is even the suggestion that he intends to benefit from the extinction of the unbranched, interbred Usher line, and his cold-blooded, macabre murder attempt makes the friend's reading of the medieval story *Mad trist* and Lady Madeline's final blood-spattered entrance even more chilling and climactic. Debussy also adds to the tension *en route* in the scenes with the resented friend (l'ami).

But the change to the character of Roderick Usher, as a result, is profound. In Debussy he is a victim of the doctor's machinations, whilst in Poe he is the central character, identified in detail with the sentient House of Usher, who is responsible for the premature burial of his sister, for whom he has no guilty passion. Debussy rather tells us that his Roderick 'looks a bit like E.A. Poe' himself, and it is Lady Madeline who sings *Le palais hanté* at the start of the opera, though Roderick is permitted a snatch of it by Debussy 'in a very low voice' near the end. As Andrew Porter says (p. 134), Debussy 'by implication, applied the Béranger couplet set over Poe's story . . . to Madeline, not Roderick, by making the doctor exclaim angrily that Usher plays upon his sister as if she were a lute'.

The time-scale in Poe is far more extended than in the opera. In Debussy, the friend does not have several weeks to become properly acclimatised to the

House of Usher or gradually to begin to understand its effects on the minds of its inhabitants. The music of this forty-five- to fifty-minute opera is continuous, and thus the action appears to be so too. Whereas the macabre dénouement comes on 'the night of the seventh or eighth day after the placing of the lady Madeline within the don-jon' in Poe, in Debussy it takes only a matter of minutes, though his final pages *are* extremely close to the text of the original.

In scene 1 of libretto C the doctor appears mysteriously from behind an arras as a servant shows the friend into an empty, dimly lit room. Lady Madeline is glimpsed crossing the stage and is heard singing the first verse of *Le palais hanté*. The doctor is hostile to the friend, seeing his intrusion as a threat to his plans, and he tries to persuade him that the destiny of the decadent Usher line is fixed. He also hints at his own love for Lady Madeline whilst condemning that of Roderick. Nevertheless the friend still demands to be taken to see Roderick.

Scene 2 begins with Roderick's monologue: he is dishevelled and, as if in a trance, sings of the 'endless torments' he suffers from the 'ancient stones' of his ancestral home. He has been wakened by what he is certain is his sister's voice, and his desire for 'light' and 'life' makes an odd contrast to the portrait painted by Poe. The doctor's attempts to dissuade the friend from rousing Roderick prove futile: after dismissing him brusquely, Roderick and his friend embrace.

With Roderick's welcome to the House of Usher, Debussy's known musical sketches for the start of scene 2 end. In the unset portion of libretto C Roderick pours out his troubles, overjoyed to have someone that he can trust at last. Not unnaturally, he fears the imminent collapse of his entire world as he grows prematurely old (at thirty-five). He dare not leave the house and continues to lament at a length necessary for the development of the libretto, but which, with all its rhetoric and repetition, must have overawed Debussy when he came to set it. Roderick breaks down in tears and then leaves the room. The doctor enters with the news of Lady Madeline's death and transportation to the vault directly below the room they are now in. He describes the route to it, as if with the end of the tale in mind. The friend again resists the doctor's insistence that he should leave the house and Roderick to his care. Roderick returns singing a snatch of his sister's song and carrying a book. He is aware of the doctor's sinister 'raven-like' nature and of his love for Madeline; but not of her premature burial.

As they read the antique book, which tells of 'ancient African satyrs and aegipans', we hear in the distance the music that Roderick imagines will accompany their strange ceremonies: an 'impassioned, funereal dance' (C, p. 14). An isolated sketch headed only 'Page 13.14 de . . .'[23] (Ex. 29) may belong to *Usher* for it has rhythmic, harmonic and textural affinities with other parts of the opera. It could well represent Debussy's only surviving music for the middle of scene 2, and to my mind it offers a superior substitute for pp. 34-5 of Allende-Blin's vocal score, which at this point introduces an extravagantly high and florid setting for Lady Madeline of verse 4 of *Le palais hanté*, which Debussy later rejected as stretching the bounds of character credibility too far. Any repeated reference to this song would, in any case, have been more appropriately transcribed for Roderick Usher.

Ex. 29. *La chute de la Maison Usher*, *F-Pn* MS 17727, unnumbered first page headed 'Page 13.14 de . . .'

Scene 2 continues with a spectacular storm, and as it mounts the friend reads the story of Ulrich's fight against the 'wonderful dragon ... before the palace of gold', the growing horror being paralleled by what Roderick hears in the vaults below. As he screams out 'Madman! madman! I tell you she is now behind this very door!', the windows crash open in the gale. The gory Lady Madeline falls heavily on her brother (who has advanced to meet her with outstretched arms), dragging him to the floor and his death. Debussy, in his excitement, almost forgot to allow the friend to flee as the House of Usher disintegrates, and only added the direction as an afterthought (C, p. 17).

He did, however, set a considerable part of these chilling final pages, as might have been expected, but in melodrama form;[24] Ex. 30 shows some of this strikingly imaginative music. Much more of the text can be incorporated than Allende-Blin provides, given the pauses indicated by Debussy and his practice of putting in only the odd word at the starts of sections to give a reference for the melodramatic synchronisation. The manuscript shows the

precise placing of the text as Debussy intended it in the passage quoted here
as bars 3–6 of Ex. 30a (cf VS, p. 36, bars 339-40); it also shows that Debussy
originally meant this music to come later in the scene, for one can just read
the start of the sentence: 'Alors! Ulrich [leva sa massue et frappa sur la tête
du dragon]' which suggests that the passage once belonged at the parallel
point shown as bar 3 in Ex. 30b. Carrying the implications of this discovery

Ex. 30. *La chute de la Maison Usher*

(a) *GB-Lbm* Add. MS 47860 (3), f. 25, bars 1-9

(b) *F-Pn* MS 17727, p. 1, bars 1-5

L'AMI

L'AMI

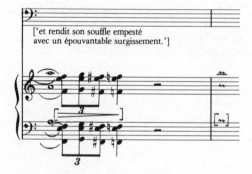

through to a logical conclusion would mean that only a relatively short passage of the final section of the libretto remains unaccounted for in Debussy's short score.

There is, however, no music for pp. 9-14 of libretto C and much of that written for the start of Roderick's monologue (pp. 6-8) is gapped and unsatisfactory. The page in the collection of Arthur Hoérée, of which the previously unpublished Ex. 31 represents the farthest Debussy got with this section, shows him skipping lines and setting these eight bars *before* the earlier line: 'Soyez le bienvenu dans la vieille Maison Usher'. Debussy then realised his omission,[25] crossed out Ex. 31 and left the score as printed in the VS on pp. 32-3.

Of the two earlier librettos for *Usher*, A[26] demonstrates the complex process of sketching and expanding from a prose synopsis, which led Debussy to the three-scene format of B (see Appendix). Scene 1 of B has Roderick alone in his chamber calling to his sister, who is heard singing no fewer than

Ex. 31. *La chute de la Maison Usher*, *F-Phoérée*, bars 6-13 (crossed out)

three of Poe's six verses (1, 4 and 5) of *The haunted palace* before she disappears and Roderick launches into the monologue which was later compressed and transferred to scene 2 in C.

Scene 2 of B contains the doctor's attempt to persuade the friend to leave immediately; the story of the doomed Usher lineage; the death and burial of

Lady Madeline in the room below; and the suggestion of the doctor's love for Madeline. The friend, not to be dissuaded from seeing Roderick, is left alone at the end of the scene, voicing his deep suspicions about the doctor and wondering what exactly is going on 'behind this mask of hypocrisy'.

Scene 3, between Roderick and the friend, tells the remainder of the well-known story, and a brief appearance by the doctor in the first draft of libretto B (p. 9) was later crossed out to leave only the two main characters. Obviously much subtle rearrangement was required to arrive at libretto C,[27] which puts the small cast to better dramatic use. Besides cutting out much redundant material, Debussy divided scene 2 of B in two, part going into scene 1 of C and the rest into the middle of scene 2 (with some minor re-ordering). C is less prosaic, flows more naturally and succinctly, and has more frequent and evenly distributed stage directions.

Some other curious differences exist between the three librettos which help to confirm their chronological order and the dates of some of the musical sketches. In Poe and Baudelaire the ancient story read by the friend (which does anything but calm Roderick's final moments) is the *Mad trist* by Sir Launcelot Canning. Its hero, Ethelred, slays a dragon and wins the shield of shining brass, which falls noisily to the floor just as Lady Madeline dislodges her coffin lid in her subterranean agonies. Debussy, however, either got a bit confused or made some deliberate substitutions, for he called the *hero* 'Sir Launcelot' in A, 'Sire Ithilrid' in B, and finally 'Sire Ulrich' in C! Lady Madeline had no song at all in the first plan of A, then she graduated to verses 1 and 4 of *The haunted palace* as A took shape, expanding to verses 1, 4 and 5 in B, before finally being restricted to verse 1 only in C. Up to 1910 Debussy also spoke of the House of 'Uscher' (spelt as pronounced in French), only converting systematically to 'Usher' after this.

* * *

Most of the *Usher* sketches in an advanced compositional stage date from 1916 and it is difficult to tell exactly what work Debussy did on the opera in 1911-12. Other compositions seem to have been an intrusion from which he escaped back to Poe as soon as possible, yet it is strange that these were finished and *Usher* was not. He abandoned the orchestral *Images* for Poe on 13 July 1909 (DUR, p. 77); only left him 'for the moment' for *Le martyre de Saint Sébastien* in November 1910 (CAP, p. 50); and was back to his old ally immediately after reworking the end of *Jeux* for Diaghilev early in September 1912 (DUR, p. 111). But there were many 'blind alleys' and 'brick walls'. As he told Caplet on 22 December 1911 (CAP, p. 57), when he felt forced to abandon Poe, probably for *Khamma*: 'I have not yet managed to finish the two little Poe operas, and everything strikes me as boring and empty. For a single bar that is alive, there are twenty stifled by the weight of what is known as tradition, whose hypocritical and shameful influence I nonetheless recognise there, despite my efforts.'

There are at least three major reasons why the Poe operas were (ironically) buried alive like Lady Madeline Usher. The first reflects Debussy's disregard of his promises to Durand and Gatti-Casazza and his desire to put quality before quantity in his dramatic music, especially after what *Pelléas* had suffered in indifferent theatrical hands. Thus in *Excelsior* on 18 January 1911 Debussy admitted to Georges Delaquys that the Poe operas were 'quite advanced, but as I have neither a director nor a collaborator to harass me into finishing them, I can work in peace' (LCr, pp 295-6). It is to Diaghilev's 'harassment' in 1912 that we largely owe the completion of *Jeux*.

The second reason comes in an undated letter from Dukas to Paul Poujaud, probably late in 1916,[28] which deserves quoting at length.

> Poor Claude [Dukas lamented], the two Poe tales haunt him continually. I have heard the first fruits of the scenario of the House of Usher (which he reads much better than d'Indy reads his [*Légende de*] *Saint Christophe*).[29] I find his dramatic idea entirely to my liking and [hope] the music arrives as he wishes . . . But I believe it is the music, above all, which does not satisfy him, even though he has written so much of it. I get the impression that his *editorial work*[30] has impaired that marvellous musical intuition which directed his energies in the past, and that he no longer possesses that conviction which gave us [*L'après-midi d'un*] *Faune* and *Pelléas*.

Debussy's practice of trying out his theatre works on his friends had not altered since *Pelléas*, though he seems not to have done this with *Usher* until he was satisfied with libretto C in 1916.

The third possible reason for the unfinished state of *Usher* concerns its similarity to *Pelléas*. Debussy even told Emily Bauer on 6 August 1908 in an interview for *Harper's weekly*[31] that he would not write his Poe pieces

> in the form of an opera, because I do not want to write anything which in any way resembles *Pelléas*. I cannot understand the object of a writer who creates a second work along the same lines which made the first successful . . . The inspiration I have through E.A. Poe is totally different in its elements from that which I felt through Maeterlinck.

By the time he was interviewed in Budapest for *Azest* on 6 December 1910, *Usher* and *Le diable* were called operas and Debussy confessed himself to André Adorjan 'very pleased' with his two subjects

> not only because the secret atmosphere, the feelings, the tensions and the emotions contained in the tales of Poe have never before been translated into music, but also because one cannot find a more complete contrast than between Poe and Maeterlinck.
>
> Furthermore, I believe that it should be the aim of every artist to depart as far as possible from the nature and subject of his success.

> I have been successful with *Pelléas et Mélisande*; that is why I shall never write another piece similar in subject and atmosphere.

Was Debussy trying to convince himself as well as maintain a public image? Probably, for both *Pelléas* and *Usher* are set in ancestral homes in stifling atmospheres 'where the action passes into subterranean vaults, where a pale, mysterious maiden suffers' (Porter, p. 133). And when Debussy told Durand that Roderick's monologue was 'sad enough to make the stones weep', it was from *Pelléas* and not *Usher* that the image came.[32]

So, too, the musical innovations of *Pelléas* are carried to their logical extreme in *Usher*, whose first scene consists almost entirely of the sort of swift *parlando* recitative found in Act 1 scene 2 of *Pelléas*. Mussorgsky's influence is even more evident, though there are no signs whatever of Wagner, perhaps because the overall form is so much simpler than in Pelléas, where there are many Wagnerian moments. Orchestral links are pared to an absolute minimum and the moments of lyricism, linked only with Lady Madeline, are brief, occurring in her opening song and the poignant evocation of her decline by the doctor to the friend (Ex. 32a). Whilst there are no thematic similarities to *Pelléas*, there are plenty of moments when its precise musical atmosphere is recalled: Roderick Usher's monologue, like Act 3 scene 2 of *Pelléas*, is characterised by a low bass pedal on C; Ex. 32a surely breathes the same air as Ex. 32b from *Pelléas*, Act 2 scene 2, and both are examples of one character

Ex. 32.

(a) *La chute de la Maison Usher*, *F-Pn* MS 9885, p. 12, bar 10 – p. 13, bar 2

(b) *Pelléas et Mélisande*, VS, p. 88, bar 7 – p. 89, bar 3

describing another to a third party (here Mélisande describes Pelléas to Golaud). Further, the start of Lady Madeline's song (bars 24-5) strongly recalls Mélisande's 'Elle est si loin de nous' from Act 2 scene 1 (VS, p. 68, bars 7-8), and the first main climax of Roderick's monologue, in which he recalls how, cruelly, he 'laughed on the day his mother died', discordantly crushes a main motif (contrary chromatic motion is a feature of *Usher*) into a savage string *tremolando* (Ex. 33), which instantly recalls the moment when Golaud kills Pelléas in Act 4 scene 4 (see Ex. 20h, last six bars).

The sudden introduction of the main idea of the prelude (Ex. 34a) into the middle of Roderick's monologue (VS, p. 22, bar 195), together with its earlier returns (bars 43, 46 and 100), its subtle transformation in bars 148-51 and the closing bars, and its various experimental reharmonisations in the manuscripts, shows that Debussy was much concerned with the unity of his opera. Dissatisfaction with this may be another reason for the incompleteness of *Usher*.

Again, as in *Pelléas*, the prelude is a microcosm of what is to follow in *Usher*. From it we know that the augmented fourth outlined by the starting motif, with its attendant sinister whole-tone harmonies, pedal-point and triplet

Ex. 33. *La chute de la Maison Usher*, *F-Pprunières*, bars 6-10

RODERICK USHER

Pour - tant   le jour où ma   mè - re mou - rut,

RODERICK USHER

j'ai   ri

rhythm (Ex. 34a),[33] is to play an important role. Much of *Pelléas* is unified texturally by close-spaced low chords, and in *Usher* the same principle, extended to cover quietly the whole orchestral compass, is first introduced in bars 11-12 from an extension of the chord in bar 5 of Ex. 34a. These dissonant, wide-spaced chordal aggregations, whose 'modernity' is inextricably linked to their spacing and scoring in Debussy, can also be found in the late theatre work *No-ja-li* (see Ex. 50). The unforgettable string chord heard at the start of Roderick's monologue (Ex. 35) serves both to unify this and to recall the opening prelude. And such is Debussy's compositional skill that one only notices afterwards that it is simply a C major chord with the main augmented fourth interval of the opera superimposed upon it.

In *Usher*, as in all Debussy, the scoring is of consummate importance, but we have only the barest hints of what the composer intended, and here the two recent stage versions also flounder. The version by Carolyn Abbate, orchestrated by Robert Kyr using the forces of *Pelléas*, tends to lack clarity (especially in the bass) and imagination, whereas that of Juan Allende-Blin, which makes the wiser choice of using the larger orchestra of *Jeux*, tends to overuse the brass and underuse the percussion. Neither has those marvellous internal details

Ex. 34.

(a) *La chute de la Maison Usher*, *F-Pn* MS 9885, p. 1, bars 1-5

(b) String Quartet, 2nd movement, bars 3-4

Ex. 35. *La chute de la Maison Usher*, *F-Pn* MS 9885, start of scene 2, p. 16, bar 14 –
p. 17, bar 1

which Debussy added only at the orchestration stage and which enrich the
opening of *Khamma* but are absent from the rest, which Charles Koechlin
orchestrated (literally) from the piano reduction.[34] Overall I find the Allende-
Blin version of *Usher* superior as it has some of that 'illuminated from behind'
quality that Debussy sought to transfer from *Parsifal* to *Jeux*. His professional
skill as an orchestrator (as opposed to an instrumentator) shows in the chordal

spacing in particular, and as an established composer he is more easily able to take advantage of Debussy's slender clues. Carolyn Abbate, on the other hand, retains five bars in the prelude that Debussy crossed out,[35] puts the melody in bars 20-1 in the wrong (treble) clef, and transfers a misread indication made in Debussy's copy of *Usher*[36] (which should apply to the climax of the *Mad trist* in scene 2) to the very start of the opera.[37]

Both performances, it must be said, were badly received by their audiences and *La chute de la Maison Usher* was critically deemed a speculative curiosity rather than a major discovery to enrich the operatic repertory. This it can never be, and its inchoate state reveals elements both more advanced and more crude than those in other, contemporary theatre scores. The crudities would have disappeared as Debussy orchestrated, but perhaps he never got this far because by 1916 his style was becoming purer and more Classical: the light, almost whimsical intermezzo element was perhaps what really interested him in his final chamber sonatas, and there was little scope for this in *Usher*, particularly in scene 2. He might also have wondered who would attend (or produce) such a gloomy piece after the horrors of the Great War. And how could Claude Debussy, 'musicien français', make his return to the operatic stage with an 'oeuvre Américaine'?

* * *

One curiosity remains: the inscription 'Le Scorpion oblique et le Sagittaire rétrograde ont paru sur le ciel nocturne' in the *No-ja-li* sketchbook (Ex. 36a), which I have shown to apply to the music accompanying the first entry of the evil doctor in *Usher* (*MQ*, 1976, pp. 547-8). This is one of the only identifiable settings of libretto B, for it leads into the words: '[Vous] voyez en moi son médecin dévoué depuis long[temps]'. As such it probably dates from 1909-10. The same passage in the 1916 version (Ex. 36b) begins 'Qui êtes-vous? Que voulez-vous?' The inscription is particularly exciting because of Debussy's links (mentioned earlier) with the occult and Rose-Croix movements, to which *he* probably introduced Erik Satie rather than vice versa.[38]

Positive information about Debussy's occult activities after *Pelléas* is very hard to come by. He spoke to Durand on 8 July 1910 about his 'insurmountable need to escape from himself through adventures which might seem inexplicable, because through them I reveal myself as a man that no one knows, and there is perhaps something better in me!' René Peter (PET, p. 31) speaks of the Jekyll and Hyde 'duality' of Debussy's existence, which went further than the conflict between the amoral man and the artist of genius. Maggie Teyte in an unguarded moment once mentioned his contacts with the occult and Egyptology around 1908-9, which both she and Emma apparently disliked. Debussy is also mentioned as an admirer of the works of Éliphas Lévi, whose *Dogme et rituel de la haute magie* proved a revelation to Stanislas de

Ex. 36. *La chute de la Maison Usher*

(a) *F-Pn* MS 17726, p. 2 *r*, bars 1-3 (1909-?1910)

La Scorpion oblique et le Sagittaire rétrograde ont
paru sur le ciel nocturne

(b) *F-Pn* MS 9885, p. 5, bars 7-11 (1916)

LE MÉDECIN

LE MÉDECIN

Qui ê - tes - vous?   Que vou-lez - vous?

Guaita[39] when it was introduced to him in 1883 by none other than Catulle
Mendès (Billy, p. 37). Debussy's music is also cited in the chapter of Jean
Lorrain's *Pelléastres*[40] that concerns the 'Black Masses' of November 1903,
though this should not be taken too seriously. Shared interests may help to
explain the bond which developed between Debussy and Gabriele d'Annunzio,
one of whose recurring poetic themes was none other than Sagittarius.[41]
Finally, the importance of the rose, the symbol of beauty, regeneration and
pure love favoured by alchemists, was carefully chosen and named by Debussy

as the most important symbol, even *character*, of the ballet *La boîte à joujoux*, where André Hellé's scenario simply mentions 'a flower'. Debussy wrote to Hellé on 29 July 1913,[42] begging him 'to put the rose on the cover of the album in the centre. This rose has as much importance as any of the characters, and I even beg you to include it amongst the characters.' Which Hellé did, as Fig. 9 shows. Similarly, Maeterlinck, who later went much farther in his mystic and occult writings, used the rose as the symbol of the innocent love between Pelléas and Mélisande.[43]

Fig. 9. Characters in *La boîte à joujoux* and their musical motifs (lay-out by Debussy) from the Durand short score (Paris, Durand et Cie, 1913)

The implication of Debussy's *Usher* inscription, as one might expect for anything associated with the doctor, is evil and impending doom. Its explanation can be found in the Tarot cards, with which Debussy must have been familiar through séances. According to Alfred Douglas (pp. 91, 94, 128, 222), the Hermetic Order of the Golden Dawn (to which Jules Bois belonged) was the only one to formulate astrological links with the Tarot alphabet, which again suggests that Debussy went farther than Lévi. To take each section of the inscription in turn:

Le Scorpion	Tarot trump XIII: Death
oblique	Somewhere between the upright position (destruction as a blessing in disguise) and the reverse position (the chance element: the wilful aspect of destiny which takes without reason). Elements of both are implied by the slanting position of Scorpio, and the links with *Usher* are obvious.
et le Sagittaire	Tarot trump XIV: Temperance
rétrograde	The reverse position of Sagittarius implies opposition created by ineptitude (the friend blocking the doctor's plans?), also frustration and the wastage of creative energy: the evil of prejudice founded on narrow, constricting rules of life (both apply to the doctor and to Roderick Usher).
ont paru sur le ciel nocturne	The night sky is found only on the cards of the eight of cups (disillusion) and the seven of swords (danger, opposition).

For the Order of the Golden Dawn, Temperance was also the 'Daughter of the Reconcilers, the Bringer forth of Life': thus Scorpio and Sagittarius together would symbolise the struggle between death and life. Mumbo-jumbo perhaps, but it is strikingly applicable to *The fall of the House of Usher* and to the position of the doctor in Debussy's interpretation at the point where the friend appears as a threat to plans which inevitably bring disaster and death in their wake.[44] Can Debussy possibly have been ignorant of all this when he added this fascinating and relevant inscription, which is certainly no stage direction, to his *Usher* sketches?

5   *Khamma* (1911-13)

This season I shall present a very important new play-dance. It is
entitled *Khamma*. I took the story from one of the old Egyptian
legends, to the translating of which, Gaston Maspéro, the French
author, devoted his life. It is a stirring human story of a dancing girl,
a story full of human emotion. When I finished working out the plot
I submitted my ideas to Claude Debussy, who was enthusiastic about
writing the music. I was overjoyed, as I was of the opinion that he
was the only living man who could do the story justice.

(Maud Allan in the *New York review* (16 Sept 1916))

She has paid [for *Khamma*], she can therefore do anything she likes
with it. An arrangement for piccolo and bass drum might please her
perhaps? In any case, it will be *most* Egyptian!

(Debussy to Durand, 17 August 1916; *F-Pdurand*)

Debussy's final remarks on the vexed question of his 'légende dansée' (or
'ballet pantomime', as he preferred to call it) were made as *Khamma* went
through a second stormy stage in 1916. They reveal the extent to which the
tantalising, globe-trotting Miss Allan — 'la "Girl" anglaise' — had worn his
patience down over the years.[1] That summer she had demanded a second
score for her forthcoming New York appearances with forty (instead of ninety)
musicians. In 1912 she had wanted 'six or seven dances' (*F-Pn* Rés. Vm.
Dos. 13 (24)) instead of the three Debussy had provided, and the score made
twice as long (forty minutes)! Whatever satirical jibes Debussy made about
Maud Allan's vacillations, absenteeism and lack of *politesse*, much of the
trouble stemmed from the imprecise and unprofessional contract which increasing financial pressures induced him to sign with her in 1910, behind his
publisher's back.

What Debussy needed at any time after his marriage to Emma Bardac was a
long-term financial saviour such as Saint-Saëns found in 1877 in the Postmaster-
General Albert Libon. Neither Claude nor Emma was even remotely capable
of living within their financial means, and when the anticipated legacy from
Emma's uncle Osiris did not follow his death on 4 February 1907,[2] matters

gradually deteriorated. Debussy was repeatedly forced to leave *Maison Usher* and works of his own choosing to undertake detested foreign conducting tours and commissions, although this means that we have the ballets *Khamma* and *Jeux* even if the Poe operas remain incomplete. On 25 September 1910 Debussy thanked Durand for yet another loan – for the 'river of gold which has . . . irrigated my banks in the nick of time' (DUR, p. 92) – and it is not surprising that when the Canadian-born dancer Maud Allan offered him 10,000 francs in the same week to compose her a ballet called *Isis* he readily agreed.[3]

Maud was then at the height of her fame. She had packed the 1700-seat Palace Theatre in London's Cambridge Circus from her first appearance on 17 March 1908 until her last that November with her *Vision of Salome*, danced to an original score by the Belgian composer Marcel Rémy (see Figs. 10 and 11). As Isadora Duncan's main European rival, she could command a salary of £500 a week, which put her in the same 'Caruso' bracket to which Debussy aspired when holding out for a fee of 200 guineas to conduct the Queen's Hall Orchestra in a single concert that same year. And it may have been at this performance of *L'après-midi d'un faune* and *La mer* on 1 February 1908 that she became acquainted with Debussy's music (or perhaps even met him).[4]

Miss Allan's scanty Grecian robes and undoubted feminine charms probably had as much to do with her box-office success as her imaginative dancing, and in 1908 she numbered among her patrons King Edward VII and Bernard Shaw. But she had been trained as a classical ballet dancer and had researched

Fig. 10. Maud Allan as Salome with the head of John the Baptist in *The vision of Salome* at the Palace Theatre, London, ?March 1908

extensively the history of the dance and callisthenics. Further, she was an accomplished pianist who had studied with Busoni in Weimar and Berlin in 1901. Her real name was Beulah Maud Allan Durrant[5] and she was intelligent, independent and highly motivated, though her book *My life and dancing* reveals that she was no militant feminist, being 'sufficiently old-fashioned to believe that the rightful destiny of every woman is to be the wife and mother, to make that inner sanctuary known by the sweet name of "Home"' (p. 114)! She herself never married and, whilst she had many admirers of both sexes,[6] her main interest lay in her stage career for which she abandoned her official musical studies in 1902. After her début in Vienna the following year, her repertoire came to include interpretations of Mendelssohn's *Spring song*, Chopin's *Valse* in A minor and *Marche funèbre*, Rubinstein's *Valse caprice* and Grieg's *Peer Gynt* suite.

The musicality and rhythmic nature of her dancing were often singled out for critical praise. As she told Philip Richardson in June 1916 (p. 275) in her characteristically informal English:

> Well, I think I told you that I have studied music very thoroughly, consequently you will understand that I am able to tell at once if a piece of music is suitable for a dance. Having selected the music, I decide upon the general idea of the dance – that is to say, the story which I wish to convey. If this happens to be of a historic nature it will mean a lot of research in order that the costume may be accurate, and the dance in keeping with the character who is being portrayed. Having arranged the general idea, I take the music in phrases and see what emotion each one conveys to me. That is about as far as I go – everything else is spontaneous.

Mrs Doris Langley Moore, who travelled with her and kept her press books between 1923 and 1925, kindly told me that as a dancer Maud was 'extremely graceful and musical, but that she lacked the essential technique for dancing below the waist . . . She had the most beautiful and unblemished feet',[7] and photographs invariably reveal these to the best advantage, though with her legs covered (see Figs. 10 and 11).

William Leonard Courtney, the co-author of *Khamma* (formerly an Oxford philosophy don), probably first met Maud Allan in connection with his work as drama critic and literary editor of the *Daily telegraph*. Reviewing *My life and dancing* to commemorate her 250th consecutive performance at the Palace Theatre on 14 October 1908, he wrote in adoration:

> The main virtue of Maud Allan is that she is utterly and entirely Greek; Greek when she represents Botticelli.[8] Greek also when she puts before us the languorous and seductive charm of Salome.
> When she dances she strikes upon the harp of life, and sets us dreaming. She is, above all, the interpreter of strange, half-remembered thoughts.

As such she would have appealed to Debussy had he seen her dance.

Fig. 11. Maud Allan as Salome with the head of John the Baptist in *The vision of Salome* at the Palace Theatre, London, ?March 1908

Isis was soon renamed *Khamma* and the scenario was probably compiled in London in mid-1910 after Maud Allan's first American tour. Censorship troubles with her notorious *Vision of Salome* may have prompted her to seek an equally exotic and sensational alternative, for she was forced to give *Salome* before a private subscription audience only in Munich in April 1907 (Allan, p. 84), and in January 1910 she found the Metropolitan Opera unavailable to her following the withdrawal of Strauss's operatic version in 1907 by the outraged owners after only one performance. Loie Fuller, another contemporary rival, had also been attracted to the Salome story. She performed it in the Théâtre des Arts in Paris in November 1907 with a specially commissioned score by Florent Schmitt, *La tragédie de Salome*, and the *succès de scandale* everywhere achieved by Oscar Wilde's play of 1893, with its 'Dance of the seven veils', may well be the reason why Maud Allan wanted seven dances in *Khamma*.

The precise genesis of the scenario of *Khamma* is impossible to trace, for the only surviving copy is in French in Debussy's hand (see Appendix). To summarise, the action takes place in the inner temple of the ancient Egyptian sun god Amun-Ra on an overcast late afternoon. Besieging hordes surround the city as the high priest prays to the stone god for deliverance. No answer is forthcoming, but the high priest has an intuition that the dancer Khamma may hold the secret of victory. In scene 2 Khamma enters, veiled (as in *Salome*). She wishes to escape from the present troubles. As moonlight floods the temple she prostrates herself before Amun-Ra and performs three dances to persuade him to deliver his people from the invaders. When the hands of the statue begin to move, she performs an ecstatic fourth dance of delirious joy, at the climax of which she falls dead to the ground, accompanied by a flash of lightning and a thunderclap. In scene 3 the high priest and the now-victorious worshippers of Amun-Ra approach the temple at dawn. The gates are opened to reveal the prostrate body of Khamma: when they realise that she has died to save them, they curtail their celebrations as the high priest blesses Khamma's corpse.

The story, as the opening quotation to this chapter suggests, derives from Sir Gaston Maspéro's 'La fille du prince de Bakhtan et l'esprit possesseur', one of his *Contes populaires de l'Égypte ancienne.*[9] The original tale was discovered by the Egyptologist Jean-François Champollion on a stone tablet in the Temple of Khonsu at Thebes, and this was brought back to the Bibliothèque Nationale by Émile Prisse d'Avennes in 1846. To simplify considerably, the story is about the spirit possession of the prince's beautiful eldest daughter and its exorcism through Khonsu, god of destiny, by means of an 'approving nod of the head to his prophet'. Maspéro informs us that Rameses III began the practice of consulting the statue of the god Amon under all circumstances, and explains how (p. 165, n. 1) in ancient Egypt statues like that of Khonsu were normally made of wood with movable limbs. Thus head and hand movements by a god are mentioned in both source and scenario, although no precise textual transference is involved. The name 'Khamma' may derive from Khonsu, or more probably from Satni Khamoîs, a son of Rameses II who acted as regent of Egypt for his aged father; 'Khamma' might have been devised as a feminine form of 'Khamoîs', though Debussy probably hit the nail on the head when he referred wickedly to Miss Allan as '*Khamma* . . . (soutra)' in a letter to Emma of 3 December 1910 (BAR, p. 89). Certainly 'Khamma' must have been chosen for its exotic appeal by Courtney or Allan, for in Hindustani it means a reed-pen (*Kh*ama), whilst its Egyptian (Arabic) meaning is a putrid stench![10]

The idea for the ballet probably came from Courtney, who, during his wide reading, came upon a potentially ideal subject for the dancer he so admired. Maud Allan may have lacked the expertise to collate a full-length ballet scenario and translate it into French, and so Courtney probably assisted her, though the naïve enthusiasm and frequent expostulations in the scenario suggest Allan rather than Courtney, who was a model English stylist of his period. Maud Allan's letters are contradictory as usual: in the first instance on 30 September 1910 she presumed it was 'not necessary' that she and Debussy 'should go through the scenario together'; whilst on 26 June 1912,[11] after she had studied the score Debussy sent her, she told him 'I do not find it altogether in accordance with the full text and thought which was submitted and verbally explained to you, and which was the outline upon which you were to build up the music, even to enlarging on the given scenario.'

This implies that Debussy may have played some part in fleshing out an initial summary scenario for *Khamma* into a format which he could respond to musically. As in *Jeux*, he stuck closely to his text in an almost cinematographic manner. This would perhaps explain why he felt free to cross out an episode at the end where 'four priests slowly carry Khamma's body on interwoven branches through the flower-throwing crowds' (p. 8 of the scenario), and his rudeness in letters about the scenario perhaps reflected his distaste for its basic conception, which he told Robert Godet (6 February 1911; GOD, p. 126) 'was childishly simple and without the interest that it ought to have'.

According to the original contract, providing the scenario reached Debussy by 6 November 1910, he was to send Maud Allan her score by the end of February 1911. She then had the exclusive right to use the music in special dances in all European theatres, as well as those in North and South America, South Africa and Australia.[12] The 1910 contract also gave her the right to perform *Khamma* in a 'single Music Hall', Charles Morton's Palace Theatre, and she clearly envisaged a triumphant return there in 1911. This has unfortunately given rise to the notion that Debussy's score was 'a piece of hack work . . . a short music-hall number':[13] nothing could be more misleading or false.

For the ballet rights to *Khamma*, Maud Allan was to pay Debussy no less than 20,000 francs: 10,000 on signature of the contract, 5000 when the score arrived, and 5000 after the fourteenth performance; in addition, Debussy was to receive 50 francs after each of the first 500 performances. These terms show that before the advent of the film score the theatre offered the best opportunities for a composer, and that Maud Allan saw *Khamma* as a second *Vision of Salome*. Debussy retained the publishing rights to the score, the royalties from which were to be shared equally between Miss Allan and himself, but the concert rights (without the ballet) were to go to Maud Allan for England and America and to Debussy for all other countries.

It is not certain how much of *Khamma* Debussy composed in 1911. When the proposed submission date in February arrived it is doubtful if he had even started, and at this point his attention was diverted for three months by *Le martyre de Saint Sébastien* which, unlike *Khamma*, had a definite production date. Naturally Debussy did not refer to *Khamma* in his letters to Durand before any problems arose, and 1911 found him occupied variously with his Poe operas, *Gigues* and the orchestration of the clarinet *Rapsodie*. But by November the cat was out of the bag, and on the 18th Debussy was forced to show Durand the incriminating Maud Allan contract (which was a direct breach of his exclusive arrangement with Durand made in August 1905). The short score, probably under way by then, seems to have been completed during January 1912 when Debussy told his publisher that he was 'in a fever trying to find what was missing and in the agony of trying to finish something at any price!' (DUR, p. 107). Nonetheless, he soon hoped to play *Khamma* to him, and he may even have made two versions of parts of it for he asked Durand on 1 February (DUR p. 108): 'When can you come and hear the new version of this curious ballet with its trumpet-calls which savour of revolt and fire and send a shiver down your back?' This is about as enthusiastic as Debussy got with what he otherwise called his 'wretched little Anglo-Egyptian ballet' (GOD, p. 126), and his desire to dedicate it to Mme Durand was probably a peace-offering to compensate for his double-dealing over the contract.

Maud Allan, meanwhile, had been touring South Africa, and her return to Europe in April 1912 'in a feverish haste to work on *Khamma*' spurred Debussy into action. A piano reduction[14] was printed, but was not put on sale for legal reasons till August 1916. He also began the orchestration, but his 'anxious life' meant that he got only as far as bar 55 of scene 1, and the remaining five-sixths was orchestrated by Charles Koechlin between 6 December 1912 and the end of January 1913.[15] Debussy thanked Durand for this part of his 'elegant solution' to the Maud Allan affair,[16] and the full score was delivered to him on 5 February. Unbeknown to both of them, however, 'la "Girl" anglaise' still had quite a few tricks up her capacious sleeves.

As a favour to Debussy, Durand had taken over the *Khamma* contract with its expensive attendant problems on 22 April 1912. After Maud Allan had allowed a text to be printed for a fee of 3000 francs, they sent her a proof copy of the piano reduction. Her objections after studying this were three. First, she feared that an orchestral performance of *Khamma* might be given *before* she had staged her ballet, thus detracting from its novel impact. Second, as she had paid for *Khamma*, she wanted it dedicated to her and not to Debussy's publisher's wife. Third, she thought that the music 'although beautiful in itself, should be sufficient for a scenario lasting forty minutes',[17] that is, twice as long! 'I presume, however', she added as a closing blow to an incredulous Debussy on 29 May, 'that you will lengthen it for me.' As we say, she supposed wrong, and despite threats on 26 June that she would have the revisions done by someone else,[18] Debussy refused to alter his score. There had been no mention of timing in the contract or scenario. But the stubborn Miss Allan remained undaunted. 'As the music now stands', she informed Durand on 9 September, 'believe me, it could *never* be a success. I know the public sufficiently well, and also that all of Debussy's music is *not* beloved, and this would certainly be the least successful of all. I cannot jeopardise my reappearance here or anywhere with it as it stands.' On the same day she wrote emphatically to Debussy: 'Believe me, dear Mr Debussy, *Khamma* needs alteration and I ask you again to realise this now and not cause further delay and possible trouble, but agree to *get at it at once!*'

The 'Girl' and her 'offensiveness' lashed Debussy into a fury.

> It is inadmissible [he told Durand on 12 September] that she should pronounce judgments absolutely without authority, and in the manner of a bootmaker who has misconstrued his orders . . . My dose of philosophy is probably not strong enough, for I have a profound loathing for the whole business . . . And here comes this little madam to give *me* lessons in aesthetics . . . who talks of her sense of taste and that of the English, which passes all understanding! On the one hand you want to cry; on the other – better still – you want to give her a good spanking! Finally, without going to either extreme, one should perhaps give her a lesson in courtesy at the very least.

So much for the *entente cordiale* which, as Debussy put it earlier, had 'been well and truly overbalanced' by Maud's rude requests.

Durand then offered Miss Allan back the 10,000 francs she had paid Debussy, provided they could keep the world rights to the music of *Khamma*. She could have new music composed for her scenario 'by one of those genius musicians that exist only in England' and performed under the same title if she so wished. At this juncture, matters seem to have gone temporarily into arbitration, as letters from a solicitor (Th. Verveer) in the Durand archives reveal. A delay of one year was proposed to Maud by Durand in January 1913 before Debussy's score was performed, to allow her time to get new music composed. But in mid-February 1913 she was still awaiting the return of the manager of the Palace Theatre, Alfred Butt, whom she needed to consult about her ballet plans. Then, without making a decision on *Khamma*, she left for an extended (and somewhat intrepid) tour of India, the Malay States, China, the Philippines, Australia, Tasmania, New Zealand and America.

Désiré-Émile Inghelbrecht showed interest in conducting *Khamma* in September 1913 (perhaps after the success of the concert version of *Le martyre*), and on 18 September Debussy told Durand (DUR, p. 116) that 'the few essential orchestral modifications were finished'. But they decided that they had better do nothing until word came from Miss Allan. Debussy supposed she was 'dancing for the negroes in darkest West Africa' and was no doubt secretly relieved that she could not get near enough to a postbox to mail any more of her infuriating demands.

1916 found Maud temporarily 'resting' at her luxurious Regent's Park mansion in London and planning yet another tour through the principal cities of America, beginning in New York in September.[19] She planned to perform *Khamma* on her nation-wide progress, and as she told Philip Richardson (p. 274):

> In one way this will be a new departure for me, for there will be one or two others included in the cast in addition to a chorus or *corps de ballet*.
> Debussy difficult? Yes, I suppose he is. His music can never become popular in the usual acceptance of the term. I have another new number, however, which is arranged on more popular lines, and will appeal to all.[20]

This indicates the sort of woman Debussy was up against. The next shock came on 26 July when she told Durand that 'Mr Debussy promised to be kind enough to make two scores for me – one for large orchestra and one for small orchestra – as the music will sometimes be given with a full symphony orchestra, and often with one of forty musicians.' Ernest Bloch had suggested double woodwind, four horns, two trumpets (thus invalidating most of the vital distant fanfares), three trombones, timpani, harp and strings.[21] To this Debussy replied (at first kindly) on 28 July that 'there are dances in *Khamma* whose effect is based upon a multiple division of strings', and that the proposed number of players was insufficient. Feeling too ill to do anything himself, he left matters to Bloch, though he wrote to him in a letter on the same day:[22] 'If Maud Allan had warned me of the small forces at her disposal, I would have orchestrated *Khamma* in an entirely different manner.' However, he thought that

> if the strings were really 'first-class', they might still manage . . . In the situation where we now find ourselves, it is best if I leave you a completely free hand: any advice I might give you will be contradicted by reality. But I should like to point out that you cannot, despite all your skill, multiply one violin by four . . . There is a piano in my score, and it is there perhaps that you will find your salvation!

But by 30 July 1916, when he had studied the score in greater detail, Debussy was in a much angrier and less compromising mood. Asking him to reduce *Khamma* from ninety to forty players was like asking her to 'dance with only one arm and one leg', he told Maud in no uncertain terms. 'There is some analogy between a crime like that and the [musical] amputation you desire.' If she went ahead with such a charade, he washed his hands of it.

Maud Allan made one last attack on Durand, claiming erroneously (perhaps desperately) that Debussy knew all along about the smaller orchestras most theatres could accommodate.

> The contract shows [she wrote on 7 August] that the Palace Theatre, London, was in mind, and this theatre, in fact no theatre, has an orchestra of ninety, or even half that number; at the most forty musicians. These points were discussed at length before I placed the order with Mr Debussy. Had it not been agreeable to him to write a

work that could be played by forty musicians I should certainly never have placed the order and pay [*sic*] a large sum of money for a work, no matter how beautiful, that I could not use other than in the largest opera houses. Even in theatres one rarely finds place in the orchestra pit for forty musicians, not to speak of ninety, and a piano too. Besides, how does Mr Debussy expect to have this work played 500 times to get his royalty, when he makes things so difficult to arrange?

Apart from the last point, this of course was all nonsense, as the Maud Allan Orchestra was specially formed for her 1916 tour and could have been any size she could afford. In addition to which, Debussy habitually scored for a theatre orchestra of full symphonic proportions and there is no evidence at all that he was ever asked to do otherwise in *Khamma*. 'The truth is', he told Durand on 17 August, 'that *Khamma* does not please her at all, and she is looking for a reason to put me in the wrong and extricate herself.' And then came the exasperated postscript about the Egyptian 'arrangement for piccolo and bass drum' with which this chapter began.

In September Maud Allan told reporters that she had had scenery made for *Khamma* which had been exhibited at a New York gallery. In the *Musical courier* on 21 September (p. 22) she also showed that she had at last faced up to orchestral reality when she wrote: 'I shall be able to do the work only in the larger cities and then with a minimum force of eighty.' She even took pains to correct a misconception begun by the *Courier* report of 27 April (p. 10): 'A mistaken notion seems to obtain', she explained, 'that *Khamma* is another form of Debussy's *Faun* prelude. That is not so. The subject of this pantomime is Egyptian, and the music was written for it . . . It is remarkable music, the best Debussy has done since his *Pelléas*.' But on 16 October Maud Allan was forced to begin her New York season without *Khamma* and Fig. 12 (a photograph taken at one of her performances in November 1916) shows her once again in her costume for the *Vision of Salome*. As far as I know, *Khamma* has never been performed in America in its original ballet form.

In December 1919 Emma Debussy tried to trace the 'nomadic Miss Allan' through Durand, when P.-B. Gheusi was planning a performance of *Khamma* at the Théâtre Lyrique du Vaudeville (see Fig. 4). But by then Miss Allan was again in America, having travelled abroad after losing her extraordinary criminal libel case against the MP Noel Pemberton-Billing in 1918 (see Kettle), together with her European reputation. She ended up accused of sadism by association and heredity, and suspected of pro-German sympathies, again as a result of a performance of *Salome*, but this time in Oscar Wilde's play.

On 11 October 1921 Maud sent her friend Mrs George Millard to Paris to collect from Durand the score and scenario that she had paid for, as she hoped to interest Henri Malherbe in her ballet for the Opéra-Comique. But this proposal met with no success. In 1923 Percy Pitt apparently enquired about a stage performance for the following London season; now that someone else

Fig. 12. Maud Allan as Salome in *The vision of Salome* in New York, November 1916, probably at B.F. Keith's Palace Theater

was prepared to foot the bill she changed her tune about the difficulties of mounting the ballet, writing to Pitt on 2 April:[23]

> I have all the orchestral parts for ninety-two musicians . . . I should be very glad to give the first performance of *Khamma*, which is my own property, under your direction and feel sure it would be an added attraction for your next London season. I also have the stage set model done by Dulac and the costume designs also by Dulac.

But again nothing came of this, perhaps because she announced in the same letter that she was leaving the following Friday for a series of concerts in Gibraltar, Malta, Cairo and Alexandria!

In the end *Khamma* was first performed in a concert version in Paris conducted by Gabriel Pierné on 15 November 1924. Percy Pitt must have alerted Maud Allan about this beforehand, perhaps in case she was interested in hearing her commission. But her reply on 19 October (*GB-Lbm* Fr. Egerton 3304, no. 15) suggests the reverse. Referring once again to her original contract, she wrote: 'Durand . . . has the concert rights *only* for a few countries but should not have it performed ere I give the first stage performance.[24] This having dragged on so long I suppose Durand thinks he will go ahead. However I will write him about it.'

Thereafter Maud Allan seems to have lost interest in her exotic brain-child and was not present when it received its ballet première at the Opéra-Comique on 26 March 1947 (see Fig. 13) with choreography by Jean-Jacques Etcheverry and with Geneviève Kergrist as *Khamma*. Miss Allan had by then retired to her suitably extravagant Frank Lloyd Wright house in Pasadena, California, and she died (sadly alone) in a rest home in Lincoln Park Avenue, Los Angeles, in 1956. As she left no will, the whereabouts of Debussy's manuscript score (presumably the missing manuscript of the piano reduction) remain unknown.

Charles Koechlin, however, did see *Khamma* as a ballet in 1947 (indeed, he was the only representative of the original team of creators to do so). He attended the performance on 24 April and liked the work so much that it inspired him to go ahead with a ballet of his own.[25] He went to several more of the twenty-two performances given, and on 24 May 1948 tried to persuade his friend François Berthet to go and hear his orchestration, 'which sounded really good'.[26]

* * *

But why did Debussy complete his music for *Khamma* if he was so disparaging about the ballet? The scenario of *Khamma*, if less 'sumptuous' than that for *Le martyre*, has more substance and variety than the inconsequential *Jeux*, and is more theatrically viable than *Masques et bergamasques*, which Debussy constructed for Diaghilev in 1909 (see Chapter 6). There may even have been an element of jealousy in Debussy's attitude to the *Khamma* scenario: he had always wanted to be his own librettist, but as Marcel Dietschy points out

(1962, p. 209), he had 'neither the assured style nor the theatrical experience to write himself a libretto or a scenario which would inspire the appropriate musical clothing'. Thus there is no score for *Masques et bergamasques*, and *Maison Usher* remains an incomplete edifice, apart from the libretto to which Debussy devoted so much time.

Debussy's condemnation of *Khamma* arose, I feel, for three reasons. First, because he felt compelled to write it, 'for reasons of domestic economy', as he put it to Robert Godet (GOD, p. 126). Second, because he hated Maud Allan's impudence, unreasonable demands and the resulting embarrassment with his publisher. Third, because he disliked the plot she had concocted with Courtney. 'Have you ever thought of the effect that a ballet scenario can have on the intelligence of a female dancer?', he quizzed Durand in January 1912 while finishing the ballet. 'When considering that of *Khamma* you sense a curious vegetation invading and swamping your brain, and you make excuses for dancers in general.' Eight months later he complained in wickedly racist terms that the scenario was 'so shallow and dull that a negro could do better'!

But this does not mean that once Debussy got inside his subject he did not give of his musical best: he was too much of a professional to do otherwise. In the same letter he told Durand that 'aided by I know not what providence, I nonetheless found the necessary inspiration to write my music'. His enthusiasm for his score shone through as he summoned his publisher to hear the chilling trumpet-calls in 1912, and the idea of underlying menace expressed through sinister distant muted trumpets is one that *Khamma* shares with *Usher* – a work he took perhaps too seriously.

Then there is Debussy's adamant refusal to modify *Khamma*. 'Such music as I have composed will remain exactly as it is', he told Maud emphatically on 16 July 1912. Answering her demand for a reduced orchestration in July 1916, Debussy admitted to her that she could never know how much he was 'heart-broken' to be unable to find a solution to her problems. But 'poor *Khamma*', he added, 'has waited so long that she can afford to grow a little older', though neither of them envisaged just how much older that would be! Koechlin's account of his orchestral collaboration reveals the care Debussy took to preserve the orchestral transparency of the subterranean prelude, a factor which allies it to the diaphanous and subtle orchestration of *Jeux*, which Debussy described to Caplet (CAP, p. 60) as being 'without feet'. Koechlin also considered *Khamma* to be superior to *Jeux* 'because it was less sectionalised, and at times more vigorous, without losing its inimitable Debussyist charm' (p. 36). The legend that Debussy told Koechlin 'write *Khamma* yourself and I will sign it' (LO, 2, p. 156) is, in fact, approximately true. Koechlin recounts in his autobiography[27] that Debussy asked him one day to his surprise to 'write a ballet for him that he would sign'; but Koechlin considered that orchestrating *Khamma* had been daring enough, and declined to take up the offer.

* * *

Both *Khamma* and *Jeux* work on two levels. Superficially they provide music appropriate to the events in their detailed scenarios, and on a higher level they are unified in themselves, though by very different means. Instead of the continual motivic renewal in *Jeux*, which uses at least twenty-one different motifs against a more or less constant rhythmic pulse, *Khamma* has just four main themes (Ex. 37 A-D). A and B represent the idea of distant revolt and, in a striking transformation from the whole-tone scale to the transposed dorian mode, A_2 represents the deliverance from this.[28] C, on trombones, represents the high priest of Amun-Ra. D is Khamma herself. Her three dances form a sort of intermezzo in the middle of the work, and each has its own sinuous theme which is subtly linked with either C or D from Ex. 37. Ex. 38, coming as an identifiable motif before Ex. 37 D, is the hardest idea to account for as it has allegiances with A, B and C and foreshadows the end of D. It probably derives from Ex. 37 C as it is first associated with the high priest (a case where the scenario can help with the formal analysis).

Khamma differs principally from *Jeux* in that its themes develop symphonically, especially C and D. These two combine and are used in varying

Ex. 37. *Khamma*, principal themes

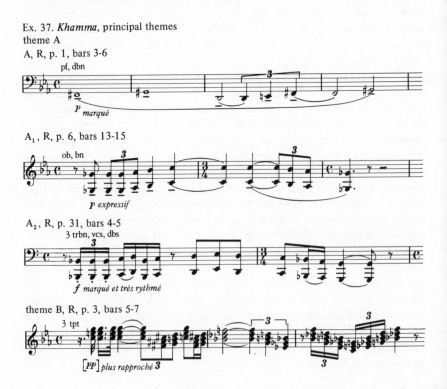

theme A
A, R, p. 1, bars 3-6

A_1, R, p. 6, bars 13-15

A_2, R, p. 31, bars 4-5

theme B, R, p. 3, bars 5-7

theme C, the high priest's theme

C, R, p. 4, bars 4-6

C_1, R, p. 9, bars 9-10

C_2, R, p. 18, bar 6

C_3, R, p. 25, bars 6-11

C_4, R, p. 30, bars 1-4

theme D, Khamma's theme

D, R, p. 8, bars 4-8

D_1, R, p. 9, bars 15-17, Khamma's entrance

D$_2$, R, p. 13, bars 12-16

D$_3$, R, p. 32, bars 7-10

D$_4$, R, p. 32, bars 16-18

Ex. 38. *Khamma*, R, p. 7, bars 13-14

forms of skilful augmentation and diminution at different points in the score, but chiefly as the ballet reaches its main climax and Khamma destroys herself in the ecstatic final dance that brings the sign of deliverance from Amun-Ra (R, pp. 25-9). The themes also have purely musical functions: B is a linking and unifying theme, leading flexibly into scenes 1 and 2, into Ex. 38, and into Khamma's first and second dances and the final victory celebrations, whereas C is the theme with which the three scenes and the final section begin (C, C$_1$, C$_4$ and C$_3$), having an assertive authority which links it with the high priest and which contrasts it with the fluid, feminine grace of the Khamma theme (D).

The skill with which the themes are transformed to meet the exigencies of the drama and with which they interlock into the basic ongoing structure in *Khamma* is quite breathtaking (see Exx. 37 and 38). As Hirsbrunner says (p. 120), 'individual elements are interchangeable and rearrangeable', though the Germanic criticism that 'Debussy is not concerned to achieve a stringent logicality of musical association' is not appropriate to his art-concealing art.

Each work represented to Debussy a new challenge to be met with a new, non-traditional formal solution: his themes relate to the drama and to each other with their own particular logic and are far from being musical 'spare parts'. The analytical difficulty lies in the skill with which Debussy covered his tracks,[29] and any attempt to uncover his secrets from a formally conventional standpoint is only likely to breed frustration.

The use of C_4 to evoke the dawn at the start of scene 3, and the augmentation of the Khamma theme into D_3 and D_4 at the very end of the ballet are just two examples of the technical skill which makes the listener instinctively realise that Debussy's works are unified, but leads him to imagine this as being achieved in some strange way that defies explanation. Unprejudiced study and listening, however, prove the truth to be otherwise, and it would be churlish to deny that Debussy's use of the various intervals up to the perfect fourth in *Khamma* was at least as musically and dramatically productive as either Stravinsky's three-note melodic cells in *Les noces* or any Schoenberg note-row. Theme A is characterised by the major second or whole tone; C uses minor and major thirds; and D the chromatic minor second. B has wider leaps and a dotted rhythm which links it with D. D itself uses the minor and major third both in outline (bar 88) and at 'x'; it also uses the major second, especially in its transformations D_1 to D_4, and thus Debussy combines features of all the other main themes into one, appropriately the Khamma theme itself. One further subtlety is that Ex. 37 D appears before Khamma does, at the moment when the high priest suddenly realises that there *is* hope of divine deliverance from the marauding mob outside the city. By introducing the Khamma theme at this point, Debussy makes clear, as soon as she enters with the same rising scale a few bars later (Ex. 37 D_1), that Khamma was the subject of the high priest's vision. Thus Debussy cleverly plants the idea of Khamma as the instrument of deliverance in our minds by both theatrical and musical means.

The other remarkable aspect of *Khamma* is its Stravinskian influence, and Koechlin (p. 51) comments on its 'harsher chords, verging on bitonality like those of "Surgi de la croupe et du bond"'.[30] He must surely have had in mind the distant trumpet fanfares of Ex. 37 B which briefly use the same combination of keys (C and F sharp major) that form the basis of part 2 of *Petrushka* (OS, pp. 58ff). They also occur in *The firebird* and Debussy heard both these scores at their Ballets Russes premières[31] before he began the music of *Khamma*. The only difference is that Debussy's bitonality is less clearly defined than Stravinsky's; its wider spacing and the absence of parallel seconds makes the end result far less strident. But it is hard to believe that Debussy did not have Ex. 39a from *Petrushka* in mind when he wrote Ex. 39b in scene 1 of *Khamma*: the triplet and 'scotch snap' rhythms; held treble C and B flat; key combination (C and F sharp/G flat major); and implied use of the same descending whole-tone scale in the lowest part are all common factors.

Ex. 39

(a) Stravinsky, *Petrushka*, OS, p. 58, figs. 95-6

(b) *Khamma*, R, p. 7, bars 10-11

Ex. 37 A$_2$ would not sound out of place in the Shrovetide Fair scene in *Petrushka*, and the fanfares in *Khamma* regularly juxtapose major and minor triads (Ex. 37 B), a device favoured by Stravinsky in his early Russian ballets.[32]

Significantly, in the same week as Debussy told Durand he was working on the orchestration of *Khamma* (DUR, p. 109), he also wrote to Stravinsky. In this letter of 13 April 1912 (Souris, p. 46) he says:

> Thanks to you I have passed a most enjoyable Easter holiday in the company of Petrushka, the terrible Moor and the delightful Balle-rina . . . I don't know many things of greater worth than what you call 'le Tour de Passe-Passe': there is a kind of sonorous magic within it, a mysterious transformation of mechanical souls which become human by a sorcery which is, until now, uniquely your invention. Finally, there is an orchestral infallibility that I have encountered only in *Parsifal*.

This refers to the passage in the first tableau (OS, pp. 35-8) where the show-man suddenly reveals the three marionettes and, by a conjuring trick with his flute ('le Tour de Passe-Passe', p. 35), brings them to life. Debussy's admiration of these novel orchestral effects was reflected in the similarly important roles he gave to the piano, celesta and muted trumpets in the opening section of *Khamma* which he orchestrated. Ex. 40a shows a celesta figure added only during orchestration which is missing in the 1912 piano reduction (R, p. 6, bars 13–14). It is also directly comparable with Stravinsky's celesta figure on pp. 37-8 of the miniature score of *Petrushka* (Ex. 40b).

Ex. 40

(a) *Khamma*, R, p. 6, bars 13-14

(b) Stravinsky, *Petrushka*, OS, p. 37, bar 2

On 18 December 1911, Debussy had written excitedly to Robert Godet (GOD, p. 129) about Stravinsky's 'instinctive genius for colour and rhythm ... His music is worked out in a full orchestral style, without an intermediate stage, and from a sketch that is charged with the dictates of his emotion. There is neither precaution nor pretension: it is childlike and barbarous.' For the moment Debussy in his established position felt equipped to cope with the rising star of Stravinsky's genius. But the danger can perhaps be seen in his indulgence in a little of the 'sincerest form of flattery' in *Khamma*, and in 1913 *The rite of spring* was to make him feel a lot less secure as he saw his own theatrical efforts and reputation eclipsed by a *succès de scandale*.

Khamma, nonetheless, provides a compendium of Debussy's harmonic procedures and is a better example of 'the latest discoveries in the chemistry of harmony' than *Reflets dans l'eau*, to which the epithet originally applied. Between the uneasy prelude, which is worlds away from *Pelléas* in scoring and content, to the final celebrations with their Stravinskian seven-beat phrases (Ex. 37 A$_2$) and gamelan-like orchestral sonorities, the keys of B flat minor and C major form the main tonal centres. But, almost as if the two were meant to be seen as a dissonance which finally resolves, *Khamma* ends in A minor, or rather on an open A, just as *Jeux* and *La chute de la Maison Usher* do. The satisfactory nature of this ending is a tribute to Debussy's skilful tonal planning, for A as a tonal centre is heard only twice before: once in the minor at the start of scene 1 (when it introduces Ex. 37 C), and once in the major (in passing) during Khamma's final ecstatic dance (R, pp. 27-8). Otherwise A minor is achieved only in the last thirteen bars, and then via E flat minor (see Ex. 37 D_3) rather than E minor, which is never used as its dominant.

Khamma also offers supporting evidence to Roy Howat's theories about Debussy's use of the 'golden section' and proportional structuring (see Howat, 1979 and 1983). Whilst he was prepared to lengthen *Jeux* for Diaghilev in 1912, Debussy was not prepared to lengthen *Khamma* for Maud Allan. In fact he *cut* a short passage from the end of the scenario, as we have seen, which suggests that he knew in advance that it would make the final scene too long and upset his proportions. The main climax of the *revised* version of *Jeux* (OS, p. 113) comes precisely at the golden section point between the start of the final section (bar 565) and the end. But in *Khamma*, proportionally perfect when Debussy allowed the piano reduction to be printed in 1912, the climax with the death of Khamma (bar 407) was already precisely placed at the golden section point between the start of the final section (bar 344) and the end. Whilst this is no proof that Debussy deliberately used this proportional device, it is yet another in a mounting collection of intriguing coincidences.

Khamma is a superbly structured and imaginative ballet and its greatest misfortunes are its neglect and the absence of a published orchestral score. It is as different from *Jeux* as chalk from cheese, and certainly does not lack 'musical meaning, purpose and inner continuity', as David Cox suggests (p. 61). If he can call others to task (p. 50) for considering *Jeux* 'elusive', then he falls into his own trap with *Khamma*, which need be 'fragmentary and elusive' no longer, and will, I hope, soon achieve the universal recognition it so richly deserves.

6   Nijinsky and Diaghilev's Ballets Russes
(1909-13): *Masques et bergamasques,*
L'après-midi d'un faune and *Jeux*

> As soon as I receive *Jeux* in a suitable proof state, I will send you a copy . . . for I should like your opinion on this 'badinage' . . . à trois! You were astonished at *Jeux* as a choice of title and would have preferred 'Le parc'! Please allow me to persuade you that *Jeux* is better: on first acquaintance it is neater, and it also conveniently expresses the 'horrors' which take place between these three characters.
>
> (Debussy to Stravinsky, 5 November 1912; LL, p. 233)

Debussy's relations with Diaghilev, 'the Maecenas of the arts', on the one hand provided him with a powerful theatrical stimulus; on the other they were fraught with mistrust and conducted at an artistic distance. Debussy resisted interference in his creations and refused to play Diaghilev and Nijinsky excerpts from *Jeux* during composition, just as he wrote his own scenario for *Masques et bergamasques* when Louis Laloy was Diaghilev's preferred librettist. Whilst the Ballets Russes appealed to Debussy and his contemporaries for their fusion of the arts of music, dancing, drama and painting, Debussy in particular was unsuited to their new, twentieth-century team-work approach. As Theo Hirsbrunner points out (p. 119), his individualistic attitude remained firmly implanted in the later nineteenth century and left the composer in complete artistic control, though it is precisely that uncompromising attitude which gives his works their enduring strength: *Khamma* and *Jeux* have survived as masterpieces in their own right, though in the concert hall rather than the theatre.

Stravinsky on the other hand, like Cocteau, *was* prepared to fulfil Diaghilev's command to 'astonish' him, though his *Rite of spring* fell foul of Nijinsky's Dalcrozian choreography (as encouraged by Diaghilev) and can never be reproduced exactly as it stunned its audience in May 1913. If one looks back on the Ballets Russes as a vital artistic force created as a reaction against Wagnerism and the Wagnerian approach to art, an important point is missed, for there were many similarities 'between the aims of the Symbolist movements, which had evolved under the influence of Wagner, and those

149

of Diaghilev' (LO, 2, p. 168). Indeed, the writer Camille Mauclair in his study *Karsavina and Mallarmé* showed how 'the Wagnerian ideals which first took root in the world of drama at the Théâtre d'Art of Lugné-Poë were eventually to find their complete expression in the Diaghilev ballet'.

Diaghilev first came on to the Paris scene with his exhibitions of Russian painting at the Salon d'Automne in 1906.[1] Between 16 and 30 May 1907 he put on five 'historic' concerts of Russian music at the Opéra beginning with Rimsky-Korsakov conducting his *Christmas eve* and Arthur Nikisch the first act of Glinka's *Ruslan and Ludmilla*. Debussy, however, told Gabriel Astruc on 23 May (LL, p. 160) that he thought the 'programmes smacked of nepotism and had noticeable omissions if they were to be called "historic"'! On 19 May 1908 Diaghilev introduced Mussorgsky's *Boris Godunov* and Chaliapin to Western Europe and during the final rehearsals displayed his now famous talent for achieving the impossible through sheer audacity, and his brilliance in inspiring others by pushing them to their artistic limits. Indeed, it is a tribute to his extraordinary co-ordinating abilities as an impresario that he managed to secure the only commissioned orchestral score from Debussy that was entirely his own work. And only three weeks late, too.

During the autumn of 1908, Diaghilev began to plan an opera and ballet season, as a result of which Fokine, Nijinsky, Karsavina and the Russian Ballet first came to the West. Vastly exceeding his budget as ever, Diaghilev had Astruc completely refurbish the dowdy Théâtre du Châtelet and nine rows of stalls were removed to accommodate a larger orchestra. The public dress-rehearsal on 19 May 1909 was the social event of the year, which was planned even down to the precise composition of its distinguished audience, though *le tout Paris* did not include Debussy who was in London supervising *Pelléas* rehearsals at Covent Garden. The programme, adapted from the St Petersburg repertoire of the Mariinsky Theatre, consisted of Benois's ballet *Le pavillon d'Armide* followed, in complete contrast, by the Polovtsian act of Borodin's *Prince Igor* and *Le festin*, a *divertissement* to music by various Russian composers including Rimsky-Korsakov, Mussorgsky, Glazunov and Tchaikovsky.

The triumphant opening season also included Chaliapin in Rimsky's *Pskovitianka*, renamed *Ivan le terrible* by the shrewd Diaghilev. This was the only purely operatic venture of the season (25 May) and, contrary to Astruc's expectations, it proved less successful than the ballets. This no doubt confirmed the format of the all-ballet seasons which were to follow. The third (mixed) programme, which opened on 4 June, included the first act of *Ruslan and Ludmilla* again, Fokine's *Les sylphides* and *Cléopâtre*, with Ida Rubinstein, later Diaghilev's *bête noire*, in the title role. *Cléopâtre*, if Maud Allan saw it, may have given her ideas for *Khamma*, for Benois's melodramatic ballet, revolutionary in its departure from classical technique, had a final temple scene with a high priest in which the dead body of Cleopatra's lover Amoun was discovered at dawn (see Buckle, 1980, p. 119).

Debussy did, however, manage to see *Ivan le terrible* and *Le festin* at the Russian Ballet on 11 June 1909, when he found fault with the fantastic costumes designed by Léon Bakst. As he told Astruc the following day (LL, pp. 176-7):

> I counted on seeing you this morning with M. Gatti-Casazza to thank you for yesterday evening's performance . . . Chaliapin was truly astounding, despite the fact that the character of Ivan suits him less well than Boris.
> As to the ballet, it is probable that I have completely forgotten the meaning of this sort of spectacle, since I was bored by it. All the same, what a peculiar way to dress people! It seems to me that we have better than that at the Folies-Bergère?

Debussy must have had in mind Karsavina's bird costume in *Le festin* 'with a head-dress and skirt of orange and scarlet ostrich feathers', and Nijinsky's 'mustard, lime-green and gold tunic sewn with pearls and topaz' for the character of the turbaned prince (see Buckle, 1979, p. 143; 1980, p. 103). His opinion was clearly that gaudy, suggestive window-dressing had been employed to cover up inadequacies in the *divertissement* at a deeper level. The public and critics, however, loved it.

Diaghilev was never one to rest on his laurels, and as soon as the season ended on 18 June he began commissioning ballets from established French composers, even though he was bankrupt and Astruc had been forced to seize the sets and costumes (and Diaghilev's personal effects) as surety against a deficit of some 38,000 francs. *Daphnis et Chloé* was commissioned from Ravel; then, at Calvocoressi's suggestion,[2] Fauré was approached, but he was too busy with his opera *Pénélope* to write a ballet. However, considering that for René Fauchois in 1919 Fauré engaged in 'a more complete realisation of a musical event that took place in the home of Madeleine Lemaire' in June 1902[3] it is surprising that the idea did not occur to him ten years earlier. Coincidentally with Debussy's theatrical career, Madeleine Lemaire's original collection of fashionable *tableaux vivants* in 1902, with music by Fauré, was entitled *La fête galante*, and his *divertissement* of 1919 was called *Masques et bergamasques*, an anachronistic[4] but evocative title which derives from Verlaine's *Clair de lune*:

> Votre âme est un paysage choisi,
> Que vont charmant masques et bergamasques.

Fauré set this poem in 1887 and Debussy set it twice, first in 1882, and then in 1891 as the third of his first series of *Fêtes galantes*, a title he was also to give to an 'opera-ballet' planned with Louis Laloy in 1913-14 (see Chapter 9).

* * *

Masques et bergamasques (1909-10)

Diaghilev next approached Jean Cocteau and Reynaldo Hahn, who started
work on *Le dieu bleu* in 1910, but for once it was Debussy who was quickest
off the mark. The Chinese scholar and critic, Louis Laloy, whom Debussy
once described as 'the most intelligent man I ever met',[5] proposed that the
two of them should collaborate on a ballet, and Diaghilev willingly agreed.
The historic meeting which introduced Debussy to Laloy and Diaghilev probably took place on 17 July 1909, for Debussy wrote to Durand on the 18th
(DUR, pp. 77-8):

> I have seen M. S. de Diaghilev accompanied by Laloy. As the second
> speaks French too fast for the first, a certain amount of trouble
> arose during the conversation.
> Naturally, I have no particular preferences for a ballet subject, but
> lo and behold they are speaking to me of eighteenth-century Italy!...
> For the Russian dancers, that seems somewhat contradictory! In
> short, they do not need the piano score till 10 January 1910 and the
> orchestral score till the first fortnight of May.

As this seemed some way away, Debussy agreed in principle, no doubt
tempted by the prestige of the Ballets Russes, Diaghilev's financial promises
and the prospect of performances in 'Rome, Moscow etc.' But what happened
next was that Debussy wrote the scenario for this 'Ballet rosso-vénitien' himself on 24 and 25 July (see Appendix).[6] Writing to Laloy on the 27th (*RdM*,
1962, pp. 33-4), he explained

> I humbly confess that I was impelled to proceed so abruptly by what
> I know to be an unfortunate trait in my character: a sudden rush of
> enthusiasm which soon disagreeably returns to square one. Besides
> [he added in an attempt to placate his frustrated librettist], I keep
> in a secret corner of my heart, the project for us to work together on
> *L'orestie* of Aeschylus[7] . . . There we shall be absolutely our own
> masters, have all the time we need, and not be bothered either by
> Russia or by Durand (*la place de la Madeleine*).

Laloy, however, did not accept this *fait accompli* and talked of going to
meet a male dancer in Venice with Diaghilev! To bring him down to earth,
Debussy spelt out the genesis of his scenario for *Masques et bergamasques*
step by step on 30 July (pp. 34-5):

1   You came to see me with Diaghilev. Various projects were discussed,
    but no clear decisions were reached.
2   I met Diaghilev *chez* Durand and he discussed a possible collaboration
    with P.-J. Toulet[8] (a further complication). At the same time he told
    me that as he was leaving for Venice in three days to meet a choreo-
    grapher,[9] he would like to take a scenario to show him.
3   As it was only a question of a *divertissement* lasting fifty minutes at
    the outside, I saw no point in turning you or the world upside down,

so I wrote the scenario myself, involving only the minimum amount of business necessary to link up the danced sections. Diaghilev found it charming and it was at once decided that Nijinsky and Karsavina should be the main characters [Arlequin and Barbarina]. So you see how simple the whole thing was!

I should add that I see no reason why my writing the scenario rules out the possibility of your intervention in the project, and if this is to be 'formal' – in the way that you choose – or 'friendly', it is only a question of words . . . though I would prefer the latter . . . So things are going ahead: we are dealing with a Russian who speaks our language and I give you my word that he will understand everything I want. I shall not expect Nijinsky's legs to depict symbols, of course, nor Karsavina's smile to interpret the doctrine of Kant.

I intend to enjoy myself writing this ballet – an excellent state of mind for a *divertissement* – and I hope that you will find as much pleasure in it as I do.

Debussy was here using Diaghilev as an excuse for his own behaviour towards Laloy. He may even then have seen him as a useful future collaborator, for he played up to him again on 2 August, writing:

Our Russian friend imagines that the best method to get his way with people is to lie to them at first. He may not be as clever as he thinks, and I tell you in all friendship that I do not play this sort of game.

However, nothing has changed between us, and that is what matters.

Whether Diaghilev, for his part, did discuss the scenario for *Masques et bergamasques* with Nijinsky in Venice in August 1909 amidst all their other pleasurable activities is not known.

Debussy's rather slight scenario in three scenes for *Masques et bergamasques* is really little more than a cross between a conventional *commedia dell'arte* story and Rossini's *Barber of Seville*. It is set on the Piazza San Marco in eighteenth-century Venice, and as the prelude finishes, the curtain rises on a group of young masked cavaliers accompanied by a group of musicians performing a serenade on guitars and viols. Barbarina, daughter of a Bolognese doctor, appears at a window dressed as a cavalier, to the admiration of those below. But she will only yield to the one who gives her 'l'eau d'or qui danse' and 'la pomme qui chante' (the waltzing golden waters and the singing apple, if you like). As the cavaliers commiserate, various masked *commedia dell'arte* characters enter furtively: Tartaglia with his enormous glasses; his valet Truffaldini; Scaramouche with his unstrung guitar; Brighella; and Arlequin, who mocks the passion of the cavaliers as the others drown the serenade with their wooden trumpets. In the confusion, Arlequin makes a sign to Barbarina to come and join him and the others, and by a ruse they outwit the cavaliers, reaching the back of the stage before they realise and begin pursuit.

Scene 2 opens with the Bolognese doctor meditating alone in his palace (rather like Roderick Usher) on matters he reads in an ancient book. However, Captain Firibiribombo, complete with moustache and curved sword, soon shatters his reverie. He asks how Barbarina is, which leads the doctor to discover her flight. The captain declares that he will find her before dawn. During the scene fishermen can be heard approaching from the distance, and they and their wives (or girlfriends) on stage form an antiphonal chorus. When they land, group and ensemble dances commence and they cavort round the doctor and mock him as he begs for news of Barbarina.

In scene 3 Scaramouche arrives dressed as an astrologer, landing from a mysterious black gondola. The doctor asks him to help find Barbarina, and while he mumbles and makes magic signs Arlequin and Barbarina step out of the gondola dressed as masked dancers and perform a *pas de deux*. The doctor does not recognise his daughter, but Firibiribombo does. He urges her to take off her mask and embarks on a grotesque pursuit. Scaramouche trips him up and Barbarina takes refuge in Arlequin's arms. The doctor rushes towards the dancer who he now realises is his daughter, but Scaramouche cuts him off and makes him look towards the gondola from which the symbolic figures of 'l'eau d'or qui danse' and 'la pomme qui chante' emerge dancing, first separately and then together, as Arlequin and Barbarina withdraw.

The young cavaliers and musicians from scene 1 return and remove Scaramouche's disguise.[10] Tartaglia, Truffaldini and Brighella intervene, but suffer the same fate. The doctor, seeing he has been ridiculed, curses his daughter. At that moment, a procession consisting of Barbarina, an unmasked Arlequin, the fishermen, l'eau qui danse and la pomme qui chante appears. The last two beg the doctor to forgive Barbarina, whereupon Captain Firibiribombo dances a *forlane* with her in which the entire company joins. Arlequin and Barbarina return to the gondola while Scaramouche and his fellow actors who have rejoined them resume their noisy fanfare on wooden trumpets.

Only the openings of scenes 2 and 3 are recognisably Debussian and it would have been interesting to see how he responded musically to Scaramouche's occult 'incantations' in the latter. No music is known to survive, other than possibly one bar marked '(Angelus)' (Ex. 41), which might apply to the 'Angelus heard sounding in the distance' as *Masques et bergamasques* begins. It appears on p. 96 of the sketchbook in the Robert Owen Lehman

Ex. 41. *Masques et bergamasques, US-NYpm* Lehman deposit, *Images* sketchbook, p. 96

collection (on deposit in the Pierpont Morgan Library) in the middle of sketches for *Rondes de printemps* and *Gigues*, and near a sketch for *La fille aux cheveux de lin*. So it could date from 1909, though it would have to be before 23 October when Debussy told Laloy that he had 'completely renounced the ballet, for this year at least' (*RdM*, 1962, p. 37).

As the scenario has nothing to do with either Verlaine or moonlight, it is easy to see why Debussy remained undecided about its title, only deciding on *Masques et bergamasques* on 17 May 1910 (DUR, p. 83) when it was about to be printed. Even then he was still considering less 'awkward' alternatives such as *L'éternelle aventure* and *L'amour masqué*. Debussy received a proof copy on 2 June and the scenario was then put on general sale, presumably because a production was still envisaged by the Ballets Russes,[11] although by then Diaghilev's deadline for the score had passed. After this, perhaps fortunately, *Masques et bergamasques* sank without trace into the murky waters of its Venetian lagoon.

* * *

L'après-midi d'un faune (November 1910 – May 1912)

Debussy was the principal victim of Nijinsky's ambitions as a choreographer in 1912-13 and Diaghilev could hardly have chosen less appropriate vehicles for his experiments than Debussy's diaphanous scores. *L'après-midi d'un faune* was selected in 1910 for Nijinsky's trial run, and whilst its 1892-4 genesis is not relevant here, it is perhaps worth remembering that it was announced in 1893 as the *Prélude, interlude et paraphrase finale pour l'après-midi d'un faune* for performance in Brussels at the Libre Esthétique of Octave Maus, possibly in conjunction with a dramatic reading of Mallarmé's Symbolist eclogue. Thus it began life in much the same category as the 1901 *Chansons de Bilitis* (see Chapter 11), though the last two parts were soon abandoned and its conception changed. The links between poem and prelude, as Debussy saw them, are also worth mentioning in the light of what was to follow. As with Nijinsky's choreography, no precise equation was intended between the art forms, as is made clear in the programme note for the première in 1894, which was either written or at least approved by Debussy. The prelude did not

> by any means pretend to be a synthesis of [Mallarmé's] poem: but rather a series of successive scenes across which the dreams and desires of the faun pass in the afternoon heat. Then, tired of pursuing the timid flight of nymphs and naiads, he succumbs to intoxicating sleep in which he can at last realise his dreams of possession in communion with universal Nature.

Moreover, to the request of Henry Gauthier-Villars for information for a review of *Faune*, Debussy replied on 10 October 1896:

The *Prélude à l'après-midi d'un faune*, my dear Sir, is perhaps what remains of the dream at the end of the faun's flute. More precisely, it is a general impression of the poem, for if music were to follow more closely, it would run out of breath like a cab-horse competing for the Derby (*Grand Prix*) with a thoroughbred!

The stylised, two-dimensional choreography for *L'après-midi*, planned by Nijinsky and his sister Bronislava in November–December 1910, may, according to Richard Buckle (1980, p. 185),[12] have been inspired by seeing Egyptian paintings and reliefs in the Louvre in the summer of 1910 'in which the head, arms and legs are shown in profile, the torso full on'. Early in 1911 the result was shown to Diaghilev and Bakst, who had recently returned to St Petersburg after disloyally staying behind in Paris to design scenery and costumes for the rival *Martyre de Saint Sébastien*. *L'après-midi*, described by Nijinska as being like a moving Greek frieze, contained only one leap and was otherwise 'made up of walks and stiff-armed poses in profile'. Diaghilev, perhaps fearing a walk-out by his chief choreographer, Michel Fokine, and also facing considerable pressure from his right-wing advisers about the dangers of this dehumanised choreography (which was at odds with Debussy's score and virtually made it redundant), postponed the ballet until 1912. It was replaced in 1911 by the comparatively classical *Le spectre de la rose* which Nijinsky's celebrated final leap helped to make legendary.

If February 1912, while the Ballets Russes were appearing at the Royal Theatre in Dresden, Diaghilev and Nijinsky made a special excursion to the suburb of Hellerau to investigate Jaques-Dalcroze's School of Eurhythmics (they had probably seen the eurhythmic system demonstrated in St Petersburg in 1911). It was at this point that Grigoriev heard about the choreography that Nijinsky had earlier devised for the *Faune*, which he wrongly associated with Jaques-Dalcroze's system in his subsequent book (pp. 72–3; and see Buckle, 1979, p. 216).

Coincidentally Diaghilev planned another Debussy ballet with Alexandre Benois in the spring of 1912 (Benois, 1941, pp. 343-4) based on the suitably theatrical *Fêtes*. As the music lasts only about six and a half minutes, it is possible either that Diaghilev intended to include additional material from the *Nocturnes*, or that he had the recently premièred *Ibéria*[13] with its 'matin d'un jour de fête' in mind. *Les fêtes* may have been intended as a replacement for *Masques et bergamasques*, or Diaghilev may have been intending to find a substitute for *L'après-midi* in 1912 as he had in 1911. But as Benois is the sole source of information, it is unlikely that we shall ever know.

Benois, summoned to Vienna from St Petersburg, conceived his 'Veronese ballet' with décor representing

> a Palladian villa somewhere on the Brenta. A sumptuous banquet was to be in progress; the Doge himself was to arrive and be received with unheard-of splendour.

> Unfortunately the music was too short to produce the final effect. Diaghilev did not doubt that he would be able, without trouble, to get the twenty or thirty bars that he needed from Debussy, but he was mistaken. The composer stubbornly refused to add anything to his music. In consequence Diaghilev suddenly cooled off towards the whole idea, although he was delighted with my designs for the costumes and décor. That is why my 'Veronese ballet' never reached the footlights.

Richard Buckle, however, believes (1979, p. 217) that the profusion of Benois's Venetian designs were seen by Diaghilev to swamp Debussy's score which was 'much too short for a *ballet d'action*' and had 'absolutely nothing Venetian or Renaissance about it'. This is supported by the complete absence of anything resembling this project in Debussy's correspondence for 1912, and the inappropriateness of Benois's sets sounds like a characteristic excuse on Diaghilev's part for abandoning *Fêtes*, even if it was one which he either invented or magnified after he had lost enthusiasm for the ballet. Benois's decision to lay the blame at Debussy's door seems to have been a totally unfounded face-saving exercise.

Another ballet based on Debussy's *Nocturnes* (*Nuages* and *Sirènes*) was, however, performed by Fernand Ochsé and Loie Fuller in May 1913, and Inghelbrecht describes a visit by the composer in late April to an orchestral rehearsal for this at his favourite Théâtre des Champs-Élysées[14] (Fig. 14) – 'the only place where music is sincerely loved', as Debussy sadly told its founder Gabriel Astruc in October 1916. As Inghelbrecht says:

> We had not yet ventured to ask Debussy to come to the theatre, and he had so far only made one discreet appearance at the avenue Montaigne for the inaugural concert [conducting *L'après-midi d'un faune* on 2 April]. We were rehearsing the *Nocturnes*. Suddenly, in the opening doorway, appeared Claude de France, as d'Annunzio so aptly named him.
> 'Why did you not call me sooner?' Debussy asked. 'I have made many modifications to my score which you should know about before going any further' [as on the Royaumont score]. 'Moreover, another work of mine has already been played here without my being asked to come and hear it' [presumably the *Marche écossaise* on 19 April].

Inghelbrecht goes on to recount that several weeks later, when Debussy felt more at home in the new theatre, he suffered himself to be presented by Loie Fuller to her 't'children' at an apparently sacrilegious rehearsal of the *Nocturnes*. 'Half-opening the door to the dance foyer, where in a jumble of multi-coloured abandon "sirènes" and "nuages" were nibbling sandwiches and oranges, Loie cried imperiously: "T'children! Miste' Debioussy!" And the *t'children* immediately began to shout at the tops of their little out-of-tune voices the siren's song [Ex. 42].' It is no wonder that Loie Fuller and her troupe were not allowed to get their grubby little hands on *La boîte à joujoux*

Fig. 14. Gabriel Astruc's Théâtre des Champs-Élysées in the avenue Montaigne, Paris

Ex. 42. *Nocturnes*, OS, p. 80, bars 1-2

SOPRANOS

La, la,   la, la, la, la,   la, la,   la, la, la, la, la, la, la, la,

during the war, even though no singing was involved. On this occasion Emma Debussy tactfully used her husband's illness as an excuse to avoid granting permission.[15]

* * *

Meanwhile, back in March 1912, rehearsals for Nijinsky's choreographic début were beginning in Monte Carlo. They proceeded slowly, both because of the non-balletic nature of the movements and because Nijinsky was better at demonstrating than explaining his requirements. But in performance Bakst's costumes made the characters stand out well against his vague, mottled backcloth, and Nijinsky looked most faun-like in piebald tights with his long pointed ears extended with wax (Fig. 15). Briefly,

> the idle Faun observes seven Nymphs [Fig. 16], and his desire is aroused by one who undresses to bathe in the stream; but when he confronts her, she flees, and he has to console himself with the scarf she has left behind . . . The Faun's token love-making with the scarf, which he carried back to his rock, culminated in a stylised jerk of the pelvis, which suggested orgasm. (Buckle, 1979, p. 224)

The action did not attempt to synchronise with the music, other than at the moment of the Faun's realisation of his passion for the seventh nymph (missing in Fig. 16) as she escapes, which corresponded to the *fortissimo* climax in bar 70 of the score. But Richard Buckle maintains (1979, p. 225) that 'although the movement for the most part ignores the music, they go marvellously together – as even Fokine conceded'.

The private dress-rehearsal on 28 May 1912 was greeted with silence and was repeated on Diaghilev's orders to scattered applause. After the première the following day, the audience was similarly stunned by the Faun's 'first sexual experience' at the end, and for the first time the Russian Ballet was booed. Again Diaghilev had the ballet repeated, both to persuade the public and to encourage Nijinsky, but it took a carefully orchestrated press battle between Gaston Calmette, the editor of *Le figaro* (who headed his condemnation 'UN FAUX PAS' on 30 May), and Odilon Redon and Auguste Rodin (whom Diaghilev persuaded to write in support) to make the ballet a sell-out.

Fig. 15. Vaslav Nijinsky in *L'après-midi d'un faune* at the Théâtre du Châtelet, Paris, May 1912

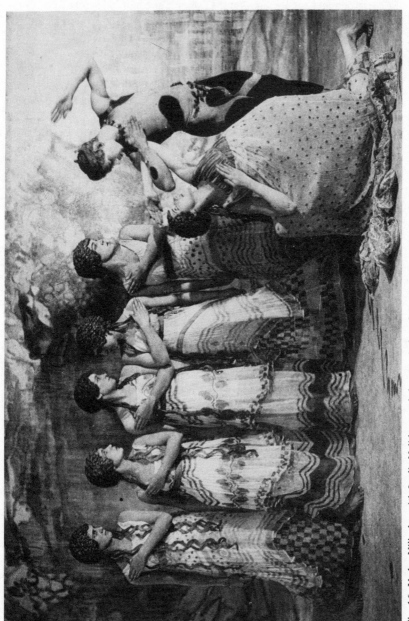

Fig. 16. Vaslav Nijinsky with Lydia Nelidova and the remainder of the seven nymphs (excluding Bronislava Nijinska) in *L'après-midi d'un faune* at the Théâtre du Châtelet, Paris, May 1912

Indeed, the extent of the scandal in the context of the Franco-Russian alliance was such that the police were present at the second performance. To meet the huge demand for tickets, Ravel's *Daphnis et Chloé* was postponed till the very end of the season (8 June), and even then an extra performance of *L'après-midi* prevented *Daphnis* having a dress-rehearsal.

Debussy reserved his own comments about Nijinsky till after the performance of *Jeux*, and Diaghilev's publicity seeking further increased the mistrust between them. 'I have not given up hope that the popularity of *L'après-midi d'un faune* will match that of [the popular song] "Mandolinata"', he wrote sarcastically to Gustave Doret on 12 December 1912 (*Lettres romandes*, 1934, p. 7), but by then he had again succumbed to Diaghilev's promises and charms and composed *Jeux*.

* * *

Jeux (1912-13)

The Diaghilev company began its third London season at Covent Garden on 12 June 1912, and the first sign of *Jeux* comes on the same day as the first performance of *The firebird* (18 June). It takes the form of a contract with Debussy signed by Diaghilev[16] for a ballet on a subject by 'M. Nijinski' for the spring 1913 season. For this, Debussy was to be paid 10,000 francs: 5000 for the piano score, to be delivered by the end of August 1912, and 5000 for the orchestral score, due by the end of March 1913. On Wednesday 2 July Debussy told Durand that 'until now I have received nothing from the suave Diaghilev except a telegram promising me the scenario of *Jeux* for the end of next week' (*F-Pdurand*). As this implies Saturday 12 July it is scarcely possible that the tennis party attended by Nijinsky, Bakst and Duncan Grant *chez* Lady Ottoline Morrell in Bedford Square, London, that same day had any influence on the scenario (which had almost certainly been written before 12 July, perhaps by Diaghilev himself from an idea by Nijinsky). However, as Richard Buckle suggests (1979, p. 234), the scene at Lady Ottoline's Georgian house that afternoon may well have inspired Bakst's set (see Fig. 17), for we know that both he and Nijinsky as spectators were 'so entranced by the tall trees against the houses and the figures flitting about playing tennis that they exclaimed with delight "Quel décor!"' (Morrell, p. 228).

Jacques-Émile Blanche's account of Nijinsky hitting on the idea for *Jeux* in the grill-room of the Savoy Hotel[17] should be taken with a pinch of salt, as his autobiographical imagination often runs riot to fill gaps in the truth. Apparently, Blanche was summoned from Lady Ripon's party to join Diaghilev, Bakst and an inspired Nijinsky, who was drawing on the table-cloth when he arrived. As Blanche explains (1937, p. 258):

Fig. 17. Design for *Jeux* by Léon Bakst, 1913

The 'cubist' ballet — which became *Jeux* — was a game of tennis in a garden; but in no circumstances was it to have a romantic décor in the Bakst manner! There should be no *corps de ballet*, no ensembles, no variations, no *pas de deux*, only girls and boys in flannels, and rhythmic movements. A group at a certain stage was to depict a fountain, and the game of tennis (with licentious motifs) was to be interrupted by the crashing of an aeroplane.[18]

The conception of Blanche acting as an intermediary with Debussy (who is said to have declared *Jeux* 'idiotic and unmusical' and to have consented to compose the ballet only when his fee was doubled) is completely false. Debussy's negotiations were with Diaghilev and for a fixed fee from the outset.

Debussy's initial surge of enthusiasm was for once maintained, even in the stifling Paris heat (made worse by the close proximity of the railway tracks to his home in the avenue du Bois de Boulogne). On 23 July he was almost certainly at work on *Jeux* when he complained to Durand (DUR, p. 109) that it was '32 degrees [centigrade] in the shade', for he speaks of an unfortunate accident to the score of *Gigues* (whose orchestration he broke off to compose *Jeux*) in the following paragraph.

Diaghilev's successful London season ended on 1 August 1912, and with five performances to give at Deauville between 6 and 22 August, he and Nijinsky called on Debussy in Paris *en route*, Diaghilev postponing a visit to Richard Strauss at Garmisch on 3 August to do so. On 9 August, Debussy described the auspicious event to Durand:

> I have received a visit from Nijinsky and his 'Niania'[19] (S[erge] de D[iaghilev]) . . . We have usefully settled some details which needed clarification. They were in a great hurry to have the music for *Jeux* on which Nijinsky wished to work during his stay in Venice! — the calm and scent of the lagoons stimulating happy choreographic dreams, it seems. I denied myself the experience of playing what I had already written, not wishing these barbarians to poke their noses into my experiments in personal chemistry! But *at the end of this month* the ballet will have to be 'executed', in the most unpleasant sense of this word! I pray that God, the tsar and my country will come to my aid on this painful occasion. (*F-Pdurand*)

There was not a moment to lose, and resorting to a frequent natural image that he associated with his own creativity and well-being, Debussy added: 'This year the sea has retreated so far that one despairs of finding it again!' But find it he did, for on 25 August he told Caplet (CAP, pp. 59-60):

> I have finished composing *Jeux* . . . How did I manage to forget the cares of this world to write a score that is almost joyful with the rhythm of these droll exploits? It is necessary, all the same, to believe that Nature, such an absurdly harsh mother, sometimes takes pity on her children!
>
> I must find an orchestra 'without feet' for this music. Don't believe that I am considering an orchestra made up exclusively of

legless cripples! No! I am thinking of that orchestral colour which seems to be illuminated from behind, of which there are such marvellous examples in *Parsifal*!

This refers to the orchestral sketch for *Jeux* made between 23 August and 2 September, the full score being written out between 28 March and 24 April 1913. The orchestral links with Wagner are discussed in full by Robin Holloway (pp. 167-94), who also gives the full scenario in French and English (pp. 162-3).

But before he came to write out the full score, Debussy was twice asked by Diaghilev to modify the ending of *Jeux*. This did *not* involve reintroducing the slow opening chords as has been thought, for *F-Pn* MS 1088 shows that they were always there (see Appendix). On 5 September 1912 Debussy told Durand (DUR, p. 110) that 'the few bars requested by Diaghilev have obliged me to modify – quite happily – the end of *Jeux* . . . it is *better in place now* and the voluptuousness oozes out freely (the Russians are like Syrian cats)'. On 12 September he added (p. 111):

> You will find considerable changes in the end of *Jeux*. I have worked at it until the very last minute. Success has not been easily achieved, for the music must fit a rather *risqué* situation! It is true, however, that when it is a question of ballet, immorality escapes through the legs of a female dancer and winds up in a pirouette.

Debussy, in fact, added only eight bars to his 'violent' section (OS, pp. 109-12), but in the process almost completely rewrote this and the *risqué* triple kiss climax of the ballet (OS, pp. 113-14). Ex. 43 shows the music originally composed for pp. 110-14 of the orchestral score, and is best compared with p. 39, bar 13, to the end of p. 41 in the published piano reduction. In addition two bars were cut out in the revision which originally formed a sequence with bars 5-6 of the 'violent' section (OS, p. 109/R, p. 39, bars 11-12). Thus, in Debussy's first scheme, the 'violent' section was sixteen bars long; in the final version it was twenty-four. The following *très modéré* climax and *diminuendo* remained the same length but were made much subtler by the return of the rhythmic idea first heard in bar 43 of the score (cf Ex. 43, bars 9ff, with R, p. 41, bars 5ff). (Ex. 43 leads straight into OS, p. 115/R, p. 42.)

Ex. 43. *Jeux, F-Pn* MS 1088, p. 21a, bars 5ff

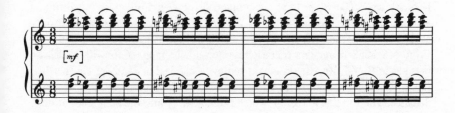

Then at four o'clock on the afternoon of 31 October, Diaghilev visited Debussy again (DUR, p. 111) 'accompanied by a diminutive lady as biting as a mosquito, who was in charge of rehearsals. He seemed satisfied, and only asked me to lengthen the end a little, at which I have been occupied all day.'[20] From MS 1088 it appears that Debussy originally ended *Jeux* with a surprise crash as in Ex. 44. Revising it meant removing the last bar and adding the final three bars as we know them, so that the ballet vanished mercurially into the distance. The top line in Ex. 44, which found its way into the piano reduction[21]

Ex. 44. *Jeux, F-Pn* MS 1088, p. 22

but not into the orchestral score, was probably removed because of its similarity with the dawn start of scene 3 of *Khamma* (Ex. 37 C_4). It is interesting
to consider that the similarly titled 'Jeux de vagues' (*La mer*) also needed two
attempts to get its final poetic disintegration just right.

On 4 April 1913, Debussy complained to Émile Vuillermoz[22] of being
'hard pressed by Durand et Cie who are extracting, one by one, the pages of
the orchestration which M. S. de Diaghilev's company await to improve their
footwork!'. Perhaps with *Pelléas* in mind, Debussy asked his publisher to
check the score and parts very carefully on 5 May. On 13 May, the day before
the public dress-rehearsal, Debussy complained to Durand (DUR, p. 114) that
'the music is beginning to emerge, but as for the choreography, I have until
now seen nothing but a formal sketch'. Naturally, he counted on Durand and
his wife (to whom *Jeux* is dedicated in lieu of *Khamma*) to come to the dress-
rehearsal, and arranged to meet them at the Théâtre des Champs-Élysées
'towards 8.30 p.m.', adding: 'You will enter with me, through the wings.'

Debussy had reason to be worried about the choreography. Nijinsky had paid a further visit to Jaques-Dalcroze at Hellerau in the first half of December 1912, and *The rite of spring* and *Jeux* were to be his first stiffly eurhythmic essays. In fact, one of the few pupils of Jaques-Dalcroze who actually had anything to do with dance, Miriam Ramberg (the late Dame Marie Rambert), was hired to help Nijinsky and to acquaint the company with Jaques-Dalcroze's methods.[23] According to Bronislava Nijinska, Nijinsky invented the choreography for *Jeux* with a volume of Gauguin reproductions in front of him, and what limited time remained to rehearse it (with the far more difficult *Rite of spring* due to be performed on 29 May) was largely wasted in argument and confusion. As Nijinsky apparently never played tennis until the summer of 1916 in New York, it is not surprising that the composite movement he created for the flirting tennis players was more suited to golf. As the white ball used was also nearly the size of a football, great hilarity resulted on the opening night, a point which Erik Satie was quick to seize on in his sarcastic criticism which appeared in the *Revue de la Société Internationale de Musique* on 15 June 1913:[24]

> *Summer sports.* Several readers have asked about the rules of Russian tennis which will be all the rage in country house-parties this season. They are as follows: the game is played at night on floodlit flower beds; there are only three players; the net is done away with; the ball is replaced by a football and the use of the racquet is banned. In a pit at the end of the court one conceals an orchestra which accompanies the games. The purpose of this sport is to develop an extreme suppleness in the movements of the wrists, neck and ankles; it has the blessing of the Academy of Medicine.

Then Bronislava Nijinska, who was to dance with Karsavina in *Jeux*, was discovered to be pregnant and had to be replaced by Ludmilla Schollar late in the day. Troubles also arose because of the vast differences in effect between the piano and orchestral scores of *Jeux*, which in reality was far less reducible than *The rite*. When Bakst's set and costumes were revealed on the over-large stage (Fig. 17) and Nijinsky appeared at the first dress-rehearsal in red wig, red tie, knee-length red-edged shorts held up by red braces, and red-topped white stockings, Diaghilev exploded. A furious row with Bakst ensued and at the last minute 'Diaghilev redesigned Nijinsky's costume himself, retaining the white shirt and red tie, but abolishing the braces and giving the dancer white trousers . . . which ended just about the ankle and were buttoned tight round the calf' (Buckle, 1979, p. 249, and see Fig. 18).

The public were somewhat baffled by the inconclusiveness and triviality of the ballet, in which few noticed the music. Henri Quittard in *Le figaro* (17 May), perhaps remembering *L'après-midi*, observed that 'composer and choreographer take absolutely no notice of each other in this ballet' and that Nijinsky 'manages to turn even the insignificant into absurdity'. But if Nijinsky was

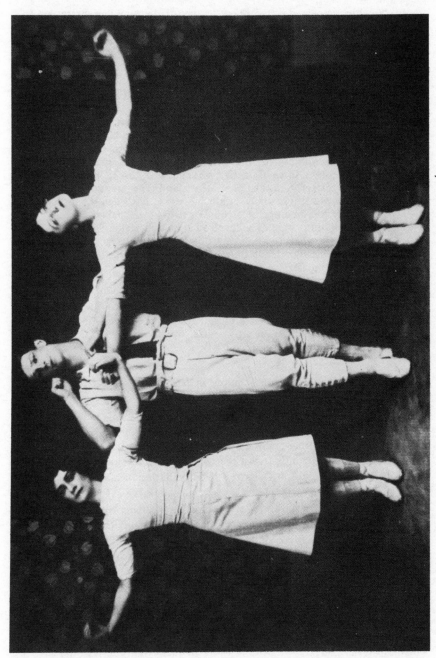

Fig. 18. Tamara Karsavina, Vaslav Nijinsky and Ludmilla Schollar in *Jeux* at the Théâtre des Champs-Élysées, Paris, May 1913

disappointed in the ballet's reception, Debussy was livid. In an open letter to *Le matin* which appeared on 15 May, the day of the première, he set out to dissociate himself from the choreography in the sort of ironical understatement at which he was a pastmaster. He also gave a neat summary of the plot in the process (LCr, pp. 236-7):

> I am not a man of science and I am thus ill-equipped to speak about dancing, since today nothing can be said about this light and frivolous subject without assuming the airs of a doctor. Before writing a ballet, I had no idea what a choreographer was. Now I know: he is a man who is very strong on arithmetic. I may not be particularly erudite, but I have remembered some of my lessons from school. This one, for instance: one, two, three; one, two, three; one, two, three, four, five; one, two, three, four, five, six; one, two, three; one, two, three (a little faster). And then one tots it all up. This may sound like nothing, but it is really most moving, especially when the problem is set by the incomparable Nijinsky. How then, being naturally reserved, did I come to be involved in an undertaking so fraught with repercussions? Because one must dine well, and because one day I dined with Serge de Diaghilev, a terrible but irresistible man who could even make stones dance. He spoke to me of a scenario devised by Nijinsky, made up of the subtle 'sweet nothings' which I suppose should always form the basis of a ballet. There was a park; a tennis court; the chance meeting of two young girls and a young man seeking a lost ball; a mysterious nocturnal landscape with that suggestion of something slightly sinister which the twilight brings; some leaps and turns and nimble footwork – in fact, all the necessary ingredients to bring *rhythm* alive in a musical atmosphere.

It is in the polyrhythmic combinations in *Jeux* and its mosaic construction from some twenty-one different motifs (which cover virtually every possible rhythmic permutation within a two-bar unit) that its modern significance lies. All kinds of waltz movement flash past our eyes and ears in cinematographic manner, though external realistic events (like the bouncing ball at the start) are never allowed to conflict with the ballet's inner development. More than any other score *Jeux* fulfils Debussy's 1907 definition of music as made from 'couleurs et de temps rythmés'.[25] 'As in "Jeux de vagues" from *La mer*, the title "games" seems to have suggested to Debussy a framework of rules which was but the starting-point for the substance of the game itself, consisting of an infinite variety of strokes and gestures.' (Nichols, 1980, p. 299)

Underpinning the structure of *Jeux* and highlighting its fleeting motifs is the three-note *acciaccatura* idea (Ex. 45a) first heard as the lower strings introduce the false start at fig. 1. The chromatic Ex. 45a emerges from the whole-tone chords at the start and also serves to confuse and contrast with the gradual emergence from a series of undulating fragments of the main lyrical theme (Ex. 45b) at bar 565 (OS, p. 95). This is really no more than a diatonic scale made rhythmic, and in its gradual evolution lies the secret of what Debussy meant when he spoke about making the various episodes in *Jeux* more homogeneous. 'The bond which ties them together is perhaps subtle, but it exists nonetheless', he told Gabriel Pierné on 5 March 1914 (LL, p. 251). And he singled out for Pierné's special attention the entry of the cellos and basses at fig. 53 (OS, p. 80, Ex. 45c), which 'indicates a new change of direction', rather than the return (two pages earlier) of the clarinet motif (Ex. 45d) from the start of the main *scherzando* section. The reason is that the former marks an important *rhythmic* preparation for the start of the main lyrical theme (Ex. 45b). Further, it is the rhythmic links between sections which have been the downfall of many conductors of *Jeux*, and the need to feel a more or less constant pulse through the continual variations is not assisted by misprints in the Durand score. The quaver is constant throughout the orchestral score, p. 51, for instance, according to Debussy's revisions in the copy now at Royaumont.

When Pierné conducted *Jeux* for the first time in concert on 29 February 1914, Debussy got a measure of the 'revenge' he desired on the 'display given by the over-ingenious Nijinsky', who had, 'with his cruel and barbarous choreography . . . trampled my poor rhythms underfoot like weeds'.[26] Debussy had earlier written just as explicitly of his distaste for Nijinsky's 'peculiar mathematics' to Robert Godet (letter of 9 June 1913; GOD, p. 136).

Ex. 45. *Jeux*, themes and motifs

(a) OS, p. 2, bars 2-3

(b) OS, p. 95, bar 1 – p. 96, bar 3

(c) OS, p. 80, bars 1-3, fig. 53

(d) OS, p. 8, bars 3-4

> This man [he complained] adds up demi-semiquavers with his feet
> and proves the result with his arms. Then, as if suddenly paralysed
> on one side, he watches the music go past with a disapproving eye. It
> seems that this is called 'stylisation of gesture'. It is ugly! It is in fact
> *Dalcrozian*, and I consider M. Dalcroze one of the worst enemies of
> music! And you can imagine what havoc his method has caused in
> the soul of this young savage, Nijinsky!

Nijinsky himself finally gave his own account of *Jeux* in his diary early in
1919 (1937, pp. 154-5). While there is much to suggest incipient mental breakdown in his pathetic self-deification and a schizophrenic leaping from one
subject to another, what he has to say about the homosexual undertones of
Jeux has a certain ring of truth about it, especially if one considers Diaghilev's
proclivities and the extent to which he arranged its creation and its climax in
the triple kiss.

> Diaghilev likes to say that he created the ballet, because he likes to
> be praised. I do not mind if Diaghilev says that he composed the
> stories of *Faun* and *Jeux*, because when I created them I was under
> the influence of 'my life' with Diaghilev. He wanted to have two
> boys as lovers. He often told me so, but I refused . . . In the ballet,
> the two girls represent the two boys and the young man is Diaghilev.
> I changed the characters, as love between three men could not be
> represented on the stage . . . Debussy did not like the subject either,
> but he was paid 10,000 gold francs for this ballet and therefore had
> to finish it.

As Robin Holloway rightly concludes (p. 194): 'The music of *Jeux* is insepa-
rable from its subject, which is sexual pleasure.'

Both the music and the orchestration of *Jeux* owe much to the scene involving Kundry and the flower-maidens in *Parsifal*,[27] similarly set in a magic
garden. Debussy took unusual care with his orchestration, making two extensive preparatory versions in order to achieve the marvellous transparency
of the final score (which is a calligraphic miracle too). When one considers the
way Debussy was moving towards an orchestra in which the strings played a
less important thematic role than the wind, it is curious to find in the preparatory score in the Pierpont Morgan Library (see Appendix) that the string
and horn parts seem to have been completed first, and the woodwind (especially the oboes, flutes and piccolos) added later. The important percussion
parts are also missing, apart from the beginning and the end, and the cellos
and basses are mostly written, in Classical manner, on the same stave. The
larger orchestra with quadruple woodwind (which never all play together)
seems to have grown in the process of orchestration, for the three trombones
and tuba appear for the first time on a specially added stave at bar 413 (OS,
p. 69), followed by the sarrusophone at bar 474 (OS, p. 80). Once the instruments have been introduced, however, Debussy remembers them till the end.
He seems at the pre-orchestral stage to have considered bars 563-4 (the lead

into Ex. 45b/OS, p. 94) as more of a main climax than the triple kiss at fig. 78 (OS, p. 113). The latter (which is none other than bar 1 of Ex. 45d in augmentation) is scored much more lightly than in the final version, whereas bars 563-4 were originally accompanied by conventional down and up pentatonic *glissandi* on harps, leading to Ex. 45b doubled on trombone. The revisions in the Royaumont score, the last orchestral work Debussy did, show him improving the continuity and making his Mussorgskian thematic thread clearer.[28]

The Stravinskian influence in *Jeux* is far less marked than in *Khamma*, and a parting of the ways had already begun before *The rite of spring* eclipsed the performance of *Jeux* a fortnight later on 29 May 1913. Whereas in December 1911 Stravinsky had had 'an instinctive genius for colour and rhythm' (GOD, p. 129), Debussy found *The rite* 'primitive with every modern convenience' (CAP, p. 64), and he told Ernest Ansermet in 1914 that Stravinsky was 'trying to make music with non-musical means'.[29] Part of the reason was that Stravinsky was more receptive to Diaghilev's new artistic developments in ballet and was more willing to enter into the necessary co-operative spirit than Debussy, taking rehearsals and forming part of Diaghilev's inner circle. Stravinsky even approved of a 'form of rhythmic gymnastics' on stage, as Romain Rolland reported in September 1914, though they had to be 'more artistic than those of Dalcroze'. Some reasons why he came so close to Debussy and then departed to such a distance can be seen in another extract from Rolland's *Journal des années de guerre* (LO, 2, p. 184). '"Speaking for myself", says Stravinsky, "colour is an inspiration to me when writing music. But when it is written, the music is self-sufficient; it is its own colour."' They disagreed too over Wagner, with whom any link was anathema to Stravinsky, and by 1915 Debussy considered that Stravinsky was leaning dangerously in Schoenberg's direction. No doubt rivalry between the two was allowed to cloud their judgment of each other, especially during the war which they viewed so differently. From 1913 onwards it was Stravinsky's star that was in the ascendant: he had no time for the dream-world of the subconscious that meant so much to Debussy and which essentially belonged (with the Wagnerian *Gesamtkunstwerk*) to the nineteenth century. Stravinsky's extroversion, financial acumen, and lack of dependence on a single publisher also made Debussy jealous. Asking Durand to register *Jeux* with the Société des Auteurs et Compositeurs on 13 May 1913, Debussy continued: 'As it is not a question of a state-subsidised theatre, the division of royalties can take place thus: two-thirds for the composer; one-third for the librettist. At least, that is how Stravinsky arranges things.'

As we have seen, it was Nijinsky's choreography that Debussy most objected to in the Ballets Russes. But after condemning this in *Le matin* on 15 May 1913, he still had kind words for the parent organisation (LCr, p. 237):

I must confess that the Russian Ballet have so often delighted me because they are always unpredictable. Nijinsky's spontaneity, whether natural or acquired, has so often moved me that I am now awaiting the production of *Jeux* like an excited child who has been promised a visit to the theatre as a reward . . . It seems to me that in our dull classroom of music, presided over by a stern teacher, the Russians have opened a window which looks out onto the open countryside. And then, for one who admires Tamara Karsavina as I do, is it not delightful to have this tenderly drooping flower as an interpreter and to see her with the exquisite Ludmilla Schollar playing so ingeniously with the shadows of night.

Later that year, on 6 December, Debussy dined with Diaghilev in Moscow, when the latter amusingly recounted the events of the Ballets Russes' tour of South America, in which 'he omitted mentioning Nijinsky very skilfully'.[30] Then they went to the theatre to see Mussorgsky's *Sorotchinsky Fair* which Debussy liked, despite its having too much dialogue. Afterwards he took the opportunity to go backstage and talk to the theatre's director and to M. Sarrine, the producer, about their plans to stage *Pelléas et Mélisande* in 1914.

Debussy seems to have forgotten that, following the performance of *Jeux* on 6 June, he had complained to Caplet (CAP, p. 66) about there being 'too many Russians' in Paris, and about the snobbery shown by artists and public alike towards them, to the detriment of art. In contrast Debussy was upset in May 1917 that Diaghilev should think him indifferent to the Ballets Russes after he had been noticeably absent from the première of Satie's *Parade* on the afternoon of the 18th. So that same day he obtained Diaghilev's address from Dandelot, and wrote nostalgically to him two days later (Auguste Martin, p. 79, no. 420): 'I would like you to know of my joy at rediscovering the singular beauty of the Ballets Russes. "It is an old dream beginning again . . .", and it makes me very melancholy because too many horrors have since overtaken everyday life.' Debussy had probably been to see Stravinsky's *Firebird* on 11 May for the opening of Diaghilev's only Paris season during the war, and he went back to see the première of Massine's ballet *Las meninas*. He wrote to Diaghilev on 26 May (*F-Po*, fonds Kochno) of 'the distinctly French charm of Fauré's *Pavane* which assumes a Spanish solemnity. It is a *tour de force* on which yourself and the prodigious Massine must be congratulated.'

Fortunately there is no record of what Debussy thought about the dance Nijinsky arranged to his *Golliwogg's cake walk* in New York in the summer of 1916, entitled *Le nègre blanc*: perhaps he never even heard about it. By the time that Nijinsky was devising a version of his *Chansons de Bilitis* in St Moritz in January 1918 which 'obeys the same basic choreographic laws as the "Faune"' (Buckle, 1980, p. 482), he was too ill to care.

But in his last active year as a composer Debussy had one further unpleasant round of experiences with *Jeux* over its authorship and a performance venue. Jean d'Estournelles de Constant (Under-secretary of State for Fine

Arts), wishing to stage a charity matinée performance of *Jeux*, wrote to Maurice Bernard (legal intermediary with the Society of Authors) on 12 March 1917 on the subject of its scenario.[31] Diaghilev's exclusive rights to the stage presentation of *Jeux* had expired in 1916 and Constant had ascertained that Diaghilev, Debussy and Durand were willing for him to proceed. The problem was that the text printed on the piano reduction appeared to be by Debussy (though it had been supplied to him by Diaghilev and was based on an idea by Nijinsky), and this was not assisted by a clause in the 1912 contract which decreed that Debussy need not share his royalties on the sales of this score with any librettist. Also, if the choreography was by Nijinsky and he was in America, who could authorise and arrange its revival? On 14 April 1917 Maurice Bernard replied that Nijinsky's name must appear on the posters as author of the 'poème dansé', and that he must collect his author's rights. But as Debussy was the most important collaborator in *Jeux*, he could authorise the performance, even if Nijinsky's consent was not forthcoming. Debussy could even arrange the *choreography* if Nijinsky was in America!

But on the same day Debussy was facing a very different problem and wrote to Durand (DUR, p. 178):

> The programme of d'Estournelles de Constant astounds me! . . . I cannot begin to understand why *Jeux* should be performed at the Trocadéro [Palace], in an auditorium a hundred times too big for it, and not at the Opéra, where it would be better suited . . . You have more skill and diplomacy than I to make M. d'E. de C. understand this.

The following day, doubtless not knowing about the free hand he could have with the choreography if he chose, Debussy again appealed to Durand (p. 180): 'One must not forget that "Nijinskian" productions have not left very good memories; one should therefore not begin again without certain "assurances".' The last we see of the affair in the correspondence is on 19 April, when M. Constant wrote to Jacques Rouché (who was in charge of its artistic side) telling him of Maurice Bernard's decision, and adding: 'But as I have told you, we *shall* have a written authorisation for *Jeux*, thanks to Mme Edwards [Misia Sert] :[32] this is a much better solution.'

However, in the end, no gala performance of *Jeux* took place in 1917 at either the Trocadéro or the Opéra. Neither does Diaghilev ever seem to have considered reviving the ballet, especially after the break with Nijinsky and Nijinsky's subsequent mental collapse. But around Christmas 1919 Emma Debussy wrote to P.-B. Gheusi about a possible revival at the Théâtre Lyrique du Vaudeville with M. R. Quinault (who had produced *La boîte à joujoux*) and Bakst's décors.[33] But it was left to Jean Borlin and the Ballets Suédois to mount the next Paris production, in October 1920, which Charles Koechlin told the conductor Roger Désormière had been a most successful interpretation.[34]

Thanks to Eimert's analysis and the position of *Jeux* as Debussy's last orchestral work, it has assumed at least as much significance for the present century as *Pelléas et Mélisande*. From the formal viewpoint, Robert Sherlaw Johnson has compared it directly with the collage technique of Messiaen's experimental *Cantéyodjayâ* of 1949 which 'uses a large variety of material, only about a quarter of which is repeated or transformed'.[35] From the literary angle *Jeux* has been seen as closely linked with *L'après-midi d'un faune*, and Laurence Berman (1980, p. 227) maintains that

> both with respect to formal ingenuity and expressive intention, *Jeux*, and not the prelude, seems to be the true musical counterpart of Mallarmé's poem. It is as if Debussy, twenty years after his first effort, finally realised in musical terms the open shapes and modifications of imagery that Mallarmé had worked out in his own art form.

Certainly it is Debussy's most successful portrayal of a dream-like experience in theatrical terms, and if its inspiration did indeed derive from Mallarmé, it is greatly to be regretted that Nijinsky (according to his wife) never read his celebrated eclogue.

7 *La boîte à joujoux* (1913)

> You see it is simplicity itself – even childish! But how do you put it over in the theatre – its natural simplicity, I mean? The characters must retain their angular movements, their burlesque appearance as cardboard cut-outs, without which the work would become meaningless. I cannot see how this project could possibly be put on at the Opéra-Comique. But nothing is impossible, after all!
>
> (Debussy, interview with Maurice Montabré in *Comoedia*
> (1 Feb 1914); LCr, p. 308)

The 'children's ballet' *La boîte à joujoux* has received scant attention amongst Debussy's later works, perhaps because it has seldom been performed or recorded, and it was Debussy's own doubts about its style of production, together with the intervention of the war, which prevented its being staged during his lifetime. The project originated as an illustrated story by the artist André Hellé, who was also a specialist in children's books. By February 1913 *La boîte à joujoux* had been converted into a pleasant little ballet scenario for which Debussy agreed to write the music. Contracts were signed with Hellé on 1 and 15 July (*F-Pdurand*) and, following his usual practice, Debussy then began a piano score, having had a suitable time to recover from the rigours of *Jeux* before he began a second round of 'games' of a more congenial nature.

The composition of the first two tableaux of *La boîte* seems to have gone smoothly, most of the music being inspired in August and September by Debussy's seven-year-old daughter Chouchou and her toys. On 25 July he told Durand (DUR, p. 115) that he was getting himself in the mood for the ballet by 'extracting secrets from Chouchou's old dolls' and was 'learning to play the side-drum' in preparation. He was 'forever inside the *Toybox*' on 11 August, and by 5 September the first tableau ('Le magasin de jouets') had only its stage directions to be added. 'I have tried to be straightforward and even "amusing"', he told his publisher (p. 116), 'without pose or pointless acrobatics.' As usual, he was concerned about the printing of the score already, as it needed different typefaces for the musical directions and for the scenario text.

By 27 September the second tableau ('Le champ de bataille') was complete, but the third (and then final) tableau ('La bergerie à vendre') was causing some problems.[1] 'The soul of the doll is more mysterious than even Maeterlinck imagines, and does not easily put up with the humbug which so many human souls tolerate', Debussy explained (DUR, p. 117). On 26 October he apologised for making Durand wait for the end of *La boîte*, owing to an unexpected rehearsal of the *Nocturnes* the previous day. But on 30 October Debussy triumphantly announced that 'nothing remained but to find a theatre' (p. 118), and a final contract was signed with Hellé on the following day.

The simple triangular love-story is perhaps best told in Debussy's own words:

> A cardboard soldier falls in love with a doll; he seeks to prove this to her, but she betrays him with Polichinelle. The soldier learns of her affair and terrible things begin to happen: a battle between wooden soldiers and polichinelles. In brief, the lover of the beautiful doll is gravely wounded during the battle. The doll nurses him and . . . they all live happily ever after.[2]

But this was not to be the case with the ballet as a whole, as with so many of Debussy's theatre projects. Debussy referred in the same interview with Montabré to *La boîte* as a 'pantomime', a 'work to amuse children, nothing more'. But he also called *Khamma* a 'pantomime', and as Henri de Régnier referred to the Ballets Russes' transformation of *L'après-midi d'un faune* in the same terms (1913, p. 85),[3] it is clear that the term in France implied a varied entertainment without spoken dialogue rather than the traditional Christmas romp beloved by England.

The first major problem to arise with *La boîte* was Debussy's opinion, expressed to Durand on 30 October 1913 (DUR, p. 118), that 'only marionettes will be able to convey the meaning of the text and the expression of the music', which would explain some of the difficulties he envisaged in the quotation which opens this chapter. The idea of a performance by marionettes derived from Maeterlinck, who called *L'intruse*, *Les aveugles* and *Les sept princesses* 'little plays for marionettes' in 1890-1, when the aim was to 'present his vision in even purer and more universal terms' (Warnke, p. 27). On 16 January 1914 Debussy was at war with P.-B. Gheusi over his conception of *La boîte à joujoux* for the Opéra-Comique, and he lost no time in putting Durand in the picture as follows:

> You should certainly know the news about the well-intentioned but curious projects of M. Gheusi . . . They are typical of our times in which people produce grand designs out of nothing at all! Do you see these poor marionettes in the same *locale* where the demands of Ariane [in Dukas's *Ariane et Barbe-bleue*] or the rages of Golaud habitually disturb the peace? — the truth is that they very seldom do such a thing.

> In the case of *La boîte*, it is necessary to separate it from its 'pretty-pretty' aspect and present it in a manner which is itself pretty new! (*F-Pdurand*)

But by April 1914, Debussy had come round to Hellé's (equally problematic) viewpoint that the ballet should be performed by children.

> It is agreed [he told Durand (DUR, p. 121)] that Gheusi will produce *La boîte* . . . As for the orchestral score, I have begun a very full sketch of it which could, if the case arises, easily be completed. What is important in this affair is to know exactly what Gheusi's intentions are. This is not easy, I assure you, with all his amiable shilly-shallying!
>
> Hellé has left for the Ile [d'Oléron]. However, we are in agreement on the following points: he will arrange the décors and costumes, and the characters will be played by children. As for the production, there is no need for a ballet-master since, more often than not, *movements* rather than traditional *ballet steps* are involved. A skilful producer – there is only one such at the Opéra-Comique – will suffice.

But the war intervened before any production got off the ground and Debussy never completed his orchestration. In fact the full score (see Appendix) shows that he did not even get as far as he had with *Khamma* before he abandoned it (perhaps for *Le palais du silence*, or because of conducting engagements in Rome, The Hague and Amsterdam in February–March 1914). He appears, however, to have followed his usual practice of steadily producing a definitive version, which in this case progressed as far as bar 37 of the first tableau (Fig. 19), approximately a twelfth of the way through. On 12 March 1915, whilst discussing the possible authorisation of a private performance of the ballet, he told Durand (DUR, p. 133) that he would rather 'wait for the eventual production in Paris', and in his last letter to his publisher on 1 November 1917 (p. 190), Debussy was still thinking of *La boîte à joujoux*, though he lied when he claimed that the orchestration was 'nearing completion'. But, he added, 'at the first opportunity [of a production] do not hesitate any longer. In waiting too long, we risk never being able to participate in this little work which, all the same, is conceived in a true French spirit.'

In the end André Caplet was asked by Gheusi to complete the orchestration after Debussy's death, though Caplet told Jacques Rouché[4] that he would not get round to this 'before 15 October [1919]' for he had 'no intention of interrupting his own production'. Caplet signed a contract with Durand on 21 October and the première took place at the short-lived Théâtre Lyrique du Vaudeville on 10 December 1919. Durand later wrote (1925, p. 106) that the orchestration was completed 'with such mastery that it is impossible for the most alert musician to perceive the join'. It is hard enough even to *see* it, as Figs. 19 a and b demonstrate. The main clue lies in the instrument names preceding the first system, where Debussy uses 'H^b', 'Bass' and 'C^{ni}' on p. 7, but Caplet uses 'Htb', 'B^{on}' and 'Cors' on p. 8.

Fig. 19. *La boîte à joujoux* (*F-Pn* MS 979): (a) p. 7 by Debussy, spring 1914

Fig. 19 (b). p. 8 by André Caplet, October 1919

P.-B. Gheusi, now co-director of the new theatre, arranged the première with Désiré-Émile Inghelbrecht as conductor. M. R. Quinault, who played Polichinelle, also produced and choreographed it, and André Hellé at last got the chance to see his scenery and costume plans come alive. In the end, though, adult dancers were used, as they were when the ballet was eventually produced at the Opéra-Comique and by the Ballets Suédois. *La boîte à joujoux* was not performed with marionettes as Debussy intended until 1962, as part of the centenary celebrations in Holland. The idea sprang from the research of Hans Henkemans, who played the original piano accompaniment at this successful 'second première'.[5]

By a tragic irony, Chouchou died of diphtheria on 16 July 1919 even before Caplet's commission: what began as Debussy's effort to amuse his beloved daughter ended almost as her obituary.

* * *

In his *Comoedia* interview in 1914, Debussy claimed that his score for *La boîte* was based on 'music that I have written for Christmas and New Year albums for children! . . . These album pieces will be brought together and made into three tableaux.' (LCr, p. 307) But even though *La boîte à joujoux* is a veritable Aladdin's cave of snippets from popular songs, Classical themes and references to his own compositions, there is no similarity to any of the musical gifts he made to Emma Bardac before 1913 (see Orledge, 1974). However, the arpeggio motif of the soldier as transformed in the second tableau (Ex. 46a) recurs almost exactly to end the *Noël pour 1914*[6] (Ex. 46b) written for Emma some fifteen months after the second tableau. Both occur in a distant bitonal context, as Ex. 46 shows. No 'Christmas and New Year albums for children' exist, as far as I know: the nearest thing to this, the *Petite cantate sur grand papier* composed in *June* 1907 (*F-Pn* MS 14519), which includes a part for Chouchou, has no musical similarities whatsoever with *La boîte*. Thus, by and large, *La boîte à joujoux* followed Debussy's normal compositional practice; unused themes for Arlequin and Polichinelle were listed in a sketchbook, which was put on sale by Emma in 1933 (AND, p. 34, no. 182), together with Hellé's original designs and scenario, and autograph proof corrections by the composer.

The score contains music of great subtlety, particularly in its opening and closing passages, and never approaches vulgarity or bombast even in the parodies of the 'Soldiers' chorus' from Gounod's *Faust* (R, p. 28, and in inversion on p. 29) and Mendelssohn's hackneyed 'Wedding march' (R, p. 44). *La boîte* does, however, contain the only direct piece of self-borrowing that I know of in Debussy, for the music of le soldat anglais (R, pp. 9-10) is surprisingly that of *The little nigar* (1909), bars 1-14, transposed up a perfect fourth, though with a different (ostinato) accompaniment using major seconds in its first eight bars.

Ex. 46

(a) *La boîte à joujoux*, R, p. 31, bars 16-17

(b) *Noël pour 1914*, F-Pn MS 14521, p. 3, bars 25-7

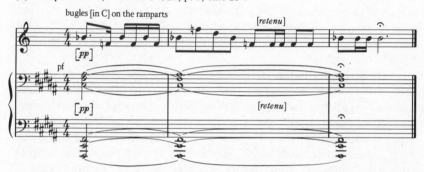

The 'Danse de la poupée' (R. pp. 13-16) begins in a style recalling the *Serenade for the doll*, and the *Children's corner* suite (1906-8) is also approached in Ex. 47, which looks like a cross between the *Golliwogg's cake walk* (bars 22-5) and *Minstrels* (bars 28-31) from the first book of preludes (1910). The 'Pas de l'éléphant' in the first tableau (R, pp. 7-8) has no connection with *Jimbo's lullaby*, though the opening prelude (R, pp. 1-2), when the toybox is closed and its inhabitants asleep, is based on motifs from this piece (notably bars 1-5 and 33-40) and shows how much more subtle Debussy's harmony had become in the intervening years. What the 'Pas de l'éléphant' does contain is a curious exotic arabesque which Debussy claimed in a footnote was an 'old Hindu chant still used today in the taming of elephants. It is constructed on the scale of "five o'clock in the morning", and must therefore be in 5/4 time.' It and its accompaniment are, however, pure Debussy and it may derive from an abandoned piece for the second book of preludes inspired by Kipling's *Jungle book* entitled *Tomai des éléphants*, which Debussy mentioned in a letter to Durand on 7 January 1913 (see Orledge, 1981, p. 24).

Other passing musical similarities in *La boîte* are to *La soirée dans Grenade* (1903) in the chords at the end of the second tableau (R, p. 36), and to

Ex. 47. *La boîte à joujoux*, R, p. 11, bars 13-16

various other preludes from the second book (1912-13), notably: *Les fées sont d'exquises danseuses* ('Danse de l'Arlequin', R, pp. 8-9); *Bruyères* (R, p. 41, line 3); and *Général Lavine − excentric* [*sic*] (R, p. 12). In the third tableau ('La bergerie à vendre'), Debussy uses the French folk-song 'Il pleut bergère' in various subtle harmonic contexts (R, pp. 37-8, 43), and the final dance (R, pp. 46-7) uses another popular French tune: 'En avant Fanfan-la-tulipe'.

Unity is attained in this sectional ballet score through the recurring use of three sharply contrasted motifs for the three main characters. The soldier has a reveille-type bugle call, the doll an attractive waltz, and the wicked Polichinelle a strident, angular idea in major seconds. Debussy illustrates all these in the score (see Fig. 9), not of course forgetting the all-important rose which has a silence coupled with a *diminuendo*! Only the Polichinelle idea is not in the opening prelude, whose repetitive, elliptical theme (Ex. 48, bars 1-2) recurs in the epilogue as the scene of the first tableau gradually returns.

La boîte à joujoux is scored for chamber orchestra (double woodwind) with harps, celesta and a fairly extensive percussion department including a *crisette*. Paap (p. 349) considers that the orchestration, though ingenious, is overdone, the ballet losing some of its intimate character because of it. His article is, however, in support of a production with piano accompaniment, and he seems unaware that the orchestral forces and style were established by Debussy in the opening pages. As with *Khamma*, Debussy included an important part for the piano, though in this light-hearted score the harmonic influence of Stravinsky's early Russian ballets is less evident. The Petrushkan element in Hellé's scenario has often been mentioned and may suggest one reason why Debussy accepted the project so readily. It is tempting to compare a passage like the final joyous polka danced by the doll's children in *La boîte* (R, pp. 46-7) with passages from the first part of *Petrushka* (OS, pp. 15-16, figs. 23-6), but the most Stravinskian moment occurs in the prelude (Ex. 48). Debussy also makes prominent use of the rising fifth, and it is difficult to believe that he did not once consider the opening of *Petrushka* when writing a passage like that shown in Fig. 19 at the point where Caplet took over the orchestration.

Ex. 48. *La boîte à joujoux*, R, p. 3, bars 7-10

La boîte was the last work Debussy completed for the theatre (apart from *Syrinx*, see Chapter 11). As Lockspeiser points out, it is a 'minor, unpretentious work' (LO, 2, p. 178) without the 'sophistication' of the Ravel/Colette children's opera *L'enfant et les sortilèges* (whose 1925 vocal score also used a design by Hellé). *La boîte à joujoux* presents fewer production difficulties than *L'enfant*, but it was by no means merely 'thrown off as a musical work for a children's party' as Lockspeiser maintains. Debussy's last untroubled pre-war work deserves to be performed more often, with or without stage action.

8   The Alhambra Theatre: *No-ja-li* or *Le palais du silence* and *Printemps* (1913-14)

I have received a letter from M. André Charlot: he speaks to me of
No-ja-li (formerly *Le palais du silence*) as if he intended to perform
it this year! That seems premature to me. Besides, I should not like
this music to be played until the fate of France is decided, for she
can neither laugh nor cry while so many of our people are being
heroically mutilated!

(Debussy to Durand, 9 October 1914; DUR, p. 128)

Debussy's associations with England were more extensive than is generally
realised. He first planned to visit London in October 1890, but did not
finally get there until 12 July 1902, shortly after the première of *Pelléas*,
when he stayed at the Hotel Cecil (accompanied by Mary Garden) at the
invitation of Messager. In all he went seven times between 1902 and 1914,
mostly to fulfil financially necessary conducting engagements, and it was for
financial reasons that he signed the contracts for *Le palais du silence* in 1913.

There are several similarities between Debussy's two 'English' ballets. First,
they both changed title during the course of composition: *Khamma* began life
as *Isis*; *Le palais du silence* ended up as *No-ja-li*, again named after the focal
female character in the scenario. Second, both ballets were concerned with
exotic subjects of the sort that appealed to Debussy in his post-*Pelléas* period
(cf *Siddartha*, see Chapter 12). Third, both ballets had chequered careers and
neither was performed in Debussy's lifetime, *No-ja-li* remaining incomplete
for reasons which will become apparent. Last, both ballets were intended for
performance in London music halls: *Khamma* in Charles Morton's Palace
Theatre in Cambridge Circus; *Le palais du silence* in André Charlot's Alhambra
Theatre in Leicester Square.

It was by no means out of character for music-hall programmes of this
period to contain serious items, especially those with exotic or spectacular
appeal, and there is nothing to suggest that Debussy lowered his sights in
either case. The 'other side' of his nature often brought him into contact with
vaudeville in the 1890s and this popular experience was used to fertilise such

compositions as *Général Lavine – excentric* and *Golliwogg's cake walk*. Debussy admitted his attraction to the music hall in *Gil Blas* on 1 June 1903 (LCr, p. 178) after visiting the Empire Theatre – 'the London equivalent of our Folies-Bergère' – as a reward for good behaviour in sitting through Richter's *Ring* cycle at Covent Garden!

Indeed, the main body of his account of the *Ring* cycle sometimes makes it resemble a music-hall entertainment and the reader is left in no doubt as to which performance Debussy would rather return to, despite the 'unforgettably beautiful moments, beyond criticism' which emerged from the periods of boredom in the Wagner. The mental strain of the four performances even caused Debussy to imagine the *Ring* as a

> leitmotif quadrille in which the motif of 'Siegfried's horn' did a very curious dance opposite that of 'Wotan's spear', whilst the 'curse' motif performed obsessively on its own . . . The *Ring* has its childish fairy-tale side . . . the dragons sing; the birds give valuable advice; a bear, a horse, two ravens, and two black sheep (which I almost forgot) all intervene in a charming manner . . . perhaps one is supposed to wade valiantly up to one's neck into this sea of improbability, without worrying about the intrusion of feelings of human weakness. (LCr, pp. 175, 177)

But if Debussy's mind wandered in the tedious passages in the *Ring* (when 'one really no longer knows whether to cling on to the music or the drama'), then it also wandered in the Empire Theatre. In the supposedly 'spiritual' dancing of a ballet by the current maestro, Léopold de Wenzel (which Debussy thought smacked too much of the 'tactical exercises of strictly disciplined Pomeranian regiments'), he found himself reflecting on what the true

> atmosphere of a ballet should be like . . . How the action within it should be regulated only by means of the language of ballet itself, a language whose mysterious and delightful calligraphy is inscribed in the winged grace of a ballerina's leg (which becomes by turns as delicate as a flower and as tender as a woman) as her whole body is transformed by rhythmic tension. (LCr, p. 179)

Although Léopold de Wenzel's choreography had its faults, his justly renowned orchestra 'could have performed the *Ring* quite as well as his own music', and their obvious expertise and size support Debussy's resolution to adhere rigidly to his orchestral conception of *Khamma* in the face of Maud Allan's peremptory demands.

Le palais du silence was, on the surface, a much more practical venture than *Khamma*. On the one hand Debussy had a ready-made scenario in French by Georges de Feure; on the other he had, in André Charlot (who had taken over from Alfred Moul as co-manager of the Alhambra in 1912), an eager producer, known to his publisher. The Alhambra had begun as a popular museum: the Royal Panopticon of Science and Art. Despite a Royal Charter from Queen Victoria in 1850, it failed, and was bought by E.T. Smith and renamed the Alhambra Palace. After a short period as a circus, it first incorporated ballet into its programmes in December 1860, and this aspect became increasingly popular under the proprietorship of the showman and entrepreneur Frederick Strange (1864-72). The Alhambra and its nearby rival the Empire (founded 1887), together rescued ballet from neglect and the exclusivity of the opera house, and brought it in a spectacular manner (and with legendary stage effects) to the general public in a relaxed music-hall atmosphere. A new period of artistic growth at the Alhambra in the first decade of this century, under ballet-master Alfredo Curti, was unfortunately cut short by the arrival of the Diaghilev company in June 1911. Despite heavy competition from the Alhambra and elsewhere, it was Beecham who finally secured their services for Covent Garden and made a change of policy inevitable at the Alhambra.

Between 1912 and the halcyon decade of the 1920s, André Charlot, with George Grossmith as his 'advisory director of productions', instituted a series of extravagant and flexible revues like *8d. a mile*,[1] most of which featured costumes by the *avant-garde* couturier Paul Poiret, who had revolutionised and simplified female fashion in the previous decade. Charlot's first production in 1912 was *The guide to Paris*, a modernised version of Offenbach's *La vie parisienne*, and most of his subsequent revues contained French items. It was therefore natural that Charlot should look to Paris for a new ballet to end the first half of his revue *Not likely!*, which was scheduled to open on 4 May 1914. The unusual factor was that Debussy should have become involved in this, as most of Charlot's revues used individual numbers of the popular song type, or tailor-made arrangements of recent 'classics' in the longer ballet sequences.[2] Probably the whole ballet was the brain-child of Feure himself, for amongst the papers in Maurice Ravel's library (now in the Bibliothèque Nationale) two scenarios by Feure were found: *Le masque terrible* (based on Edgar Allan Poe's *The masque of the red death* and received by Ravel from the Alhambra on 17 March 1914) and *Les jardins d'Antinoüs* (dated 'London, 1 June 1914').[3] Perhaps Feure intended to gain access to Charlot's revues by means of these ballets commissioned from prestigious composers: he worked with Charlot increasingly after *Not likely!* but is nowhere mentioned in the programmes of revues before this.

Georges van Sluijters (*dit* de Feure), a Parisian of mixed Belgian and Dutch origins, remains a particularly elusive and fascinating character of the sort one expects to find associated with Debussy. He rose to prominence as an illustrator and lithographer through the Art Nouveau movement and enjoyed considerable acclaim during the period 1895 to 1905, especially for his decorative work for the gallery owner Samuel Bing in connection with the Paris Exhibition of 1900. His elongated, slightly sinister figures owe something to Aubrey Beardsley, and Gabriel Weisberg claims (p. 229) that 'he rendered in visual terms the world of poets and novelists of the Symbolist age'. Certainly his mysterious women, who seem lost in a dream-world or metaphorically in rapport with their strange, elaborate landscapes, reveal clear links with the poetry of Baudelaire and the novels of Georges Rodenbach. Feure seems to have shown considerable talent for all the many forms of art to which he applied his highly developed craftsmanship. He decorated porcelain for Gérard in Limoges, produced exquisite water-colours (like that of the dancer Loie Fuller), designed furniture for the house of Fleury, and some time after 1905 transferred to England, becoming known as a theatrical designer and producer. He was also something of an author, and his earliest known work (probably written in Holland before he went to Paris in 1890) was the play *Le palais du silence*. This he remodelled into a one-act ballet scenario in October–November 1913 (see Appendix) which has a prelude and eight scenes and is set in ancient China on the island of Formosa.

The page marked 'prelude' contains an emotive, poetic summary of the Formosan *status quo*, presumably to be read aloud over an orchestral introduction (see Ex. 49). The poetry is remarkable for the controlled length of its lines which form an elaborate visual design:

> Le Prince HONG-LO est muet
> Le Prince HONG-LO a maudit le destin
> et se venge du sort
> il impose dans ses domaines
> *'Le Silence'*
> Un serment solennel garde la loi sévère
> Tout est mélancolie en son âme épeurée
> Que tout soit sombre à ses yeux!
> Plus de chaudes couleurs!
> Plus de douces nuances!
> Le 'neutre'
> Sur les murs
> et le 'gris' sur les hommes –
> le 'noir'
> sur lui!
> Il aime – pauvre prince – la petite Princesse
> NO-JA-LI
> Douce esclave faite idole
> Pour elle il n'est de loi
> Que celle du serment:
> Qu'elle se pare de teintes carillonnantes!
> Qu'elle se pose comme une fleur!
> Elle est la seule lumière
> Sur cette tristesse.

As the prelude tells us, the main character is Prince Hong-Lo who loves the young captive princess, No-ja-li. Unfortunately Hong-Lo was born dumb, and to avenge his cruel fate imposes a decree of silence throughout his domains, with special guards (whom we meet in scene 1) to enforce this. The penalty for speech is death. Scene 2 introduces little No-ja-li, followed by the old man who carries her dolls. She is naturally upset at being divorced from the joys of life and conversation. In scene 3 Hong-Lo himself appears with his Malayan jester Malang-Malang, who mimics the tragedies of life with a series of traditional masks and gestures. Scene 4 shows No-ja-li alone, miserable and frustrated, and in scene 5 Hong-Lo prostrates himself before her on her throne as if she were an idol, begging for a 'gesture of compassion' from her in scene 6 (presumably in mime). She, however, longs for laughter and life and remains cold towards him, so he devises a means of communicating his love without breaking his own law of 'silence'.

In scene 7 the Malayan 'gamelan' orchestra with 'strange bells, horizontal harps and deep-toned drums' appears, and in scene 8 it accompanies the allegorical 'Ballet of the flame of love' that Hong-Lo has devised, in which hope and fear, joy and tears, confidence and jealousy, triumph and despair battle with each other. Predictably, the 'flame of love' rules supreme in the end. But No-ja-li pretends not to understand the significance of the ballet and feigns sleep at the moment of its triumphant conclusion. The prince, exasperated, draws his sword in rage and rushes towards No-ja-li, but is stilled by her frail innocence and beauty as she sleeps. His anger is diverted towards the hapless ballet troupe and he attacks Love and her cortège. However, Love and the human sentiments, filled with courage and justification, symbolically fight back and vanquish Hong-Lo, who then withdraws his decree of silence and expels the hated guards from his palace. All sing a hymn of joy and thanksgiving for the return of life and for No-ja-li, and the little princess no longer spurns the love of the poor dumb prince.

All things considered, the scenario, though slight, is by no means untenable. The use of non-speaking participants, communication through music and mime, and an allegorical ballet-within-a-ballet are clever ideas: the overall conception has a greater *raison d'être* and scope than many other short ballet scenarios. There is also a well-controlled progression from traditional oriental statuesqueness and cruelty towards humanity and love in the final scene, when the dramatic pace appropriately increases. Perhaps Feure knew of Debussy's predilection for things oriental and he may have introduced the gamelan orchestra to Formosa (from distant Malaya) for scenes 7 and 8 with the deliberate intention of attracting him. Indeed, earlier in 1913 when he wrote his article on taste,[4] Debussy had in mind his Indo-Chinese theatrical experiences at the 1889 Universal Exhibition. He even compared the powerful simplicity of the Annamite (now South Vietnamese) theatre favourably with the extravagances of Wagner:

> The Annamites perform a kind of embryonic opera, influenced by the Chinese, in which one can recognise the formula for the *Ring* cycle – only there are more gods and less scenery! An explosive little clarinet transmits the emotion; a tam-tam invokes terror . . . and that is all! No special theatrical effects; no hidden orchestra. Nothing but

an instinctive desire for the artistic, ingeniously satisfied, and without a hint of bad taste!

A good deal of geographical confusion seems to have gone on all round in 1913, and even if Debussy had composed music for the final scenes of *Le palais du silence*, it is extremely unlikely that he would have tried literally to recreate the effects he had so admired in 1889.

Some time in early November 1913 Feure approached Debussy with his scenario and seems to have had no trouble persuading him to collaborate,[5] for a contract was signed between the authors and Durand on the 21st which gave André Charlot exclusive rights to theatrical representations of *Le palais du silence* anywhere in the world. Then, on the 27th, Debussy signed his own contract with the Alhambra Society,[6] in which he agreed to send the piano reduction and orchestral score of the ballet to them by 2 April 1914 for a fee of 25,000 francs: 10,000 on signature, 10,000 on delivery of the scores, and 5000 on the first performance. The length was to be that preferred by Debussy for all his ballet scores, fifteen to twenty minutes, and the Alhambra were made to guarantee that the orchestra would be of the same size if the ballet was performed outside London. (This again makes it look unlikely that Maud Allan's claims about Debussy knowing the reduced size of orchestra needed for *Khamma* before he composed it were correct.)

In November 1913 Debussy was busy composing *Syrinx* for Gabriel Mourey (see Chapter 11), and the first half of December was spent in successful but exhausting conducting engagements in Moscow and St Petersburg at the invitation of Koussevitzky. But on 6 January 1914 Debussy wrote to Durand (DUR, p. 120), as an excuse for not going to Brussels, that '*The palace of silence* is taking up all my time.' This was not strictly true, however, for he wrote on the same day to Charles Gruet, Mayor of Bordeaux, recommending Edgard Varèse as musical director for his opera house (LL, p. 248). The sketches in the Bibliothèque Nationale (see Appendix) almost certainly date from early January 1914, for by the middle of the month Debussy had abandoned his Chinese ballet to arrange *Minstrels* for violin and piano,[7] and to rehearse this and other pieces for a recital with Arthur Hartmann on 5 February.

Perhaps it was the brick wall that Debussy encountered in *Le palais du silence* which established 1914 as his least productive year since 1906; his creative depression can be seen in a letter to the financier Bertault as early as 24 January.[8] He writes miserably: 'I cannot work as I would like to; at times I envy people who are dying of cold.'! Conducting engagements in Rome (18-23 February) and in The Hague and Amsterdam (26 February – 2 March) only made matters worse, though neither these nor the lucrative Alhambra contract saved Debussy the necessity of writing to Bertault again on 12 March to ask him to bring a loan of 4800 francs surreptitiously to a Colonne concert that he had to review.[9] With all these worries, Gheusi's production of *La boîte à joujoux*, and accompanying Ninon Vallin in the first performance of his *Trois poèmes de Stéphane Mallarmé* on 21 March, it is perhaps not surprising that the completion of *Le palais du silence* by 2 April became increasingly unlikely.

By mid-March Charlot was beginning to worry that he would have no French ballet at all for his forthcoming revue. No doubt because of his excellent work on *Khamma*, Charles Koechlin was summoned to visit Debussy on 26 March to talk about 'collaborating on a ballet for London'.[10] This was almost certainly the celebrated occasion (mentioned towards the end of Chapter 5) when Debussy asked Koechlin to 'write a ballet for him that he would sign' (see Chapter 5, n. 27), but which Koechlin thought was going *too* far.

Fortunately, early in 1912 Henri Büsser had completed a reorchestration (under Debussy's supervision) of the composer's second *envoi* from Rome – *Printemps* of February 1887. The original orchestration (condemned by the Académie des Beaux-Arts for its 'vague impressionism') is supposed to have been destroyed in a fire, and Debussy had actually begun to reorchestrate *Printemps* himself in September 1908, incorporating the piano duet parts from the 1904 published version as he did so (DUR, p. 65). Büsser (1955, p. 178) recalls how he was asked to complete the operation on 5 July 1909 because Debussy, as usual, had got bored with a 'job' that was of Durand's rather than his own choosing.

Despite Debussy being 'so simple and modest' and a joy to work with, Büsser seems not to have completed his task until three years later, and the new, approved *Printemps* only received its première at the Société Nationale on 18 April 1913. Debussy, in fact, intended to conduct it himself on his Russian tour that December, but decided against including it in his Moscow programme, lest it 'produce a false impression. There should be no doubt in the public's mind whether or not I have made any progress', he reasoned to Emma on 5 December (BAR, p. 106).

But *Printemps* was in 1914 a published *fait accompli* which was just the right length (fifteen minutes) for a ballet. So, giving ill-health as his justifiable reason (in the form of a letter from his doctor, M. Crépel), Debussy proposed to the Alhambra Society (through Durand) a modification of his original contract, offering as compensation the exclusive rights for England to adapt *Printemps* (Spring) for the stage in 1914.

Charlot replied to Durand on 1 April[11] that, with modifications, *Printemps* would be suitable, but that it was not merely a question of its

> purely and simply replacing *The palace of silence* . . . When you put Debussy's repertory at my disposal on my last trip to Paris, your only object was to save me embarrassment. But it is now necessary to face the problems and remedy them, and to this end I have drawn up a codicil to our contract of 27 November which seems to offer the best solution to our common problems.

The codicil[12] effectively sold *Printemps* to Charlot for 5000 francs for 1914 and 250 francs per week thereafter. One month after its first performance the Alhambra Society were to decide whether they wished to produce *Le palais du silence* or not. Perhaps they had heard about Debussy's cavalier attitude towards contracts, for a clause was added stating that

> in the case of the Alhambra taking up this option, M. Debussy undertakes not to send any ballet to England between the signature of the present codicil and the first performance of *The palace of silence*, nor during the two months after the London première of *The palace of silence*, which is to be not later than 1 June 1915.

Thereafter various complex financial clauses followed, based on the 25,000 francs offered on 27 November 1913. If the Alhambra Society did take up the option, Debussy was to deliver the piano and orchestral scores of *Le palais du silence* to them within one month of receiving notice of their decision.[13]

This last condition, however, was hardly likely to go down well with Debussy, who wrote to Durand:[14]

> It seems to me that the Charlot affair, given that one concedes the idea of delay and the case of *absolute necessity* (stated in a letter sent by Dr Crépel to M. A. Charlot), becomes extremely simple.
> In my opinion, the sum of 250 francs per week for *Spring* is quite insufficient.
> The *Temple* [*sic*] *of silence* trouble remains unaltered. I cannot wait in suspense to see what it will suit the Alhambra to do with a composition I have already done a lot of work on, and it is precisely because we have surrendered *Spring* for their consideration and *await their pleasure* that they should not be creating complications.
> I remain convinced that André Charlot will put an end to all these tiresome matters in the best interests of the Alhambra and ourselves.

Obviously with the idea in mind that Charlot would let him keep the 10,000 francs he had received on the signing of the contract, but at the same time would not insist on a new ballet, Debussy cheered up a little, and on 4 May we find him inviting Pasteur Vallery-Radot (p. 138) 'to come and hear [Verdi's] *Othello* tomorrow evening.[15] You have lost nothing in missing *Manon*', he adds wickedly.

With the comforting thought that Durand would always extricate him from legal entanglements, as he had done with *Khamma*, Debussy then reverted to the more straightforward task of redesigning his *Chansons de Bilitis* into the *Épigraphes antiques* for piano duet in July, but overall it proved a depressing summer. On 14 July he wrote despairingly to Robert Godet (GOD, p. 141): 'For a long time now I have felt lost, my powers frightfully diminished. Ah! Where is the magician you so loved in me? This is nothing more than a morose acrobat who will soon break his back in a final graceless pirouette.' Debussy 'did not write a note or touch a piano' (DUR, p. 126) whilst at Angers in August and September, being much distressed by Germany's declaration of war on France on 3 August, by the nearby practising of soldiers on trumpets and drums, and by his own inability to make any useful contribution to the war effort.

However, Charlot had not given up hope of producing his Chinese ballet, as the opening quotation to this chapter shows. Whether the change of title to *No-ja-li* had anything to do with Debussy is not known, but what is certain is that Debussy was ironically saved by the war he so detested from having to complete it. He never mentioned the matter again, and Charlot appears not to have pressed his legal claim further or tried to find another composer for Feure's scenario.

One pendant to the story is that Feure himself attempted to interest Jacques Rouché and the Paris Opéra in June 1923 in the 'two [*sic*] ballets' he wrote 'for Claude Debussy, for which he was, by contract with Durand, to write the music. Unfortunately, my friend Debussy died at the beginning of this work', Feure told Rouché, 'and the matter remained there.'[16] Feure had another musician in mind now to compose these ballets, and Rouché, having expressed interest, arranged to meet him on 6 July with, 'in support, Debussy's correspondence'. What happened, where the Debussy correspondence now is, and what the second ballet was, I should very much like to know. Perhaps Feure was thinking of one of his unset Ravel ballets as well?

* * *

To return to *Printemps*: Büsser's orchestration seems to have reached London by the end of March 1914, for in his letter to Durand on 1 April Charlot remarked that he had just heard the score after only two hours orchestral rehearsal and that it seemed extremely 'suitable' for his requirements. 'One can certainly achieve something of great interest in staging this delightful symphony, though there are a quantity of "buts"', he added ominously. Chief amongst these was that the second part was scenically perfect, but too short (six and a half minutes) on its own. With Part 1 added, however, the whole ballet (fifteen minutes) was too long! So Charlot wanted to use the first part up to fig. 5 (OS, pp. 1-11, two minutes) as an overture, and then he wanted a section lasting 'just under a minute' during which 'a poem of sixteen to twenty verses' was to be recited, plus another section of 'three minutes at most' for 'a poetic scene involving two or three people'. The whole of the second part was to be retained as a grand ensemble for the full Alhambra *corps de ballet*.

Charlot wanted the cuts to be suggested and authorised by Debussy immediately as rehearsals had to commence on the following Monday (6 April). He hoped that Debussy (despite Dr Crépel's sick note) would feel well enough to do this. But he strongly hinted that, failing this, he would make the cuts himself and he hoped that Durand knew him well enough to trust him not to do anything artistically sacrilegious. This was precisely the opposite problem

Fig. 20. The *corps de ballet* of the Alhambra Theatre, London, in Part 2 of *Spring*, Friday 14 May 1914; costumes by Georges de Feure

to that which Debussy had faced with Maud Allan in 1912, but there is no reason to suppose that he even seriously considered removing the requested two and a half minutes from the latter half of the first part of *Printemps* (OS, pp. 11-43), even though he was less attached to this early score than to *Khamma*.

With or without cuts to *Printemps*, *Not likely!* – a new revue in two acts and twelve scenes by George Grossmith and Cosmo Gordon Lennox (produced by Grossmith and Charlot) – opened on Monday 4 May 1914. It proved to be the longest-running of Charlot's pre-war revues, enjoying 305 performances in all. Debussy's *Spring* ballet with Jack Morrison as Winter, Carlotta Mossetti as the youth and Phyllis Monkman as the maiden in the 'poetic scene involving two or three people' in Part 1, and the full *corps de ballet* in Part 2, was performed as scene 4 of the revue in a prestigious spot immediately before the main interval. The scenario is credited on the programme[17] to Messrs Ronsin, Marc-Henri and Lavardet, with head-dresses by Maison Lewis and, ironically, costumes by none other than Georges de Feure! A picture of the rather crowded second part, showing that Feure was well acquainted with Poiret's lampshade style of 1909 and his harem (or pleated) skirt of 1911, can be seen in Fig. 20. Other gloriously camp moments from the performance on Friday 14 May are shown in Fig. 21 and 22.

On the day following the opening of *Not likely!*, the critic of *The times* singled out the Debussy ballet for special praise, though neither the composer nor the title was mentioned. The following extract offers a fascinating (if romanticised) account of the production:

> There is one scene in the first act which stands out as the gem of the entertainment. Winter, with mournful tread, passes from a Grecian glade, a delightful picture of many shades of green, and as he goes, the flowers and grass burst forth in the joy of spring, and the fancy of the young men and maidens, led by Miss Phyllis Monkman and Miss Carlotta Mossetti, lightly turns to thoughts of dancing. As they dance, the spirit of spring, of love, and of life enters into their hearts, and the curtain falls in a riot of colour and motion. Brief as the interlude was it furnished the most pleasant moments of the evening.

Following the example of the Diaghilev ballet, Debussy intended both his English exotic ballets to be played by a full symphony orchestra, and there is no reason to suppose that the instrumental requirements for *Printemps* (see Appendix) were not met, for the music hall did not then have to survive on the restricted budgets that most theatres endure today. The short passages of *Le palais du silence* that exist suggest that its orchestral dimensions may well have been of the size of *Jeux* (see Ex. 50), and Richard Howgill, who worked at the Alhambra as a répétiteur in 1914, told Lockspeiser in 1965[18] that

Fig. 21. Carlotta Mossetti (the youth) and Phyllis Monkman (the maiden) in Part 1 of *Spring* at the Alhambra Theatre, London, Friday 14 May 1914

Fig. 22. Carlotta Mossetti and Phyllis Monkman with the *corps de ballet* in Part 2 of *Spring* at the Alhambra Theatre, London, Friday 14 May 1914

the orchestra was then quite large and capable to deal with Debussy [*sic*]: . . . We had given *Printemps* and *Danse profane* as ballets and I had played most of Debussy's piano music written up to that time to Charlot (also some Ravel and Satie). John Ansell went to Paris to arrange the commission and Debussy sent me back a signed photo.

After *Not likely!*, Feure featured increasingly in Charlot's wartime revues, producing his own *Temple of the Sun* ballet, which included Erik Satie's first *Gymnopédie* (in Debussy's 1897 orchestration?), in *5064 Gerrard!* (19 March 1915). He also wrote and designed the 1917 Christmas pantomime *Aladdin* for Drury Lane. Late in 1928 Feure returned to Paris permanently, and his disappearance from the English theatre scene and his use of a pseudonym have led biographers to assume that he died in 1928. Virtually nothing is known of his last Parisian period, other than that he registered at the *Hôtel de ville* of the *16ᵉ arrondissement* on 6 June 1929 and died at 20 rue Caulaincourt, Paris 18, on 26 November 1943 at the age of 75.

In *Not likely!* Debussy's ballet rubbed shoulders with an early song by Jerome Kern called *Honeymoon Lane* (scene 1), as well as 'A Revue of the Music Hall Songs from 1864-1914' (scene 8). The finale consisted of a 'Revue Parisienne', featuring the celebrated dancers Maurice and Florence Walton, and a cake-walk with an introductory verse by Elsa Maxwell. Although Debussy's name was included in large type below scene 4 on the programme, while none of the other composers' names was listed, his was the only name not included on the main advertisement on the front page: he was rightly recognised as being in a different musical class altogether (not that that helped the staying power of his ballet). As the revue was such a flexible format, the solo dancers in *Spring* began to be varied from July 1914, and in the week ending 29 August the whole ballet was withdrawn and its position taken by a scene called *The sloping path*, with a set modelled on the ziggurat of Ur and featuring the rather *risqué*-sounding 'pass along girl'! Most of the more spectacular or topical numbers in the revue were retained, however, simply being shuffled about from time to time.

If Debussy's actions in 1903 are anything to go by, there is a possibility that he saw his *Spring* ballet at the Alhambra. In earlier days he often frequented the music hall, and between 16 and 19 July 1914 he made his final visit to London to conduct the Queen's Hall Orchestra in a concert of his own works at the home of Sir Edgar Speyer (17 July). This concert included the *Danses sacrée et profane* and the *Prélude à l'après-midi d'un faune*. Debussy stayed with the Speyers at 46 Grosvenor Street, W1, and could easily have attended the performance at the Alhambra on Saturday 18 July, when Mr Colverd played Winter and Miss Broadwood the maiden. On that night, before the main revue, he would have been treated to such delights as the overture *Chispagos* by a Mr Reeves, Minnie Kaufmann the trick cyclist, and Chinko the Chinese juggler, all of which escapist fare he would surely have relished.

* * *

The existing music for *No-ja-li* amounts to a collection of ideas, mostly with the implied key signatures of B minor or major, though Debussy (as usual) disdains such mundane details. At least fifteen different motifs are discernible, some with developments and harmonisations indicated: none of them recurs elsewhere in Debussy. The longest continuous section (some thirty-five bars in all, discounting revisions) is for the opening prelude. Ex. 49 gives the start of this and includes two of the main ideas for the ballet: A, an arch-shaped motif in 'oriental' parallel fourths over fourth- and fifth-based side-stepping chords (marked 'x'); B, an undulating bass idea associated by Debussy with 'Le Silence'. B recurs in parallel fifths on pp. 13 *v* and 14 *r*. Debussy marks the 'Commencement du Ballet' with a cross (where the curtain presumably rose), and indicates that A was to be scored for flute and clarinet. Theme A is preceded by what looks like an arabesque for solo cello (or bassoon) in triple time from which some accompanying treble (I_4^7) chords have been carefully removed.

A single bar's rest at the top of p. 10 *v* is marked 'La petite princesse No-ja-li'[19] by Debussy, although the following bar is crossed out and the subsequent motif is unclear and is nowhere repeated. It seems as though Debussy's vision of the continuity of *No-ja-li* first fatefully faltered at this point, ironically the 'silence' of *No-ja-li* herself (end of Ex. 49).

The continuous sketch for the prelude stops altogether shortly after the four repeated bars shown in Ex. 50, which introduce a new motif (C) in major seconds and some wide-spaced and very advanced bitonal chords which are harmonic extensions of x from Ex. 49. The aggressive rhythms suggest that it may represent the dreaded guards who enforce Hong-Lo's decree of silence.

The A and B motifs and further harmonic extensions of x recur in varying forms in the remainder of the *Palais du silence* sketches. C from Ex. 50 is less used in its original rhythmic form, but together with the perfect fourth and fifth, the major second as an interval pervades the whole score, both harmonically and melodically. Ex. 51 shows an ostinato figure built from a major second and a perfect fourth, covering a perfect fifth in all. Over this, off-beat quaver chords in superposed fourths lead to a return of A from Ex. 49. Ex. 52 shows seconds and fourths again in prominent use, and Debussy might well have had his earlier piano piece *Pagodes* (1903) in mind when he sketched this passage, the main harmonic bases of the ballet being wide-spaced triads of B major and D sharp minor. However, the ten-year gap between *Pagodes* and *No-ja-li* is everywhere apparent, the latter being less repetitive and pentatonic, producing a barer, more genuinely oriental sound.

In addition there are some less immediately 'oriental' passages, often more chromatic and sometimes based on sliding thirds. From p. 20 *v* onwards the

Ex. 49. *No-ja-li*, *F-Pn* MS 17726, pp. 9 *v* – 10 *v*

202

Ex. 50. *No-ja-li*, *F-Pn* MS 17726, p. 11 *r*

Ex. 51. *No-ja-li*, *F-Pn* MS 17726, p. 13 *r*

Ex. 52. *No-ja-li*, *F-Pn* MS 17726, p. 19 *r*

melodic line is often like an arabesque for violin, though the second- and fourth-based chords in the accompaniment and the odd references back to earlier motifs to my mind identify these passages as belonging to *No-ja-li*. Even if they bear no resemblance to the opening bars of the score, then neither do they contain anything resembling the published version of the Violin Sonata.[20]

One further idea (Ex. 53), found in various harmonisations on pp. 14 *v* to 17 *r*, might also be surmised to be for the Violin Sonata were it not surrounded by *No-ja-li* material, and were it not for the start of the ballet (Ex. 49) which shows that a chromatic arabesque around middle C was intended as an integral feature. The first bar of the sinister Ex. 53 might be thought similar to bars 8-10 of the prelude to *La chute de la Maison Usher* (Ex. 54), though the latter has an initial semiquaver figure which turns in on itself, is constructed in one- (as opposed to two-) bar units, and is much sparser and more pedal-based harmonically. Ex. 54 also evolves from the main *Usher* motif itself (Ex. 34a, x), whereas Ex. 53 is a self-contained idea. The first bar of Ex. 53

Ex. 53. *No-ja-li, F-Pn* MS 17726, p. 17 *r*

Ex. 54. *La chute de la Maison Usher, F-Pn* MS 9885, p. 1, bars 7-11

Ex. 55. *F-Pn* MS 17730, unnumbered page

Cette nuit de Mars et de clair de lune

also recurs in the extra, unnumbered gatherings (in pencil) of *F-Pn* MS 17730, which are not part of the blue-ink sketches for *Fêtes galantes* (see Chapter 9). As there is no full libretto for *No-ja-li* it is impossible to confirm whether the following underlay, found elsewhere in MS 17730, is from this ballet or not: 'Dans ma main votre main s'attardant . . . yeux'; 'Cette nuit de Mars et de clair de lune' (Ex. 55); 'Délivrez-moi . . . mon amour'.

In the end *Printemps*, written in Italy for the French Académie, was ironically the only English ballet by Debussy to be performed in England during his life-time, and one can only conjecture what the completed score for *No-ja-li* would have been like, with its scenes for gamelan orchestra and its final dramatic dénouement. From the existing sketches it seems likely that it would have been an exciting score from the harmonic point of view, with a timeless simplicity and a distinct oriental flavour not found in *Khamma*. It is also freer from the influence of Stravinsky, and its closest contemporary is the prelude to *La boîte à joujoux*. There is no sign of any compromise as far as audience or players are concerned, and it was probably external factors — conducting tours, concerts, ill-health and the war — which led Debussy first to lay aside and then to abandon his most exotic theatrical venture.

The change of title from *Le palais du silence* to *No-ja-li* indicates a change in focus by its authors towards a more human approach, although the idea of 'silence' was a central one for Debussy, first appearing in the context of *Pelléas et Mélisande*. Debussy told Pierre Louÿs on 17 July 1895 that 'Silence is a beautiful thing . . . the empty bars in *Pelléas* are evidence of my love of this sort of emotional expression' (LOU, p. 56), and as Jarocinski points out (p. 152), 'Almost all Debussy's music emerges from silence, fades away at times, and then relapses once more into silence.' Some eighty per cent of his music is marked *piano* or *pianissimo* and Debussy effectively reduced the dynamic level of music, using many terms which refer to dying away, vagueness and distance. The idea of silence appealed increasingly to him during the war years, and his letter to Godet (GOD, p. 142) written on New Year's day 1915 shows the value he attached to this all-too-rare commodity. 'You are probably

the only man who understands that silence does not simply mean oblivion',
he lamented. 'But these offensive times make delicacy a rare flower, so sweet
to inhale!' On the other hand, Debussy would have known Poe's apocalyptic
tale about the *terrors* of 'desolation' and 'silence' from his copy of Baudelaire's
Nouvelles histoires extraordinaires. Only in *Le palais du silence* is 'silence'
incorporated into the title of a work, and Debussy may have been loth to lose
it for *No-ja-li*. As Ex. 49 shows, however, it is curiously the appearance of the
little princess that is accompanied by the silent bar (cf Mélisande), for the
'silence' itself has a distinct musical motif (B)!

Five days later on 6 January 1915, Debussy told Vallery-Radot (p. 140)
that his 'silent' year was over:

> I have slowly begun to write music again, mostly so as not to forget
> how to compose altogether, and only a little for my own satisfaction.
> It seems to me that the time is right to return not to a narrow and
> ultra-modern French manner, but to the true French tradition which
> begins with Rameau – at which point it began to get lost!

Debussy was already entering his final creative period and the restrained world
of the chamber sonatas: for his little Anglo-Chinese ballet, *No-ja-li*, this meant
the final curtain.

9   *Crimen amoris*, later *Fêtes galantes*
(1912-15)

It was enough, as you have shown, to have the taste and sensibility
to reject the *tours de force* in which Moriceoblat managed to uproot
the verses of poor Verlaine like bad teeth!
(Debussy to Louis Laloy, 30 November 1913; *RdM*, 1962, p. 39)

'Moriceoblat', alias Charles Morice, seems to have begun preparing his entertainment based on the poetry of Verlaine in the spring of 1912, for Debussy
sought to consult him on 19 April about various changes before a final version
of *Crimen amoris* was drafted. A contract was signed with Morice and Durand
on 21 May[1] for a 'conte lyrique' in three acts intended for the Paris Opéra, and
it seems likely that the piece was centred on the long, diabolical (even occult)
poem of the same title dedicated to Villiers de l'Isle-Adam in the 'Naguère' section of Verlaine's *Jadis et naguère*.[2] Verlaine described his 'mystery' to Charles
de Sivry in January 1881 as 'entirely evil and at odds with Christianity', and it
would be fascinating to know if the suggestion for the 1912 collaboration
came from Debussy himself. Certainly, the opening stanza with its echoes of
Poe must have appealed to him:

> Dans un palais, soie et or, dans Ecbatane,
> De beaux démons, des Satans adolescents,
> Au son d'une musique mahométane,
> Font litière aux Sept Péchés de leurs cinq sens.

The poem depicts an orgy of the seven deadly sins with the most beautiful
of the 'fallen angels', a young boy of sixteen, in a deep depression from which
the other demons seek to divert him. This has come about because he can no
longer distinguish between good and evil: both have suffering at their root
and he wishes to sacrifice them in favour of universal love. To this end he sets
light to the hell in which the satans are cavorting (his 'crimen amoris') and all
exult (especially in the first version) in the deliberate immolation. Nothing
remains of the palace and the poem ends with a view of the paradise of Nature
on earth and the love of God 'who will protect us against evil'.

Presumably other Verlaine poems were to be involved, but it seems that from fairly early on all did not go well with the Debussy–Morice partnership. This can be seen from the opening quotation to this chapter, which is directly at odds with Verlaine's own tribute to the poet of December 1887, coincidentally published in *Amour*,[3] which ends:

> Artiste pur, poète où la gloire s'assure;
> Cher aux femmes, – cher aux Lettres, – Charles Morice!

It also made it extremely unlikely that in particular the multiple performance clause in Debussy's contract (shades of *Khamma*) would ever be brought into operation. According to this, 5000 francs was to be paid for the score of *Crimen amoris*, with 5000 francs after the first, twentieth, thirtieth, fortieth and fiftieth performances, which all had to take place within ten years of the first! All payments were to be made through Durand who, as usual, was to publish and sell Debussy's score, though, to be on the safe side, he carefully added a clause stating that he was not to be held financially responsible for the terms of the contract if no performing rights were ever paid to him by the Paris Opéra.

In the initial surge of enthusiasm, the ballet was even announced in *Musica* in November 1912, but as early as 15 January 1913 Debussy had decided to replace Morice with his friend Louis Laloy, though he had yet to inform Morice of the details. As he told Durand:

> Charles Morice . . . who thinks that everything in the garden is rosy, knows nothing of my decision, other than that it will cause a delay! I replied to him in a non-committal manner, not giving definite details or any date, and promising to speak 'sympathetically' to you of his request. It is clear, though, that the hard-up belong to the same family as myself, but you know the situation and will not do other than what suits you best. (*F-Pdurand*)

Presumably Debussy, being notoriously cowardly, had told Morice that pressure of other commitments would prevent his working on the score of *Crimen amoris* for the time being, and that he could not guarantee the date of its completion. His reply, however, has unfortunately not survived. Morice's 'request' to Durand must have been for an advance payment for his libretto before Debussy had set it to music.

But within the week Morice had discovered the truth. Sticking to his contract, he placed Debussy in something of a quandary for Debussy wrote to Durand on 21 January 'enclosing a note from the sinister Ch. M[orice] who is insisting without pity, as you can see. You are perhaps going to find me stupid, but I do not know how to reply to him, and I would be most grateful if you could provide me with a good argument by return.' (*F-Pdurand*) As with *Khamma*, Debussy had for reasons of artistic principle fallen foul of his contract and needed Durand to help him out. It is unfortunate that Morice's libretto for *Crimen amoris* has not survived, as this might provide reasons for Debussy's disenchantment, though it would appear that Morice's own 'crimes' lay in seeking to rewrite Verlaine's poetry, or in combining the verses in an insensitive manner which altered their character through their context.

Something seems to have been worked out eventually, for just before he left for Moscow, Debussy wrote enthusiastically to Laloy about the new version of *Crimen amoris* which was to be officially retitled *Fêtes galantes* in January 1914. 'It offers excellent opportunities to compose real music and I am very pleased', he told Laloy on 30 November (*RdM*, 1962, p. 39), adding in a characteristic postscript: 'the end of the third tableau is perhaps a little melancholy. Could you envisage a return to the start of the first tableau with a general movement towards the boat (*galère*), singing all the while?'

On 5 January 1914, Debussy was busy trying to find music with a 'charm equal to that of *Fêtes galantes*' (p. 40) and thought that if he could, it would promise 'some most agreeable soirées'. But when he told Maurice Montabré about his theatrical projects at the end of January (LCr, p. 308), Debussy was afraid publicly to admit the author substitution and still named Charles Morice as the author of what had now become an 'opera-ballet'. Like *Le palais du silence*, which also occupied Debussy's thoughts at the outset of 1914, it was 'far from being finished', and the division of his attention between the two projects may be one reason why neither ballet progressed beyond its opening scene.

On 27 January, just before his *Comoedia* interview with Montabré, Debussy signed another contract with Laloy, Durand and Charles Morice.[4] The conditions of the 1912 contract were to stand, but Laloy, having made 'certain modifications to the original idea of the libretto' was named (with the otherwise redundant Morice) as a collaborator on the project. Laloy was even made to renounce all payment for his part as librettist, to be compensated with one quarter of Debussy's foreign rights as composer! He was evidently something of an optimist, if not a masochist!

But this was not the end of the matter. As with the heirs of Mallarmé, who were reluctant to authorise Debussy's publication of the *Trois poèmes* in the summer of 1913,[5] so Verlaine's heirs wanted payment for the use of his verses and the title *Fêtes galantes* two years later. On the advice of Jacques Rouché, a M. Remacle was called in to sort out the legal tangle. As usual Charles Morice had a hand in stirring up trouble and was probably the one who informed Verlaine's heirs of Debussy's activities as a form of revenge. Debussy, who had returned to *Fêtes galantes* in late June 1915 (DUR, p. 134), told Durand on 27 September:

> Charles Morice is a sly fellow, and seems to me to be the Jesuit agent in this plot . . . but then these bailiff types are not worth much any more! Legally this is nothing but a case of written documents which have gone astray. It would therefore be interesting to know if these

people can produce a document substantiating their claims. Without this, it seems that all that is left for me to do is to pay rights to [Verlaine's] heirs, and that the prohibition of using these poems and the title *Fêtes galantes* is purely arbitrary. Finally, let us leave Remacle to worry about the semiquavers, and the others to their disappointed hope of cheating us out of large sums of money. For my part, I have other librettos to struggle with.

This meant completing the libretto of *La chute de la Maison Usher*, and *Fêtes galantes* was unfortunately sacrificed to this more important project during the fortnight that remained of Debussy's last productive summer at Pourville. Perhaps impending legal difficulties worried him more than he cared to admit in both *No-ja-li* and *Fêtes galantes*, or perhaps in both cases it was the constraints of trying to find inspiration in other people's librettos that led him to seek refuge in his own.

Either in January 1914 (concurrently with *No-ja-li*) or in September 1915 before he decided to abandon Laloy's rather undramatic libretto too (see Appendix), Debussy began composing music for the start of the first tableau: 'Les masques'. This extrovert, dance-like fragment (Ex. 56) turns out to be none other than a setting of stanzas 1 and 3 of Mezzetin's opening song in the one-act comedy *Les uns et les autres* (also from *Jadis et naguère*), which Debussy had considered setting as far back as 1896 (see Chapter 12). From *Les uns et les autres* Laloy borrowed the idea of placing the action in a park

Ex. 56. *Fêtes galantes, F-Pn* MS 17730, ff. 1-2

* Debussy writes 'corsages' in error (cf bars 37-8)

212

MEZZETIN

yeux   Et   bat - tre les cœurs jo - [yeux,___]

MEZZETIN

À l'é - troit **dans les cor - [- sa - ges...]

[((Déjà on ne l'écoute pas. Des couples
se lèvent et esquissent des pas.
D'autres masques entrent à gauche. Saluts.)]

[((Une danse s'organise—Menuet.)]

** 'sous' in Verlaine

à la Watteau late one summer afternoon. He also adopted the character of
Mezzetin, giving him the same unenviable role of entertaining a group of
nonchalant, languid masqueraders with only the aid of his mandoline. But
whereas in Verlaine Mezzetin appears only in the first and last scenes, in
Laloy's libretto he is allotted a more substantial role and emerges as the most
stimulating and spirited character of all. A subtle musical touch of Laloy's is
that the tuning of Mezzetin's mandoline is made to reflect the transient moods
of his masquers on the Island of Love. All the names of the masqueraders
are otherwise changed, and Laloy christens them with those from the familiar
Italian *commedia dell'arte*, perhaps in memory of *Masques et bergamasques*.

Debussy's sketch was obviously made from Laloy's libretto as both omit
the second stanza of Mezzetin's song found in *Les uns et les autres*. The first
bar of Ex. 56 suggests that a longer prelude to the first tableau of *Fêtes
galantes* existed, but has since disappeared. Mezzetin can be heard strumming
his mandoline, first on the off-beat (bars 2-9) and then incisively on the beat
(bars 10-27). At the end of Ex. 56, Debussy leaps past the first stanza of *À la
promenade* (from Verlaine's own *Fêtes galantes*) to the point where the assembled company begins to dance a minuet, and bars 42-7 in particular seem to
echo the spirit, if not the precise material, of *L'isle joyeuse*. Perhaps this hark-
ing back to an earlier musical period was another reason why Debussy abandoned *Fêtes galantes*; to my mind he rejected the original version of the étude
Pour les arpèges composés in that same summer of 1915 for similar reasons.[6]

It is possible that the third folio of *F-Pn* MS 17730, in the same blue ink as
the extract quoted in Ex. 56, is a sketch for the first two lines of *À la promenade* (Ex. 57), for the poem fits Debussy's vocal line quite well. But it is difficult to see how the music fits into Ex. 56 *before* the minuet, as Laloy's
libretto intends. Ex. 57 with its French overture dotted rhythms is clearly the
work of Debussy 'musicien français', and is a not-too-distant (if less dynamic)
relative of the prologue to the Cello Sonata in the same key of D minor (Ex.
58), which suggests that both date from the summer of 1915.

Ex. 57. *Fêtes galantes*, *F-Pn* MS 17730, f. 3

[*Lent e sostenuto*]

Ex. 58. Cello Sonata, 1915, prologue, bars 1-3

With *Usher*, these sketches represent the last theatre music Debussy composed. Nothing could be further from the sparse, sinister atmosphere of the late Poe opera, and Exx. 56 and 57 provide ample testimony that for Debussy each work entailed a new beginning, the creation of a new musical world. Both were rejected precisely because they did not provide Debussy with the opportunity to achieve this goal, and Laloy's libretto as a whole invited just the sort of reference to the past that Debussy sought to avoid.

Laloy's libretto is divided into three tableaux: 'Les masques', 'Les rêves' and 'La vérité', and in reality all he contributed was the plot and some stage directions. The rest is made up from Verlaine's exquisite poetry, with extracts or complete poems from *Fêtes galantes* (9), *Ariettes oubliées* (3), *Aquarelles* (1), *Sagesse* (2), *Amour* (1), *La bonne chanson* (1), *Poèmes Saturniens* (3) and *Jadis et naguère* (2, including *Les uns et les autres*, scenes 1 and 10), though no extracts from *Crimen amoris* were included. The skill lay in arranging Verlaine's poems into a developing and varied scenario, and overall Laloy handles this side of things with sensitivity and acumen. He introduced three texts (*Pantomime*, *En sourdine* and *Green*) which Debussy had set in the 1880s, plus a short extract from *Colloque sentimentale*, the last of the second series of *Fêtes galantes* songs of 1904. But there was probably no intention on the part of either collaborator that existing settings should be used, as only two lines from the middle of *Colloque sentimentale* are involved, and the first stanza only of *Green*. In the case of *En sourdine* Laloy uses the first two stanzas in his central tableau, then includes a reprise of the second stanza towards the end of tableau 3, to which he adds stanzas 3 and 4 only, the last two being separated by a dance for the assembled company. The crucial fifth stanza, in which Debussy so cleverly ties the thematic threads together in his second setting of 1891, is missing entirely; a cumulation of points like this, together with the considerable length of the project (far in excess of his usual fifteen- to twenty-minute ballets) may have contributed to Debussy's abandoning of *Fêtes galantes* for *Usher*.

The treatment of *Pantomime* and *Colombine* (both complete) from Verlaine's *Fêtes galantes* provides further examples of Laloy's skill. The four stanzas of the former are divided into two equal groups, which are inserted between the three verses of *L'heure du berger* from the *Poèmes Saturniens* (part of the collection *Paysages tristes*). And the six stanzas of *Colombine* are used at strategic moments in the outer tableaux, with the third recurring as a sort of refrain. The musical associations ('Do, mi, sol, mi, fa') of the third stanza were perhaps meant to stimulate Debussy's imagination into providing them with a less obvious and simplistic harmonic background than that implied by Verlaine. Despite the risk of reverting to earlier styles, it is to music's great loss that Debussy never made settings of some of the masterpieces that Laloy included, like *Un grand sommeil noir* (from *Sagesse*), *À Clymène* (from *Fêtes galantes*) and *L'hiver a cessé* (from *La bonne chanson*). During the singing of this final poem, there is 'a general movement towards the boat' and a sort of return to the festive mood at the 'start of the first tableau', as requested by Debussy in November 1913. Laloy did his best to oblige, and it is simply unfortunate that the poem he chose is about spring, being thus a good four months premature in a libretto set in late summer!

Briefly, the plot of *Fêtes galantes* concerns the love of Lélian and the dancer Colombine and the ups and downs of their affair. Lélian has a somewhat ineffective jealous rival in Arlequin, who plots to stab him as he dreams in the central tableau, aided and abetted by Pierrot and Léandre. The former invents a ruse whereby Arlequin is to attack Lélian: when Colombine comes to the rescue, the ensuing struggle is to be arranged so that it ends in an embrace in full view of the awakened Lélian. When the miscreants make their escape, Colombine is left holding the dagger she has wrested from Arlequin, all of which demands a good deal of understanding on Lélian's part next day.

Daybreak finds the flirtatious masquers in quarrelsome mood and Mezzetin has little success in amusing them. It is Lélian's lifting of Colombine's mask in the final tableau that has the desired effect on the company: all are struck by her beauty, and the mists shrouding the Island of Love suddenly clear. After general festivities, the lovers and masqueraders depart. Lélian and Colombine leave the island last, not without a certain regret at quitting the scene of the sufferings that have served to strengthen the bond between them.

Poor, obliging Laloy, having also been disappointed over *Masques et bergamasques* and *L'orestie*, finally received some satisfaction when Debussy, after the battles of Verdun and the Somme, asked him for an *Ode à la France* in 1916 and drafted a complete short score for soprano (in the character of Joan of Arc), mixed choir and orchestra the following year.[7] Again Debussy raised difficulties over the text of this dramatic ode, and he evolved the idea for a soldiers' song, providing Laloy with a rhythmic model for his words. Several versions were made of parts of the text and Laloy did not discover which Debussy had chosen in 1917 as war work kept him away from the composer until December of that year, by which time 'music had completely deserted him'.

10   *Le martyre de Saint Sébastien* (1911)

> I should tell you that I wrote in two months a score that would
> normally take me a year, and that I put into practice my theories —
> if I can call them that — on incidental music, which should be
> something other than the vague background murmurs which usually
> accompany verses or prose, and which should be closely at one with
> the text.
>
> (Debussy, interview with René Bizet in *Comoedia* (18 May 1911);
> LCr, p. 305)

Le martyre de Saint Sébastien is Debussy's longest theatre score after *Pelléas*,
containing about fifty-five minutes of music in its original stage version,
nearly three times as much as any of his ballets. It is also his only completed
score of incidental music, and being so often maligned it merits special consideration here.

The catalyst in the whole enterprise was the wealthy Russian dancer Ida
Rubinstein, who wanted to mount a spectacular showpiece of her own after
her successes with the Diaghilev company in 1909-10. Gabriele d'Annunzio,
adventurer, patriot, poet and hedonist *extraordinaire*, arrived in Paris in the
spring of 1910, chased from his Tuscan villa by his numerous creditors. There,
like Comte Robert de Montesquiou, he was stunned by la Rubinstein's performance as Cléopâtre and as the Sultana Zobeïda in *Schéhérazade*. She was
equally theatrical off stage, an intense and domineering beauty who lived
mostly on champagne and biscuits and was every inch a queen in her starring
roles. Her imposing presence received as much attention as the dancing of her
negro slave lover Nijinsky in *Schéhérazade*, and Fokine wrote of her performance as the faithless Zobeïda:[1]

> Everything was expressed with one single pose, with one movement,
> one turn of the head ... Every single line was carefully thought out
> and felt ... She stands in front of a door through which her lover is
> momentarily due to emerge. She waits for him with her entire
> body. Then ... she sits utterly still while slaughter takes place

around her. She majestically awaits her fate in a pose without motion . . . I consider this one of the most successful accomplishments among my ideas of the new ballet.

Whilst as far back as 1883 d'Annunzio had written a pagan sonnet *La mort du dieu*, which described the death of Adonis in the same florid and decadent style as *Le martyre*, he claimed that it was only Ida Rubinstein who really focused his attention on Saint Sebastian in 1910. According to Tosi (ANN, p. 10), the Paris papers announced that this project by d'Annunzio would inaugurate the new Théâtre de Fête on the Esplanade des Invalides in 1911, and in August he was busy researching the subject in depth with the assistance of Georges Hérelle and Gustave Cohen. The latter, an authority on Roman and early Christian literature, maintained in June 1911 (p. 705)[2] that d'Annunzio's greatest debt to his medieval mystery play sources was his use of repetitive octosyllabic metre, and that his 'French vocabulary is at least as rich as his Italian vocabulary' (p. 708).

D'Annunzio was fascinated by the primitive and masochistic elements in early Christianity, as is reflected in his treatment of the torture of the chained twins Marc and Marcellian, Sebastian's ecstatic dance on the burning embers (Act 1), and his exquisite pleasure as he faces death from the archers of the Emperor Diocletian, which he formerly commanded (Act 4). He was also curious to find out from Cohen (see 1957, p. 31) about nudity and sexual role reversal in the ancient mysteries, and was slightly nonplussed to hear that the latter usually involved men appearing as women rather than *vice versa*, for which he had intended to use the ideally 'flat-chested and slender' Ida Rubinstein. But beyond the bare facts which underlie the various episodes in *Le martyre*, d'Annunzio derived little from his sources. In fact he claimed early in May 1911 (Handler, p. 1) that 'the action was ordered by *biographical unity* alone, developing in a series of episodes similar to those one sees in stained-glass windows'. It is true that Sebastian was a favourite of Diocletian and that miracles followed his conversion to Christianity, but the magic chamber with its occult undertones (Fig. 23), the curing of 'la fille malade des fièvres', and the appearance of the Virgin Mary who transforms everything with the light of the new faith (including the astrological significance of the zodiacal signs in Act 2) are pure d'Annunzio. So is Diocletian's decision in the 'council of the false gods' court scene in the third act to have Sebastian stretched out as if crucified and his beauty suffocated with flowers[3] by the women of Byblos when he persists in proclaiming his belief in the Christian faith.

Cohen later claimed (1938, p. 370) that the final scene in paradise, which was to cause so much trouble in rehearsal, had been his own suggestion on 21 December 1910.[4] All the while, he tells us, d'Annunzio had in mind Ida Rubinstein and the Ballets Russes (where he had discovered her): he viewed her 'as a great *tragédienne* as much as a great dancer' (p. 371). She, in turn, described her first meeting with d'Annunzio as follows:[5] 'I danced, I mimed . . .

Fig. 23. *Le martyre de Saint Sébastien*, Act 2, 'La chambre magique', at the Théâtre du Châtelet, Paris, May 1911

I can say that he gave me a voice . . . He led me to a complete discovery of myself, of all that I did not know about myself.'

The Catholic writer Charles Péguy described the charismatic d'Annunzio as 'capable of miracles',[6] but it was a financial rather than a religious one that tempted Debussy. In fact, he was only third choice as a composer, being suggested by Robert de Montesquiou after Jean Roger-Ducasse and Henry Février had refused.[7] In his poetic letter to Debussy on 25 November 1910 (ANN, pp. 51-2; trans. in LO, 2, pp. 158-9) d'Annunzio maintained that Gabriel Mourey was the link between them, but his own flattering and somewhat general overture produced the desired result. On 30 November Debussy replied from the Hotel Krantz in Vienna (whither he had gone to conduct *Ibéria* and *La mer*) that 'the thought of working with you fills me with feverish anticipation' (ANN, p. 52). But three days later in Budapest he was less enthusiastic. 'This proposal contains nothing of any worth', he told his wife (BAR, pp. 88-9), 'and besides, I shall seem to exert a special attraction for female dancers.'[8] But d'Annunzio had cunningly won Emma round to his cause, and her help in persuading her husband to accept and produce was also valued by the impresario Gabriel Astruc.

Debussy returned to Paris on 7 December and on the same day that d'Annunzio wrote to Emma to arrange a persuasive dinner party at the Café de Paris to introduce Ida Rubinstein, Debussy apparently accepted the commission, for his contract with Astruc is dated 9 December.[9] The amount of detail in this is as much of a mystery as the 'mystery' itself when one considers how little of *Le martyre* was actually written at this juncture. Perhaps Ida was the severely practical partner in the trio, for the plan included three important dances which were to be delivered to Astruc separately by the end of February 1911 so that she could arrange suitable choreography with Michel Fokine. For this a special fee of 6000 francs was to be paid, plus 8000 francs on signature and a further 6000 when the score and parts were delivered at the end of April for the first rehearsals. The première in the 'saison lyrique' at the Théâtre du Châtelet was to be around 20 May 1911 (it actually took place on the 22nd), and special clauses were added (probably on Debussy's insistence) to ensure that *Saint Sébastien* could not be performed without his music (which formed 'an integral part' of it); if the contract was broken, Debussy was not to be financially liable in any way.

At this stage the drama was in four acts and contained the following items:

Act 1 ['La cour des lys']	*Prélude symphonique* [VS, pp. 1-5]
	'Danse des charbons ardents', 'accompagnée du choeur des séraphins' [VS, pp. 15-24, with two contraltos representing Marc and Marcellian, and coryphées instead of séraphins]
	Madrigal 'à 5 voix' (optional) [VS, pp. 24-9, actually à 4 for divided sopranos and altos]
Act 2 ['La chambre magique']	*Prélude symphonique* [VS, pp. 30-8]
	'Danse des planètes' [? VS, pp. 43-5]
Act 3 ['Le concile des faux dieux']	*Prélude symphonique* [VS, pp. 47-9]
	'Danse de la passion de Notre Seigneur' [probably VS, pp. 52-5]
Act 4 ['Le laurier blessé']	*Prélude symphonique* [VS, pp. 73-5]
	Lamentations des femmes veuves et finale [VS, pp. 78-86 and 87-104, printed as Act 5]

There was thus to be rather less music, and especially less singing, in the original conception of *Le martyre*. All the vocal items that occur in the second and third acts of the final version are missing, and the mystery eventually became less of a dancing showcase for Ida Rubinstein, with the loss of the separate 'Danse des planètes' in the magic chamber act. Debussy had even at this stage decided on his orchestral forces, which remained fixed right to the final version (including 'three harps and a celesta (large model)'), for a letter, in which Debussy says that there are still 'six more months to write the music',[10] lists everything but the fourth trumpet.

Act 3, which d'Annunzio considered to be 'musically the most important', was the first to reach Debussy – on 11 January – after considerable delays. After Debussy and d'Annunzio had discussed it at dinner that evening, d'Annunzio told Astruc to pay Debussy a visit, adding 'he understands everything marvellously: it is a rare joy to work with such an artist'.[11] On 21 January d'Annunzio told Astruc that Debussy was about to start on the 'Virgins' chorus in Act 1',[12] and on the 23rd Debussy was offered the traditional *Te Deum* as an alternative to d'Annunzio's final chorus, which was based on Psalm 150.

Debussy refused this offer on the 29th and in the same letter expressed his doubts and fears in tackling such a rich poetic tapestry (ANN, pp. 63-4):

> I have reached the point where all music seems useless beside the unceasingly renewed splendour of your imagination. Thus it is not without a certain amount of terror that I see the moment approaching when I shall positively have to write something. Will I be able to? Will I find what I want? This fear is perhaps salutary, for one cannot penetrate mystery shackled by conceited pride.

He was rather more optimistic when he told Robert Godet on 6 February (GOD, p. 126) that *Le martyre* was 'much more sumptuous' than *Khamma*. 'I have no need to tell you that in it the cult of Adonis joins that of Jesus; that it is very beautiful . . . and that . . . if I was allowed the necessary time, there are some rather beautiful discoveries that could be made.' The 'necessary time' would normally be two years rather than two months, he informed Edgard Varèse on 12 February (Lesure, 1965, p. 335), and on the previous day he had been trying to pin down d'Annunzio as to where exactly Ida's dance on the burning embers began (ANN, p. 66):

> There are words spoken during this dance, are there not? When you are near me I hear the music that your speech suggests, but all the same I need practical landmarks to guide me. Your notes for the painter [Bakst] and the musician resemble an enchanted forest full of images, in which I sometimes feel like Tom Thumb (*le 'Petit Poucet'*).[13]
> The rhythm of the *Chorus of seraphim*[14] pleased me enormously. I believe that the start of the Assumption of Saint Sebastian [Act 4] will perhaps need a more expansive form: over-repetition of the same musical sounds introduced by the same poetic rhythms could become a danger.

When the complete first act arrived on 13 February, d'Annunzio explained that the dance began when the saint entered the 'burning parallelogram . . . I believe that the mystery of the second act will please you', he informed a

Fig. 24. *Le martyre de Saint Sébastien*, Act 2, the group of female magicians (Mlles Ch. Barbier, Gonzales, Marion, Jane Mea, Neith-Blanc, Rafaële Osborne), at the Théâtre du Châtelet, Paris, May 1911

kindred occult spirit (ANN, p. 67). 'When one opens the vast door of the magic chamber, the air is already *filled* with enchantment.' (See Fig. 23.) And on the following day he described 'the atmosphere of this liturgical drama' as 'the "incredible". The second and third acts take place on the most exalted summits of the supernatural.' (ANN, p. 68; and see Fig. 24)

That same day the 'irresistible whirlwind' of Ida and Gabriele forced open another door when Debussy hinted to Caplet that he would be needing his help with *Le martyre* as soon as he returned from Boston.[15] His letter (CAP, pp. 50-1) makes it look as if he had hardly started on the music, but that the arrival of Act 1 had brought the urgency of the situation home to him. 'Naturally, I have very little time to write a great deal of music', he confessed. 'You know how much I like that! So there is not a moment to be lost in deciding. In the output of a mine, there is a type of coal which is called unsorted (*tout venant*) . . . this is my predicament exactly.'

The idea that Caplet played any part in the *composition* of *Le martyre* in March–April 1911 is most unlikely, but he orchestrated most of Acts 2–4[16] and proved an invaluable aid at rehearsals, as Debussy later told Henry Russell, director of the Boston Opera, when recommending Caplet to him on 22 October (CAP, p. 75):

> I saw my friend André Caplet at work and it is an all-too-rare experience in the life of someone whose works are performed to have been able to attend rehearsals – generally so unpleasant – without any kind of fear. Moreover, you know his talents as a born conductor, his marvellous understanding of this complex and delicate art.

On 11 February 1911 an interview with Henry Malherbe appeared in *Excelsior* which reveals the extent to which Debussy had to rethink his religious attitudes as he composed *Le martyre* (LCr, pp. 301-3). Whilst he could maintain that he did not 'worship according to the established rites' and had rather 'made a religion from the mysteries of Nature', he still confessed that 'the subject of *Le martyre de Saint Sébastien* seduced me above all by its blend of intense life and Christian faith'. Then, in a passage which goes deep to the roots of his musical philosophy, he expanded on the way his inspiration came from Nature: how

> suddenly, without anyone's consent, one of these natural memories flows out, expressing itself in musical language . . . If I talk to you in this manner, it is not to offer you an ostentatious show of artistic morals, but precisely to prove to you that I have none. I detest doctrines and their irrelevance.
>
> That is why I want to write down my musical dreams with the greatest self-detachment. I wish to sing of my inner landscape with the naïve candour of childhood.

During the following week, Debussy found himself involved in the final rehearsals for a revival of *Pelléas et Mélisande* on 18 February. This made it 'impossible to fulfil Mme Rubinstein's demands to detach her dances from the rest of the score' (ANN, p. 70) by the end of the month. 'In truth', he informed Astruc at about this time, 'I told her that perhaps one or two dances could be ready towards 15 April . . . Besides, it would need the facility of Ganne combined with the genius of Wagner to write so much music in so little time . . . It is inadmissible that I should be held to conditions made by M. Fokine',[17] Debussy concluded, forgetting the contract he had signed the previous December. In fact it appears that Debussy, like d'Annunzio, was not composing *Le martyre* in sequential order. His request to Durand for the loan of the six-part *Missa Papae Marcelli* of Palestrina 'for a few days' in March[18] intimates that he was then busy on the choruses of the paradise scene, which the Italian journal *Il tirso* suggested on 4 June were by Caplet.

It was only on 2 March that the complete text was finally ready, and the principals assembled to read this a week later *chez* Astruc at the Pavillon de Hanovre. The relative silence from Debussy during March and most of April suggests that these were the 'two months' when most of the score was composed, the interlude before the paradise scene and the 'lamentations' at the end of the third act coming last of all.

By early May rehearsals were under way and, as everyone had feared, it was the scene in paradise which created hell. Debussy, uniquely, set down his reactions to a rehearsal at the Théâtre du Châtelet in a letter to Gabriel Astruc (ANN, pp. 74-5) which suggests that the problems involved in this hurried production were basic, to say the least. At this point the music for Act 5 was still not ready to be used in rehearsal, and Debussy protested that:

> Since the staging problems stop at the gates of paradise, the performers are convinced that, as there is no more music, they can go away — some *chez* Larue, the others *chez* Zimmer or some other inferior wine-merchants — and it would perhaps be better to scrap the paradise part altogether?
>
> But there are more serious matters which should not recur at *any* price. Amongst others, the bad co-ordination between the action and the music.
>
> It is absolutely vital to stage the end of the fourth act differently. As it is arranged now, the audience, seeing the actors exit (and this resembles a provincial funeral procession), will naturally think of it as a cue to do the same thing themselves.
>
> I have asked what can best be done during the Assumption of the soul of Saint Sebastian to bring back the seven seraphim as angel musicians [VS, pp. 92-4],[19] and during the final chorus to set the golden palms in motion! [VS, pp. 97ff] Without pretending that this should appear ingenious, it is a way of livening up the background, which at the moment remains too static and similar . . . Finally, there is still the question of paradise! One cannot manage by bringing down a backcloth with rays painted on, when the rays do not radiate [Fig. 25].
>
> One should perhaps begin the departure of Sebastian's cortège

Fig. 25. *Le martyre de Saint Sébastien*, Act 5 no. 2, the paradise scene; design by Léon Bakst

later. This should pause at the moment when the light bursts forth
[VS, p. 87] and his funeral procession should restart (less woefully)
during the unaccompanied choruses [VS, pp. 88ff]. I really believe
that all this is important and I should be obliged if you would reply
to me.

    P.S. The light on the cortège of the women of Byblos and the
followers of Adonis etc. should be lunar [VS, pp. 78ff]. It needs
torch-bearers. These torches should be put out at the end of the
lamentation: 'Renversez les torches, Éros! Pleurez!' [VS, p. 86]

    P.P.S. No one should enter during the preludes . . . From the first,
it is not polite, and it is a standard order which applies on each
similar occasion.

    P.P.P.S. Thank you for the box which you have put at my disposal.

In effect, Debussy was concerned about the bad co-ordination from Act 4
no. 3 onwards. What little action there was happened too quickly, leaving the
long choruses in paradise completely static. The first part of the letter suggests
that it was the music for Act 5 (which Debussy orchestrated himself) that
'arrived at the theatre page by page, hastily copied and corrected in pencil'
(Vuillermoz, 1920, p. 157). Vuillermoz also tells how moved everyone was,
including Debussy, by the first musical run-through, and that it was only then
that the real 'martyrdom' began!

    First of all, in trying to follow Caplet's beat the singers were obstructing
Armand Bour's 'impressive ensemble movement'. So they were 'parked in the
wings or behind props or between two giants, and were generally harassed
from all sides'. Inghelbrecht, Vuillermoz and Chadeigne (the chorus-masters)
tried to regroup them and, in Russian style, dressed in chorus costumes to
assist them from within the ranks. But then the designer, Léon Bakst, set
about redistributing everyone on stage so as to balance their gorgeous costume
colours. Any semblance of choral ensemble vanished and many, unsure of the
unfamiliar music, did not dare sing at all! And still Debussy was trying to
'persuade Bakst that paradise was a place universally thought to be "dazzling" ',
as he told the long-suffering Caplet.

    Then to crown everything, six days before the performance the Archbishop
of Paris, Monseigneur Amette (who was to conduct a campaign against the
fox-trot in 1913), forbade Catholics to attend Le martyre under penalty of
excommunication, and all d'Annunzio's works were put on the Papal Index!
Finally, on the morning of the public dress-rehearsal (21 May) the Minister of
War was killed in an aeroplane accident at Issy, which cast a further shadow
over the proceedings and must have seemed like yet another evil omen to the
authors.

    In an attempt to restore the balance, Debussy and d'Annunzio published a
joint protest against the archbishop's denunciation (ANN, facing p. 32) which
described Le martyre as 'profoundly religious; the lyrical glorification not
only of Christ the wonderful Athlete, but of all Christian heroism', and

Debussy in an interview with René Bizet published in *Comoedia* on 18 May (LCr, pp. 304-5) again spoke of its religious nature. Whilst there were 'no religious precedents at all' in his works and he was 'not a practising Catholic', he nonetheless assured Bizet that

> I wrote my music as if it had been commissioned for a church. I composed decorative music . . . the illustration in timbres and rhythms of an exalted text. When, in the last act, the saint ascends to paradise, I consider that I have realised all that I felt and experienced in this conception of the Ascension. Have I really succeeded? That does not worry me any more. We no longer possess the spirit of faith of old. Is the faith my music expresses orthodox or not? I ignore this question. It is mine alone; mine which sings forth in complete confidence.

Which was just as well, because its veiled mysticism needed a much more sensitive and polished performance than it received to be properly appreciated, though its *Parsifal*-like qualities were commented on by several critics. These included Pierre Lalo (*Le temps*, 30 May), who otherwise mostly disliked it because it was untrue to the *Pelléas* aesthetic and lacked that indefinable sense of unity that critics have always been so fond of praising in Debussy. Gaston Carraud (*Liberté*), on the other hand, found it superior to the intervening works since *Pelléas*, and Alfred Bruneau (*Le matin*) agreed, and liked its expansiveness and simplicity, especially in the final choruses. Paul-Jean Toulet (1926, pp. 133-4) thought that it was difficult to judge how good Bakst's costumes were because the stage was so poorly lit, but that did not prevent Marcel Proust and Robert de Montesquiou being riveted by Ida Rubinstein's legs, which Proust told Reynaldo Hahn 'were like a cross between those of Clomenil and Maurice de Rothschild' (1956, p. 206)! The young Jean Cocteau too was ecstatic about Rubinstein's androgynous incarnation of the saint (Figs. 26 and 27), which went beyond a mere 'sense of the theatre' (*Comoedia*, 1 June). Mme de Saint-Marceaux in her journal[20] was more down-to-earth though, and particularly stressed how long and incomprehensible it all was, especially Ida, who was a better actress than speaker. Henry Bidou explained at greater length in the *Journal des débats* (29 May) that Rubinstein's voice was 'flat and muted, having harshness without volume. She spoke through her nose atrociously and rolled her "r" s as if she had a mouthful of pebbles . . . She presented a series of poses which were neither linked to each other nor of any consequence.'

The critics were not all kind about d'Annunzio's poetry or conception either. Paul Crouzet published an article – 'Le vrai mystère de Saint Sébastien' – in the *Grande revue* (23 June) and F. de Nion in *L'écho de Paris* wickedly described d'Annunzio as 'a troubadour who has read Ibsen'![21] As the première lasted till past midnight (nearly five hours), substantial cuts were made in the second act before the subsequent performances, according to Louis Vuillemin (*Comoedia*, 25 May), and *Le martyre* was never performed

Fig. 26. Ida Rubinstein as Saint Sebastian

Fig. 27, Sketch by Léon Bakst for Ida Rubinstein as Saint Sebastian in Act 4 of *Le martyre de Saint Sébastien*

again in its full original state. Despite a certain social and intellectual acclaim, *Le martyre* was withdrawn after the ninth performance on 1 June to make way for rehearsals of the Ballets Russes, and as a curious hybrid it has never really proved viable in revival. It is usually performed in a curtailed concert version (as conducted by Inghelbrecht at the Société Musicale Indépendante on 14 June 1912), or in Caplet's four-movement suite (as conducted by Varèse in Prague on 4 January 1914).

Robin Holloway, elsewhere excellently perceptive, is rather harsh on *Le martyre*. Debussy, he says, used *Parsifal* as 'a model rather than an influence' being much guided by the music for Amfortas in his patchy score (pp. 147-52). He sees *Le martyre* as (p. 144) the 'most rapidly-produced yet unspontaneous of [Debussy's] works' with a 'high proportion of the music' being 'poor in quality'. He later describes the work (p. 147) as 'ramshackle, suffering from the fragmentariness that defeats almost all incidental music and all melodrama', and considers that (p. 158) the 'major strength of *Le martyre* is the unaccompanied choruses in the 1st and 5th Mansions, which represent Debussy's nearest approach to his Renaissance ideal' and whose 'effect is totally un-Wagnerian'. But he forgets that at the première Debussy's score took up only about one fifth of the time, the rest being filled by d'Annunzio's 'nearly 4000' extravagant verses. As more and more cuts were made, right down to the concert versions, Debussy's score became more and more stylistically disconcerting, as individual items were brought into closer proximity. He was, after all, writing incidental music 'closely at one with the text' in all its vagaries, and never intended that *Le martyre* should be unified in the manner of *La mer*.

But that is not to say that it is 'ramshackle', and Debussy *did* make some attempts to bind his varied score together and make it gel. On the textural side there are various instances of divided strings descending *tremolando* from on high. On the harmonic side, there are recurring passages of parallel major and minor chords, often on the woodwind in close position. From the tonal point of view the outer acts end in E major, with the second act often in the relative C sharp minor. And thematically, there is the recurring 'Sébastien!' idea (Ex. 59), a distinctive, spread dominant eleventh chord first heard in the orchestra over a pedal in bars 27-8. There are also subtle links within and between the acts. For instance, the sliding chromatic idea (Ex. 60a) recurs in Act 3 nos. 4 and 7 and is recalled in unobtrusive augmentation in Act 4 no. 3 (Ex. 60c; VS, p. 82); whereas Act 4 no. 2, at a point in the score where things are in danger of seeming fragmentary, manages to sum up the main musical arguments of Act 1 and also to recall towards the end – though in a very different context (VS, p. 77) – the marvellously expansive moment in Act 2 (VS, p. 45) when the magic chamber is flooded with light.

Ex. 60a is one of several points where *Le martyre* shows similarities with

Ex. 59. *Le martyre de Saint Sébastien*, Act 1 no. 2, VS, p. 9, bars 1-4

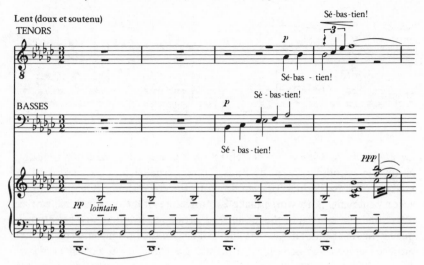

Ex. 60

(a) *Le martyre de Saint Sébastien*, Act 3 no. 4, VS, p. 57, bars 1-2

(b) *La chute de la Maison Usher*, *F-Pn* MS 9885, p. 4, bars 3-4

(c) *Le martyre de Saint Sébastien*, Act 4 no. 3, VS, p. 82, bars 4-7

La chute de la Maison Usher (cf Ex. 60b), and Lady Madeline's ensuing chromatic vocalise (VS, p. 4) finds a direct parallel in Act 3 no. 4 of *Le martyre* (VS, p. 55, line 3), even down to the *tremolando* pedal-point in the accompaniment. Both works make extensive use of melodrama for theatrical effect and the interval of the diminished fifth appears both as a *pizzicato* bass quaver figure at the start of Sebastian's dance on the burning embers, and in a more developed and eerie form to herald the entry of the doctor in *Maison Usher* (VS, pp. 4-5). The interval is, of course, synonymous with the augmented fourth which dominates the *Usher* score (see Ex. 34a, x).

Just as *Le martyre* in places looks forward (or sideways) into *Usher*, so Act 1 in particular also looks back to the fresh modal world of *La damoiselle élue* (OS, pp. 20-4), thus assuming a central point of reference in Debussy's theatrical career. Its eclecticism is more marked than in any other of Debussy's works, and as Roger Nichols says (1973, p. 70), from now on Debussy 'became increasingly selective in the type of material he used for any one work'. He is at his best in *Le martyre* when he has a vivid image to inspire him: the burning embers spit and crackle to great effect in Sebastian's first dance; the diminished seventh contrabassoon theme evokes an eerie and disturbing picture of the magic chamber beneath a string texture like that of the thematically comparable *Khamma* prelude transposed into the treble; and the music for Sebastian's suffering, death and funeral procession (Act 3 no. 4 to the end of Act 4) is poignant, deeply felt and the finest in the score. It is the more obvious and extrovert passages to which Debussy responded least well. The pentatonic fanfares announcing the Emperor Diocletian in Act 3 sound as banal now as the melodramatic effects which largely prohibit the revival of this unwieldy 'mystery', and it is only Debussy's skilful orchestration which covers up his routine response to d'Annunzio's version of the 150th Psalm in Act 5.

More than any other Debussy score *Le martyre* often feels like film music and Debussy may have realised its potential when he got so excited about M. Péquin's proposals in the summer of 1914.[22] The cinema was an art form that had long fascinated Debussy. As early as 30 March 1903 he wrote in *Gil Blas* that Richard Strauss' *Ein Heldenleben* was 'a book of images, even cinematographic' (LCr, p. 135), and his criticism in the same journal a fortnight later suggested the back projection of a film version of *Die Walküre* to his least favourite conductor Camille Chevillard, after he had found his semi-staged concert version of the opera so ridiculous. Debussy was clearly *au fait* with the latest developments in this field for he added: 'We have seen in a recent play at the [Théâtre de l']Ambigu how powerfully it can enhance the emotional effect. We must be right up to date in this matter.' The play in question, Richard Langham Smith has discovered (RLS, p. 176, n. 2), was Eugène Sue's melodrama *La juif errant*, which had previously been popular in the shadow theatre of Henri Rivière that Debussy loved to frequent at Le Chat Noir in Montmartre in the 1890s. It is worth remembering also that the interludes in *Pelléas* are the musical equivalent of a cinematographic back projection, as they subtly change both scene and mood, and Debussy told Edgard Varèse in February 1911 that he 'liked images almost as much as music' (Lesure, 1965, p. 335). In November 1913 (LCr, p. 242), he saw the 'application of cinematographic techniques to pure music' as a way of reviving the taste for symphonic music amongst his contemporaries. 'It is the film', he added, 'the Ariadne's thread, that will show us the way out of this alarming labyrinth.'[23]

On 20 June 1914 Debussy asked d'Annunzio if he had 'any news of the film man', as he would 'take great pleasure in a visit from him' (ANN, p. 96). D'Annunzio replied through Emma (ANN, p. 97) that M. Péquin 'came to Venice on Tuesday to discuss the incarnation of Saint Sebastian and he will come to Paris in a few days'. He also delivered the mouth-watering news that 'Saint Sebastian asks 200,000 francs to allow himself to be attached to the tree of Apollo' (presumably for 'shooting'!). 'The Man is ready to offer 100,000 francs, and to raise the sum if he can avail himself of ready-prepared costumes.' As Debussy had arranged to stay with the Speyers in London in mid-July 1914, he was worried on 4 July about missing M. Péquin's visit, though thanks to a telegram from d'Annunzio he almost certainly saw him on the following day, and once again it seems that Ida Rubinstein was involved. Debussy describes the visit as follows (ANN, p. 99):

> Though a business-man, [M. Péquin] is pleasant enough, only he pretends to have instructions from *la diva* who cannot go beyond the sum of 20,000 francs as a premium! I did not believe I would have to haggle, the more so because that would have involved unlimited documents! M. Péquin should return armed with a contract next Tuesday [7 July] at 6 p.m. There is in this affair someone in a great hurry: Claude Debussy. It is quite natural that M. Péquin wishes to make a profit out of this, because the art of business consists of taking advantage of the miserable poverty in which artists sometimes find themselves. But at last I shall work with you again, and that is the most important thing.[24]

However, this was not to be, for when M. Péquin called on 7 July the deal was off. Poor Debussy wrote a bewildered note to d'Annunzio to ask what had happened, and no filming of *Le martyre* actually took place until after the Paris revival of June 1922 when Ida Rubinstein's dances were recorded for posterity.

This was not the first occasion when Ida had put a spanner in Saint Sebastian's works. Debussy had tried to delay the project of Astruc and Inghelbrecht to present *Le martyre* in concert form in July 1913 because la Rubinstein still intended to resurrect it at the Théâtre des Champs-Élysées. 'Moreover', he added to d'Annunzio on 9 July (ANN, p. 89), 'I need to be assured of Mme Rubinstein's intentions from now on to be able to bring myself to write the music that we have agreed to add.' And Debussy told Gaston Choisnel (of Durand et Cie) on the 24th that he was 'at the disposition of M. H. Klein', adding 'do not forget . . . that the music of *Le martyre* will probably be enlarged, and considerably' (*F-Pdurand*). So it would seem that something approaching an operatic version was planned *before* Jacques Rouché requested this in 1914 to inaugurate his career as the new director of the Paris Opéra.

But back in 1913, there was something of a panic on because, as Debussy told d'Annunzio on 30 July (ANN, pp. 89-90):

> Astruc has still not seen Mme Rubinstein, who is leaving immediately to go lion-hunting in Africa! It is a noble sport, without a doubt, but what will become of so many worthwhile projects as a result? Is there any way of obtaining some assurance before her departure? If it is any use my intervening personally, then I am quite ready! If needs be I will go to Versailles barefoot and with my arms laden with chains!

And according to Simon Harcourt-Smith[25] something quite as dramatic actually happened! When Ida finally returned to Paris in October 1913, a meeting was arranged involving his father, Bakst, Astruc[26] and Debussy. They were ushered into the salon out of the pouring rain by a servant, and after waiting for five minutes, heard an enormous crash followed by a scream and a pause. Then the salon door was dramatically flung open and la Rubinstein (in a manner worthy of Madeline Usher) staggered in naked with blood pouring from her shoulder, trying to restrain a chained panther that she had brought back from Africa and which had previously broken loose and savaged her! Quite what the shy and sensitive Debussy made of all this we are not told!

But hopes for *Le martyre* were dashed on this occasion by Astruc's bankruptcy and surrender of the lease on the Théâtre des Champs-Élysées. Debussy tried to save the situation on 19 October (ANN, p. 91) and wrote firmly to Astruc:

> After rethinking the matter carefully, I believe that you are wrong to give up *our* theatre [see Fig. 14]. People will certainly descend on you because of this desertion. It would [be better], in my humble opinion, to continue the struggle, and if you go under it is worth more to do so in the cause of beauty.

You have not given sufficient thought to the fact that the transfer
of our company to the Opéra is absolutely impossible. They do not
go in for revolutions there, believe me. You have already found
many supporters; it is impossible that you will not find others!

From a letter to Inghelbrecht on 3 June 1915 (*US-NYcobb*) it would
appear that Astruc once again had plans for putting on *Le martyre*, but 'it
seems that the habitual spokes have been put in our wheels . . . Decidedly no
one likes music in Paris', Debussy complained bitterly.

Then on 3 December 1916 Debussy told Robert Godet (GOD, p. 163) that
Jacques Rouché, 'perfumer–director, has asked me to make an opera of Saint
Sebastian, keeping the music already written'. When asked his advice, however,
his 'only friend – alias Roderick Usher' proved less than enthusiastic. On 5
January 1917 Godet replied saying (*RdM*, 1962, pp. 82-3):

The musical ideas are not rich enough to guarantee you the option
and quality of their development . . . If the "lyrification" . . . of this
hieratic mystery requires that you should destroy the harmony of its
musical proportion either by curtailment or by introducing into it
entirely new and anomalous elements (through the quality of the
inspiration), that would seem to me to be a great pity. Everything
depends on knowing what the poetic alterations would consist of,
and if they would add incentives to the action.

But Debussy apparently went ahead and his last letter to Durand, on 1
November 1917 (DUR, p. 190), shows that he was thinking exclusively of his
theatrical projects at the point when the advanced state of his rectal cancer
forced him to give up music for ever. As he told his publisher: 'Laloy and I
have worked on the lyric version of *Le martyre de Saint Sébastien*; it is
strange that in these 3,995 or so verses, there is little that is austere. Just
words . . . words . . . I believe that we shall come through it all the same.'
According to Durand (1925, pp. 24-6), Rouché had asked for the operatic
version before the war, then declared it impractical, then revived the idea in
1916 due to the wartime celebrity of d'Annunzio's exploits, by which time
Debussy was too ill to do very much. The whereabouts of what he and Laloy
did manage to achieve is unknown.

Finally, Rouché did stage a revival of *Le martyre* with Ida Rubinstein and
Bakst's sets at the Opéra on 18 June 1922,[27] when the second (magic chamber)
act was cut completely, the fifth act choruses were sung from the wings, and
Caplet had to be replaced at the last moment as conductor by the chorus-
master Henry Defosse. Charles Tenroc wondered in *Comoedia* (19 June)
whether this was from 'an excess of devotion to the memory of a great composer whose score [Caplet] now believes to be sacrificed to and drowned by
the sumptuousness of its surroundings'. He also summed up the general verdict
when he concluded that 'In this long and slow-moving spectacle which lacks
profundity, the abundance of words and images submerges the music.' Only

those ever faithful to Debussy, like Laloy, still had kind words for Ida Rubinstein's brain-child as it tried to adjust its unwieldy frame to face up to the new brevity and changing aesthetics of the neo-classical 1920s. As Émile Vuillermoz put it (1920, p. 158), Debussy's '*Parsifal* still awaits its Bayreuth'.

11   The remaining incidental music (1899-1913) and the plays written in collaboration with René Peter

> Let me tell you that when it comes to the theatre, it is necessary to be wary of premature, over-hasty results . . . Generally a dismal, insignificant fate lies in wait for you at the crossroads of the first performance. Then there is nothing more that you can do, except weep!
>
> (Debussy to Gabriel Mourey, 30 October 1913, on the subject of the incidental music for *Psyché*; letter cited by kind permission of *US-A US*)

La tragédie de la mort, Les '*Frères en Art*' (*F.E.A.*) and the other Peter collaborations (1896-9)

Debussy's friendship with René Peter and his family began in the late 1880s. The author's elaborated reminiscences, however, make a precise date difficult to establish and the intimacy of their friendship tends to be magnified. If they met at a 'dinner at the Versailles home of the poet Maurice Vaucaire' when Debussy had just returned from the Villa Medici, then Peter would have been fifteen rather than 'eleven or twelve' (PET, p. 23). But no matter; René and Michel Peter were sons of the prominent Dr Michel Peter, 'the adversary and also the cousin of Pasteur' (LO, 1, p. 132). René had ambitions as a playwright and published several light comedies and farces written in association with Georges Feydeau, Robert Danceny and others from 1894 onwards.

Around 1896 Peter wrote a one-act verse play called *La tragédie de la mort* and 'timidly' brought it to Debussy for his opinion. According to Peter (PET, p. 211), Debussy suggested

> several improvements and even proposed a collaboration. This was the beginning of these 'theatre lessons' that a curious good fortune led me to receive from Debussy. Over a period of four years [1896-9] this enchanter in sound, with untirable patience, coped with words in my honour! And I must tell you that he took great pleasure in it.[1]

The precise chronology and even the number of the plays on which Peter

237

solicited advice is difficult to ascertain, though it would appear that the period involved is that covered by *La tragédie de la mort*, thus ending with Debussy's composition of a berceuse for it in April 1899. A process Debussy began in enthusiastic friendship became something of a diplomatic chore when his frank criticism of Peter's insubstantial comedies distressed their sensitive and insecure author. The most important result of the whole affair was Debussy's own completion of the comedy *Les 'Frères en Art'*, a *roman à clef* peopled from his own *fin-de-siècle* world, which outlines his own intense, left-wing artistic ideals in the years between the composition and performance of *Pelléas*.

After giving initial advice on *La tragédie de la mort* in 1896, Debussy persuaded his friend Pierre Louÿs to write a preface for it. This offered a welcome enhancement for Peter's fledgling career, as Louÿs had acquired a considerable poetic reputation since the publication of his *Chansons de Bilitis* in December 1894, and a certain notoriety after the appearance of *Aphrodite* in March 1896. Louÿs told his brother Georges (LOU, p. 85 n. 3) that a 'little preface for a friend' had been completed in the Hôtel de l'Oasis in Algiers on 20 January 1897, but that 'it is my first and I am less proud of it than of my sketches'. This dissatisfaction and Louÿs' nomadic lifestyle caused delays, and in December 1897 Debussy made repeated efforts to secure a finished draft of the preface before Louÿs left on another extended foreign trip. The reasons for his inaction that year also concerned the young French-speaking Moorish girl Zohra ben Brahim, whom he had met in March and had brought back to Paris the following month. She provided the inspiration for the additional *Chansons de Bilitis* (including *La chevelure* set by Debussy), and the tearful letter Louÿs wrote (LOU, p. 107) after their parting at Marseilles on 29 December reveals how close their attachment was.

But some form of preface must have reached Debussy early in 1898 because he wrote to Louÿs in Cairo on 27 March to say that proofs of it were on their way to him and that Peter was delighted with it (LOU, p. 110). However, Debussy was not of the same mind and recommended that his friend 'change the form of his preface' to use 'free verse', as in the rest of the play. So presumably publication was suspended, and when Louÿs did 'finally find a free evening to rewrite the preface' on 27 January 1899, his original had disappeared, 'undoubtedly by the hands of the spirits' (pp. 125-6). As, in true Ida Rubinstein style, he was leaving for the 'most inaccessible deserts of Africa' on the following Tuesday, Debussy obtained another copy of the play from René Peter and sent it to Louÿs; the final preface was duly delivered to Debussy at lunch on the day of Louÿs' departure (31 January). With help from Louÿs and Debussy, the complete verse drama (to whose text the latter may have contributed) was published by the Société du Mercure de France in August 1899.[2] In February 1900 Peter sent Louÿs a copy with a verse dedication in imitation of his own *Chansons de Bilitis*:

Pour le jour des Hyacinthies,
il m'a donné la plus belle préface
Sertie dans son style magique
et qui est douce à mon orgueil!
Comme le miel . . .

The composition of Debussy's incidental music was almost as protracted and probably only came about when the play was provisionally accepted for production by André Antoine. Peter tells us diplomatically that it was never performed due to a 'disagreement over the interpretation'. But early in 1898 he needed a 'berceuse for the opening scene, where an anxious mother bends over the cradle of her baby who is near to death' (PET, p. 105). On 15 February Debussy told Peter (p. 212):

> My conclusion is that a northern ballad must be found which can be adapted to the berceuse. There cannot be a question of *composing music*, that would appear too pretentious in the context. I do not think that this will be difficult and I should be only too glad to do this myself, though I haven't much time at the moment.

By 6 May Debussy had done little except think about the berceuse, but was anxious that Peter should not think him idle. 'I intend to envelop in music the ballad of the child crowned with flowers', he reported, changing his approach (PET, p. 213). 'Up till now I have scoured books of popular songs in vain; I dream, in other respects, of giving up these researches to try to find something myself which owes nothing to anyone.'

Peter then goes off at a tangent to describe Debussy's unsuccessful bet on a horse called Brahma (p. 214) which is compared with the composer's slow 'race' to complete the berceuse. Debussy, in his April 1899 dedication, excused himself for 'momentarily taking up a "poitevin"[3] accent', which Peter tells us (p. 105) was a typical Debussy hoax to cover for all the time he had supposedly spent in his folkloric research, for *La tragédie de la mort* was not even set in a specific country. In any event, Debussy advised Peter that 'one should not think that the berceuse is designed to put the audience to sleep! I believe that it will work, being as simple as a blade of grass and singable in any situation.' (p. 105)

Sadly, it was sung in no 'situation' whatsoever and the monodic *Berceuse pour la 'Tragédie de la mort' sur une vieille chanson poitevine* remains in manuscript form (see Appendix) with its text suitably apostrophised to make it look authentic (see Ex. 61). Its four simple strophes, sung by the mother to her dying child, tell the story of a fairy who finds a child crying because his flowers have faded. The fairy showers flowers from her own white sceptre over the child's head and shoulders, scattering the child's first faded blooms. But the child throws these new garlands to the ground angrily and the fairy tells him, 'as some flowers die, others are born; it is your good fortune you are parting with'.

The start, Ex. 61, is typical of Debussy's seventy-one-bar setting in the

Ex. 61. *La tragédie de la mort*, *US-Wc*, p. 1, bars 1-8

Ex. 62. *Berceuse*, verse 2, from *La tragédie de la mort*, *US-Wc*, p. 1, bars 25-7
[LA MÈRE]

dorian mode, which covers a range of only an octave from c' to c''. Phrase B (twelve bars) answers A (Ex. 61) and is extended simply to fourteen and seventeen bars at the end in the overall form: A B B B$_1$ A B$_2$. At times the words seem fitted to the preconceived melody, rather than *vice versa*, as the unnatural prosody of Ex. 62 (from section B) suggests. This repetitive piece, devoid of any musical characterisation, is unique in Debussy's output: perhaps one day Peter's play will be performed so that it can be heard in its proper context for the first time.

Debussy's 'theatre lessons' seem to have been even less organised and technical than his contemporary piano tuition.[4] 'His way of constructing a scene, of arranging an entry or special effect owed little to the rigorous technique of a Scribe or a Sardou, and my theatrical débuts suffered cruelly from this', Peter recalls (PET, p. 77). After André Antoine had been bewildered by a protracted three-act drama by Peter, he too offered some fairly basic suggestions. But Debussy did not want to hear about them, having 'never shown more than a passing interest in the flights of fancy of the Théâtre Libre'. Surprisingly, Peter tells us that Debussy was 'little drawn towards modern dramatic productions . . . having only contempt for the "sham" theatre of Henri Bataille and making an exception only for that of [Maurice] Donnay,[5] which enchanted him'. Bearing in mind his interest in Maeterlinck and Ibsen, all this seems most unlikely, and we know that Debussy went to first performances of new plays by his friends at least, such as *La possédée* by Victor-Émile Michelet at the Théâtre des Arts in 1909.[6]

In this imperfect state of affairs Debussy and René Peter began their next collaboration, a fairy-tale in fourteen tableaux which progressed no further than its derivative title: *Les mille et une nuits de n'importe où et d'ailleurs* (PET, pp. 77-8). This was followed by the more significant dramatic satire *Les 'Frères en Art'*[7] whose subject was the formation of a secret society of same name designed to promote unity rather than rivalry between the arts and artists, and to promulgate their works in their best interests, by-passing commercial agents. As Richard Langham Smith points out (RLS, p. 8), 'This pipe dream is interesting not only as a curious echo of the Pre-Raphaelite Brotherhood, which was becoming widely publicised in France during the nineties, but also as an artistic counterpart to the militant anarchist unions.'[8] Camille Pissarro, amongst others, held similar views even earlier than Debussy (see Lockspeiser, *RdM*, 1970, pp. 170-1).

Some time in 1897, in the early planning stages of *Les 'Frères en Art'* (to which Debussy referred on several occasions as *F.E.A.*), Debussy wrote to René Peter's sister-in-law Alice, to whom he seems to have been attracted,[9] expressing his reservations about the play (PET, p. 87).

> Naturally, I have done nothing about *F.E.A.*! The excitement of the first few days has transformed itself into something to be mistrusted, and the possibility of looking at things dispassionately has led me to reflect, perhaps too deeply. It seemed to me that to set such an enterprise in motion, it was necessary to be more anxious to get to know the minds of all these people better. One is inventing nothing, alas, and the knowledge of the human heart represents the sum total of innumerable experiences. The characters of the comedy, themselves, conspire to make the task difficult by varying their points of view in such a way that it is impossible to maintain an opinion about them for longer than the space of an evening!
>
> Therefore, one must generalise to excess. At least in taking the characters in groups one has more chance to express the truth about some of them. On this observation, I beg you to consider *Les tisserands*[10] as a much more perfect masterpiece than is generally thought. To tell you the truth, I do not yet consider myself stalwart enough to muck out the stables of Augeas, and it is necessary to do a bit of that here!
>
> There is no need for René to be upset about all this, nor should it prevent him from seeking more immediate glory. Me, I am an old romantic who flings any cares about success out of the windows! That is why I am not writing to him: I prefer to avail myself of you.

Most of the characters in *Les 'Frères en Art'* are portraits of prominent people of the time, thinly disguised under fictional names: Maltravers, the painter, is Debussy himself; Marie, his mistress, is Lilly Texier (according to Peter); the English art critic, James Redburne, is probably Swinburne (with elements of George Moore and Ruskin); Hildebrand, another painter, is probably the art historian and sculptor Adolf von Hildebrand; St Diaz, the art critic, may represent Diaz de la Peña, a pupil of Delacroix; and so on (see

Lockspeiser, *RdM*, 1970, pp. 172-3). The society is the brain-child of M. Durtal in the first tableau, and its name (we are told in scene 5) was invented by his wife.

Like many communistic enterprises, Les Frères en Art begin with ideals of liberty, equality and fraternity. But somehow the reality always proves different, and in this case it is Maltravers himself (whom we meet in scene 6 of tableau 1) whose strongly held views (a mixture of intellectual anarchy, meritoriousness and pantheism) threaten the stability of the new society at its first meeting in tableau 3. Maltravers's artistic anarchy can be seen in his wish to destroy all libraries because they contain only 'changing aspects of the same truth, which is rather to be found in a tree or the colour of a sky than in books'. His meritoriousness appears in scene 3 of the second tableau in his speech to Raland in which he says 'talent serves only to designate the mediocre . . . Leave this word for the so-called amateurs in art . . . we are dying of mediocrity!' And in the third and final tableau he claims pantheistically: 'Art is the flame in the young, new light of the morning; it is when sometimes the sun shines gently, or in the days which finish in an orgy of gold and blood like the Egyptian kings . . . It is liberty and *you* make a formula out of it', he concludes (with allusions to Ruskin and Turner), destroying the harmony at the first gathering of the artistic brotherhood as he demolishes the argument of the composer Valady. The loosely constructed text ends with the wives of the members discussing the meeting, though like the first tableau this is incomplete.

When René Peter published the first three scenes of the second tableau (PET, pp. 78-85), he maintained that he and Debussy got no farther with this because a theatre director (? Antoine) expressed interest in the play and Debussy did not wish to make his theatrical début with a non-musical work (p. 85) – that is, before *Pelléas et Mélisande* reached the stage. The Peter extract is thus a first version, probably dating from 1897 and is not the same as the Meyer manuscript text, which may date from about 1903[11] as it mentions telephones and cinematographic techniques. Some of the names are changed slightly in this later (completed) version (Durtel becomes Durtal; Heldebrand becomes Hildebrand) and Debussy cuts out a discussion by Maltravers and Marie (PET, pp. 82-3), both to bring Maltravers's friend Raland back on the scene more quickly, and to avoid exposing Maltravers's serious reservations about Durtal and his new society until the final tableau. This, incidentally, is the only point in the play where there is any specific reference to music (in this case Boieldieu's opera *La dame blanche*) and Raland even decides to follow the more knowledgeable Maltravers's advice and describe the composer Rollinat as a 'poet' rather than a 'musician' in future.

Les 'Frères en Art' is also of interest because it affords, at the start of the second tableau, a glimpse into Debussy's domestic arrangements with Lilly Texier. One line added by Debussy in his revision is Raland's remark that the couple 'are as silent as little goldfish', implying that they have little to say to each other and live an enclosed, goldfish-bowl existence. Marie is 'a delightful woman and nothing more', with an ideal of cosy domesticity that threatens to stifle the creative Maltravers. It is also significant that Marie's role was pruned by Debussy, which further suggests that the revision took place after he had decided to leave Lilly. At the only moment when the couple embrace, Debussy adds the cool direction 'nothing more, nothing less', which is not found in the early Peter version.

Debussy's views as expressed in his other writings are everywhere apparent in the character of Maltravers, who has by far the profoundest observations in the play. 'I come from the working classes', he reveals in the final tableau,

> and I do not seek to hide the fact. I also believe that from this
> melting-pot of suffering and hatred, and only from this strength
> represented by the people will the most beautiful works of art arise.
> The only problem is that the common people do not like art . . .
> They feel rather like intruders or poor relations! You see traces of
> this in almost all anarchical schemes which apply to them: the
> propagation of art is not included. Is this a bad thing? I don't think
> so. One will never stop people genuinely born to love art from
> satisfying their passion, it will simply become more disinterested.
> And I maintain that Art, with a capital A, will eventually regain all
> her beauty and will no longer serve to conceal opinions or non-
> entities, as it so often does nowadays.

In reality, Debussy refused to give details about his early life, and it was only beneath this cloak of anonymity that he felt free to express himself so bluntly. He did not mention the reactions to his upbringing, later encouraged by Emma, which made him a luxury-loving capitalist *par excellence*, who avoided 'people' and the market-place like the plague after his privacy was threatened by the success of *Pelléas et Mélisande*.

Next, according to Peter (p. 88), came the comedy *Le roman de Rosette*, for which Debussy gave his customary advice and even designed an original frontispiece (see Auguste Martin, p. 52, no. 219). There is a possibility that Debussy's long critical letter of 24 October 1898 (LL, p. 96), for once written direct to René Peter, refers to this project. In any case, it is worth quoting in full for the light it sheds on Debussy's attitudes to their collaboration and to the theatre in general. He writes:

> To say to someone 'you have made a mistake' has never been easy for
> the one who has to say it, nor pleasant for the one to whom this blunt
> statement is addressed. Moreover, I do not really know where one
> acquires the right to assert that anyone has made an error? . . . To
> start at the beginning, the kinship of your work with the theatrical
> genre that I detest the most is a reason for me to deplore it. Whilst I
> am on the subject, the characters are somewhat hastily drawn, the
> whole thing is hasty and dry, and the style, whilst containing some
> pretty details, does not appear to me to be sufficiently theatrical. In

addition to which, I believe that the masterpiece written according to this formula will be a long time in coming! . . . Do you see, one is not dealing here with the daily routine of life, which is both too awful and too profoundly beautiful; the transformations wherein one tries to encapsulate its mystery or its banality will always be wrong. Observe how the beauty of Ibsen's theatre is an exception. Now . . . I can make a mistake . . . and before going on with this adventure I should like to see you consult someone better informed than me, to whose judgment you should commit yourself.

For myself, the success that you would gather here seems injurious to me and would not make me take an interest in you. You can and should do better. It is only the mediocre who are discouraged by bad experiences, the others derive new strength from them to arrive at a definite and special alchemy. It should be your aim at any price to be a party to this.

Also in 1898 another comedy, *L'utile aventure*, came close to performance because Debussy happened to be in Reynolds' Bar at the same time as the actor M. Chautard, recently appointed director of the Théâtre du Gymnase, who was persuaded to consider it (PET, pp. 218-21). But there seems to have been trouble with this collaboration too, and Debussy told another mutual friend Mme Dansaert:[12]

> every time one tries to explain even the slightest opinion, one falls into the most regrettable misunderstandings! Nevertheless, *L'utile aventure* should not become *La noire aventure*. Therefore, please explain to René that there is not any tragedy involved, and that *L'utile aventure* can and should remain a well-executed piece of work.
>
> The trouble is that I have the disagreeable habit of perhaps saying things rather too assuredly because it seems necessary to me *that they should be said thus*, all for the greatest good of *René Peter*! This is worth much more than the watery opinions of heaps of people, whom it is not necessary to name as they are too many. Reassure René and assure him of my ardent and 'troublesome' friendship.

Despite several dinners and pressure from Peter, by the time it came to making a decision Chautard's associate director Alphonse Franck had become sole director of the Théâtre du Gymnase and the comedy was dropped, to be renamed by its authors *L'inutile aventure*!

Then, probably in 1899, there was the unfinished comedy collaboration *L'herbe tendre*, which included the character Julien Grippon (PET, p. 222, n. 2), and the farce *Esther et la maison de fous*, which, as Dietschy puts it (1962, p. 132), 'petered out'! A letter to Pierre Louÿs (*US-AUS*) mentions Michel Peter sending Debussy's short story *La grève des fous* to the 'concours du *Journal*', but the only sign of the project is a brief synopsis by Debussy in the collection of Mme René Peter (cited in Dietschy, 1962, p. 136, n. 1). It runs, improbably, as follows:

Esther had always been devoted to the service of the State, as her original position as courtesan proves . . . However, one day when her latest lover commented rather cruelly on the dilapidated state of her bosom, she pronounced the historic words: 'Farewell, beasts of burden! The days of wine and roses are over!' From then on she was known as the Lady in Black and invested the fruits of her nightly labours in the purchase of the lunatic asylum (*maison de fous*) at Bécon-les-Bruyères . . . From there emerged most of the world's famous madmen . . . like Prince Hamlet . . . and Roderick Usher.

Esther et la maison de fous was yet another product of Debussy's fertile theatrical imagination which never got beyond the drawing-board. And before *Pelléas* took up all his time, he turned his attention in 1900 away from Peter towards a friend he held in higher literary esteem, Pierre Louÿs. Peter continued in his own superficial way, though *Chiffon*,[13] his first comedy to be performed (in 1904), was, inevitably, approved by Debussy (PET, p. 196).

Pierre Louÿs and the *Chansons de Bilitis* (1900-1)

Debussy had already set three of Louÿs' evocative *Chansons de Bilitis* in 1897-8 before the question of an accompanied recitation arose. *La chevelure* was composed from a copy sent to him by the author in May 1897 in advance of its publication in *L'image* (no. 11, Oct 1897, p. 339), and the songs were first performed as a group by Blanche Marot and Debussy on 17 March 1900. In the same year a recital of eleven other poems was planned with synchronised incidental music for two flutes, two harps and celesta at the Théâtre des Variétés (letter to Debussy of 25 October 1900; LOU, pp. 150-1), though the true origins of this date back to October 1898 when Debussy attended a lecture on Louÿs' poems by M. A. Segard. After this he had cause to doubt whether his vocal settings added anything to a 'pure and simple reading' of the poems, and he even told Louÿs (LOU, p. 118) that the music served 'clumsily to dispel the audience's emotion' which the poetry had stimulated. 'What is the use', he continued on 16 October, 'of harmonising the voice of Bilitis, either in the major or the minor, when she herself has the most persuasive voice in the world?' He found the 'other [musical] décor' he sought, which allowed Bilitis to 'speak alone', in the later conception of recitation interspersed with music, mime and *tableaux vivants*.

By 15 January 1901 Debussy had finished his incidental music, but now the Salle des Fêtes of *Le journal* was causing as many problems as the Théâtre des Variétés had the previous year.[14] While Louÿs wrote to his brother about afternoons happily spent in rehearsals with 'nude female models who are going to represent the eleven *Chansons de Bilitis*', Debussy was complaining that with only a fortnight left, the organisers of the *Journal* were 'drunkards, or rather "journalists" '! No instrumentalists had been hired, no music copied; everything remained in their imagination. 'Assuredly there is something rotten in *this* state of Denmark!'[15] he told Louÿs on 31 January, and he thought it vital to have at least one ensemble rehearsal before the dress-rehearsal. 'Without this, the result with be little short of scandalous!' he justly complained.

But in the end the series of *tableaux vivants*, performed *chez Le journal* on 7 February with Mlle Milton as reciter, was enthusiastically received by its élite private audience. *Le journal* reported on 8 February (LOU, pp. 195-6) that 'M. de Bussy's [*sic*] gracious and ingeniously archaic music ... accompanied Mlle Milton's voice and combined with her in a soothing rhythm, whose charm added to the antique beauties of the poetry.' Just what Debussy had set out to achieve, in fact. The 'impeccable figures' of 'Mlles Loulii, Marcel, Darcy, Marie Chaves, Lucienne Delbeau etc.', beneath their artistic drapes, helped create the 'ideal dreamed of by the poet', and doubtless the lesbian undertones of the poetry added a certain fascination and spice to the 'soirée privée'. However, only ten tableaux were listed in the review in *Le journal*, with *Chanson* (no. 4)[16] and *Le souvenir de Mnasidica* (no. 11) being omitted, and *L'eau pure de bassin* (no. 9) coming before *Les courtisanes Égyptiennes* (no. 8).

No music was performed while the poems were recited, but Ex. 63 gives some idea of the careful way the fragile atmospheric music was inserted into breaks in the poetry. After the final two lines, five more bars in similar arabesque vein add the second harp and celesta (in Boulez's realisation) to complete *Le tombeau sans nom* (no. 7). Perhaps for practical reasons the 1901 score was kept extremely simple (mostly modal or whole-tone melodies with filigree accompaniment), and it was not until their July 1914 expansion as the *Épigraphes antiques* for piano duet that any development or formal complexity appears. In 1901 only nos. 4, 10 and 12 contained two different sections: in the first two cases the second sections are elaborations of the first,

Ex. 63. *Chansons de Bilitis*, no. 7: *Le tombeau sans nom*, *F-Pn* MS 16280, score pp. 9-10

Mnasidica m'ayant prise par la main
  me mena hors des portes de la ville,
  jusqu'à un petit champ inculte
  où il y avait une stèle de marbre.
  Et elle me dit:
  'Celle-ci fut l'amie de ma mère.'

Alors je sentis un grand frisson,
  et sans cesser de lui tenir la main
  je me penchai sur son épaule,
  afin de lire les quatre vers
  entre la coupe creuse et le serpent:

'Ce n'est pas la mort qui m'a enlevée,
  mais les Nymphes des fontaines.
  Je repose ici sous une terre légère
  avec la chevelure coupée de Xanthô.
  Qu'elle seule me pleure.
  Je ne dis pas mon nom.'

Longtemps nous sommes restées debout, et nous n'avons pas versé la libation.
Car comment appeler une âme inconnue d'entre les foules de l'Hadès?

* doubled by fl II in parts (added in pencil, not by Debussy)

whereas the final section of *La pluie au matin* is a cyclic reprise of the opening *Chant pastoral*. The following table shows how a mere 100 of the 158 bars written in 1900-1 became 273 bars in 1914 when new central sections were added to *Épigraphes* 1–4, and nos. 5 and 6 were completely recomposed. The titles do not always correspond either, as one might expect them to.

1901	1914
1 *Chant pastoral*	1 *Pour invoquer Pan, dieu du vent d'été* bars 1-16, 33-6
2 *Les comparaisons*	unused
3 *Les contes*	unused
4 *Chanson*	3 *Pour que la nuit soit propice* bars 1-11
5 *La partie d'osselets*	unused
6 *Bilitis*	unused
7 *Le tombeau sans nom*	2 *Pour un tombeau sans nom* bars 1-2, 5-6, 8-12
8 *Les courtisanes Égyptiennes* flute 1 bars 5-9	2 *Pour un tombeau sans nom* bars 28-32

9 *L'eau pure du bassin*	unused
10 *La danseuse aux crotales*	4 *Pour la danseuse aux crotales*
bars 1-14	bars 1-14
bars 19-28	bars 52-61
11 *Le souvenir du Mnasidica*	
start	5 *Pour l'Égyptienne* cf rhythm
	bars 27ff
flute bars 5-13[17]	2 *Pour un tombeau sans nom*
	bars 25-7
12 *La pluie au matin*	6 *Pour remercier la pluie au*
	matin
bars 2-3	bars 5-6
bars 13-15, 18-21	cf bars 55-63
(cyclic recall of no. 1)	

Le Roi Lear (1904)

René Peter unhelpfully gives two accounts of how Debussy's incidental music intended for Antoine's production of *King Lear* came into being. One is that just before rehearsals began for *Pelléas et Mélisande* in 1902 he obtained the commission for Debussy, who refused to follow the matter up (PET, p. 221). The other, more likely explanation is that Debussy heard about Antoine's proposed production and asked Peter (who knew him better) to arrange matters (PET, p. 155). This is also borne out by Antoine's memoir of 8 January 1904 (1928, p. 228):[18] 'I shall need incidental music for *Le Roi Lear*, but I should like something of character. My friend René Peter suggested Claude Debussy to me and it would fulfil my dream if the young master would accept.' The account Peter gives of a backstage conversation between Antoine and Debussy (cap in hand, taking insults about musicians and composers in general) seems highly spurious. It is hardly likely that Debussy would have written as much as he did for a director who was 'bored' by music and musicians, considered composers 'complete cretins', and would only consider music for *Lear* if it 'didn't take up too much room, and didn't get in the way of the text or distract the audience's attention'! The fact that Antoine used a youthful score by Edmond Missa[19] for the delayed opening on 5 December 1904 shows that he *was* concerned that music should play a part in his Shakespearean adaptation.

As is well known, 1904 was a turning-point in Debussy's life, and his elopement to Jersey and Dieppe with Emma left little time for composition (other than piano music) that summer. Antoine's production of *Lear* had in fact been ready since early April, but had had to be delayed due to the phenomenal success of *Oiseaux de passage* by Maurice Donnay and Lucien Descaves (see

Antoine, 1928, pp. 230-1) which was retained till the end of the season in July and also used to open the new season on 15 September. By then Antoine had managed to contact Debussy on his extended honeymoon in Dieppe and received an unoptimistic response on 20 September (1928, p. 239) about his incidental music which, 'if it does not pretend to add anything to the glory of Shakespeare', was still considered 'necessary'. Debussy, for his part, was annoyed at Antoine's continual postponements and now it appeared that he had suddenly decided he needed the score by 1 October, which for Debussy was an impossibility.

> Bear in mind that besides my writing the music, it will be necessary . . . for the musicians to rehearse at least twice before they come into contact with the stage.
> On this subject, can you assure me that there will be *thirty musicians*? Will you have the necessary room for them? This is the minimum number that I can use, without which we shall have nothing but a feeble little sound like flies rubbing their legs together!

On 26 September, Antoine decided, realistically, that Debussy could not be relied on, and took his conductor M. Bretonneau's advice about using Edmond Missa's score. Even though the première was further delayed by over two months, he probably had no wish to hire thirty musicians for what might (and did) turn out to be an extensive run. Whilst Antoine never mentioned Missa's music again, *Le Roi Lear* proved a turning-point in Antoine's career, its immense success showing him 'a new direction' (1928, p. 248) away from the 'bourgeois and contemporary comedies' that he had relied on in the past. But although the Théâtre Antoine's 3400 seats were filled at every one of the sixty performances until 15 July 1905, Antoine still managed to lose 3000 francs due to his vast production costs and his policy of cheap seats. So Debussy's benefit (had he got his thirty musicians) would have been artistic rather than financial, and perhaps his misgivings about Antoine were wise after all.

The music Debussy actually wrote for *Le Roi Lear* consisted first of a *Fanfare d'ouverture* (rather more imaginative than the one which later began the third act of *Le martyre de Saint Sébastien*), and second of the beautiful *Sommeil de Lear*, presumably the 'soft music' which is played as Lear lies asleep in 'a tent in the French camp' at the start of Act 4 scene 7. Both were published by Jobert (1926) in an orchestration by Roger-Ducasse. Of the five other movements Debussy intended to write, only a few assertive bars of a prelude have survived in short score (Ex. 64), which were dedicated to Georges Jean-Aubry in July 1908 (see Boucher, Plate 43 (2)).

Like Verdi, Debussy had great plans but achieved little with Shakespeare's *King Lear* and once the prospect of a stage performance had passed, he seems to have lost interest. Despite assurances to Durand in September–October 1905 and in August 1906 that he was working on the score, which Édouard

Ex. 64. *Le Roi Lear*, *Prélude*

Colonne was anxious to conduct, little seems to have been done. The inclusion of *Le Roi Lear* as 'in the press' in a Durand catalogue of 1910 was (to quote Lear himself) 'nothing . . . come of nothing'.[20]

L'histoire de Tristan, Psyché and the other Gabriel Mourey projects (1907-13)

The projects with Gabriel Mourey are best discussed in a group, even though the flute solo known as *Syrinx* was virtually their only tangible result in terms of incidental music. According to Mourey (p. 747), he and Debussy first met in 1889, the year in which his translation of Poe's poetry appeared. Mourey mentions Debussy's 'extraordinary charm' at this time, though he was generally 'uncommunicative . . . reserved, silent and rather mysterious . . . and not of those who talk a lot and say nothing'. Mourey himself was extremely versatile, being a skilled poet, playwright, critic and translator. He was an authority on Swinburne and Odilon Redon, a Wagnerite, and had many friends in common with Debussy in literary and occult circles, such as Villiers de l'Isle-Adam, Catulle Mendès, Jules Bois, Mallarmé and later d'Annunzio. His explicitly lesbian one-act play *Lawn-tennis*, understandably turned down by Antoine for the Théâtre Libre in May 1891, has similarities with *Jeux* but was never considered as a model. Camille and Elaine go much further than the three coy dancers in Nijinsky's supposedly daring scenario twenty-two years later, and Mourey's 'mixed doubles' were extremely short-lived!

In July 1907 Mourey offered Debussy a libretto based on *Le roman de Tristan* by the medievalist Joseph Bédier,[21] which the composer enthusiastically outlined to Victor Segalen in a discussion on 8 October that year (SEG, p. 74). In the first act the dwarf Foncin reveals to King Mark that Tristan is the queen's lover. Mark does not believe this, but Isolda's guilt is proven and she is seized and abandoned in a leper colony, from which she is rescued by

Tristan. The second act is set in a forest where the fugitives are worn out by their misery. Act 3 is set on a white moorland, though Debussy tells us nothing about the action. In the final act, Tristan becomes mad and is betrayed by 'Isolda of the white hands'. The ensuing death of Tristan moved Debussy deeply, especially the line 'Je ne puis plus tenir ma vie.' But he admitted to Segalen, 'Mourey's prose is not very lyrical and many passages do not exactly "invite" music.' Mourey (p. 748) tells of Debussy being 'strangely moved' by the project; as was so often the case with collaborators, Mourey 'admired his marvellous sense of literary requirements, of artistic fitness'.

In fact, as Debussy explained to Segalen on 26 July 1907 (SEG, pp. 62-3):

> I read Bédier's *Roman de Tristan* when it first appeared and immediately wanted to make an opera out of it, so beautiful did it appear to me, and so much did it seem necessary to restore to Tristan his legendary character which had been so deformed by Wagner . . . Then I forgot this project until recently, when Mourey (whom I had not seen for years) came to visit me and talked about his plans for Tristan. My enthusiasm, sadly asleep I admit, woke up, and I accepted!

But although Debussy did work at the libretto of *Le roman de Tristan* (which soon became *L'histoire de Tristan*) in 1907 and the project was an-nounced in the press on 5 August, he was prevented from going further by a complex literary tangle. Before Debussy and Mourey lighted on *Le roman de Tristan*, Bédier's cousin Louis Artus had prepared his own scenario from it and had secured an exclusive licence from its author to adapt it for the theatre. When he learned of the rival plans, Artus suddenly wanted Debussy, the celebrated member of the Société des Auteurs, to collaborate on his scenario instead. When Debussy declined, Artus adopted a 'dog-in-the-manger' attitude, though as Dietschy points out (1962, p. 189), Debussy would hardly have been enthusiastic about working with the '*vaudevilliste* who had written *La culotte*'. Bédier was willing for Debussy to write music for *Tristan*, but Artus remained adamant and even prevented him from collaborating direct with his cousin in April 1909.

It was at this juncture that Mourey suggested three other projects:[22] *Huon de Bordeaux*,[23] which Debussy dismissed as 'falling back on characters in helmets and ready-made legend'; *Le marchand de rêves*, which he preferred because 'in fixing nothing, it permits anything . . . there is more fairyland in our era than M. Clemenceau supposes,[24] it is simply a question of finding it'; and *Le chat botté* (after La Fontaine), a 'strong, well-known piece, which makes the transformation that one would need to employ in it more easily accessible to the public'. *Puss in Boots* was thus the second pantomime (in the English sense) which Debussy had seriously contemplated, the first being *Cinderella (Cendrelune)* with Louÿs in 1895 (see Chapter 12).

Debussy was, however, still hoping to work with Bédier in May 1910, as he told Laloy (who had first brought them together). Far from abandoning the idea in the face of Artus' selfish intransigence, or for work on *Le martyre* and *Khamma*, Debussy was still discussing the project in 1912. Henri Büsser (1955, p. 185) reports how in March 1912 Debussy saw its conception as dramatically opposed to that of Wagner, and observed after meeting Debussy and Dukas at a performance of *Tristan* at the Opéra on 20 June that year that Debussy found it 'terribly boring' as he 'doubtless had his own *Tristan* in mind'.[25] But by June 1916, he conceded to Segalen (SEG, p. 141) that 'one must leave heroes to their legends, without which they become ridiculous and bombastic', and it was the *Tristan et Iseut* of Bédier and Artus which was finally performed with incidental music by Paul Ladmirault at the Palais de la Méditerranée in Nice on 30 January 1929.[26]

Many letters survive concerning the *Tristan* project, and (as we saw in Chapter 4 where it was mentioned as *La légende de Tristan*) Debussy sold Gatti-Casazza the first option on it for the Metropolitan, New York, along with his Poe operas in June 1908. He even sent Durand one of its '363 themes' (in true Wagnerian leitmotif style) from his holiday in Pourville on 23 August 1907 (Ex. 65). This is sadly all the music that survives from a project that Debussy preferred to Segalen's *Siddartha* and to which he 'gave the maximum curiosity of which I am capable' (SEG, p. 78).

Ex. 65. 'l'un des 363 thèmes du "Roman de Tristan" ', DUR, p. 54

Finally, in 1913 Mourey again approached Debussy, this time to compose incidental music for his three-act dramatic poem *Psyché*.[27] Debussy, busy trying to finish *La boîte à joujoux*, was reluctant at first. 'Have you thought what genius would be needed to rejuvenate this tired old myth, already so exploited that it seems that the feathers of the wings of love are all whittled away by it?' he asked Mourey.[28] But Mourey persisted with the private performance he planned at the home of Louis Mors in November, and Debussy finally agreed to compose a piece to be played from the wings, representing 'the last melody that Pan plays before his death' (Mourey, p. 748). Prophetically, Debussy had written about this as he concluded his article on taste earlier that year (LCr, p. 224):

The beauty of a work of art will always remain mysterious. That is to say, one will never be able to discover exactly 'how it was done'. Let us preserve, at all costs, this magic which is peculiar to music . . . When the god Pan had assembled the seven pipes of the syrinx, he was at first able only to imitate the long, melancholy note of the toad lamenting in the moonlight. Later, he competed with birdsong.

On 30 October Debussy asked Mourey:[29]

Would it be possible for Mme Mors to postpone the dates you gave me until the month of December? Here is why: it is materially impossible that the music will be ready, and don't forget that rehearsal time must also be included. Further, on reflection, the few moans uttered by the choir will appear ridiculous if this is all the music necessary during the second act, for the simple reason that they will be connected to absolutely nothing!

Do you not see that it would be more reasonable to stick to your first idea of *La flûte de Pan*? On 14 November I must be in Lausanne to rehearse and conduct a concert which takes place on Monday 17th. So you see how little time is left.

Then followed the advice on the too-hasty production of theatre music which opened this chapter, though Debussy does not seem to have stuck to it, for on 24 November he told Mourey[30] that he had still not finished this piece which 'in truth . . . is a devil! Have you a flautist?' he asked the author, 'or do you want *me* to find one?' So most of *La flûte de Pan*, which Louis Fleury first performed *chez* Louis Mors on 1 December 1913, was in fact written in a very few days at the end of November. It was renamed *Syrinx* by Jobert for publication in August 1927, at which juncture bar-lines were added by Marcel Moyse.[31]

A perfect, self-contained monody is perhaps the most challenging of all compositions, as Debussy well knew, and his evocative flute solo has, together with *Jeux*, exercised a special fascination for contemporary analysts. Not wishing to lose touch with reality in semiotic approaches outside the framework of Debussy's experience, my own view is that *Syrinx* is a living adaptation of sonata form, with A_1 and B_1 (Ex. 66) as the main, sinuous rhythmic ideas; A_2 and B_2 as linked subsidiary motifs; and C providing a lyrical contrast as a kind of second subject. C is introduced by the end of B_2 in bar 6, which is itself an extension of A_2 (see Ex. 66). The development section (bars 9-25) is mostly concerned with aspects of B, though it often loses its triplet rhythm and thus assumes aspects of A_1, which is itself developed in bars 13 and 21. The 'recapitulation' (bars 26ff) is mostly of A_1, but this is gradually fused with the triplet rhythm of B_1 (bar 30; Ex. 67). Bars 31-5 have the function of a coda but combine this with recapitulation and further development of B_1, plus a reference to C (Ex. 67). The formal subtlety arises from the increasingly close links between the various aspects of the arabesque ideas A and B. A, B and C are differentiated only by their rhythmic character-

Ex. 66. *Syrinx*, motifs

A₁, bars 1-2

A₂, bar 4

B₁, end of bar 4

B₂, bars 5-6

C, bars 7-8

Ex. 67. *Syrinx*, bar 30 – end

istics, with the further feature that C acts as an auditory landmark to show when a section is about to end, whilst each section begins with A_1.

Gabriel Mourey later described *La flûte de Pan*, which has the same title as the first of Debussy's *Chansons de Bilitis*, as (p. 748) 'a real jewel of restrained emotion, of sadness, of plastic beauty, of discreet tenderness and poetry'. I could not wish to improve on such an eloquent description.

12 *As you like it;* Louÿs, Segalen and the projects from *Pelléas* onwards (1895-1917)

> I was dreaming . . . Should I draw myself up some precise plan? . . . Should I finish some pieces? . . . So many questions put forward by a childish conceit and the need to rid oneself at any price of an idea that one has lived with for too long.
>
> (Debussy before the first meeting with Monsieur Croche, antidilettante, in *La revue blanche* (1 July 1901); LCr, p. 47)
>
> I have this curious need to leave works unfinished, which does not satisfy the contrary 'needs' of my editor at all.
>
> (Debussy to Gabriel Mourey, 6 January 1909; letter cited by kind permission of *US-AUS*)

As you like it (1886, 1917); *Comme il vous plaira* (1902-3)

Debussy's intentions to compose music for Shakespeare's *As you like it* span an even longer period than his Poe operas and recur at key moments to frame the remainder of his theatrical career. Two of the schemes were for incidental music: first, in Rome in 1886 for an adaptation by Maurice Vaucaire about which little is known (see PET, p. 24); and second, for a production by Firmin Gémier in 1917 with a translation by Paul-Jean Toulet. As André Schaeffner observes (1964, p. 453),[1] Gémier was only the second theatre director Debussy himself approached (the first being Antoine with *King Lear*), and coincidentally both efforts concerned Shakespearean projects. Gémier, who had begun his career with Antoine in 1887, had succeeded him as director of the Théâtre Antoine in 1906 and as director of the Odéon in 1914. Like Romain Rolland, Gémier was inspired by the idea of theatre for the people, and he shared Debussy's views on the grandeur and possibilities of art in the open air.[2]

In between came the project for an opera, which alone used the French title *Comme il vous plaira*. This was planned in three acts and five tableaux in 1902-3, Toulet's libretto being completed (apart from the 'final *divertissement*') by 14 September 1903 (Toulet, 1927, p. 59).[3] But Debussy had passages to work on much earlier, for Toulet told Mme Bulteau on 26 October 1902 that he had 'completed several scenes' with which both he and Debussy were satisfied before he left for an extended visit to Indo-China which lasted from November 1902 until May 1903.

Although the only music Shakespeare actually inspired in Debussy was the few bars for *Le Roi Lear* and the piano prelude *La danse de Puck*, he was a lifelong devotee of the bard. Having had no formal education, Debussy was probably introduced to Shakespeare by evening readings in Rome in 1885 with Paul Vidal and Xavier Leroux. Pierre Louÿs, who knew his literary proclivities better than anyone, suggested they work on *Hamlet* together in May 1898 (LOU, p. 113), 'because that is precisely what would suit you best – without giving a damn about Monsieur Thomas'.[4] The idea to revive *As you like it* seems to have stemmed from Debussy, as one of the many projects considered in the wake of *Pelléas*. Perhaps because there was nothing at all Shakespearean in his writings to date, Toulet readily agreed to what proved a mutually stimulating project.[5]

Two plans were submitted to Debussy by the autumn of 1902 and his reactions show how much he wanted to break new theatrical ground (as in *Le diable dans le beffroi*), and especially to get away from the aesthetic of *Pelléas*. He told Toulet on 21 October 1902 (TOU, p. 15):

> The second plan suits me in every way. Don't you think we could heighten the interest of the first scene by the introduction of an offstage choir which would comment on the various incidents in Orlando's wrestling match? Their part could consist of varied exclamations such as: 'He's down! He's up again! Hurrah! He's no coward!' – No! Joking apart, I think that musically this could offer something quite new. I should also like to have the various songs sung by a group of people. The duke is rich enough to hire the Chanteurs de Saint Gervais[6] and their conductor for the Forest of Arden.

He wanted to use the 'scene between Charles the wrestler and Oliver (Shakespeare scene 1) as an introduction . . . Whenever you can replace the exact word by its lyrical counterpart, don't hesitate', Debussy instructed Toulet. 'This idea is to counter your fear of being too rhythmical. Rest easy, you will find all this in the music.' As we have seen, rhythm and timbre were the prime elements in Debussy's theatre music for which he needed appropriate inspiration.

Poor Toulet had envisaged *As you like it* starting with the second (garden) scene between Rosalind and Celia (TOU, p. 16), but he willingly concurred with Debussy's plan, even though he considered the characters of Oliver and the wrestler as subsidiary, to be better 'introduced later, in scenes 2 and 3. Note that a part of the scene between Celia and Rosalind which I am sending you', Toulet continued (p. 17), 'where they speak of their disguises and assumed names, is transferred to the end of the tableau to a scene where they persuade the clown [Touchstone] to go off with them'. That is, the end of Shakespeare's Act 1 scene 3 was inserted into Act 2 scene 4.

Debussy accepted Toulet's 'clarification of the tenuous and complicated intrigues' of *As you like it* with apparent enthusiasm on 25 October (p. 18), but still wanted a response to his ideas about the final betrothal scene (which he never received, and which is perhaps the most important musically).

> I see it as an opportunity for scenic development in which marvellously costumed characters would enter to strictly marked rhythms preparatory to the entry of Rosalind and Orlando [Debussy wrote of Act 5 scene 4]. All this mixed with songs in an antique manner, that is to say integrated with the action. Don't be afraid of developing the character of Touchstone, which is so fantastic and individual . . . You have made me impatient to have every detail of this little human fairy story.

But by the time he returned from Hanoi in 1903 Toulet was heavily addicted to opium, and he told Debussy (LO, 2, p. 250): 'Some of the characters of *Comme il vous plaira* have lain down on the grass and gone to sleep. Others have got lost in the forest and, God forbid, were making a disreputable place of it.' Debussy, whose theatrical focus had now shifted towards *The devil in the belfry*, nonetheless tried to revive Toulet's interest in the 'incomparable Rosalind' and they even discussed her costumes in February 1904 (Toulet, 1927, p. 70).

But thereafter there was silence[7] until June 1917, when Debussy saw Gémier in his celebrated role as Shylock in *The merchant of Venice*.[8] 'I spoke to him of my old passion for *As you like it*', Toulet learned on 7 June (TOU, p. 103), 'and I told him that if he intended to produce it, I should like to have the honour of writing the incidental music.' Gémier agreed and also wanted Toulet as translator, to which the poverty-stricken poet agreed on 9 June, though he was not sure whether his 1902-3 version would suffice, or whether Gémier wanted a literal translation. This last, he confessed to Mme Debussy, did not appeal to him and he 'distrusted' Gémier, who was, 'like Antoine, afflicted with Shakespearitis (*chexpyrite*)'. Debussy begged Toulet on 20 June (pp. 107-8) to see Gémier's point of view.

> You imagine Gémier to be rigorously Shakespearean. If you knew the translation of *The merchant of Venice* you would feel more at ease [see n. 8!]. This man . . . only wants to use his talents as a producer to rouse the audience. *As you like it* will not be of much use to him from this point of view; but he will find a way, you can be sure . . . The vocal element can play a large part in *As you like it* . . . I do not want to lose any of the songs which adorn the text . . . I recommend them to your goodwill: still more to your lyricism.

Toulet seems to have entered into his own negotiations with Gémier and come to some agreement, according to Debussy's last letter to Durand on 1 November 1917 (DUR, p. 190). But by then it was all too late and Toulet's queries about what to do with the duke and his followers in the second act remained unanswered. 'I can't send them to the cinema', he jested to the suffering Debussy on 8 November, either insensitively or with enforced cheerfulness. The 'idea of distant hunting choruses continues to fascinate my modesty', he told Debussy on 19 January 1918 (TOU, p. 124), in a letter which suggests that the extracts from *As you like it* published in 1936[9] come from this later version. But a few weeks later Debussy was dead and Toulet moved on to other things.

Projects with Pierre Louÿs and others (1895-1901)

Orphée/Amphion (c1895-?1900)

The next idea that Debussy considered after *Les noces de Sathan* (see Chapter 2) was probably a ballet with the poet Paul Valéry called *Orphée* around 1895. Valéry proposed his very advanced conception of *ballet blanc* to Debussy by letter[10] as follows:

> In my opinion, it is necessary to write the clearest ballet in the world, one without a programme, for one should say only what legs and instruments permit.
> Only, to vary the pure action, I would add several feminine mimics to the dancers. The dancers would be in their tutus and eternal tights: the mimics in light veils . . . not far removed from those of Greek figurines . . . I add one vast area: the music – yours . . . I had incidentally thought of the myth of Orpheus, that is to say the animation of everything by a spirit, the fable dealing essentially with movement and order.

Plans for a ballet were later converted to equally revolutionary ones for an opera entitled *Amphion* (c?1900), whose 'history' Valéry described in 1932:[11]

> I told Debussy that I foresaw an ambitious system built on a breakdown of available resources and conceived according to a rigorous plan. I would give to each element in opera a new function: the orchestra and the singing would play completely different roles; drama, mime and dance would be rigorously separated and dealt with independently during predetermined time periods . . . There would be numerous levels and floors with different groups in each department . . . Lighting and scenery would be subjected to the same conditions.

If Debussy had a hand in the formation of these schemes, which is likely, then they were way ahead of their time. But dreams they remained, never descending from the realms of two equally vivid and impractical imaginations. The seed planted by *Orphée*, however, may have started to grow again in 1907 when Debussy suggested the idea for what became Victor Segalen's *Orphée-roi*.

Cendrelune (April 1895 – 1898)

This musical version of the children's story *Cendrillon*[12] was planned with Pierre Louÿs for Carvalho at the Paris Opéra-Comique in Christmas 1895, though drawing up plans with ever-changing characters is all that seems to have been done, and that mostly in the first flush of enthusiasm in April–May 1895. First of all, the title of this 'conte lyrique' in two acts and three tableaux was variously *Le roi des aulnes* or *La reine des aulnes* ('The erlking' or 'The queen of the elves') before it became *Cendrelune*. Second, its heroine was progressively called 'la petite fille modèle', Geneviève, Psyché and finally Cendrelune, whilst the favourite amongst the children captured by the wicked queen of the elves was first Kundrynette, then Cendrelune (!), and then Perséphone as the queen herself changed into la dame verte in the final version.

Louÿs' first synopsis, posted to Debussy on 12 April (*RdM*, 1971, pp. 31-2, with la petite fille modèle and Kundrynette), was a jejune affair and was followed a week later by a fuller scenario (*RdM*, 1962, pp. 62-3),[13] from which all the confusion arises. Cendrelune here is busy waving her magic wand in the wicked queen's service to thwart the two saints (Agnes and Catherine) who, disguised as a woodcutter and Joan of Arc, try to assist Geneviève as she resists temptation. Louÿs' final synopsis of early May 1895 (LOU, pp. 185-9) is fleshed out into a sort of *pot-pourri* of *Cinderella*, *Babes in the wood* and *Snow White*, starring Cendrelune, Perséphone and la dame verte. The *Parsifal* element is still retained in the enchanted park and maidens, and in the search for true paradise in Act 2 scene 5. This was to be either through the Church (now represented by Saint Agnes and Saint Margaret) or in the earthly paradise of Nature as offered in the temptations of la dame verte, whom Cendrelune accepts as her long-lost mother at the end.

Debussy was highly critical of the second act in his letter of 11 May 1895 (LOU, p. 53). He found the sentimental picture of the little enchanted girls dancing and waving assorted fruit around Cendrelune and her friend Marie-Jeanne as they kneel lost in the forest snow in scene 2 'un peu 1822'. And he quickly spotted the *Parsifal* element as being beyond the scope of such a small enterprise, in which various aspects could and should be made more moving.

Louÿs, now the veteran of three versions of this insignificant folk-tale, was understandably 'not amused' and replied touchily on the following day: 'Write *Cendrelune* YOURSELF. You are perfectly capable of doing so. By dint of making so many changes to this little scenario, it has become a stranger to me.' (LOU, p. 54) Debussy even asked Louÿs if he would like André Gide to finish *Cendrelune* for him on 16 May, but he seems eventually to have persuaded Louÿs to begin the libretto of Act 1 (LOU, p. 189 n.), probably in August 1895. He did not give up hope for a long time and was still trying to get a complete libretto out of Louÿs on 27 March 1898 (LOU, p. 110). The latter, however, told him to concentrate on getting *Pelléas et Mélisande* staged at the Opéra-Comique and forget about *Cendrelune* (LOU, p. 113): which was precisely what happened.

La grande bretèche (September 1895)

The only reference to this project (which, like *The fall of the House of Usher* and *Axël*, deals with premature burial) comes in a letter to Henry Lerolle of 23 September 1895 (LL, p. 76), in which Debussy mentions 'working on the libretto of *La grande bretèche*'. Presumably he intended to make an opera out of Balzac's 1831 story[14] about Mme de Merret's lover, who was surprised one night by the return of her husband and took refuge in a convenient closet. The Comte de Merret accepted his wife's word that she was alone and grimly walled up her Spanish lover in his hiding-place within the house near Vendôme known as 'La grande bretèche'.

Daphnis et Khloé (later Chloé: November 1895 – 1898)

On 27 November 1895 Louÿs asked Debussy (LOU, pp. 64-5) if he felt he had 'the courage to write a ballet in three scenes; thirty minutes music; my scenario; title: *Daphnis et Khloé* (with a capital K); interpreters: Daphnis: Émilienne [d'Alençon]; Khloé: Khléo [Cléo] de Mérode; Lykainion: Labounskaya; Théâtre de la Bodinière?' This was one of Louÿs' many money-making plans during the period before the immense success of *Aphrodite* absolved him from the need for financial support by his brother Georges.

The idea came from Alphonse Franck[15] who had been asked to put on a show for the opening of the Théâtre d'Application[16] in the rue Saint-Lazare on 15 December, and the scenario was to be derived from Longus. Debussy at first refused, but was furious when Louÿs then offered the ballet to Massenet (letter of 18 January 1896; LOU, pp. 68-9), who also turned it down. Louÿs then persuaded Debussy to reconsider, sending him a plan of the scenario in mid-January 1896, by which time the ballet had assumed the familiar title of *Daphnis et Chloé*.

Louÿs clearly had *L'après-midi d'un faune* in mind when he said the work 'began with a flute theme' (played by Daphnis). With Wagner in mind he also wanted the theme for the first section constructed like the 'first phrase of *Parsifal*', and proceeded to give Debussy other detailed instructions about the sort of music he ought to compose (LOU, pp. 66-7). Debussy predictably did not take kindly to this taste of his own medicine (cf *Cendrelune*) and it was some while before he began to treat the ballet with the seriousness that Louÿs intended. Would the orchestra for M. Houston-Stewart Chamberlain's[17] proposed production consist of anything other than a 'xylophone, a banjo and a Russian bassoon?' he asked Louÿs on 17 January. The following day, understandably annoyed by Debussy's cavalier attitude, Louÿs sent him the details he required, though it is not clear which theatre was intended for the fifteen performances with scenery by Amable and 'an excellent orchestra' (LOU, p. 69).[18]

As usual, Debussy was a long time starting any music and the trouble was that he found the whole ballet static and uninspiring. As he told Louÿs on 20 March 1896 (LOU, p. 72): 'I absolutely must see you on account of Daphnis, who goes nowhere, and Chloé, who imitates him. The anarchist element of the music organises reconciliations in my brain and the red flag of revolution disturbs my poor spinal membranes until I no longer know what to do!' The answer to the last sentence was the inevitable 'rien', though Debussy asked for the scenario again (which had gone back to Louÿs for revision) on 27 December 1897 (LOU, p. 107). Once more Debussy did nothing and his hypocritical stance in badgering Louÿs for the preface to *La tragédie de la mort* in 1898 finally caused the poet to flare up and list all the music Debussy had promised to write for him but had never even started! And that included *Daphnis et Chloé*.[19]

Aphrodite (April 1896 – ?1898)

Given Debussy's glowing appraisal of the 'prodigiously supple' artistry of Louÿs' *Aphrodite* when it first appeared in the spring of 1896,[20] it is difficult to see why his projected score was never written. Pasteur Vallery-Radot suggests (p. 78) that it might have been because Louÿs intended it for performance at the Olympia Music Hall as a ballet or pantomime late in 1897,[21] but *Khamma* and *Le palais du silence* were intended for similar venues, as we have seen. It is more likely that Debussy was again back-pedalling because he wanted to make his theatrical début with *Pelléas* but still keep his other options open for the future, when he would know better how his career was taking shape.

Louÿs intended *Aphrodite* to follow the pantomime *Sardanapale* at the Olympia in late November 1897, and he must have anticipated an adverse reaction from Debussy since he explained that, whilst there were 'many prostitutes at the Olympia . . . there were still more in the amphitheatre of the Opéra!' (LOU, p. 101). He tried to tempt Debussy with the possible receipts from a long run of a spectacle based on his current best-seller, but he does not seem to have been aware of the time needed to write an orchestral score as opposed to a scenario. The difference between Debussy's artistic standards and those of his now-forgotten contemporaries can be seen in the *Vénus Aphrodite* affair: M. de Lagoanère, the manager of the Olympia, anxious to exploit the success of Louÿs' sensual book, managed to persuade Charles Aubert and the composer Émile Bonnamy to knock together at short notice a pantomime entitled *Vénus Aphrodite* which reached the stage by March 1898 (LOU, p. 102, n. 1). Its origins, however, fooled no one, least of all Louÿs.

But Louÿs' annoyance at Debussy's selfish indecision and idleness was probably greater, and furthermore was only just beginning. He complained to the composer Camille Erlanger on 20 October 1900 that 'during the past two years, I have turned down ten or twelve applications to authorise *Aphrodite* as an opera because my friend Debussy had asked me to reserve it for him ... Since this request is now withdrawn, I am, on the contrary, accepting all projects that anyone wishes to speak to me about.'[22] But once bitten, Louÿs never again granted exclusive rights to anyone. This later caused difficulties for Erlanger, who staged the first operatic version of *Aphrodite* in France at the Opéra-Comique on 27 March 1906 in Albert Carré's production, with Mary Garden as Chrysis and scenery by Lucien Jusseaume.[23]

Les uns et les autres (1896)

This was probably to have been an opera based on the one-act verse comedy published by Verlaine in 1884 as part of *Jadis et naguère*. It was intended for the singer Julia Robert and for production at the Théâtre Salon (LCat, p. 153). Verlaine's comedy in ten scenes in an eighteenth-century *fête galante* setting *à la* Watteau is dedicated to Théodore de Banville and was first performed on 20 May 1891 at the Théâtre Vaudeville as part of the benefit night for Verlaine and Gauguin. The Princesse Edmond de Polignac had suggested it to Fauré for musical treatment the previous month,[24] but neither he nor Debussy seem to have been particularly interested in the project. Debussy, however, set stanzas 1 and 3 of Mezzetin's song which opens scene 1 as part of Laloy's libretto for *Fêtes galantes* in 1914 or 1915 (see Chapter 9 and Ex. 56).

Le chevalier d'or (February–November 1897)

This project, with its interesting possible Rosicrucian connections, is also referred to as the 'pantomime si esthétique de Mme Forain' (PET, pp. 204-5) and was intended for private performance at her Paris home, probably for Christmas 1897. The celebrated artist Jean-Louis Forain had asked for Debussy's musical assistance early in February that year (LOU, p. 88), and on 14 September Debussy told Georges Hartmann that 'the musical plan was complete' and the score would take 'about two and a half months to finish'.[25] This revelation of the detailed planning of a dramatic project in various stages is unique to my knowledge, and suggests that Debussy may have progressed further with some 'unstarted' projects than would appear to be the case.

But on 1 November, Debussy told René Peter that *Le chevalier d'or* was 'naturally still not finished' (PET, p. 205), and when Mme Forain gave him a deadline he remarked (PET, p. 204) that it would be just as easy 'to learn Assyrian' as to comply with it! He probably never got beyond his plan, which may one day come to light and offer some positive information on the occult associations of Debussy and his circle. In Joséphin Péladan's *Le panthée*[26] the hero, Bihn, who is composing his 'Symphonie d'or' (when not obsessed with the alchemically perfect metal itself), may be modelled on either Satie or Debussy. 'You know that [Bihn] has composed a mystery according to his obsession, a "mystère d'or" ', one of the characters says of the hero (p. 272). Similarly, in the last tableau of Les 'Frères en Art' Debussy makes Talancet tell of the great success of the lithographs of his latest painting 'Le Christ à la maison d'or'. Such references are perhaps coincidental, but there are a great many of them.

La tentation de Saint Antoine (July 1897)

In 1897 a proposal was made to Debussy that he should write 'ornamental music' for the play (after Flaubert) by Vicomte Auguste Gilbert de Voisins – to which, Debussy told Pierre Louÿs, he never even replied (letter of 9 July 1897; LOU, p. 98). Voisins was a novelist whom Louÿs first met at the Hôtel de l'Oasis in Algiers in March 1897 during his stay there with Zohra ben Brahim, and Louÿs probably suggested the collaboration with Debussy. Like Segalen, Toulet and Laloy, Voisins was greatly attracted to the Far East and its culture (see Fig. 28). He repaid Louÿs by falling in love with his wife (Louise de Heredia) and finally married her by proxy at a civil ceremony in Arcachon in June 1915, two years after she had divorced Louÿs.

La fille de Pasiphaé (1898)

Debussy also positively turned down a request for a 'substantial amount' of incidental music for a tragedy written by Comte de Balbiani. 'Monsieur Victor', as Peter calls the author (PET, pp. 29-30), was a poet–financier who had based his tragedy loosely on Racine's Phèdre (1677). Dietschy (1962, p. 127) suggests that it might have been Balbiani for whom Gaby Dupont deserted Debussy after the Alice Peter affair (see Chapter 11).

Le voyage de Pausole (April 1900 – September 1901)

As with all the other Louÿs–Debussy projects, a change of title took place during the planning stage for Le voyage de Pausole. Louÿs' fantastical Aventures du Roi Pausole in the contemporary utopia of Tryphême first appeared in serial form in Le journal between 20 March and 7 May 1900.[27] The indecisive Pausole's 'voyage' is, finally, undertaken in search of his daughter Aline (who has eloped on a lesbian affair with a French ballet dancer called Mirabelle), and is essentially one of self-discovery. Both Debussy and his wife Lilly followed the episodes avidly.

Debussy began thinking of music to accompany Pausole's journey[28] in April 1900, perhaps as his benefactor Hartmann's death at this time made him think more seriously about his artistic future. But it was not until 2 September 1901 that he made definite plans for a symphonic suite. He told Louÿs (LOU, p. 165):

> I have worked for a long time in the company of that little
> neurasthenic Mélisande . . . Suddenly she said to me: 'Tonight I

dreamed of King Pausole, a very fine man, and you cannot take too much care in composing this symphony for his royal person which should bring to life again his wonderful journey (made to recover things that he had never even lost) through a fanfare of trumpets.'

But composition and imaginative description were two very different things, and the need to revise *Pelléas et Mélisande* and complete its orchestration meant that poor Pausole's epic musical journey never even began.

Projects with Victor Segalen and others (1902-10)

Le pèlerin d'amour (December 1902 – January 1903)

At the very last moment, in December 1902, Debussy was asked to write a song for the opening scene of Victor-Émile Michelet's one-act lyric verse fantasy *Le pèlerin d'amour*, which was to receive its first performance at the Théâtre de l'Odéon at 5 p.m. on 10 January 1903. *Le pèlerin d'amour* was published at the end of *La porte d'or*, a collection of poems which was awarded the first Prix Sully-Prudhomme in June 1902, and its 'workshop' performance was to be introduced by a lecture on modern poetry by young authors delivered by George Vanor.

According to Richard-E. Knowles (p. 230), *Le pèlerin d'amour* was Michelet's first theatrical work and had been written in 1899. The Parnassian poet José-Maria de Heredia had originally suggested performing the play at the Comédie-Française, but a fire there prevented any immediate plans for this in 1900. Later, when things had returned to normal, the administrator of the Comédie-Française, Jules Claretie, submitted Michelet's play to his selection committee, but they rejected it on 14 May 1901. It was André Ulrich, a childhood friend of Michelet, and by now a high-ranking official in the Ministry of the Interior, who persuaded Paul Ginisty to accept the play for performance at the Théâtre de l'Odéon. Ginisty for his part wanted a musical score added to the play, and it was for this reason that Michelet sought Debussy's assistance once *Le pèlerin d'amour* had achieved a measure of official acclaim and a performance had been firmly decided upon.

The play itself is a scaled-down version of the *fête galante* theme beloved of French authors after Verlaine, in which the adolescent *ingénu* Lélio (the pilgrim of love, played *en travestie* as was the first Pelléas) falls in love with the more experienced Faïs, watched over on the island of Cythère by the worldly-wise old woman in grey. Faïs decides to amuse herself and test Lélio's devotion, but he unfortunately overhears her complacent admission to the old woman that she is the willing and practised agent of the god of love. Lélio's ideal is shattered, and despite Faïs' assurances that their love will grow from the suffering he has experienced, he prefers to leave the island with his wounded faith in true love.

The slight but sensitively evoked plot is prefaced by a scene announced in the edition by Paul Ollendorff (1903, p. 200) as being to the 'music of M. Claude Debussy'. While an offstage voice (preferably male) sings, the old woman sits replenishing her fire on the Cytherean seashore in front of the statue and temple of love. The scene Debussy was to set runs as follows (pp. 200-1):

LA VOIX: Pèlerins d'amour, voici la patrie:
          Voici resplendir l'adorable grève;
          Elle abordera la barque fleurie,
              Au pays de notre rêve.

LE CHOEUR (ou LE CHANTEUR):
          Heureuse terre,
          Sol de féerie,
          Salut, Cythère,
          Salut, Patrie!

LA VOIX: L'idéal fuyant que nous voulions suivre
          Comme un vol léger d'oiselles prochaines,
          Nous l'avons atteint, l'idéal de vivre
              Pour des amours surhumaines.

          Ô coeurs parfumés d'immortelle fête,
          La fête d'aimer fleurira vos tombes,
          Vous qui désirez, pour seule conquête,
              L'île où viennent les colombes.

LE CHOEUR (ou LE CHANTEUR, *se rapprochant*):
          Heureuse terre,
          Sol de féerie,
          Salut, Cythère,
          Salut, Patrie!

Three letters from Debussy to Michelet[29] reveal, however, that on 31 December 1902, only eleven days before the première, Debussy was still trying to ascertain which instruments his promised 'five musicians' played!

> I can assure you that they will make a noise like flies rubbing their legs together.[30] We are not in a bar where five Tziganes[31] are in charge! The following instruments are absolutely necessary: *two violins, one viola, one cello, one double bass, two flutes, one harp.* Without them, the whole thing can only sound ridiculous. Reply to me straight away and I will try to write your song as quickly as possible.

But the response from the ever economical Paul Ginisty, the director of the Odéon, which was relayed to Debussy must have been even less forthcoming than he anticipated, for he wrote to Michelet on 3 January 1903: 'Ginisty . . . is surely making fools of us. No one sings without accompaniment except in courtyards, and even that does not happen all that often . . . Since there is so much contempt for music in this theatre, it would be better to do without it altogether.' With only seven days to go, this must have been what was decided. No music for *Le pèlerin d'amour* has come to light, and at the single performance scene 1 was simply recited.

Joyzelle (?1903)

Maeterlinck's *Joyzelle* was first performed at the Théâtre du Gymnase on 20 May 1903 with Georgette Leblanc in the title role, and it is easy to see why Debussy might have been attracted to this latter-day equivalent of *The tempest*. Joyzelle and her lover Lancéor (Merlin's long-lost son) arrive on Merlin's enchanted island by chance in a thick fog, and the various initiations and sacrifices they go through under the supervision of Merlin and Arielle before they are united can be likened to Masonic rituals, which would surely have appealed to Debussy as much as they did to Mozart in *The magic flute*. However, nothing came of the project which is only mentioned by Vallas (1958, p. 358) and Lockspeiser (LO, 2, p. 294). Perhaps Debussy wisely foresaw the dangers of setting another play by Maeterlinck so close to *Pelléas*.

Don Juan (?1903)

The only evidence of a plan to treat the Don Juan story is a letter from Albert Carré to René Peter[32] in which he says:

> My greatest regret is that Debussy, who disappeared so prematurely, never gave the Opéra-Comique another work. He dreamed about two tales of Edgar Poe . . . a *Don Juan*, an *Orphée* and a *Tristan*. But nothing was found amongst his papers after his death and I remain convinced that the painful memory of the public dress-rehearsal of *Pelléas et Mélisande* had something to do with the timidity he showed afterwards and the doubts which haunted him. The public is never aware of the crimes it unconsciously commits.

This observation goes to the heart of Debussy's theatrical inachievement, and appropriately comes from the man whose judgment he respected most.

Dionysos (1904-5)

The three-act lyric tragedy by Joachim Gasquet, on which Debussy planned to base what was perhaps to have been an opera, was first performed at the Théâtre Antique d'Orange on 1 August 1904. Only Dietschy (1962, p. 268, no. 109) mentions the project, which was presumably just another of the many that Debussy contemplated in his search for a successor to *Pelléas*.

Siddartha (August 1907)

Victor Segalen's *Siddartha* was begun during an enforced stay at Colombo in Ceylon in November 1904 and it was sent to Debussy early in August 1907, shortly after work had begun on *Le roman de Tristan* (see Chapter 11). The Buddhist drama tells the legendary Indian story of the young Siddartha's search for the secret of life, and the desires, visions and mental crises he undergoes during his long, troubled quest for Nirvana and incarnation as a Buddha. Earlier, however, in *Gil Blas* (2 March 1903; LCr, p. 106), Debussy had pooh-poohed fashionable Parisian asceticism, though his public and private views could often contradict each other, as we have seen.

> Nothing is more exciting than playing the little Buddha, living on an egg and two glasses of water a day and giving the rest to the poor, contemplating eternal cosmic and pantheistic dreams . . . and the intriguing confusion between self and non-self, all absorbed into the cult of universal consciousness. All very attractive in conversation, but unfortunately not worth a penny in practice and possibly even dangerous.

But this does not mean to say that Debussy applied the same cynical practicality to Segalen's script, even though he did reject it. In fact he digested *Siddartha* slowly and sent his considered opinion to Segalen on 26 August 1907 (SEG, pp. 66-7):

> It is a prodigious dream! However, in its present form [five acts], I cannot imagine any music capable of penetrating its depths! The most music could do would be to underline certain gestures or add definition to certain scenes. In short, an illustration rather than a perfect union between the text and the frightening immobility of the principal character . . . If I asked you to reduce your dream to more normal proportions, I would feel that I was stupidly destroying the effort of a part of your life, and that is a depressing thought.[33]

Debussy suggested instead that 'something admirable might be done with the myth of Orpheus' (SEG, p. 67), whose significance Segalen had earlier discussed in his story *Dans un monde sonore*, and so *Orphée-roi* was born. Nothing was composed for *Siddartha*, and for once Debussy quickly came to a positive decision. So it is no surprise to learn that the few bars marked 'Bouddha' in the Pierpont Morgan 1907 sketchbook are not for *Siddartha* but for bars 13-14 of the piano *Image Et la lune descend sur le temple qui fût*, as Ex. 68 shows. This may help to explain the slightly oriental feel of this *Image*, which may in fact originally have been called *Et la lune descend sur le Temple de Bouddha*.[34]

Orphée-roi (August 1907 – early 1909)

Two hours after receiving Debussy's letter turning down *Siddartha* on 29 August 1907, Segalen was reading to his wife his first sketch for *Orphée-triomphant* (SEG, pp 11-12), such was his desire to collaborate with the famous Debussy. He explained to him in a letter headed 'La naissance d'Orphée' on 4 September (pp. 68-9) that he could not

> help being upset at *Siddartha*'s failure to please you. But I feel bound to agree with what you say. Besides, something has emerged from all this which is both quite unforeseen and very good for me . . .

Ex. 68

(a) *US-NYpm* Lehman deposit, *Images* sketchbook, p. 34

(b) *Images*, 2e série, no. 2, bars 13-14

By all means let us consider Orpheus – but an Orpheus in whose creation we should destroy the popular legendary figure and explode some tedious myths and clichés: he will make a superb protagonist.

This suggestion had, however, come indirectly from Debussy, who had expressed his contempt for Gluck's operatic treatment of Orpheus on 26 August. Gluck, he complained (SEG, p. 67), 'dealt only with the anecdotal and sentimental side of the legend, omitting everything that made Orpheus the first and most sublime figure among the great misunderstood'. This opposite view to that of Berlioz was by no means new, for Debussy had delivered some stinging insults in his 'Open letter to Monsieur le Chevalier C.W. Gluck' in *Gil Blas* on 23 February 1903 (LCr, pp. 98-101; RLS, pp. 123-6). Three weeks earlier, in the same paper, he had written (LCr, p. 89):

> Gluck could not have taken Rameau's place on the French scene without thoroughly assimilating the latter's beautiful works into his own style. Why on earth is the Gluck tradition still alive? The pompous and artificial treatment of recitative is sufficient evidence that it is. There is also his habit of abruptly interrupting the action; thus it is that Orpheus, having lost his Eurydice, sings a romantic aria hardly in keeping with his own mournful state of mind . . . But that is typical Gluck!

So, in Segalen's text, to which Debussy made extensive corrections and suggestions, it is Eurydice rather than Orpheus who is the pursuer and who in the end dies from what she believes to be unrequited love. In addition to Orpheus and Eurydice, there are only three main characters: Eurydice's father (an old harpist), a priest and a warrior. In Act 4 of the lyric drama, a priestess of the Bacchantes enters the dialogue, and a chorus of her crazed tribe actually have the last words in the libretto.

There are no fewer than three versions of the text of *Orphée-roi*. The first was started in November 1907 and sent to Debussy act by act for comments up to 19 April 1908. The second, revised version was sent in similar stages up to 3 September that year. The third was completed on 23 November 1915 by Segalen alone (not surprisingly after all Debussy's 'helpful' suggestions) and was designed for publication without music. It finally appeared as a play in 1921,[35] two years after its author's premature death.

Segalen's enthusiasm began to wane as it became evident that Debussy preferred to pick at other people's drafts than to write his own words or music. The trouble his own prose cost Debussy can be seen from a letter of 26 October 1913 (in *US-AUS*) to his editor Émile Vuillermoz whilst finishing the most poetic of all his articles for the *Revue de la Société Internationale de Musique* at the last moment.[36] 'It is too well constructed', he lamented immodestly. 'If one touches a phrase, everything collapses . . . I have done scarcely anything but suppress, because it is easier.' Perhaps he should have tried to place himself in his own librettist's shoes more often.

Debussy's corrections to Segalen's text reveal first his minute attention to detail. A simple phrase for the warrior at the start of Act 1, for instance, went through five stages before it became 'Puissions-nous y voir enfin!' (SEG, p. 227 n. 2). His concern was for absolute clarity and concision with no ambiguity. Second, as with Toulet in *Comme il vous plaira*, Debussy wanted as much lyricism as possible. Early in the second act, the priest says in the second version: 'Ce n'est pas un magicien. C'est le roi: l'oracle est indiscutable.' The final word was 'not lyrical' enough for Debussy; but though whilst there was a possibility of a musical score Segalen accepted most of his friend's suggestions, he was his own master in 1915 and 'indiscutable' was reinstated. Third, anything that reminded Debussy of Maeterlinck (that is, of *Pelléas*) was condemned, like the passage in Act 2 of the first version where Eurydice finds Orpheus asleep. Its short, repetitive phrases, such as 'Où es-tu?', were singled out for criticism (SEG, p. 265), as were other little exclamations (p. 227). Last, Debussy was concerned with the effect certain passages would have in a staged musical setting. In the second extract from the libretto reproduced in *Segalen et Debussy* (p. 287), Debussy indicates that a passage for Orpheus (which could come from an aria by Massenet or Saint-Saëns),[37] was 'too balanced, too operatic'. Occasionally he expressed his approval of Segalen's efforts, most often when Eurydice had something poetic or feminine to say (as on pp. 271, 335). These added colour and lyricism to an otherwise choppy and declamatory text and thus extended its musical possibilities.

Debussy elaborated on his advice in his meetings and correspondence with Segalen. Sometimes he even discussed the music he intended to compose for

Orphée-roi, the concept of which grew gradually dimmer as time went by. On 10 October 1907 he concurred with Segalen that 'Orpheus was music itself' (SEG, p. 80), adding, 'this will allow me to carry through ideas that I should not otherwise be able to'. 'Orpheus should sing wordlessly throughout the drama', he told Segalen somewhat cryptically on 12 November (p. 84). He liked the two acts he received in the second version on 27 August 1908 in principle, though 'sometimes' he found the all-important 'rhythm more literary than lyrical. To better explain myself I would . . . cite to you certain passages of Chateaubriand, Victor Hugo and Flaubert which are usually considered flamboyantly lyrical, but which, in my opinion, contain nothing musical whatsoever.' And Debussy at this stage also wanted to enlarge the role of the crowd (a recurring tendency after *Pelléas*, which does not have one) as well as the character of Orpheus (SEG, pp. 101-2).

But all the while no music was even being sketched as far as is known. In May 1908 Segalen confessed his impatience to his wife (SEG, p. 98) and told Debussy that he had 'stayed too long in France, inactive on his behalf'. In mid-November that year Debussy became involved with a troublesome revival of *Pelléas*, and although they worked at the text together in December, Debussy was beginning to lose interest. Perhaps he got cold feet as he saw 'the moment approaching when I shall positively have to write something' (ANN, pp. 63-4), or perhaps he was really more interested in *Tristan* and was using *Orphée-roi* to polish up his skills as a librettist in preparation for *La chute de la Maison Usher*. By way of contrast, he turned to the orchestral *Images* and contrived to postpone meetings with Segalen until the latter left for China in May 1909 for an extended stay which lasted till July 1913 (Fig. 28).

On his return Debussy gave him permission to publish his text separately, but resisted any queries as to its musical future in September 1913. Segalen returned to China in October and later completed his purely dramatic version whilst working at the maritime hospital in Brest in 1915. When Debussy came to reread *Orphée-roi* early in June 1916, he 'heard the music which should accompany the drama less and less', and had completely changed his attitude towards the musical role of Orpheus. 'At first, we did not make Orpheus sing', he told Segalen in a letter of 5 June 1916 (SEG, p. 141), 'because he was song itself. This is a false conception. Nevertheless, we [*sic*] can still claim to have written a work in which certain parts are extremely beautiful.'

Drame cosmogonique (?1908)

This, according to Dietschy (1962, p. 268, no. 113), was a project with the painter Jacques-Émile Blanche which was abandoned in 1908. It is only likely because of Debussy's interest in matters astrological — he often referred to the stars Sirius and Aldebaran in his letters to Stravinsky, Godet and others.[38] Segalen's desire to pay off the debt to his earlier researches by 'reconstructing ancient myths, as well as metaphysical, cosmogonic and especial-

Fig. 28. Victor Segalen and Vicomte Auguste Gilbert de Voisins excavating a third-century tomb at Sseu-Tch'ouan, 1910

ly Orphic dramas' (SEG, p. 13) may provide a clue to the real author of this plan.

The remaining projects (1911-17)

Pygmalion (1911)

In an interview with Georges Delaquys in *Excelsior* on 18 January 1911, Debussy admitted that Rameau's *Pygmalion* was to be presented at the Théâtre des Arts in his orchestration.[39] But, he added, 'it is impossible to say when. I have no time to work on it at the moment. It is not an enormous task, certainly, but it is a very interesting one for me, in that it means restoring the true character of these enjoyable old scores which has been corrupted by the intervention of copyists and conductors.' Whether this was to be a scholarly reconstruction along the lines of d'Indy's *Castor et Pollux*, which Debussy reviewed in *Gil Blas* on 2 February 1903 (LCr, pp. 88-91; RLS, pp. 111-13), or whether it was the revival of *Hippolyte et Aricie* at the Opéra in 1908[40] which gave Debussy the idea, we cannot be certain. Debussy did, however, participate in the complete edition of Rameau's works,[41] revising Cahusac's text and the figured bass realisations of the opera-ballet *Les fêtes de Polymnie* (vol. 13, 1908). But the revival of *Pygmalion* in Paris in 1913 had no connection with Debussy, nor is his name mentioned in connection with the ballet in vol. 17, part 1, of the complete edition.

La dame à la faulx (1911)[42]

The Symbolist poet Saint-Pol-Roux (pseudonym of Paul Roux) began writing his gargantuan dramatic poem *La dame à la faulx* in March 1890 and described it in a preface of October 1895 as the 'Spectacle of Humanity amidst the multiple conflict of Life and Death . . . An *inner tragedy* in which I have *exteriorised* the constituent elements in simple, familiar and, dare I say, *popular* crystallisations.' (Briant, p. 92) It was to be set as a 'modern concept in a world of gothic colours' (Briant, p. 94). *La dame à la faulx* was completed in Paris late in 1896 and published as a 'tragedy in 5 acts and 10 tableaux' in 1899 (Paris, Mercure de France). There are three central characters: Magnus (a prince) and Divine (a young chatelaine) who represent youth and love, the ideal couple; between them comes la dame à la faulx herself – 'the most beautiful woman in the world' – to whom Saint-Pol-Roux refers simply as 'ELLE'. In addition there is a host of lesser characters: students, friends of Magnus, alchemists, woodcutters, vagabonds and so on. But beneath a veil of mysterious allegory these products of Saint-Pol-Roux's fertile and fantastical imagination serve a wider purpose: they are cogs in the wheel of 'the titanic struggle of man faced with the eternal drama of Death' (Briant, p. 91), and through them the idealistic Saint-Pol-Roux sought to bring about a 'renewal of the tragic genre' itself. Indeed *La dame à la faulx* was only the first part of a trilogy and was to be followed by *Le tragique dans l'homme* and *Sa majesté la vie*.

Like Villiers de l'Isle-Adam's *Axël*, which has certain similarities to *La dame à la faulx*, Saint-Pol-Roux's monumental tragedy was deemed unproducible at the time of its publication, though as Briant says (p. 32), it establishes Saint-Pol-Roux as 'the true precursor of *cosmic* poetry'.[43] However impractical the original end-product was in theatrical terms, there can be no doubts as to Saint-Pol-Roux's poetic genius and idealistic aims, which were held in the highest esteem by fellow poets such as André Breton, Paul Éluard and Francis Jammes, the last of whom placed him alongside Maeterlinck, Rimbaud, Gide and Claudel in 1904 (Jouffroy, p. 257).

Some time during the next decade Saint-Pol-Roux modified *La dame à la faulx* for theatrical presentation and offered it in 1910 to Jules Claretie, the administrator of the Comédie-Française. When Claretie refused it, Saint-Pol-Roux turned in December 1910 to Jacques Rouché (then the director of the Théâtre des Arts) with his 'poetic symphony', in which his aim had been 'to condense the play as well as to magnify the roles of the principal characters'.[44]

The intermediary in the affair was probably Léon Frapié, a friend of both parties, though Rouché shared many of Saint-Pol-Roux's beliefs concerning the fusion of the arts (including stage design and music) in the context of the contemporary theatre. As Yves Sandre says (p. 8): 'For Jacques Rouché, dramatic art was both "an aspect of and dependent on the plastic arts".'

Quite how enthusiastic Rouché really was about *La dame à la faulx*, however, is difficult to determine, for none of his replies to Saint-Pol-Roux's lengthy and detailed letters (see Sandre, pp. 14-45) have survived. But it seems likely that in 1911 a production of the revised version was seriously considered (by Saint-Pol-Roux at least), and as Debussy was by then amongst the most celebrated of composers for the stage, and because he shared Saint-Pol-Roux's Rosicrucian beliefs,[45] it comes as no surprise that the poet approached him for the incidental music which he intended should play a vital role in his forthcoming production. On 28 February 1911 he wrote to Debussy (Sandre, p. 46):

> I come in the names of M. Jacques Rouché and myself to ask you to do us the honour of writing the incidental music for *La dame à la faulx* (about five fully developed pieces and some ten short pieces to establish moods). We know that you are extremely busy with *Saint Sébastien*, but the director of [the Théâtre des] Arts would not need your score until 1 October [1911], and the performance of *La dame* should take place at the end of October or the beginning of November . . . On your acceptance, M. Rouché will send you a copy of the manuscript, for the work has been synthesised and modifed a little to interpret a more elevated conception of Beauty.

Saint-Pol-Roux optimistically hoped for an affirmative reply, 'today if possible', from the hard-pressed Debussy, and the fact that Debussy's only surviving letter to Saint-Pol-Roux is extremely brief and (unusually for this period) undated, suggests that it was written during the intensely busy months of March and April 1911 when he composed most of his score for *Le martyre*. It runs as follows (Jouffroy, p. 258): 'Here is – – – with my sincere joy to participate in anything which will serve to enhance the glory of the great poet which you are, my dear Saint-Pol-Roux.' Precisely what Debussy enclosed with his letter is unfortunately unknown, and as in so many other instances his initial enthusiasm never seems to have taken any practical form.

Like Ida Rubinstein when she was planning *Le martyre*, Saint-Pol-Roux hedged his bets by approaching other composers for incidental music for *La dame à la faulx*. His first choice, apparently, had been Gabriel Dupont,[46] but Rouché seems to have encouraged him to sets his sights rather higher, as the following letter from Saint-Pol-Roux to Rouché of 16 February (Sandre, p. 16) suggests: 'I shall indicate the places where music is needed in order that Paul Dukas (perhaps instead of Debussy, whose time is so taken up with *Saint Sébastien*) can immediately set to work, for if you cannot definitely accept Dupont, we should agree to choose one of these masters, given "the eternity" of the subject.' But Dukas, equally busy with his ballet *La péri*, also seems to have been put off by the sheer scale of Saint-Pol-Roux's plans.

In September, despite Rouché's misgivings, Saint-Pol-Roux reverted to Dupont, who, he told Rouché on the 14th (Sandre, pp. 24-5), had 'had his motifs all ready for a long time, for he wishes . . . to write the music for *La dame*. Hence this will be nothing but child's play for him. It would only take me a single day to annotate his manuscript (with appropriate indications), which I shall return to you by personal messenger.' Rouché, however, was still unenthusiastic about Dupont and an additional problem was that he was still clinging to the original manuscript of the play. At the end of September Saint-Pol-Roux asked him to make copies of the 'three acts in his possession' (Sandre, p. 26) and to

> send two copies to me: one for myself and one which I shall annotate for the composer. Dukas and Debussy are both overwhelmed by other works, as I told you on my last visit to the theatre, and I am going to approach the third outstanding musician whom we talked about: Maurice Ravel. Now that the text is established, Ravel (if he accepts) would be able to get down to the task in double-quick time. In two months he will certainly have put the finishing touches to the few musical passages that are required.

But Ravel also had outstanding commitments, notably the completion of his ballet *Daphnis et Chloé* for Diaghilev's Ballets Russes. So the over-optimistic Saint-Pol-Roux reset his sights on Dupont, and he begged Rouché on 10 October (Sandre, p. 28) to tell Dupont 'not to show his manuscript to anyone. The theatre contains so many indiscreet babblers!'

Elaborate stage designs and the casting of the principal roles also caused many delays, but it seems likely that Rouché used the lack of copies of the play and his insistence on a major composer for the score to frustrate Saint-Pol-Roux's ambitions. The production at the Théâtre des Arts was first post-poned until early February 1912 and then to 1 March, by which time the celebrated actor Édouard de Max would be available to play the role of Magnus. But as early as 18 January Rouché decided to cancel the production altogether (see Sandre, p. 45), and Saint-Pol-Roux finally sent his son Coecilian to retrieve his manuscript from Rouché on 27 February, together with that 'containing his musical indications' for *La dame à la faulx*.

Exactly when in 1911 these 'musical indications' were made is not known; nor does it seem that Dupont's score was completed. Predictably the play has never been staged to this day, but fortunately we do know what Debussy's 'five fully developed pieces' and 'ten short pieces' might have consisted of, for Saint-Pol-Roux's musical annotations to the earlier version of *La dame à la faulx* have survived in the collection of Mlle Divine Saint-Pol-Roux and are printed by Sandre (pp. 50-7). Amongst the major pieces there was to have been an overture to Act 1, an intermezzo before Act 2, a prelude to Act 4, and an intermezzo describing 'La course à la Mort' to cover the scene change into the final act. The shorter pieces included a song for Divine in two stanzas (with harp accompaniment) towards the end of Act 1; a nocturne (lasting one and a half minutes) early in Act 2; a chorus of offstage pilgrims in Act 2 scene 1; a 'strange march' at the end of Act 4 scene 4, accompanied by a rhythm played on knuckle-bones (*osselets*); and a choral finale to Act 5, with shouts of 'Noël' to proclaim the triumph of Magnus (p. 57), 'whilst underneath grating instruments represent the wrath of "ELLE". The final fury of the brass will break off *abruptly* at the word "Liberté", that is to say at the *coup de la faulx*. At this point the strings . . . very softly, play a lament whose beauty offers a ray of hope – and to conclude the hour strikes from below.'

Saint-Pol-Roux's meticulousness as to the length of movements and their precise instrumentation perhaps offer an additional reason why Debussy felt unable to comply with his request for incidental music for *La dame à la faulx*. For instance, in defining the three main themes of the play (which were to recur at specified points throughout the score in a somewhat Wagnerian manner), Saint-Pol-Roux instructed that the theme of ELLE (the theme of Death) was to be scored for clarinets, bassoons, string basses, hand-stopped horns (*pavillons bouchés*) and timpani; Magnus's theme (the theme of Humanity) was to be scored for harps, horns, fifes, trumpets (*fanfares*), tubas and percussion; whilst Divine's theme (the theme of Life) was to be scored for the equally unlikely combination of harps, violins playing on their top (E) strings (*chanterelles*), oboes, flutes, bugles, cornets, handbells and ordinary bells. Even if Saint-Pol-Roux's orchestral specifications had been more practical, it is extremely unlikely that Debussy would have allowed himself to be dictated to in this way under any circumstances. However high his expressed opinion of Saint-Pol-Roux as a poet was, *La dame à la faulx*, even in its modified version for the theatre, can never have been other than still-born as far as Debussy was concerned.

Drame indien (?1914)

Debussy's idea for an Indian drama (which had no connection with *Siddartha*) was brought to light by Léon Vallas in *Claude Debussy et son temps* (p. 380), where it is mentioned as a 'wartime project'. Perhaps it was the 'third drama' mentioned by Gabriele d'Annunzio in his letter to Debussy of July 1914, as has been suggested by Tosi (ANN, pp. 100, 123-4 n.). D'Annunzio also refers to it in his letter of 31 March 1928 to the *comité d'initiative* for the erection of a Debussy monument, but unfortunately gives no details.

Tania (February 1914 – March 1916)

All that is known of the author with whom Debussy corresponded about *Tania* is that he was Russian. The scheme may have been based on an adaptation of Pushkin's verse novel *Yevgeny Onegin* (1831) whose heroine, Tatyana,[47] exhibits the characteristics of ideal Russian womanhood in her love for the disenchanted Byronic hero Onegin.

Debussy must have received the scenario of *Tania* shortly after his initial period of enthusiasm for *Fêtes galantes* and *Le palais du silence*. Theatre music was uppermost in his mind early in 1914, and he wrote to the author on 25 February:[48]

> The scenario of *Tania* pleased me greatly and I am convinced that it offers the opportunity for surprising dramatic displays. Unfortunately I shall not be able to work at it for a period which will seem to you to be too long. I do not wish to prevent you seeking the aid of another composer and I can do no more than assure you of my regrets.

But the author did not give up hope, and on 19 March 1916 Debussy was forced to tell him:

> Some time ago you had the patience to emphasise in a long letter the multiple attractions of Tania from the lyrical point of view. Rest assured that I have no need of such ardent pleas on her behalf, and I am profoundly conscious of all the tragic and generally ignored humanity that this drama contains.
>
> But ... what you are after would need a sort of ... Mussorgsky. For I remain convinced that a Russian is needed to write the music for *Tania*. I am not Mussorgsky, and this long illness makes it impossible for me to know when I shall be able to return to serious work.
>
> Your impatience is certainly legitimate, and I beg you to excuse my having made you wait so long for the return of the manuscript of *Tania*.

The 'tragic and generally ignored humanity' referred to above certainly suggests that an adaptation of Pushkin is a possibility, even though Tchaikovsky's *Eugene Onegin* is nowhere mentioned.

Drame fantastique (?1917)

The information given by Dietschy (1962, p. 268, no. 114) concerning this plan was supplied to him by Eugène Berteaux. The libretto was to be by Debussy himself, so it would have been truly 'fantastic' if the work had progressed beyond the familiar stages of dream and brief initial enthusiasm.

13 Debussy in and about the theatre: some observations and conclusions

> I have no theory, no prejudice. I try to be sincere in my art and my
> opinions, that's all. Only, I believe that in art there is an aristocracy
> that should not be compromised. That is why I have little desire for
> great success or gaudy fame . . . I like only silence, peace, work and
> isolation and what is said of my work is of no importance to me. I
> do not mean my music to be imitated, nor that it should exert an
> influence on anyone. I try to remain independent and I compose, as
> I must, whenever I can. That is all I can tell you.
>
> (Debussy, interview with Georges Delaquys in *Excelsior*
> (18 Jan 1911); LCr, p. 297)

By now I hope that a balanced picture has begun to emerge of Debussy as a
composer both for and within the theatre, and that some of the complex and
manifold reasons why he contemplated so many projects yet completed so
few will have become apparent. Much depended on the focal position in
Debussy's career of *Pelléas et Mélisande*, the only theatre work he chose and
completed himself without a definite production in view. Much also depended
on his attitudes towards his librettists and on Durand's attitude towards him.
But before I return to these areas in more detail, I should like first to consider
Debussy's views about his theatrical contemporaries and forebears, and about
the Parisian institutions on which their livelihoods largely depended.

Debussy's views about his theatrical predecessors and contemporaries

Debussy's public and private opinions could often be dissimilar, as we have
seen, and he was often hypocritical through cowardice or to maintain a public
image. Nevertheless, his articles, some written with the aid of the pseudony-
mous Monsieur Croche, provide a wide-ranging panoply of his lively, often
ironical views.

A recurring theme in Debussy's writings after *Pelléas* is that French music
should remain true to itself, for he stoutly championed the operatic line of
descent from Rameau (to himself) against that passing from Gluck, through

Berlioz and Wagner, to Wagner's French imitators. Much of the tyranny of the latter he blamed on women (*Gil Blas*, 2 Feb 1903; LCr, p. 89; RLS, p. 111): Marie Antoinette's support allowed Gluck's influence to impose itself on France; whilst the Paris première of *Tannhäuser* was largely due to the efforts of another Austrian, Mme von Metternich. 'From having known you', Debussy told Gluck in his 'open letter' of 23 February 1903 (*Gil Blas*; LCr, p. 100), 'French music reaped the unexpected benefit of falling straight into the arms of Wagner.' But when he claimed that Gluck owed a great debt to Rameau, his aim was the further glorification of his French predecessor rather than any wish to appear illogical. '*Castor et Pollux* contains in embryo the original ideas that Gluck was to develop later on', he had written earlier that year (*Gil Blas*, 2 Feb 1903; LCr, p. 89). Above all he hated Gluck's 'terrible prosody': 'You turn French into an accented language, when it is, on the contrary, a language of nuances', he accused (LCr, p. 99). 'Rameau was infinitely more Greek than you . . . What is more Rameau was lyrical . . . and we French should have continued in a lyrical tradition rather than waiting a century before rediscovering it.' All this was Gluck's fault, as Debussy saw it, through the intermediacy of 'Spontini, Le Sueur, Méhul etc.'. And furthermore, his music contained 'the seed of Wagnerian formulae' which were to tyrannise music in what Monsieur Croche called the 'Who's who of the gods'.[1]

Gluck's pernicious influence had also spread to Berlioz, who was 'never, strictly speaking, a theatrical composer' (8 May 1903; LCr, p. 165). 'Despite some beautiful passages in *Les Troyens* . . . its proportional defects make performance impractical and its overall effect monotonous, even boring.' Berlioz was 'the favourite musician of those who know nothing about music', chiefly because of his 'harmonic liberties', and his 'rambling forms'. Debussy most admired *L'enfance du Christ* and Berlioz's orchestral music, and for once he shared Fauré's opinion in this as both men hated the staged version of *La damnation de Faust*,[2] though Debussy thought that the fault lay with the presumptuous and inept producer Raoul Gunsbourg[3] rather than with Berlioz.

Debussy was kinder to Berlioz as a Romantic successor to Weber, even if Berlioz was 'so in love with Romantic colour that he sometimes forgets about music' (*Gil Blas*, 26 Jan 1903; LCr, p. 83). Weber was the one German innovator Debussy really admired – far in excess of Beethoven. True admiration from Debussy always took the form of descriptions which could equally well apply to his own music. So when he described Weber's music as 'containing . . . the sort of dreamy melancholy so unique to this period', he must also have been thinking of his own parallel achievement in *Pelléas*. And the following appraisal of Weber's *Oberon* (LCr, p. 82) tells us at least as much about its reviewer as about the opera in question:

> [Weber] was perhaps the first to have been concerned about the relationship which must exist between the ubiquitous spirit of Nature and the soul of a character. Certainly, he had the idea of

using the legend as a sounding-board upon which music could express natural actions. Indeed, it is music alone that has the power to evoke imaginary scenes at will from a world both of certainty and of fantasy, which functions in secrecy in the mysterious poetry of the night with its thousand anonymous sounds of moonbeams caressing the leaves.

Debussy begged Albert Carré in the same 1903 review to revive Weber's beautiful *Der Freischütz* at the Opéra-Comique, as 'he alone is capable of understanding how its legendary scenes could be recreated'. Earlier, in a conversation with Robert Godet after the unsettling dress-rehearsal of *Pelléas* on 28 April 1902 (*Chesterian*, June 1926; RLS, p. 106), he had compared Weber's forest in *Der Freischütz* with the one he soon planned to portray himself in *As you like it*:

> Between [Weber's] forest, vibrating with the terrors and the rather heavy and childish joys of the Germanic legend, and, for example, this forest in the Ardennes, so resolutely fictitious, where the confetti of *As you like it* bursts forth like rockets, there is certainly an insuperable distance. Now, is it not all the more strange that, barely touched by the wand of the magician Weber, the realistic and natural scene for the most German of melodramas assumes a grace and freshness, a mystery even worthy of Shakespearean fantasy?

In the same article Debussy showed how much he admired Weber's orchestration too. He vowed he would use Weber's characterisation through timbre in *Der Freischütz* to explain to a 'visitor from Mars' the colouristic properties of the woodwind and horns. In direct contrast to muddy orchestrators like Wagner and Richard Strauss, 'the most daring combinations of Weber's orchestra, when he makes himself most deliberately symphonic, have in particular the tone colour preserved in its original quality: colours that are superimposed without mingling, the mutual reactions which enhance rather than abolish their individuality.' (RLS, p. 108) This is precisely what Debussy sought to achieve in his own orchestration.

Meyerbeer, on the other hand, epitomised for Debussy all that was worst in over-inflated nineteenth-century grand opera.

> To celebrate the return of spring, the Opéra has revived *Les Huguenots* . . . There is a certain irony in linking these two events, for *Les Huguenots* cannot pretend to have anything to do with 'renewal'. Rather it is one of the miseries of daily life, like epidemics, three per cent devaluation, and the excavations for the Métro . . . This opera is one of the most tiring to listen to and to perform. (*Gil Blas*, 23 March 1903; LCr, p. 127)

And the following month (*Gil Blas*, 27 April 1903; LCr, p. 155), he flattered Offenbach by saying that he 'would never have been able to write *Robert le diable*, first because he was accustomed to better librettos, and second because he never wanted to lumber himself with such grandiose boredom'.

Debussy classed Verdi's *La traviata* as a forerunner of the Italian *verismo* school, which he thought should be exported *en bloc* back to its country of origin before it could influence French opera. He did distinguish between Verdi and his lesser successors, however, insofar as

> Verdi seeks in heroic manner to tell of a life more beautiful than the attempted 'realism' of the young Italian school. Puccini and Leoncavallo pretend to a study of character, even to a sort of crude psychology, but in reality this goes no further than simple anecdote.
>
> The two *Bohèmes* are striking examples. In Leoncavallo there is only the harshness of various insignificant acts, whose sentimentality is rendered in that nasal manner peculiar to Neapolitan songs. In the other, if M. Puccini is attempting to recapture the atmosphere of the streets and people of Paris, he still manages to make an Italian noise. I would not be so pretentious as to hold his being Italian against him, but why on earth did he choose *La vie de bohème*?
>
> With M. Mascagni and the universally popular *Cavalleria rusticana*, we relapse again into triviality, only here it is made worse by the declamation which attempts to be lifelike but ends up as cunning artificiality. It's all extremely boring!
>
> In France it has become fashionable to look for subjects in much the same spirit as those of the Italians. But one cannot state too often that a good book often makes a bad play, from which it is easy to deduce that it would not improve as an opera. (*Gil Blas*, 16 Feb 1903; LCr, pp. 96-7)

Debussy maintained his anti-*verismo* views for the rest of his life. In 1914, he asked M.-D. Calvocoressi:[4] 'Why talk of modern Italian opera? That would be ascribing to it an importance of which it remains totally destitute. The greater part of the public revels in the vulgar and the meretricious, and at all times has bad taste been catered for. The Italians, well aware of what the public wants, act accordingly.' Perhaps his views had been further entrenched in the interim by reading Mascagni's judgment of *Pelléas* in *L'éventail* of July 1908 (Dietschy, 1962, p. 197): 'The music of *Pelléas*', Mascagni wrote, 'makes you think of silent film pianists who play their little tunes so timidly and modestly while the most extraordinary scenes unfold before them.'

The main exception Debussy made in Wagner's case was for *Parsifal*, an 'admirable treatise on the uselessness of formulae . . . and an ingenious contradiction to the *Ring*' (*Mercure de France*, Jan 1903; LCr, p. 64). Three months later, he expanded at length on 'the beautiful sunset mistaken for a dawn' (*Gil Blas*, 6 April 1903; LCr, pp. 137-40; RLS, pp. 164-7). Here, the 'finest character' was Klingsor and the musical zenith the prelude to the third act and the 'Good Friday spell'. Debussy praised its 'noble and strong, unique and unexpected orchestral sonorities . . . one of the most beautiful monuments in sound ever raised to the eternal glory of music'. But here and elsewhere[5] he declared himself against Wagner being performed in concert, however much the music was able to withstand this treatment. It brought *Parsifal* 'down to a simple everyday level' from its musical pedestal and there was even a danger that it would be converted into mere salon music.

But whereas Debussy defended Wagner's right as a theatrical composer to be heard in the theatre alone, he openly disapproved of the direct French imitation of the musical principles he had made his own. 'The advice of Wagner has been bad for many countries and many musicians', who have thus been diverted from 'le sens national', he told the impresario Barczy in December 1910 (LL, p. 202). 'Chabrier, so marvellously endowed by the comic muse, died in pursuit of the lyric drama, a Glucko-Wagnerian importation so contrary to our national genius', he lamented in December 1916.[6] He was kind in his review on 12 January 1903 (*Gil Blas*; LCr, p. 69) of d'Indy's *L'étranger* in Brussels precisely because 'the influence of Wagner never goes very deep: the heroic hamminess of the one is never compatible with the artistic integrity of the other. If *Fervaal* is subordinated to the Wagnerian tradition, it redeems itself by its morality and its disregard for the grandiloquent hysteria that overpowers so many Wagnerian heroes.'

But hearing *L'étranger* again in a Paris concert hall the following week caused Debussy to revise his opinions (*Gil Blas*, 19 Jan 1903; LCr, pp. 76-7). The perfection of its craftsmanship was no longer enough, and it became apparent that d'Indy 'sticks too rigidly to the plot of this drama, which is so concise and unified in itself. All his theatrical timing disappears in concert performance. The result is like pages torn from a very beautiful book whose context has been lost: even if they are still beautiful, they have no meaning.' This helps to explain why Debussy remained so opposed to any sort of concert performance of *Pelléas*, in which the model was Mussorgsky rather than Wagner in terms of its natural declamation and overall simple expressiveness within the framework of a national tradition. 'We completely ignore the theatrical works of Mussorgsky, Borodin and Rimsky-Korsakov', Debussy complained in *Gil Blas* on 28 June 1903 (LCr, p. 190),

> and they contain the sonorous expression of the Russian spirit that we are so envious of, magnified for the stage. I know that it is easier to publish a book than to put on an opera, but would it not be of interest in certain quarters to have some friendly exchanges? Despite the alliance, few modern French operas are performed in Russia: a just response to our own inertia.

But whilst Debussy thought more highly of Rimsky-Korsakov than Fauré did,[7] he had an even lower opinion than Fauré of 'superman' Richard Strauss (*Gil Blas*, 30 March 1903; LCr, p. 135), who 'must have inherited from [Nietzsche] his disdain for trifling sentimentalities and also his wish that music should not continue to illuminate our nights for ever . . . but rather replace the sun itself'. But perhaps Debussy had heard Strauss' equal and opposite reaction to *Pelléas* through Romain Rolland, in which Strauss claimed that Act 1 contained 'nothing . . . no musical phrases: no developments' (Inghelbrecht, p. 238).

Of his French contemporaries the only work Debussy consistently praised was Édouard Lalo's *Namouna*[8] and in January 1903 he recalled how M. Vaucorbeil, the director of the Opéra, had shown him the door in the past because of his youthful enthusiasm for the work.[9] If the main theme of his B minor Symphony of 1880 shows that Debussy also knew the overture to Hérold's *Zampa* well, then its second, *cantabile*, theme (Ex. 69) is just one of many instances of his early admiration for Massenet, 'that musical historian of the female soul'. Much bound up himself with portraying ideal women in music, Debussy admired a similar trait in his colleague, however different the end result usually was:

> His music is vibrant with sensations, with *élan*, and with embraces that we wish would last forever. Massenet has been reproached for having too much sympathy for Mascagni and for not worshipping Wagner enough, [but] this criticism is as false as it is unacceptable . . . [In *Manon*, Massenet] found the framework that best suited his flirtatious habits, but he should not have forced them into the Opéra. One does not flirt at the Opéra; one bawls incomprehensible words at the top of one's voice! . . . Massenet realised he could better continue to adapt his genius for clear colours and whispering melodies in works made of lightness itself. That is not incompatible with artistic depth, it only demands more subtle methods of discovery.   (*La revue blanche*, 1 Dec 1901; LCr, pp. 58-9)

But as usual, Debussy's printed opinion was not necessarily compatible with that expressed in private letters. Back in February 1893 he had written to Prince André Poniatowski (p. 308) of the

> sad sight afforded to all those who love art by today's composers: its so-called representatives. We have had a *Werther* by Massenet, where one can ascertain a curious mastery in the gratification of all the stupid whims and the poetic and lyrical needs of the dilettantes of cheap taste! Everything in this work is borrowed from someone or other, and he has this even more deplorable habit of taking a fine idea and turning it into a facile, superficially pleasing and sentimental parody of itself.

It must be remembered that, at this time, Debussy was dissatisfied with his own opera *Rodrigue et Chimène* and had not as yet begun *Pelléas*. His frank denunciation of contemporaries may thus well have been an extreme reaction to his own artistic insecurity and lack of tangible success at the age of thirty. He continued vitriolically: 'It is the same story with *Faust* as murdered by Gounod; or *Hamlet* as so unfortunately "deranged" by Ambroise Thomas', though he later wrote in *Musica* in July 1906 that the 'art of Gounod represents a moment in French sensibility', and maintained that he did not misrepresent Goethe's ideas in *Faust* any more than Wagner falsified the

Ex. 69. Symphony in B minor, 1880, R, p. 9, bars 6-14

character of the legendary Tannhäuser in opera (LCr, p. 192). For Ambroise Thomas, however, Debussy never managed a kind word, and he swore an oath to Fauré in 1910 on the 'ashes' of the former director of the Conservatoire that he would not judge their vocal classes that year! (letter of 14 May 1910; LL, p. 191)

In 1893 Debussy also had a low opinion of his Prix de Rome successor Gustave Charpentier. He told Poniatowski (p. 308) that this

> young star rising on the musical horizon . . . seems to me destined for a glory as productive as it is unaesthetic. He is a successor to Berlioz, who was, I believe, an inveterate practical joker [and] who came to believe in his own jokes. Charpentier has rather less of Berlioz's aristocratic disposition: he is of the people and is on the point of writing . . . an opera which will be called *Marie*,[10] set in Montmartre. *La vie du poète* is the work which so endears itself to the admiration of the crowds, and its cheekily Romantic title already tells us something about its author. But what you cannot imagine for yourself is the lack of taste it reveals: you might call it a bar-room triumph! . . . To give you a brief example, the last movement of this symphony depicts the Moulin Rouge, where the poet (a title one should be suspicious of) finds himself stranded. There is even a prostitute whose cries imitate orgasm!
> Ah! poor music! What filth these people drag you through!
> Naturally, all the insignificant snobs, fearing to be taken for boring idiots, proclaim it a masterpiece! . . . But, good God, music is a dream whose veils one gently draws apart! It is not the expression of a sentiment, it is the sentiment itself!

Whilst Debussy was later more generous about Charpentier's orchestral *Impressions d'Italie*,[11] his opinion of *Louise* never improved. He thought *Pelléas* should have been chosen by Carré in its place in 1900, and he told Pierre Louÿs on 6 February, four days after the première (LOU, p. 137), that Charpentier

> took the delightful and picturesquely humane street-cries of Paris, and like a true Prix de Rome winner, made sickly popular songs out of them. The underlying harmonies I shall call parasitic, to be polite . . . It is a thousand times more conventional than *Les Huguenots* . . . and people call that true to life! Good heavens, I would prefer to die immediately! . . . Naturally Mendès rediscovers Wagner in it and Bruneau magnifies the influence of Zola. In sum: a very French work, though there is certainly an error in the addition . . . which is more stupid than deliberately wicked.

Debussy assured Louÿs that in the face of such critics and an audience so blind to true beauty, he 'would rather *Pelléas* were performed in Japan' (an ironically prophetic wish in view of his recent popularity there). He was probably angry when Vincent d'Indy compared his opera with *Louise* as a work 'equally sincerely written and no less emotively powerful', however much the two works were 'diametrically opposed in their poetic inspiration and musical result' (*L'occident* (Brussels), June 1902, pp. 380-1).

Debussy's final pet hate was Camille Saint-Saëns, and from the standpoint of his later writings it is difficult to imagine anything less likely than Debussy arranging Saint-Saëns' *Caprice sur les airs de ballet d'Alceste de Gluck* for piano duet, as he did in 1889. In 1901 he had Monsieur Croche say (*ReB*, 15 Nov 1901; LCr, p. 57) that *Les barbares* was

> worse than other operas because it is by Saint-Saëns. He owed it to himself and still more to music not to set this story in such a mixed-up manner. There is even a farandole which has been praised for its archaic perfume: it is a stale echo of *The Cairo road* which was the hit of the 1889 Exhibition . . . Is there no one who likes Saint-Saëns enough to tell him that he's written enough music and would be better employed in his lately acquired vocation of explorer?

Debussy liked the above passage so much that he had his *alter ego* repeat it in *Gil Blas* on 16 March 1903 (LCr, p. 119). But two months later he was rather more charitable about *Henry VIII*, if saying that Saint-Saëns 'lacks that grandiloquent bad taste characteristic of Meyerbeer's genius' can be taken as charitable. 'He is more of a musician than a man of the theatre', Debussy continued perceptively (*Gil Blas*, 19 May 1903; LCr, p. 168), 'and he uses those facile effects permitted in this theatrical genre only as a last resort.' Saint-Saëns, for his part, hated Debussy's music from *L'après-midi* (which 'cultivated the absence of style, logic and common sense'), through *Pelléas*, to *En blanc et noir* with acid consistency.[12]

Debussy's views about theatres, from their policies and personnel to their architecture and acoustics

Debussy also wrote about various aspects of Parisian theatrical institutions with varying degrees of disapproval. The Opéra (which produced a 'peculiar noise that those who paid for it called music') predictably came bottom of the list. 'By special favour and a state subsidy', he told his readers in *La revue blanche* (15 May 1901; LCr, p. 38), 'this theatre can put on anything it likes . . . It will never change unless there is a revolution, and revolutionaries rarely bother with opera houses.' Two years later he discussed the Gailhard administration in *Gil Blas* (9 March 1903; LCr, pp. 111-14; RLS, pp. 135-8), challenging the Opéra's nomination as the 'greatest lyric theatre in the world'. He criticised its

> serious defects and simplistic lack of any precise overall policy. The Opéra relies more on bad luck than on what might be called public taste[13] . . . Once and for all, the Opéra should be a model theatre, not a place where ostentatious luxury conceals the poverty of what is performed . . . They do very little work at the Opéra, and I know from a reliable source that they revive old pieces by adding new, even unrehearsed elements because they don't want to trouble the orchestra. As for this orchestra . . . it gives shaky performances in which the uncertainty is combined with a most disturbing lack of care.

Debussy's proposed solution was to let the Opéra be

> governed by a board of people too rich to be worried about making money, but who would, on the other hand, be proud to spend lavishly on beautiful things . . . Then there should be a completely free and independent musical director, whose function would first be to bring himself up to date with artistic affairs, and then to plan in advance a programme of retrospective and carefully chosen works.

Why not have Richter to conduct Wagner operas, Debussy suggested, as they did at Covent Garden, 'where the performances are perfect in every respect'?[14] On 30 April 1903 he wrote in one of his London letters to *Gil Blas* (LCr, p. 161):

> The particular attraction of Covent Garden is that music feels at home there. You find yourself paying much more attention to the perfect acoustic than to the sumptuous decorations, and the orchestra is large and strictly attentive. In addition, M. André Messager fulfils his artistic responsibilities with perfect and assured taste and this suprises no one. You can see how strange this all is, for they actually consider that a musician can usefully run an opera house! In reality, such organisers are usually idiots or perhaps reactionaries! In any case, I will not venture any comparisons, for they would only confirm too obviously the poverty of our means, and our national pride would suffer as a result.

And in June 1914 (*The etude*; RLS, p. 320), Debussy praised the British audience too, for its

> most remarkable capacity for attention and respect. It does not think itself compelled noisily to express dissatisfaction whenever it fails to grasp at first hearing the purport of a new work. And this of course, as far as the appreciation of modern music is concerned, is the best attitude. To believe that one can judge a work of art upon a first hearing is the strangest and most dangerous of delusions.

Debussy's changing views about the Opéra-Comique before and after *Pelléas* show the extent to which personal circumstances could affect his artistic opinions. On the day after the death of its director, Léon Carvalho (30 December 1897), Jules Huret, a journalist, sent a questionnaire to various composers soliciting their views on the desirable future of Paris theatres like the Opéra-Comique. Debussy replied on 19 January 1898:[15]

> Will you permit me not to have an official opinion on the future of the Opéra-Comique? Without knowing exactly why, it will probably continue to function. As to an experimental lyric theatre, that seems like a bad joke to me, for one does not experiment with music. No one likes music enough in France, neither its performers nor its audience, for a lyric theatre to maintain itself, and you will always return to the situation where music assumes the unforeseen role of mediator.

In reality French composers including Debussy were to welcome with open arms the inauguration of Paris's third lyric theatre, Gabriel Astruc's

Théâtre des Champs-Élysées, in 1913. However, Debussy's 1898 comments on the lack of support it could anticipate unfortunately proved more accurate than his later optimism, and its role as the great white hope for Parisian theatrical standards was short-lived.

Debussy's jaundiced views in 1898, of art suffering as immoral composers sought to make their fortunes from opera, changed somewhat after Albert Carré assumed the directorship of the Opéra-Comique and *Pelléas* was successfully produced. Assessing the 'musical balance sheet' in *Gil Blas* on 28 June 1903 (LCr, p. 189), he found the Opéra-Comique a place of 'feverish activity, as methodical as a factory with work going on on every floor'. After a plea for revivals of *The marriage of Figaro* and *Der Freischütz* in addition to Adolphe Adam's *Le toréador* (for which Carré had a weakness), he praised Carré's positive role at the helm of the newly revitalised theatre. 'The public listens and the artists back him, two things that do not often go happily together', he observed, with the cautionary addition that Carré should not forget that this enviable state of affairs was invariably brief.

In 1903 his role as both critic and composer after *Pelléas* inspired in Debussy a great deal of thought on theatrical matters. He also took up the theme of art and theatre for the people. His article in *Gil Blas* of 2 March (LCr, pp. 105-9; RLS, pp. 129-32) shows him to have been well aware of Gustave Charpentier's Conservatoire Mimi Pinson and Catulle Mendès' Théâtre-Roulotte. He also read widely around his subject and criticised Adrien Bernheim's *Trente ans de théâtre* (Paris, Devambez, 1902) for 'transporting the solemnity of the Comédie-Française into the most unlikely places'. This book was also taken to task for its narrow scope by Romain Rolland, who had published his collected views in *Le théâtre du peuple* (Paris, Suresnes) that same year. Debussy's left-wing ideas were equally radical, though as always he dealt more in ideals than hard reality. His remedy for the current malaise (LCr, p. 108) was to 'unite the *Théâtre Populaire* and the *Opéra Populaire*', which could be achieved by a reversion to the

> theatrical ideas of the ancient Greeks. Let us rediscover Tragedy and enhance its primitive musical accompaniment with the vast resources of the modern orchestra and an unlimited choir! Without forgetting, of course, to include the combined effects of pantomime and dance, developing lighting resources to the extreme to make [such a performance] suitable for a large crowd of people.[16] One could gain much valuable information about this from the entertainments mounted by Javanese princes, where the imperious seduction of the wordless language of pantomime is developed to its absolute limits, because it is based on actions rather than set formulae. It is to the detriment of our own theatre that we have sought to limit it to immediately comprehensible expression alone.

Nevertheless, taking art to the people depressed Debussy in that it involved condescension and artificiality if no lessons were drawn from the past.

Roman circuses and the simply portrayed emotions of the Greek tragedians like Aeschylus and Euripides had been on the right lines. But in the Paris of Debussy's day a new, welcoming, free theatre would need to be specially constructed: adapting an existing building would not suffice. In a sense, Debussy was already in the right frame of mind in 1903 for the establishment of his Temple of Beauty, the Théâtre des Champs-Élysées, 'the only place where music is sincerely loved' (see Fig. 14).

Debussy nonetheless believed that much harm arose from the all-too-common French attitude that nothing succeeded or was artistically of much value outside Paris.[17] He was in favour of decentralisation and state subsidies for important lyric theatres in the provinces, which could do nothing but good for those in Paris as provincial theatres would both emulate their successes and encourage them to do still better to maintain their superiority. But, as always, he remained fiercely chauvinistic. German peformers of all types were more 'scientific' (by which Debussy meant less expressive and spontaneous) than French ones, and he told Adolphe Aderer on 8 October 1909[18] that whereas in Germany 'it is true that music is better treated and better listened to, this is not absolutely true in every case. Our national ingenuity should enable us to avoid the simplistic path of imitating the Germans, without stifling our passion for music with harsh discipline, which is more acceptable outside France.' 'We French', he observed immodestly in 1911 (*Comoedia*, 26 Jan 1911; LCr, p. 300), 'are an admirably intelligent and marvellously gifted people', and in January 1903 he had stated bluntly (*Mercure de France*; LCr, p. 64) that 'German influence has only ever had any ill effect on small-minded, susceptible people; or to put it better, those who take the word "influence" to mean "imitation".'

Debussy was not interested only in events inside the theatre, he had definite views about its architecture too, and complained about the face-lift the Opéra-Comique was receiving in a letter to Georges Hartmann on 6 July 1898,[19] which again suggests learning from the ancients.

> Yesterday I passed the Opéra-Comique, which is now rid of its scaffolding, and I don't need to tell you that it is extremely ugly: a cross between a bank and a railway station! [Fig. 29] . . . I see no particular objection to this and there are many similar efforts, but why upset these poor stones by continually shifting them around? And why does architecture — a most beautiful art form — persist with severe, unflowing lines when it should, on the contrary, be able to create endlessly? These people seem to ignore the effects of light, and consequently all the theory of luminous curves which provides the mysterious harmony that links the various parts of a building. Quite to the contrary, they are contriving to dig tombs where all light is pitilessly extinguished.

Debussy also took as much interest in the internal lay-out and the orchestral placing in particular. Replying to Aderer in 1909, he advised that: 'If when

Fig. 29. The front of the Opéra-Comique, Paris

you are constructing a music theatre you take more trouble with the orchestra and less with the cloak-rooms, you should be able to position the instruments where you want them. This is one of the numerous results of the force of habit often being contrary to good sense, and even to good taste.' In September 1913, replying to an enquiry by Pierre Montamet in *Excelsior* (15 Sept 1913; LCr, p. 306), he maintained that the pretentious Opéra 'should be adapted and rejuvenated . . . Better still, an entirely new form of lyric art should be created' to replace the 'decaying opera-ballets of our ancestors', he suggested, with *La boîte à joujoux* clearly in mind. 'Nothing is more difficult than to orchestrate for the Opéra', Debussy continued, 'for in this immense shell the instrumentation seems either thin or overloaded. If musicians are unable to remedy this defect, then the engineers and architects should busy themselves in trying to do so!'

Debussy was even critical of his talented designers for *Pelléas*, Lucien Jusseaume and Eugène Ronsin.[20] In March 1902 he told Albert Carré (LL, p. 114) that 'Jusseaume, after having made a great deal of fuss, has decided to co-operate, which will not be too bad! Today I must go and see the other plans *chez* M. Ronsin: I pray that God will help me in this new battle.' Debussy had clear ideas about what he wanted the sets for *Pelléas* to look like and perhaps tried to press for his own plans against the better judgment of his designers. Fig. 30 shows his sketch for Act 3 scene 1 with the 'tower' and 'lime-tree' carefully positioned: Fig. 31 shows Ronsin's final backcloth for this tableau as published in *Le théâtre* in June 1902. And after Jusseaume's marvellous work for the rest of *Pelléas* (see Figs. 6 and 7), Debussy still managed to criticise his designs for Georges Hüe's *Titania* in January 1903 (*Gil Blas*, 26 Jan 1903; LCr, p. 85; RLS, pp. 103-4), which he thought were over-elaborate and intended to promote the designer's own glory rather than that of Shakespeare.

In the same article Debussy attacked the famous librettist Louis Gallet, saying that 'he died without leaving any titles important enough for him to be considered the "father" of anything in the realm of art' (LCr, p. 83). And in November 1901 Victorien Sardou, who wrote librettos for Offenbach and Saint-Saëns (including *Les barbares*) received similar treatment (*ReB*, 15 Nov 1901; LCr, p. 56; RLS, p. 54). Debussy was rude about theatre conductors like Sylvain Dupuis, Büsser and Campanini, and singers like Rose Féart and Maggie Teyte as we saw in Chapter 3, and he answered critics of *Pelléas* (like Eugène d'Harcourt) with biting irony in *Le figaro* on 16 May 1902 (LCR, pp. 269-71):

> M. Gauthier-Villars reproaches my score because the melodic lines are never found in the vocal parts but always in the orchestra. I wished never to halt the action and to make it continue uninterrupted. I wanted to do away with parasitic musical phrases. On hearing opera, the spectator is accustomed to experiencing two

Fig. 30. Debussy's sketch for a design for Act 3 scene 1 of *Pelléas et Mélisande*, showing the tower and lime-tree

Fig. 31. Eugène Ronsin's design for Act 3 scene 1 of *Pelléas et Mélisande*, showing 'one of the castle towers'

distinct sorts of emotion: the musical emotion on the one hand, and the emotion of the characters on the other. Generally they are experienced successively, but I tried to ensure that both emotions were perfectly blended and simultaneous.

If Debussy made theatrical personalities suffer, then he was also cruelly wounded himself by Henri Bataille's *La femme nue*, which paraded his private life, loosely disguised, before *le tout Paris*, in particular the tragic breakdown of his marriage to Lilly Texier. This parody opened at the Théâtre de la Renaissance on 27 February 1908, with Berthe Bady in the title role, and it proved immensely popular. It is small wonder that Debussy wrote to Durand on 1 November that year that 'intellectuality, or, in its place, comprehension does not appear to me to have visibly increased amongst theatre folk' (*F-Pdurand*).

Towards the end of his career there is evidence to suggest that Debussy saw music as capable of increasingly realistic portrayal. He told Durand in March 1908 (DUR, p. 58) that in his orchestral *Images* he was 'attempting something different — in a sense, *realities*', and he was particularly pleased with the natural way 'Les parfums de la nuit' led into 'Le matin d'un jour de fête' in *Ibéria* during Pierné's rehearsals for the première, which took place on 20 February 1910. As he told Caplet (CAP, p. 46): '*It feels as if it was improvised (Ça n'a pas l'air d'être écrit)* . . . Everything is there in the awakening and rising of people and things . . . I see a merchant selling water-melons and street urchins whistling very distinctly.' His 1910 impression of the Hungarian violinist Radics (see Chapter 12, n. 31) provides further evidence of his belief in music's realistic powers of natural evocation, and many of his 'impressionistic' piano pieces had specific sources of inspiration.[21] To my mind they were meant to depict as much as to evoke. He was consistently against the performance of theatrical works in concert versions, and in his own works there was a considerable overlap between theatrical and non-theatrical pieces. *Fêtes*, for example, is vividly dramatic, even cinematographic, as in their own ways are *Gigues* and *Ibéria*. The 1901 *Chansons de Bilitis* were happily transformed into the *Épigraphes antiques* for piano duet, and thinking about Segalen's Buddhist drama *Siddartha* in 1907 probably led to the *Image* for piano *Et la lune descend sur le temple qui fût* (see Ex. 68).

The extent to which positive images or dramatic scenes inspired his more plentiful, 'pure' music may be greater than is realised, for he was extremely annoyed in 1916 when Louis Rosoor, one of the first interpreters of the Cello Sonata, published in a programme the descriptive commentary that Debussy had told him in confidence. This was: 'Pierrot awakens with a start and shakes off his drowsiness. He sings a short serenade to his beautiful beloved who, despite his entreaties, remains unmoved. He consoles himself for his lack of success by singing a song of freedom.' Slight maybe, but important to Debussy, as his letters of 12 and 17 October 1916 to Durand reveal.[22]

Debussy particularly admired the visual elements inspired in 'Eritaña', the fourth movement of Albéniz' *Ibéria* (*Revue de la Société Internationale de Musique*, 1 Dec 1913; LCr, p. 245; RLS, p. 301), being always impressed by the skilful use of rhythm and colour. By February 1914, however, he had come to the conclusion that because of the advances made in terms of cinematic realism and its incumbent musical possibilities 'It must be confessed that, although there will be a struggle involved, symphonic compositions for the theatre will soon become very much a dead thing of the past' (*Revue de la*

Fig. 32. André Caplet and Debussy around 1910

Société Internationale de Musique, 1 Feb 1914; LCr, p. 253). If the cinema were to be the 'Ariadne's thread' showing the way out of the 'disquieting labyrinth' of modern music, there would be inevitable casualties *en route*: one of these, as Debussy saw it, was music for the theatre.

Some reasons for Debussy's lack of theatrical 'productivity'

The reasons why Debussy contemplated so many theatre projects yet completed so few are many and complex, and it is first necessary to distinguish between immediate excuses and substantial recurring reasons. The excuses for abandoning or not even starting works differ from project to project, sometimes duplicating or overlapping as I have tried to show. They include: insufficient players for a satisfactory performance (*Les noces de Sathan*; *Le pèlerin d'amour*; *Le Roi Lear*); a dated libretto (*Cendrelune*); a too static libretto (*Daphnis et Khloé; Siddartha*); a prosaic, unlyrical libretto (*Comme il vous plaira*; *Orphée-roi*; *Crimen amoris*); authorisation problems (*La Princesse Maleine*; *L'histoire de Tristan*); abandonment for other more important work (*Le chevalier d'or* for the *Nocturnes*; *Le voyage de Pausole* for *Pelléas et Mélisande*); too many works taken on at once (*No-ja-li*, *Fêtes galantes* and *Tania* in 1914); and sheer size and impracticality which gradually dawned on Debussy after his initial burst of enthusiasm had worn off (some of the above and most of the remainder). Indeed, without a definite production date and harassment from a catalyst like Diaghilev, it was a foregone conclusion that the yogic Debussy would always prefer contemplation to action.

The first main *reason* for non-completion concerns the central position of *Pelléas et Mélisande*, a sort of 'no-man's-land' on which other works either bordered or through which they were refracted like light through a prism — just as light from Wagner was refracted in various subtle ways in Debussy's theatrical works, until it came to illuminate *Jeux* 'as if from behind' (CAP, p. 60). Debussy counted on *Pelléas* to establish him both financially and artistically, and he set such store by his only self-motivated masterpiece for the stage that before it was performed he avoided completing anything that might detract from its dramatic impact. Thus it was inconceivable that any of the Peter collaborations could be staged prior to 1902, and he deliberately back-pedalled over Louÿs' *Daphnis et Khloé* and *Aphrodite* when definite theatrical venues loomed into sight. After 1902, as Durand alleges (1925, p. 9), Debussy feared direct comparison with *Pelléas*, and however much elements from it crept into other stage works like *La chute de la Maison Usher*, his public stance remained: 'And now for something completely different.' Much of his aggressive defence was focused on his two little Poe operas, probably in the case of *Usher* because of its very similarities with *Pelléas*.

Then there was the effect of the traumatic dress-rehearsal of *Pelléas* on 28 April 1902 from which, as Carré later testified,[23] Debussy never really recovered. This intensified his love—hate relationship with the theatre as well as his natural timidity and self-doubt. Supervising numerous revivals of *one* opera was quite enough without adding to their number — a view which must have been reinforced by production difficulties with *Le martyre* and *Jeux*. The second main reason involved librettos and librettists. As Dietschy concluded (1962, p. 209), Debussy had 'neither the assured style nor the theatrical experience to write himself a libretto or a scenario which would inspire the appropriate musical clothing'. Whilst his solutions to the Poe tales were ingenious and inventive, they nonetheless destroyed the essential character of the originals. Just as the scenario of *Le diable dans le beffroi* diverted him in 1903, so that of *Usher* prevented *Fêtes galantes* from getting under way in October 1915 and absorbed much of his available composing time in later life. The effect on his theatrical 'productivity' of the war and his final illness have, I feel, been overestimated.[24]

After Maeterlinck's *Pelléas et Mélisande*, Debussy never again found his ideal poet or poem. His other librettists were mostly friends, probably encouraged because they provided company and variety for the reclusive Debussy, who shunned publicity after *Pelléas* and saw only interpreters, doctors, publishers, collaborators and a few remaining friends after his desertion of Lilly for Emma in 1904. Stimulating extra visits may have been one reason why Debussy found so much to criticise and have rewritten by his librettists, to an extent which led Louÿs to abandon *Cendrelune* and Segalen to complete *Orphée-roi* on his own.

A more likely explanation is that Debussy was working with second-rate writer friends but considered that *he* belonged as a librettist to the same front-ranking category he knew himself to be in as a composer. He fancied himself as a dramatic critic, but it was often a long while before his collaborators saw through his persuasive charm and infectious enthusiasm. In the interim most of his victims were subjected to demands for literary revisions on a scale worthy of Flaubert. It would be interesting to know if they ever met separately to discuss their mutual problem, for Segalen, Louÿs, Laloy, Toulet and Peter were all deeply interested in travel, poetry and Far Eastern culture. Planning works and envisaging their potential for new theatrical techniques must have interested his librettists too, but they, unlike Debussy, never allowed these elements to become obsessive. The more complex the libretto, the less likely Debussy was to complete or even start its score, and most of his theatrical music was composed for ballets with slight arguments that merited no literary attention, but perhaps permitted greater flexibility and a freer rein to his abundant inspiration. But like Verdi, Debussy's intense interest in the minutest dramatic points and musical possibilities of his librettos made him a true theatrical composer.

Third, there was the role of women (and finance) in Debussy's life. Whilst women absorbed a great deal of Debussy's time and energy, only Gaby

Dupont had a theatrical work dedicated to her (*Rodrigue et Chimène*) and she probably inspired the creation of Mélisande in 1893-5, a carefree period to which Debussy later looked back with nostalgia and regret. Lilly Texier inspired nothing, and Emma's main achievement was to compel Debussy to take on lucrative conducting tours and uncongenial theatrical commissions to support her in the manner to which they had become accustomed. But whilst writing *Le martyre*, *Khamma* and *Jeux* meant that time and energy was diverted from other theatre projects of Debussy's own choosing, it is quite likely that we should have an even more slender theatrical corpus were it not for Emma. Her role as intermediary between d'Annunzio and her husband in the composition of *Le martyre* was of especial importance, and Debussy dedicated Emma's copy of the vocal score in June 1911, in touching gratitude for her moral support, with the words: 'Pour ma petite mienne en souvenir de trois mois de *Martyre* qu'elle seule sût apaiser par cette jolie formule: "Qu'est-ce que c'est que cela pour toi!".' (*F-Ptinan*) It is interesting to consider that *Le diable dans le beffroi* alone of the theatre works covers Debussy's only period of relative financial security (1904 – early 1907) and even then there is no evidence that he added anything musical to it during these years.

Fourth, editorial pressure from Durand, to whom he fell increasingly in debt, led Debussy, whatever his personal preferences, to channel his creative energies into more accessible, non-theatrical music from 1903 onwards. And if Durand often provided financial advances, he was by no means generous, keeping detailed accounts of every centime involved. Although Debussy was granted a ten per cent reduction on all musical purchases, Durand nonetheless made him pay 4 francs 50 centimes for three conducting batons and buy his own score of *La mer* (15 francs) to send to Henry Wood in January 1908 before his first conducting trip to London![25] In addition Durand administered the payment of an allowance to Lilly Texier, which only increased the size of Debussy's debt to him. By April 1912 Debussy owed Durand nearly 43,000 francs (*F-Pn* Vm. Dos. 13 (15)); it is easy to see why his editor's wishes had to be obeyed, and they did not include vague impractical theatre projects. Editing the works of Chopin and Bach during the war may have delayed Debussy's theatrical ventures (like *Usher*) still further, though the former probably inspired Debussy to compose his *Études*.

Whilst Debussy's inspiration came mostly from extra-musical natural or literary images, the cross-fertilisation that took place between theatrical and non-theatrical works could still mean that we really have more 'theatre' music than we imagine if ideas inspired by the theatre projects were transferred into contemporary chamber or orchestral works. The most obvious example is the piano piece of 1904 for the spot-the-composer competition in *Musica*, which comes direct from the sketches for *La diable dans le beffroi*. But the process was a two-way one, as the self-borrowing from *The little nigar* and the *Children's corner* suite in *La boîte à joujoux* shows, though since all Debussy's cake-walk movements had theatrical origins in the music hall, the pattern is, more strictly speaking, circular.

Fifth, the amount of theatre music Debussy composed was limited by the high standards he set for himself, so that it should survive even the most unsympathetic treatment. This Bachian attribute of musical self-sufficiency can be seen in the deceptively solid construction and superb craftsmanship in which 'art conceals art'. As Debussy told Louis Laloy during rehearsals for the Covent Garden *Pelléas* on 18 May 1909 (*RdM*, 1962, p. 33):

> They are trying to do the work of a month in three days. The
> directors are charming and full of goodwill. I shall end up believing
> that it is all the fault of the composers, who beneath a pretext of
> wanting their music played, consent to terrible approximations in
> performance, a state of things which directors are getting used to.
> This is why it is so vital to write the best music possible, because bad
> music always has to put up with whatever comes along.

He spent a great deal of time thinking about his short contribution to Gabriel Mourey's *Psyché* in 1913 for this very reason, as we saw in Chapter 11.

Sixth, whilst Debussy's style began to change with *Khamma* in response to the virile creative genius he recognised in Stravinsky's *Firebird* and *Petrushka*, it is possible that further stylistic changes may account for the non-completion of some later theatrical works like *Fêtes galantes* and especially *La chute de la Maison Usher*. After the heights of rhythmic complexity in *Jeux*, a neo-classical reaction set in with the final chamber sonatas. Just as he returned to the libretto of *Usher* at the end of his Pourville 'holiday' in 1915, he wrote to the Italian conductor Bernardino Molinari on 6 October (Paoli, p. 204), in tones that were ominous for the future of his Poe operas and *Fêtes galantes*: 'What beauty there is in music all by itself which has no set purpose . . . For many people [the six sonatas I am writing] will not have the importance of an opera . . . But it seemed to me that they would serve the cause of music better!' With 'pure' music he also ran less risk of direct comparison with Stravinsky, whose career he saw largely in terms of the Diaghilev ballets. The alluring and rather Romantic idea of long, secret hours spent in isolation on an incomplete masterpiece like *Usher* must have crossed his mind at some stage or other too. Godet's letter to Debussy of 16 December 1917 (*RdM*, 1962, p. 89) speaks of his 'new manner' as if it was something discussed by Debussy himself in a letter which has since been lost. Quite how *Usher* would have been completed, or *As you like it* composed, in the spirit of this late renewal, we can thus only vaguely conjecture.

Lastly, Debussy's 'compulsive inachievement' (Holloway, p. 233) in the theatre was not entirely unconnected with his own laziness. Whilst his nineteenth-century attitude of artistic exclusivity did not fit in with the new spirit of collaboration instigated by the Ballets Russes, and he was rightly mistrustful of the precedence of choreography and spectacular staging over music,

Debussy nonetheless 'farmed out' as much work to outside orchestrators as his supposedly less orchestrally minded contemporary Fauré did over the same period. This principle of beginning to orchestrate a work and then apparently growing tired of it is most surprising for the composer who revolutionised the role of timbre in music. The practice was not restricted to the theatre works either, for the *Rapsodie* for saxophone and orchestra had to be completed by Roger-Ducasse after Debussy's death. The only explanation is that this last stage of composition was the hardest for Debussy, and it is our loss that large proportions of works like *Le martyre*, *Khamma* and *La boîte à joujoux* lack those felicitous extra details that Debussy added as he orchestrated.

Had it not been for Diaghilev's insistence, the miracle of *Jeux* might have been still-born because, whether we like it or not, Debussy was self-indulgent, self-centred, impulsive and indolent. His multiplicity of interests and jackdaw mind, which operated on so many levels, did not favour concentration on a single project for any length of time, which made completion unlikely. The grass must always have seemed greener in a new project, and the attraction of planning it and assessing its theatrical potential must often have tempted him away from the problems of the matter in hand.

And so Debussy's search for total renewal, both of himself and of the lyric drama, continued, together with his quest for lyrical librettos that would inspire the vital ingredients of rhythm and colour in living, perfect theatre music. *Orphée-roi* and *Comme il vous plaira* failed to inspire him for the same reason that he found Gluck inferior to Rameau: insufficient lyricism. Sadly, Debussy died at an age when Rameau was only just beginning to compose for the theatre, which makes his frustration at being unable to complete his Poe operas in 1916-17 all the more understandable. Being certain that he planned more theatre music than he ever notated is no consolation to us, and Debussy was being wholly honest and sincere when he wrote after the death of the more obviously fulfilled Massenet in 1912 (*Le matin*, 14 Aug 1912; LCr, p. 204): 'In art the person one most often has to struggle against is oneself: the victories thus won are perhaps the most marvellous of all.'

But had *Pelléas et Mélisande* not been internationally acclaimed, or had Debussy been left financially secure in 1907 after the death of Emma's financier uncle, or had he not had the organisation of Durand et Cie behind him after 1903, it is dubious whether many of the post-*Pelléas* masterpieces in other genres, which changed the course of twentieth-century music, would ever have seen the light of day at all. We might, of course, have had a lot more theatre music instead, but on reflection I seriously doubt it.

* * *

Epilogue

As Charles Koechlin observed in his unpublished study of *Pelléas* in 1949,[26] Debussy was not 'theatrical' but rather 'of the theatre', and his only opera represented 'ideal theatre' in the liberty of its conception and in its overriding humanity. *Pelléas* was the late and most perfect flowering of the Symbolist movement, in which simplicity of plot was turned to advantage in that it provided Debussy with the opportunity to create through music the often unexpressed feelings of its characters. Music took over at the point where words became powerless, and seldom before or since has there been such a perfect wedding of the two, a point which Hugh Macdonald's new crystal-clear English translation for the English National Opera's production in November 1981 has now revealed to a great many more people. The plot, with its similarities to Wagner's *Tristan und Isolde*, automatically demanded new means of expression; and it is not surprising that, amongst all his unstarted theatre projects after *Pelléas*, Debussy appeared most interested in Bédier's *L'histoire de Tristan*.

Just as Debussy's entire career had revolved around the theatre, so appropriately it was the subject of his final wish. When Louis Laloy visited him on his death-bed on 21 March 1918, Debussy regretted being unable to go to the dress-rehearsal for a revival of Rameau's *Castor et Pollux* at the Opéra that afternoon (Laloy, 1943, p. 3). 'Trying to smile', Laloy writes, 'he said to me in a faint voice on seeing me leave: "Bid good-day to Monsieur Castor!".' In February 1903 (*Gil Blas*; LCr, p. 91) Debussy had even apologised for continuing at such length about the 'elegant . . . unaffected' music of this favourite opera of his. As if writing from one 'musicien français' to another, he had explained: 'Moments of true joy in life are rare: I would not wish to keep them to myself.' Debussy's own moments of true joy in the theatre had indeed been few and far between, but, like Rameau, his devotion to the stage has resulted in renewed pleasure for others worldwide, and has immeasurably enriched the repertory of both music and the theatre.

Appendix
Chronological catalogue of theatre works and projects

In order to give as comprehensive a picture as possible of Debussy and the theatre, the following catalogue embraces everything from complete operas to ideas that probably did little more than temporarily enter his fertile brain. It also includes the plays written in collaboration with René Peter and projects mentioned in the text that he swiftly rejected. Prix de Rome and other cantatas for concert performance are omitted, though exceptions are made for *L'enfant prodigue* and *La damoiselle élue* which received stage performances in their revised orchestral forms after 1904. Ballet projects in which Debussy was not involved, like the Diaghilev/Benois *Fêtes* of 1912, are omitted, even though they are mentioned in the text. Only the ballet choreographed by Nijinsky for *L'après-midi d'un faune* is included, because of its importance.

The Appendix gives the following information: date of composition or consideration; title; description and author of the text; publication details of the text; details of the first performance of the text in its original form (if applicable); description of the music; dedication; locations and contents of the manuscript(s); publication details of the music; details of the first performance of the music. As far as is possible the numbered entries for manuscripts and librettos are arranged in chronological order. The first date or dates given in the left-hand column show when Debussy was most involved with a project or actually composed its score, and the works are listed chronologically by their dates of starting rather than completion. A second date or dates in parentheses below indicates the total time-span of the project, including revisions and adaptations. None of the works have opus numbers and their usually progressive tonality makes the attempt to list even principal keys or key-centres futile.

The system of abbreviations used in the Appendix is that of *The new Grove dictionary of music and musicians*, ed. Stanley Sadie, 20 vols. (London, Macmillan, 1980), with a few additions. The key to abbreviations for manuscript sources and bibliographical references may be found at the start of the book (pp. xv-xvii). The place of first performance is Paris unless otherwise stated. In most cases only the present locations of manuscripts are given; details of past locations may be found in LCat.

Abbreviations

A	alto, contralto (voice)
acc.	accompaniment, accompanied by
B	bass (voice)
b	bass (instrument)
Bar	baritone (voice)
bn	bassoon
cat.	catalogue
cel	celesta
Cie	Compagnie
cl	clarinet
cond.	conductor, conducted by
cymb	cymbals
cymb ant	cymbales antiques (antique cymbals)
db	double bass
dbn	double bassoon
ded.	dedication, dedicated to
eng hn	English horn (cor anglais)
esp.	especially
f., ff.	folio, folios
facs.	facsimile
fl	flute
gr c	grosse caisse (bass drum)
harm	harmonium
hn	horn
hp	harp
inc.	incomplete
incl.	includes, including
lib	libretto
M.	Monsieur
Mez	mezzo-soprano
movt	movement
MS, MSS	manuscript, manuscripts
ob	oboe
orch	orchestra, orchestration
orchd	orchestrated by
orig.	original, originally
OS	orchestral score
perf.	performance, performed by
pf	piano
pic	piccolo
PLU	present location unknown
prem.	première
pubd	published
pubn	publication

recit	recitative
R, red.	(piano) reduction
repr.	reprinted
Rés.	Reserve collection (*F-Pn*, *F-Po*)
rev.	revised
S	soprano (voice)
sar	sarrusophone
sc.	scene
SMI	Société Musicale Indépendante
SN	Société Nationale (de Musique)
str	strings
T	tenor (voice)
tamb	tambour de basque (tambourine)
timp	timpani
tpt	trumpet
transcr.	transcribed
trbn	trombone
tri	triangle
unacc.	unaccompanied
unperf.	unperformed
unpubd	unpublished
v, vv	voice, voices
va	viola
vc	cello
vn	violin
VS	vocal score
ww	woodwind
xyl	xylophone

c1882 **Florise**
text: comedy in 4 acts by Théodore de Banville
(Paris, Alphonse Lemerre, 1870)
no music survives

c1882 **Hymnis**
text: lyric comedy in 7 sc. by Théodore de Banville
(Paris, Tresse, 1880); prem. Théâtre Nouveau
Lyrique, 14 Nov 1879, with incidental music by
Jules Cressonnois
music: Debussy set parts of sc. 1, 2 and 7 at least
ded.: Marie-Blanche Vasnier
MSS: 1 *CH-Gbodmer* (4 pp.): sc. 1, 'Il dort encore,
une main sur sa lyre'
2 *US-NYhorowitz* (11 pp.): sc. 7, *Ode bacchique*,
2vv, pf
3 PLU (29 pp.): sc. 1, 2 (inc.), 7, and an unnumbered sc., all in VS (sold Hôtel Drouot, Paris,
1 Jan 1926; see cat. by Kra, no. 38)
unpubd
unperf.

Paris, 1883-4; Rome, **Diane au bois**
1885-6 text: heroic comedy in 2 acts by Théodore de Banville
(Paris, Michel Lévy, 1864); prem. Théâtre de
l'Odéon, Oct 1863
music: Debussy set parts of Act 2 sc. 3 and 4 as a duo
for Eros (T) and Diane (S) with short score acc.
MS: *US-NYpm* Robert Owen Lehman deposit (29 pp.).
Facs. of p. 5, see Fig. 2; facs. of p. 9, *The new
Grove*, vol. 5, p. 295
pubn: extracts in LO, 1, pp. 78-81
prem.: BBC Radio 3, 9 Nov 1968

24 May – 8 June 1884 **L'enfant prodigue**
orch rev. 1906-8 text: lyric sc. by Édouard Guinand (Paris, Institut de
with André Caplet France, 1884)
music: set for Lia (S), Azaël (T), Siméon (Bar), orch
(3 fl, 2 ob, eng hn, 2 cl in A, 2 bn, 4 hn in F, 2 tpt
in F, 3 trbn, tuba, timp, cymb, tamb, 2 hp, str)
ded.: Ernest Guiraud
MSS: 1 *F-Pn* MS 968 (88 ff.): orig. orch
2 *F-Pn* MS 1021 (8 ff. and 13 pp.): 'Cortège'
and 'Air de danse', with rev. orch (1906)
3 *F-Pn* MS 1013 (13 ff.): recit and aria for Azaël,
with rev. orch (1908)
pubn: VS (Paris, Durand, Schoenewerk et Cie, 1884)
rev. VS and OS (Paris, Durand, 1908)
prem.: concert perf.: Institut de France, 27 June
1884. Rose Caron (Lia), Ernest Van Dyck (Azaël),
M. Taskin (Siméon), Debussy and René Chansarel
(pf duet)

partial stage perf.: Salle Gaveau, 12 Dec 1907.
'Cortège' and 'Air de danse'. Charlotte Lormont
(Lia)
complete stage perf.: London, 28 Feb. 1910 (in
French)

1886

Salammbô
text: ?Debussy, after novel by Gustave Flaubert
(Paris, Michel Lévy, 1863)
music: ? opera or symphonic commentary
no music or scenario survive

1886

As you like it
text: comedy by Shakespeare, adapted by Maurice
Vaucaire
no incidental music or text survive

Feb 1887
(1887-1914)
orch rev. early 1912
by Henri Büsser

Printemps
music: symphonic suite in 2 parts, pf duet, orch (pic,
fl, ob, eng hn, 2 cl in A, 2 bn, 4 hn in F, 2 tpt in C,
3 trbn, timp, cymb, tri, tamb, hp, str)
pubn: OS (Paris, Durand, 1913)
prem.: concert perf.: SN, Salle Gaveau, 18 April 1913,
cond. Rhené Bâton
stage perf.: as a ballet *Spring* (scenario by Ronsin, Marc-Henri, Lavardet) in André Charlot's revue
Not likely!, sc. 4, Alhambra Theatre, London, 4
May 1914. Jack Morrison (Winter), Carlotta
Mossetti (the youth), Phyllis Monkman (the
maiden), Alhambra *corps de ballet*; with costumes
by Georges de Feure. See Figs. 20-2

1887-8
(1887-1904)
reorchd 1902

La damoiselle élue
text: lyric poem by Dante Gabriel Rossetti, trans.
Gabriel Sarrazin, pubd in *Les poètes modernes de
l'Angleterre* (Paris, Paul Ollendorff, 1885)
music: set for la damoiselle (S), une récitante (Mez),
female chorus (SSAA), orch (3 fl, 2 ob, eng hn, 2
cl in B flat, b cl, 3 bn, 4 hn in F, 3 tpt in E, 3 trbn,
2 hp, str)
ded.: Paul Dukas
MSS: 1 *F-Pn* MS 984 (14 pp.): sketches
2 *US-NYpm* Mary Flagler Cary collection (cat.,
no. 100b) (15 pp.): VS with orch indications,
dating from May 1893
3 PLU (4 pp.): A part with pf red. (cat. C.
Hopkinson, London, May 1954)
4 *F-Pn* MS 985 (60 pp.): rev. orch (1902)
pubn: VS (Paris, Librairie de l'Art Indépendant, 1892)
VS (Paris, Durand et Cie, 1902)
OS (Paris, Durand et Cie, 1903)

prem.: concert perf.: SN, Salle Érard, 8 April 1893.
Julia Robert (la damoiselle), Thérèse Roger (une récitante), cond. Gabriel Marie
    stage perf.: Opéra-Comique, 4 Feb 1904. Mary Garden (la damoiselle), cond. André Messager

*c*1887-9   **Axël**
text: drama in 4 parts by Villiers de l'Isle-Adam, pubd in *La jeune France*, viii (Nov 1885 – June 1886), no. 88, pp. 193-221; no. 89, pp. 257-83; no. 90, pp. 385-420; no. 92, pp. 453-65; no. 93, pp. 517-33; no. 95, pp. 649-66; prem. Théâtre de la Gaîté, 26 Feb 1894, with incidental music by Alexandre Georges
music: Debussy set 1 sc. according to Vallas (1958, p. 140)
MS: PLU
unpubd
unperf.

1890-1   **L'embarquement pour ailleurs**
text: 1st edn, 2 playlets by Gabriel Mourey with songs by S.P. Blundell (Paris, Albert Savine, 1890); 2nd edn, journal of the poet Damon followed by the 2 playlets from the 1st edn (Paris, H. Simonis Empis, 1893)
music: symphonic commentary as a 'frontispiece' probably to the 1st edn
Debussy's score was never started

1890-2   **Rodrigue et Chimène**
text: lib by Catulle Mendès, after Guillén de Castro: *Las mocedadas del Cid – comedia primera* (1618) and Pierre Corneille: *Le Cid* (1637)
music: opera in 3 acts, for Don Diègue de Bivar (B/Bar); Don Rodrigue de Bivar, son fils (T); Don Hernán, frère du Cid (T); Don Bermudo, frère du Cid (T); Don Gomez, [Comte] de Gormaz, père de Chimène (Bar/B); Chimène, fille de Don Gomez (S); Inèz, servante de Chimène (Mez); Le Roi Ferdinand de Castille (B); Don Juan d'Arcos (T); Don Pedre de Terruel (T); chorus (hommes de Gormaz et Bivar, filles de Bivar etc.); orch (unspecified)
ded.: Gabrielle Dupont, dated 'Avril 90' on Act 1
MS: *US-NYpm* Robert Owen Lehman deposit: Act 1 (inc.; 55 ff.); Act 2 (40 pp.); Act 3 (28 ff.). Short score. Facs. of part of the Act 2 duet, Boucher, Plate 24; facs. of Act 3, ff. 18 *r*, 17 *v* (Chimène's aria), see Figs. 1 a and b
unpubd and unperf. (both were planned in 1979 by

Harold House (Oklahoma) and Carolyn Abbate (Princeton)

1891   **La Princesse Maleine**
text: drama in 5 acts by Maurice Maeterlinck, pubd serially in *La société nouvelle* (Brussels) (1889), and in 1 vol. (Gand, Louis Van Melle, Dec 1889)
music: opera
project abandoned when Maeterlinck refused authorisation to Debussy in favour of Vincent d'Indy (23 June 1891)

1892   **Les noces de Sathan**
text: verse play in 1 act and 5 tableaux by Jules Bois, pubd in *La revue indépendante* (April–June 1890), rev. edn (Paris, P. Chamuel, 1892); prem. Théâtre d'Application, 28 March 1892, with incidental music by Henri Quittard
music: incidental music
Debussy's score was never started

1892 – Sept 1894   **L'après-midi d'un faune**
(1892–1912)
text: poem by Stéphane Mallarmé, pubd as *L'après-midi d'un faune: églogue* (Paris, Alphonse Derenne, 1876)
music: very free symphonic commentary scored for orch (3 fl, 2 ob, eng hn, 2 cl in A, 2 bn, 4 hn in F, 2 hp, cymb ant, str)
ded.: Raymond Bonheur
MSS: 1 *US-NYpm* Robert Owen Lehman deposit (6 ff.): orch sketch. Ded. Gabrielle Dupont, worded 'À ma chère et très petite Gaby, la sûre affection de son dévoué Claude Debussy, October 1899'
    2 *F-Pjobert* (15 ff., 26 pp. of music); OS, dated '1892' (title) and 'Septembre 1894' (end)
    3 *F-Pjobert* (6 pp.): transcr. for 2 pf by Debussy
    4 *US-NYpm* Mary Flagler Cary collection: OS, R and some orch parts (with annotations) used by Sergei Diaghilev for the production by the Ballets Russes in 1912
proofs and printed scores with autograph corrections: see LCat, p. 86
pubn: OS (Paris, Eugène Fromont, 1895)
    2 pf red. (Paris, Eugène Fromont, 1895)
prem.: concert perf.: SN, Salle d'Harcourt, 22 Dec 1894, cond. Gustave Doret
    stage perf.: Théâtre du Châtelet, 29 May 1912, by the Ballets Russes. Vaslav Nijinsky (le faune), Lydia Nelidova, Bronislava Nijinska and 5 others (les nymphes); stage designs by Léon Bakst; choreo-

graphy by Vaslav Nijinsky and Bronislava Nijinska (first planned in Nov 1910 and early 1911, finalised by Nijinsky between March and May 1912), see Figs. 15 and 16

Aug 1893 – 17 Aug 1895; ?1898; Jan 1900; Sept 1901 – April 1902 (?summer 1892 – 1902)

Pelléas et Mélisande

text: drama in 5 acts and 12 tableaux by Maurice Maeterlinck, pubd as *Pelléas et Mélisande* (Brussels, P. Lacomblez, 4 May 1892); prem. Théâtre des Bouffes-Parisiens, 17 May 1893, by Théâtre de l'Oeuvre company: Émile Raymond (Arkel), Georgette Camée (Geneviève), Marie Aubry (Pelléas, *en travestie*), Aurélien-François Lugné-Poë (Golaud), Mlle Meuris (Melisande), Georgette Loyer (le petit Yniold), Mme Louis France (la vieille servante), M. Boulay (un médecin), M. Grange (le portier), Mmes Poraye, Inès-Netza, Millet, Lemarié, Arnold (servantes, pauvres etc.); with scenery by Paul Vogler and costumes by Lugné-Poë; Mélisande's song in Act 3 sc. 2 by Gabriel Fabre, set March 1893, see Exx. 1 and 2

'lib': *F-Ptinan*: copy of 1st edn of Maeterlinck's play, printed on Holland paper and bound in vellum, with Debussy's autograph annotations (Auguste Martin, p. 40, no. 130)

music: opera in 5 acts and 12 tableaux, for Pelléas (T), Golaud (B/Bar), Arkel (B), le petit Yniold (S), un médecin (B), Mélisande (S), Geneviève (Mez), orch (3 fl, 2 ob, eng hn, 2 cl in B flat, 3 bn, 4 hn in F, 3 tpt in F, 3 trbn, tuba, timp, cymb, tri, 2 hp, str)

ded.: Georges Hartmann and André Messager worded 'À la mémoire de Georges Hartmann et en témoignage de profonde affection à André Messager'

MSS: 1 *F-Pmeyer* (52 ff., 61 pp. of music; in black, green, blue and orange pencil and black ink): Act 1 sc. 1 and 2 (5 pp.); Act 2 sc. 1 (7 pp.); Act 2 sc. 2 (11 pp.); Act 2 sc. 3 (7 pp.); Act 4 sc. 4 (9 pp.); Act 5 (22 pp.). Rough sketches mostly on 3-4 staves, dated at the end 'pour H. Lerolle . . . Juin– Juillet 95'. Facs., LPm, pp. 19-84

2 *US-NYpm* Robert Owen Lehman deposit, formerly in the private collection of Robert Legouix (12 ff., 15 pp. of music; in black ink): draft of Act 4 sc. 4, dated 'Septembre–Octobre 93' at the end. Short score (acc. on 3 staves) ff. 1-4. Pelléas: 'C'est le dernier soir . . . J'aurais presque peur de te tou[cher]' (VS, pp. 232-9/OS, pp. 320-8). Incl., on f. 2, Pelléas: 'Mon père est hors de danger, et je n'ai plus de quoi me mentir à moi-même' (insert in VS, p. 233, between bars 7 and 8). Facs., see Fig. 5

ff. 5-12. Mélisande: 'Je ne songe qu'à toi' – end
(VS, p. 254, bar 3 – end of p. 267/OS, p. 345, bar
6 – p. 364). Incl., on ff. 5-6, Pelléas: 'On est triste,
souvent quand on aime . . . Nous attendons tou-
jours; et puis' (insert in VS, p. 255, between bars 2
and 3). Also incl., on f. 10, Pelléas: 'Il restera là
tant qu'il croira que nous ne voyons pas' (insert in
VS, p. 263, between bars 3 and 4)

ff. 7 *v* – 9 *v*. Sketches for Act 4 sc. 4
The missing pages of this manuscript (corresponding to VS, pp. 240-54) were probably removed by
Debussy and inserted into the Bréval manuscript,
cited below (see LPm, pp. 99-110)

3 *F-Pn* MS 1206, Bréval manuscript (19 ff., 29
pp. of music; in black ink with corrections in black,
red and blue ink, and blue, red, purple, black and
green pencil): Act 4 sc. 1 (3 pp.); Act 4 sc. 4 (26
pp., complete). Short score (acc. on 3 staves).
Facs., LPm, pp. 87-120

4 *F-Ppolignac*: decorated Japanese fan given to
Yvonne Lerolle in Feb 1894 with bars 1-5 of Act 1
sc. 3 (VS, p. 39) (sold Hôtel Drouot, Paris, 14 Dec
1979; see cat. by Thierry Bodin, frontispiece and
no. 32)

5 *CH-B* (7 ff.; 12 pp. of music, some – '104',
'108', '112', '115' – only numbered by Debussy;
in black ink): Act 4 sc. 1 and start of sc. 2. Fair
copy of the pf red. (between 1898 and 1901) of
Act 4 up to VS, p. 205, bar 11 (Golaud: 'Pelléas
part ce soir'), now bound with the manuscript of
the suite *Pour le piano*. This MS was rev. in 1901
as part of no. 7 below, where there are 4 fewer
bars in the prelude to sc. 1, the pace of the dialogue
is tighter with a few minor textual cuts, and there
are some thematic changes and more silence in the
accompaniment. (I am grateful to David Grayson
for providing me with this information.) Facs. of
p. 105, Tilman Seebass: *Musikhandschriften in
Basel*, Veranstaltet vom Kunstmuseum Basel (Basel,
Basel Berichthaus, 1975), p. 79.

6 *US-Bc* (131 ff., rectos only): Act 1 (22 pp.,
numbered 4-23), dated 'Déc. 93, Janv.-Fév. 94' at
the end; Act 2 (19 pp.), dated 'Juin – 17 Août 95'
at the end; Act 3 (36 pp.); Act 4 (36 pp.), dated
'Sept.–Oct. 93, Mai 95, Janvier 1900, Sept. 1901'
at the end; Act 5 (18 pp.). Short score (acc. on 3-4
staves). Facs. of 2 pp., Emanuel Winternitz: *Musical
autographs from Monteverdi to Hindemith* (Princeton, Princeton University Press, 1955; repr. 1965),
Plates 173 and 174; the last 5 bars of Act 5 are
included in facs. in Denis, p. 31, as part of the
letter sent to Henry Lerolle on 20 June 1895.
(This manuscript is now on deposit in *US-NYpm*.)

7 *F-Pn* MS 17686 (18 ff., numbered 103-20): VS prepared for Fromont edn (1902) of Act 4 sc. 1 and most of sc. 2 (Durand VS, pp. 189-219)

8 *F-Pn* MS 17683 (23 ff., numbered 121-43): VS prepared for Fromont edn (1902) of Act 4 end of sc. 2 – end of sc. 4 (Durand VS, p. 219, last bar, plus 14 bars' interlude, then pp. 223-67)

9 *F-Pn* MS 17686 (21 ff., numbered 144-64): VS prepared for Fromont edn (1902) of Act 5 (Durand VS, pp. 268-310)

10 *US-AUS* (3 ff., in black ink and blue pencil): sketches for orch of Act 1

f. 1 (numbered '40'). Part of Act 1 sc. 3 (OS, p. 48, bar 4 – p. 49, bar 1)

ff. 2-3 (unnumbered). Part of Act 1 sc. 1 (which occurs in Fromont VS between p. 21, bar 7, and p. 22, bar 3); this passage is the orig., shorter interlude linking sc. 1 and 2 (corresponding to Durand OS, p. 24, bar 6 – p. 25, bar 1, then cutting to p. 28, bar 13)

unidentified sketch (1 f., in black ink), possibly for Act 3 sc. 1 (OS, p. 178) or for an interlude, as bars 5-6 and 13-14 contain the Pelléas motif (Ex. 22d)

11 *F-Pn* MSS 961-5 (402 ff., 406 pp. of music): Act 1 (MS 961; 55 ff., 64 pp. of music); Act 2 (MS 962: 103 ff., 101 pp. of music); Act 3 (MS 963: 88 ff., 86 pp. of music); Act 4 (MS 964: 109 ff., 108 pp. of music); Act 5 (MS 965: 47 ff., 47 pp. of music). OS used for printed edn and by Messager and Büsser in 1902 (with some alterations by them)

12 *F-Pn* Cons. Rés. 2729 (1 p.): Act 3, the change from sc. 2 to sc. 3 (OS, pp. 197, bar 2 – p. 198); the first 2 bars in the manuscript are those missing in the VS, p. 148, between bars 6 and 7 (see also 'printed OS with autograph corrections' no. 3, below)

Proofs of Fromont OS (1904) with autograph corrections: 1 *F-Pn* MS 1029: first proofs of Act 1, second proofs of Act 3

2 *US-NYpm* Robert Owen Lehman deposit: second proofs of Acts 1-2, first proofs of Acts 3-5 (409 pp.)

3 PLU: 4 pp. of corrected proofs of Act 1 (numbered 65-8) (listed in the cat. *Spectacles* (Paris, Coulet, Faure, 1972), p. 175, no. 1045)

printed OS with autograph corrections: 1 *F-ASO*: Fromont edn (1904, 409 pp.) with extensive corrections in red ink, many not incorporated into later Durand edns

2 *F-Pn* Rés. Vma. 281: Fromont edn (1904, 409 pp.), with corrections which were incorporated into the Durand edn (1905) on pp. 167-380. Ded. at

start, worded 'À MadaBardac . . . Ces quatre cent neuf pages de timbres variés qui valent à peine l'ombre que fait ta petite main sur ce gros livre . . . juillet 1904.' This score could be considered as a final proof stage, for Debussy wrote on p. 1 'Bon à tirer . . . 29 juin 04'

 3 *F-Pn* Cons. Rés. 2729: Durand edn (1905, 409 pp.) with corrections in blue ink on pp. 1-5, 10-18. Ded. Emma Bardac, April 1908 (see also MS no. 12, above)

pubn: VS (Paris, Fromont, 1902, 283 pp.), plate number E. 1416, F: lacking extended interludes

 VS (Paris, Durand et Cie, 1907, 310 pp.), plate number D et F. 6953: incl. interludes in full, but lacking 15 bars in Act 3 sc. 4 (p. 184)

 OS (Paris, Fromont, 1904, 409 pp.), plate number E. 1418, F

 OS (Paris, Durand et Cie, 1905, 409 pp.), plate numbers D et F 6577 (on p. 1), E. 1418, F 6577 (on p. 1), E. 1418, F

 pf red. by Gustave Samazeuilh of interludes (Paris, Durand et Cie, 1905)

prem.: Opéra-Comique, 30 April 1902 (dress-rehearsal on the afternoon of 28 April 1902). Jean Périer (Pelléas), Hector Dufranne (Golaud), Félix Vieuille (Arkel), Blondin (le petit Yniold), M. Viguié (un médecin), Mary Garden (Mélisande), Mlle Gerville-Réache (Geneviève), cond. André Messager; produced by Albert Carré; scenery by Lucien Jusseaume and Eugène Ronsin; costumes by Bianchini; stage manager Albert Vizentini; chief répétiteur Louis Landry; chorus-master Henri Büsser

c1895–?1900

Orphée/Amphion
experimental ballet, *Orphée*, planned with Paul Valéry; converted to experimental opera, *Amphion*, c?1900.
Valéry's scenario and Debussy's score were apparently never started

April-Aug 1895
(April 1895 – March 1898)

Cendrelune (also known as *Le roi des aulnes* and *La reine des aulnes*)
text: lyric fairy-tale in 2 acts and 3 tableaux by Pierre Louÿs, intended for the Opéra-Comique, Christmas 1895. Scenarios pubd *RdM*, lvii no. 1 (1971), p. 32 (version of 12 April 1895); *RdM*, xlviii no. 125 (1962), pp. 62-3 (version of 19 April 1895); LOU, Appendix A, pp. 185-9 (version of May 1895). 10 pp. of manuscript lib for Act 1, ? Aug 1895, PLU (sold Hôtel Drouot, Paris, April 1932, see cat.

by Kra, no. 26)
Debussy's score was never started

Sept 1895   **La grande bretèche**
text: lib by Debussy, after story by Honoré de Balzac
pubd in *Scènes de la vie privée*, vol. 3 (Paris, Mame,
1832)
music: opera
Debussy's lib and score were apparently never started

Nov 1895 – March   **Daphnis et Khloé** (later *Daphnis et Chloé*)
1896   ballet
(Nov 1895 – 1898)   scenario: in 3 scenes by Pierre Louÿs, after Longus,
Daphnis and Chloe
scenario retained by Louÿs and probably destroyed;
Debussy's score was never started

April 1896 – ?1898   **Aphrodite**
ballet
scenario: based on Pierre Louÿs: *Aphrodite. Moeurs
antiques* (Paris, Société du Mercure de France, 28
March 1896); ballet intended for the Olympia
Music Hall, Paris, late Nov 1897
Debussy's score was never started and Louÿs' scenario
does not survive

1896   **Les uns et les autres**
text: verse comedy in 1 act by Paul Verlaine, pubd in
his *Jadis et naguère* (Paris, Léon Vanier, 1884);
prem. Théâtre Vaudeville, 20 May 1891
music: ? opera, intended for perf. by Julia Robert at
the Théâtre Salon
Debussy's score was never started (but see *Crimen
amoris*, later *Fêtes galantes*, 1912-15)

1896 – April 1899   **La tragédie de la mort**
text: verse play in 1 act by René Peter, with 'improvements' suggested by Debussy in 1896, pubd with a
preface by Pierre Louÿs (Paris, Société du Mercure
de France, Aug 1899)
music: incidental music
MS: *US-Wc* (2 pp.): sc. 1, *Berceuse pour la 'Tragédie
de la mort' sur une vieille chanson poitevine*, 'Il
était un' fois une fée qui avait un beau sceptre
blanc', A, unacc.; see Exx. 61 and 62
unpubd
unperf. in the context of the play

Feb–Nov 1897   **Le chevalier d'or**
text: ?Rosicrucian pantomime by Mme Jean-Louis

Forain, intended for perf. *chez* M. Forain, ? Christmas 1897
Debussy completed a 'musical plan' by 14 Sept 1897 but the score was never started

July 1897

La tentation de Saint Antoine
text: drama by Vicomte Auguste Gilbert de Voisins, after a drama by Gustave Flaubert (Paris, Bibliothèque Charpentier, 1874)
music: incidental music
Debussy refused this commission, which may have come through Pierre Louÿs

? 1897

Les mille et une nuits de n'importe où et d'ailleurs
fairy-tale in 14 tableaux planned with René Peter
Peter's text and Debussy's score were never started

1897–8
(1897–?1903)

Les 'Frères en Art' (also known as *F.E.A.*)
text: satirical comedy in 3 tableaux (7, 6, 7 sc.) by Debussy and René Peter, completed by Debussy alone probably in 1903. The characters, modelled on contemporary figures, are as follows: Maltravers (painter; Debussy), Marie (his mistress; Lilly Texier), M. Durtal (president of the Frères en Art), Mme Durtal (inventor of the title 'Frères en Art'), une domestique *chez* Durtal, M. Hildebrand (painter; probably Adolf von Hildebrand), Mme Hildebrand, James Redburne (English art critic; probably Swinburne, George Moore or Ruskin, or a mixture of all three), St Diaz (art critic; probably Diaz de la Peña), M. Raland (sculptor), M. Talancet (painter), Mme Talancet, M. Valady (composer), Mme Valady, M. Pardieu (printer), M. Anculac (amateur art-lover)
MS: *F-Pmeyer* (43 ff.): final version in 3 tableaux (11, 9, 19 pp.) (typed copy in the Lockspeiser collection, University of Lancaster). Meyer collection cat. (1961), Plate 12, shows a list of sc. and characters in Debussy's handwriting
pubn: tableau 2, sc. 1-3 (1897-8 version), PET, pp. 78-85; excerpts from the final version, Lockspeiser, *RdM*, 1970, pp. 165-76

1898

La fille de Pasiphaé
text: tragedy by Comte Victor de Balbiani, after Racine: *Phèdre* (1677); unpubd
music: incidental music
Debussy refused the commission

*c*1898

Le roman de Rosette
text: comedy by René Peter, with advice and a frontispiece by Debussy
unpubd, unperf. and probably unfinished

c1898
L'utile aventure
text: comedy by René Peter with Debussy, intended for M. Chautard at the Théâtre du Gymnase
unpubd, unperf. and probably unfinished

c1899
L'herbe tendre
text: comedy by René Peter with Debussy, including the character Julien Grippon
unpubd, unperf. and probably unfinished

c1899
Esther et la maison de fous
text: farce by Debussy, ? with René Peter
MS: PLU, formerly in the private collection of Mme René Peter (4 ff.): synopsis by Debussy, undated, see Dietschy, 1962, p. 136, n. 1
Debussy's text was probably never started

c?1900
Amphion
experimental opera planned with Paul Valéry, see *Orphée*, 1895

Oct 1900 — Feb 1901
(1898-1901)
Chansons de Bilitis
text: 11, later 12, poems by Pierre Louÿs (1 *Chant pastoral*; 2 *Les comparaisons*; 3 *Les contes*; 4 *Chanson*; 5 *La partie d'osselets*; 6 *Bilitis*; 7 *Le tombeau sans nom*; 8 *Les courtisanes Égyptiennes*; 9 *L'eau pure du bassin*; 10 *La danseuse aux crotales*; 11 *Le souvenir de Mnasidica* (probably the late addition); 12 *La pluie au matin*)
music: incidental music scored for 2 fl, 2 hp, cel, to accompany the recitation of the poems with *tableaux vivants*
MSS: 1 PLU: score, given to Louÿs
  2 *F-Pn* MS 16280: instrumental parts, mostly in the hand of a copyist; cel part by Pierre Boulez for 1954 re-creation
pubn: score with poems interspersed, and cel part by Arthur Hoérée (Paris, Jobert, 1971)
prem.: Salle des Fêtes of *Le journal*, 7 Feb 1901. Mlle Milton (reciter); with *tableaux vivants* by Mlles Loulii, Marcel, Darcy, Marie Chaves, Lucienne Delbeau. In the review (*Le journal*, 8 Feb 1901) only nos. 1-3, 5-7, 9, 8, 10 and 12 were listed (in that order), though the orig. parts suggest that all 12 poems were perf. in the order given above (under 'text')
  re-created at the Théâtre Marigny, 10 April 1954, at a Domaine Musical concert. Madeleine Renaud (reciter)

Sept 1901 (March 1900 — Sept 1901)
Le voyage de Pausole
text: *Aventures du Roi Pausole* by Pierre Louÿs,

serialised in *Le journal* (20 March – 7 May 1900)

music: suite for orch to accompany King Pausole's fantastical journey through his kingdom of Tryphême

Debussy's score was never started

June 1902 – Sept 1903

(1902-?1912)

Le diable dans le beffroi

text: lib in 1 act and 2 tableaux by Debussy, after Edgar Allan Poe: *The devil in the belfry*, trans. Charles Baudelaire, pubd in *Nouvelles histoires extraordinaires* (Paris, Michel Lévy frères, 1857). The tableaux are set respectively in Dutch and Italian villages, and the characters are as follows: the devil (? whistling only), a bell-ringer, his son Jean, the mayor, his daughter, villagers.

MS: *F-Pmeyer* (6 pp.): 'Notes pour L. D. d. l. B. – 1er cahier', dated 25 Aug 1903; Debussy's notes consist of a scenario in 2 tableaux. There is also a copy of the printed text in Baudelaire's translation

pubn: scenario, POE, pp. 60-3

music: opera with orch (incl. cimbalom and solo vn)

MSS: 1 *F-Pmeyer* (3 pp.): sketches for ? tableau 1. Facs., as 'Esquisses inédites', III, in POE. Bars 1-8, 19-22 of the *Morceau de concours*, pf, pubd *Musica* (Jan 1905) in the 'Album musical', no. 6, p. 9, also ed. Roy Howat (Paris, Durand et Cie, 1980), derive directly from these sketches

    2 PLU (1½ pp.): description of scenery, a song for tableau 1, 1p. of music (listed in AND, p. 35, no. 185)

Debussy's lib and full score were apparently never started

autumn 1902 – Feb 1904

Comme il vous plaira

text: lib in 3 acts and 5 tableaux by Paul-Jean Toulet, after Shakespeare: *As you like it*, trans. and adapted by Toulet with advice from Debussy. MS: PLU, formerly in the private collection of Mme Cahen Martineau: lib, completed 14 Sept 1903 apart from the 'final *divertissement*', with the passages Debussy wanted changed underlined in pencil

Debussy's score was never started

Dec 1902 – early Jan 1903

Le pèlerin d'amour

text: lyric verse fantasy by Victor-Émile Michelet, pubd in *La porte d'or* (Paris, Paul Ollendorff, 1903), pp. 197-227; prem. Théâtre de l'Odéon, 10 Jan 1903, with Mlle Rabuteau (Lélio), Mlle Brille (Faïs), Mlle Even (la vieille)

music: song for sc. 1 planned by Debussy to be scored for offstage male v, optional chorus, and at least 2 vn, va, vc, db, 2 fl, hp

Debussy's part in the project was abandoned when Paul Ginisty (director of the Odéon theatre) stipulated in early January that the song must be unacc.

?1903 **Joyzelle**
text: after play in 5 acts by Maurice Maeterlinck (Paris, E. Fasquelle, 1903); prem. Théâtre du Gymnase, 20 May 1903, with Georgette Leblanc (Joyzelle)
music: ?opera
neither the lib nor Debussy's score was ever started

?1903 **Don Juan**
text: after ? Byron or Molière
music: ?opera
project mentioned by Albert Carré; neither the lib nor Debussy's score was ever started

1904 **Le Roi Lear**
(1902-?1908) text: Shakespeare: *King Lear*, trans. Pierre Loti and Émile Vedel; prem. Théâtre Antoine, 5 Dec 1904, produced by André Antoine, with an early score by Edmond Missa
music: incidental music in 7 movts
MS: PLU: 3 pp. of orch sketches for a *Fanfare d'ouverture* (18 bars) and *Le sommeil de Lear* (28 bars for the start of Act 4 sc. 7), 2 half-pp. giving the plan of the 7 movts Debussy intended to write (listed in AND, p. 35, no. 184); 4 bars of a *Prélude*, ded. Georges Jean-Aubry, dated July 1908 (see Ex. 64). Facs. of *Prélude*, Boucher, Plate 43 (2)
pubn: *Fanfare* and *Le sommeil de Lear*, orchd Jean Roger-Ducasse (Paris, Jobert, 1926)
prem.: pf perf.: in a red. of Roger-Ducasse's OS, Salle Gaveau, Musique vivante series, 22 Oct 1926, Léon Vallas (pf)
orch perf.: in Roger-Ducasse's version, Concerts Pasdeloup, 30 Oct 1926, cond. Albert Wolff
the concert suite requested of Debussy by Édouard Colonne in 1905-6 was never completed

?1904-5 **Dionysos**
text: lyric tragedy in 3 acts by Joachim Gasquet (Paris, Charpentier et Fasquelle, 1905); prem. Théâtre Antique d'Orange, 1 Aug 1904
music: ?opera
neither the lib nor Debussy's score was ever started

July 1907 – April **L'histoire de Tristan**
1909 text: lib by Gabriel Mourey, after Joseph Bédier's
(1907-12) adaptation of a twelfth-century Breton romance

by the Anglo-Norman poet Thomas pubd as *Le roman de Tristan* (Paris, Firmin-Didot, 1902-5). MS: PLU: letter from Debussy to Segalen of 8 Oct 1907 outlining the lib, pubd in SEG, p. 74
music: opera in 4 acts
MS: *F-Pdurand*: letter from Debussy to Durand, dated Pourville, 23 Aug 1907, incl. one of the '363 thèmes du *Roman de Tristan*' (see Ex. 65)
pubn: DUR, p. 54
no other music survives

4-26 Aug 1907 (1906-7)	**Siddartha**

text: lib by Victor Segalen, based on his Buddhist drama in 5 acts, written in Colombo (Ceylon), Brest and Paris, Nov 1904 – 1907. MS: PLU
music: ?opera
Debussy rejected the project in a letter to Segalen of 26 Aug 1907 (SEG, pp. 66-7) in order to concentrate on *Orphée[-roi]*

29 Aug 1907 – early 1909 (1907 – June 1916)	**Orphée-roi** (orig. *Orphée-triomphant*)

text: lib by Victor Segalen in four acts ('La montagne'; 'Le bois et le fleuve'; 'Le portique de la mer'; 'Le temple sous la terre et l'antre') with a prologue and an epilogue ('La montagne et les airs sonores'). The characters are as follows: Orphée, Eurydice, le vieillard citharède, un prêtre, un guerrier, une prêtresse-ménade, peuple en rumeur, ménades en folie. MS: private collection of Annie Joly-Segalen. Facs. of pages showing Debussy's criticisms as noted by Segalen, SEG, pp. 269, 287. Pubn: lib rev. as a play, 1915 (Paris, Georges Crès, 1921). This version pubd in SEG, pp. 219-341, with annotations by André Schaeffner showing how the two versions of the lib of 1907-8 differed
music: opera
Debussy's score was never started

?1908	**Drame cosmogonique**

project, planned with ? Jacques-Émile Blanche, of which nothing survives

June 1908 – 1917 (1890-1917)	**La chute de la Maison Usher**

text: lib in 1 act and 2 (orig. 3) sc. by Debussy, after Edgar Allan Poe: *The fall of the House of Usher*, trans. Charles Baudelaire, pubd in *Nouvelles histoires extraordinaires* (Paris, Michel Lévy frères, 1857). The characters are as follows: Lady Madeline Usher, le médecin, l'ami, Roderick Usher
MSS: 1 *US-AUS* (22 ff., 27 pp. of writing): first version of the lib, incl. complete draft in 3 sc. (13 pp.);

dating from ?1908 – June 1909 (this version is called 'A' in Chapter 4). Extracts and variants, POE, pp. 53-5, 57-8, 85-97

2 *F-Pn*, formerly *F-Ptinan* (12 pp.): second version of the lib in 3 sc. but with sc. 2 redesignated sc. 1 in a revision; dated 'VIII/09 – VI/10' (version 'B' in Chapter 4). Also 2 pp., undated but contemporary, the first numbered '8' (cf no. 6 below); these may be part of lib A as they refer to 'Sir Launcelot' in the story-telling sequence near the end

3 *F-Pn* MS 9885 (17 pp.): final version of the lib in 2 sc., Pourville, Oct 1915 – Sept 1916 (version 'C' in Chapter 4). Pubd in POE, pp. 85-97

Also:

4 *F-Pn* Rés. Vmd. 41: Debussy's annotated copy of extracts from Baudelaire's *Nouvelles histoires extraordinaires*, with *La chute de la Maison Usher* on pp. 86-111; 24 passages are marked in pencil and there are 3 minor annotations in black ink; the brown paper cover is marked 'D.L.M.' in Debussy's handwriting

5 *US-NH* Gimbel estate (1 p.): prose scenario

6 *F-Pdavid* (1 p.): page from the end of the lib, numbered '12', dated 'VIII/09' (cf no. 2 above; see also music MS no. 3 below)

music: opera set for Lady Madeline Usher (S), le médecin (Bar), l'ami (Bar), Roderick Usher (Bar), orch (unspecified, but probably the same size as that of *Jeux*)

[1909-15] MSS: 1 *F-Pn* W. 54 (2) (22 pp.): *carnet* with sketches for *Usher* on pp. 7-8 (VS, bars 23, 26-7, 31-5); these probably date from May 1909 for they are close to notes on the production of *Pelléas et Mélisande* at Covent Garden, which was being prepared in that month

2 *F-Pn* MS 14520 (1 p.): 18 bars presented to Emma Bardac on her birthday, 11 June 1909, marked 'Ce qui sera peut-être le prélude à *La chute de la maison Uscher* [*sic*]' (cf VS, bars 1-6, 199-202, 7-13)

3 *F-Pdavid* (1 p.): 9 bars from the end of the opera, classed with lib MS no. 6 above; probably dating from 1909 (VS, bars 383-91; they probably belong earlier in the sc., cf VS, bars 199-201, which are themselves misplaced, being bars 7-9 of Debussy's sketch for the prelude (see no. 2 above))

4 *F-Pn* MS 17726, *No-ja-li* sketchbook: sketches for *Usher*, mostly for Lady Madeline's song *Le palais hanté*, stanzas 1 and 4, appear on pp. 1 *v* – 8 *r* (and ? 8 *v*); incl., on p. 2 *r*, 'La Scorpion oblique

et le Sagittaire rétrograde ont paru sur le ciel nocturne' (see pp. 124-7)

5 *F-Ptinan* (1 p., framed): 14 bars of stanza 4 (discarded in lib C) of *Le palais hanté* (VS, pp. 34-5, wrongly transferred from the start of sc. 1 to the middle of sc. 2 by Allende-Blin, so that it occurs after Roderick Usher's monologue)

[1916-17 (in lib C order)]

6 *F-Pn* MS 9885 (21 pp.): sc. 1 and part of sc. 2 up to VS, bar 223 (20 pp.); p. 21 is an 8-bar sketch for the end of the opera, see no. 14 below. Short score, dating from 1916. Facs., as 'Esquisses inédites', II, in POE

7 *F-Pprunières* (1 p.): part of sc. 2 (following that on p. 20 of *F-Pn* MS 9885, see no. 6 above) (VS, bars 225-47). Facs., Lockspeiser, 1936, p. 111

8 *F-Pn* MS 17727: sketches for the first part of sc. 2 appear on pp. 2 *r–v*, 3 *r* (VS, bars 248-95)

9 *F-Ppincherle* (1 p.): first part of sc. 2 (VS, bars 296-312). Facs., POE, Plates 26-7 (following 'Esquisses inédites', II, see no. 6 above)

10 *F-Phoérée* (1 p.): first part of sc. 2 (VS, bars 313-22). This manuscript also incl. a setting (crossed out) of the words 'Des flambeaux . . . allumons les flambeaux . . . c'est à peine si je vous vois! Cher Roderick . . . je n'ai eu be[soin de personne]' (lib C, end of p. 8) which is as far as Debussy progressed with continuous music for sc. 2; see Ex. 31

11 *F-Pn* MS 17727: 18 bars of music for the middle of sc. 2 ('Page 13. 14 de . . . [lib C]') appear without text on the unnumbered first page of the manuscript; see Ex. 29

12 *GB-Lbm* Add. MS 47860 (3): sketches for sc. 2, start of the final melodrama ('Sire Ulrich, coeur vaillant . . . [un bouclier d'airain brillant]') (VS, bars 337-62) appear on f. 25; see Ex. 30a

13 *F-Pn* MS 17727: sketches for the end of sc. 2 ('Alors! Ulrich leva sa massue . . . mais tomba à ses pieds', lib C, p. 16) (VS, bars 363-82) appear on p. 1; see Ex. 30b

14 *F-Pn* MS 9885: an 8-bar sketch for the end of the opera appears on p. 21; its words, 'Ah! damné! tu me l'as volée', are not those of lib C (VS, bars 392ff). For facs. and further details of the contents of this manuscript, see no. 6 above

there are reported to be other *Usher* manuscripts in the estate of Ferruccio Busoni but at the time of writing (May 1981) I have no confirmation of this

pubn: VS in the version by Juan Allende-Blin (Paris, Jobert, 1979, 41 pp., 400 bars) prem.: partial concert perf.: part of Roderick Usher's monologue in sc. 2, perf. with pf acc., Société Française de Musicologie, Paris, 27 Nov 1959

stage perf.: in the version by Carolyn Abbate, orchd by Robert Kyr, with double ww as in *Pelléas et Mélisande*; Jonathan Edwards College, Yale University, New Haven, Connecticut, 25 Feb 1977, cond. C. William Harwood; directed by Graf Mouen. From the point early in sc. 2 where the continuous musical material breaks off, the production was spoken

stage perf.: in the version by Juan Allende-Blin, orchd with quadruple ww as in *Jeux*; Berlin Opera, 5 Oct 1979, cond. Jesus Lopez-Cobos; directed by Nikolaus Lehnhoff. Sung throughout, with pauses representing the gaps in Debussy's music. (This version was first heard in a concert perf. on Hessischer Rundfunk, Frankfurt-am-Main, 1 Dec 1977, with Irène Jarsky, Bruno Laplante, Walter Köninger, Michael Leighton-Jones, cond. Eliahu Inbal)

29 March 1909	**Huon de Bordeaux** text: lib by Gabriel Mourey, ? after Wieland music: ?opera Debussy rejected the project
29 March 1909	**Le marchand de rêves** text: lib by Gabriel Mourey music: ?opera Debussy rejected the project
29 March 1909	Le chat botté text: lib by Gabriel Mourey music: ? fairy-tale opera or pantomime Debussy rejected the project
17 – 25 July 1909 (July 1909 – June 1910)	**Masques et bergamasques** (in May 1910 Debussy also suggested the titles *L'éternelle aventure* and *L'amour masqué*) ballet 'rosso-vénitien' scenario: in 3 sc.; ballet intended for the 1910 season by the Ballets Russes. Though Louis Laloy was asked to write the scenario, Debussy did so. The characters are as follows: Arlequin (to have been danced by Vaslav Nijinsky), Barbarina (Tamara Karsavina), le docteur bolonnais, Capitaine Firibiribombo, Scaramouche, Tartaglia, Truffaldini, Brighella, l'eau d'or qui danse, la pomme qui chante, jeunes cavaliers, pêcheurs et leurs femmes MS: *US-AUS* (4 pp.): scenario, dated 'VII.09', written on 24-5 July 1909

pubn: (Paris, Durand et Cie, 1910)
music MS: *US-NYpm* Robert Owen Lehman deposit, *Images* sketchbook: 1 bar, marked '(Angelus)' (see Ex. 41) on p. 96 may be a sketch for the opening of the ballet
with the possible exception of this bar, Debussy's score was never started

27 July 1909   **L'orestie**
text: lib by Louis Laloy, after Aeschylus
music: ?opera
Laloy's lib and Debussy's score were never started

Jan 1911   **Pygmalion**
ballet in 1 act by Jean-Philippe Rameau, 1748, to have been reorchd ? and edited by Debussy for perf. at the Théâtre des Arts, early 1911; see Chapter 12, pp. 273-4
Debussy never started work on the project

late Jan – May 1911   **Le martyre de Saint Sébastien**
(25 Nov 1910 –   text: mystery in 5 acts ('La cour des lys'; 'La chambre
Nov 1917)   magique', substantially cut after the prem. and omitted in the revival of June 1922; 'Le concile des faux dieux'; 'Le laurier blessé'; 'Le paradis', added last on Cohen's suggestion of 21 Dec 1910 and often referred to as the second part of Act 4), by Gabriele d'Annunzio with 'advice' from Gustave Cohen and Ida Rubinstein; pubd in *L'illustration théâtrale*, no. 181 (27 May 1911) and (Paris, Calmann Lévy, 1911). The characters are as follows: le saint, la mère douleureuse, la fille malade des fièvres, l'empereur [Diocletian], le préfet
music: incidental music set for anima Sebastiani (S), la voix de la vierge Erigone (S), les deux jumeaux Marc et Marcellian (2 A), chorus (chorus séraphicus, citharèdes, femmes de Byblos, coryphées, chorus syriacus, and in Act 5 chorus martyrum/virginum/ apostolorum/sanctorum omnium), orch (2 pic, 2 fl, 2 ob, eng hn, 3 cl in B flat, b cl, 3 bn, dbn (orig. sar), 6 hn in F, 4 tpt in C, 3 trbn, tuba, 4 timp, gr c, cymb, tam-tam, cel, 3 hp, harm (off stage), str)
MSS: 1 *F-Po* Rés. MS 2004: full score in black ink and pencil; a collation of three scores in the hands of Debussy, André Caplet and three other copyists (incl. M. Colombin)
Act 1
prelude and duet (les jumeaux) (8 ff.) by Debussy (OS, pp. 1-18)
no. 2 (5 ff.) by Debussy (OS, pp. 19-26)
no. 3 (21 ff., numbered '21'–'42'): ff. 21-31 by

Debussy in black ink; ff. 32-42 by Caplet in pencil (from OS, p. 47, bar 4: 'Je danse sur l'ardeur des lys') (OS, pp. 27-63)

Act 2

nos. 1-3 (8 ff., 7 ff., 10 pp.) by Caplet (OS, pp. 64-98); a few tempo and other perf. indications by Debussy as elsewhere, and some vocal parts in no. 3 in a third hand

Act 3

nos. 1-5 by Caplet (OS, pp. 99-132); in no. 3 (p. 5, bars 4-5) Debussy altered the text of the bass part (les citharèdes), though the new text ('Beau roi chevelu de lumière') was not incl. in OS, p. 106, bars 1-2

no. 6 (6 pp.) by Caplet (OS, pp. 133-40); instrument names (pp. 1-2), str *tremolando* parts and corrections to hp *glissandi* (pp. 2-3), and vocal parts (p. 4, figs. 3f) by Debussy

no. 7 (6 pp.) mostly in a fourth hand, though some of this very sketchy movt could be by Caplet (OS, pp. 143-8)

Act 4

prelude (6 ff.) by Caplet (OS, pp. 149-55)

no. 2 (4 pp.), by same hand as Act 3 no. 7, with alterations (e.g. to str, hn parts on p. 4) by Debussy (OS, pp. 156-60)

no. 3 (16 pp.) mostly by Caplet, but vocal parts in a fifth hand ? M. Colombin (OS, pp. 161-75)

Act 5

nos. 1 and 2 (23 pp.) by Debussy (OS, pp. 176-202), but vocal parts in no. 2 in the same hand as Act 2 no. 3

2 *GB-Lrussell* (1 p.): corrections to the hp and cymb parts at the end of the prelude to Act 4 (OS, p. 155), sent by Debussy to Caplet, probably in May 1911. Facs., CAP, between pp. 56 and 57. See also Orledge, 1974, p. 1033, Ex. 1

3 *GB-Lrussell* (1 p.): 4 bars in short score for the end of Act 2 no. 3 ('Tous les astres louent sa clarté, Ah!'; VS, p. 46, bars 1-4), sent by Debussy to Caplet and marked 'Hoc varietur' ('This may be changed'). Facs., CAP, between pp. 56 and 57

printed OS with corrections: *F-Po* A 742a: used as a conducting score by Caplet in 1911, with some 'modifications' by him, esp. to the brass on pp. 61-3, 99-103

pubn: VS, prepared by Caplet (Paris, Durand et Cie, 1911, 104 pp.)

OS (Paris, Durand et Cie, 1911, 202 pp.)

prem.: complete stage perf.: Théâtre du Châtelet, 22 May 1911. Ida Rubinstein (le saint), Adeline

Dudlay (la mère douleureuse), Véra Sergine (la fille malade des fièvres), Maxime-Julien Desjardins (l'empereur), Henry Krauss (le préfet), Rose Féart (anima Sebastiani), Eugénie [Ninon] Vallin (la voix de la vierge Erigone), Mmes Courso and Chadeigne (les deux jumeaux Marc et Marcellian), cond. André Caplet; produced by Armand Bour; scenery and costumes by Léon Bakst; choreography by Michel Fokine; chief répétiteurs Marcel Chadeigne, Émile Vuillermoz; chorus-master Désiré-Émile Inghelbrecht

, abridged perf.: SMI, 14 June 1912, cond. Désiré-Émile Inghelbrecht

orch perf.: symphonic suite, arranged by Caplet ('La cour des lys' (Act 1 prelude); 'Danse extatique et final du 1er acte' (Act 1 no. 3); 'La passion' (parts of Act 3 no. 4); 'Le bon pasteur' (Act 4, nos. 1 and 2)), Prague, 14 Jan 1914, Czech Philharmonic Orchestra, cond. Edgard Varèse

film plans: M. Vidal-Hult (in Dec 1913) and M. Péquin (in June–July 1914) made plans for film versions, but the first filming (of Ida Rubinstein's dances) took place during a revival at the Opéra, June 1922

at the request of Jacques Rouché, director of the Opéra, Debussy and Louis Laloy worked on an opera version in 1914 and Dec 1916 – Nov 1917; the project was never completed and no material for it is known

Feb–Oct 1911

La dame à la faulx

text: tragedy in 5 acts and 10 tableaux by Antoine Saint-Pol-Roux (pseudonym of Paul Roux) (Paris, Mercure de France, 1899); rev. 'version théâtrale', ?1910, ed. Yves Sandre (Mortemart, near Limoges, Rougerie, 1979)

music: incidental music (5 longer and 10 shorter pieces), intended for a production of the rev. version by Jacques Rouché at the Théâtre des Arts, late Oct or early Nov 1911

MSS: private collection of Divine Saint-Pol-Roux: text and plans by Saint-Pol-Roux for the incidental music

Debussy's score was never started, nor did Dukas or Ravel (who were also approached in 1911) write any music, though some may have been composed by Gabriel Dupont; Rouché abandoned the stage production early in 1912

Dec 1911 – April 1912

Khamma (orig. *Isis*)
ballet pantomime or 'légende dansée'

(30 Sept 1910 –
Aug 1916)
orch, bars 79ff (R,
p. 7, bars 10ff),
completed by Charles
Koechlin under
Debussy's supervision,
5 Dec 1912 – 31
Jan 1913

scenario: in 3 sc. by Maud Allan, William Leonard
Courtney and ? Debussy. The characters are as
follows: Khamma, the great god Amun-Ra, high
priest of Amun-Ra, crowd of besieged Egyptians
MS: *F-Pn* Rés. Th. b. 126 (9 pp.): scenario in French,
titled 'Ballet pantomime en trois scènes', in Debussy's hand
music: scored for orch (pic, 3 fl, 3 ob, eng hn, 3 cl in
B flat, b cl, 3 bn, dbn, 4 hn in F, 3 tpt in C, 3 trbn,
tuba, timp, gr c, cymb, gong, cymb ant, pf, cel,
2 hp, str)
MSS: 1 *F-Pn* MS 17728 (1 p.): sketches for the
'Khamma' theme, see Ex. 37 D
2 PLU, formerly in the private collection of
Maud Allan, sold after her death on 7 Oct 1956 by
public auction: R by Debussy, dating from 1912
3 *F-Pn* MS 15470 (41 pp.): 28 pp. of preliminary
sketches for orch by Charles Koechlin (complete
version from sc. 2, bar 18: 'La peur de Khamma')
probably dating from 5-14 Dec 1912; 13 pp.,
numbered 30, 34-5, 48-9, 58-9, 62, 67-9, 72, 80,
from the first version of the OS by Koechlin, with
a few corrections by Debussy, probably dating
from 26 Dec 1912 – 13 Jan 1913
4 *F-Pdurand* (80 pp.): full score, pp. 1-10 by
Debussy in pencil, probably dating from April
1912; pp. 11-80 by Koechlin in ink, copied 4–31
Jan 1913, see Orledge, 1975, p. 31. (Copy in *F-Pn*
Gr. Vma 289)
pubn: R (Paris, Durand et Cie, 1912, 32 pp.), not put
on sale, for legal reasons, until Aug 1916
prem.: concert perf.: Concerts Colonne, 15 Nov 1924,
cond. Gabriel Pierné
    stage perf.: Opéra-Comique, 26 March 1947.
Geneviève Kergrist (Khamma), Michel Gevel
(Amun-Ra), Dany Markel (high priest of Amun-Ra),
cond. Gustave Cloez; scenery and costumes after
maquettes by Luc-Albert Moreau, see Fig. 13;
choreography by Jean-Jacques Etcheverry

Feb 1912

Ballet persan
planned with Paul-Jean Toulet, ? as an alternative to
Masques et bergamasques for Diaghilev (see Chapter
6, n. 8)
no music or scenario survive

1912

L'après-midi d'un faune
ballet version by Vaslav Nijinsky, see pp. 308-9

April 1912 – late
Sept 1915

Crimen amoris (reworked as *Fêtes galantes*)
opera-ballet, intended for the Opéra

text: *Crimen amoris*: lib (lost) for a lyric tale in 3 acts by Charles Morice, probably after Paul Verlaine's poem *Crimen amoris* pubd in *La libre revue* (1-15 May 1884) and in the 'Naguère' section of *Jadis et naguère* (Paris, Léon Vanier, 1884)

Fêtes galantes: in Jan 1913 Debussy decided to replace Morice by Louis Laloy who in late 1913 reworked the project as *Fêtes galantes*, an opera-ballet in 3 tableaux ('Les masques'; 'Les rêves'; 'La vérité'). This used poems by Verlaine from *Jadis et naguère* (incl. sc. 1 and 10 of *Les uns et les autres*; see p. 313); *Fêtes galantes* (Paris, Alphonse Lemerre, 1869); *Romances sans paroles* (*Ariettes oubliées*, *Aquarelles*) (Paris, Sens, 1874); *Sagesse* (Paris, Société-Générale de Librairie Catholique, 1881); *Amour* (Paris, Léon Vanier, 1888); *La bonne chanson* (Paris, Alphonse Lemerre, 1870); and *Poèmes Saturniens* (Paris, Alphonse Lemerre, 1866) (see Chapter 9). The characters of *Fêtes galantes* are as follows: sung roles Lélian, Mezzetin, chorus (masqueraders, fairies, lovers); danced roles Colombine, Arlequin, Pierrot, Léandre, Cassandre, le marquis, l'abbé, 2 Italian girls, masqueraders in French and Italian costume. MS: *F-Pn* Rés. Vmb. 33 (14 pp.): typed lib of *Fêtes galantes*, undated (? Nov 1913) with a few corrections in black ink, probably by Laloy; described as a 'ballet en trois tableaux d'après Paul Verlaine par Claude Debussy'

music: to have been set for Lélian (Bar), Mezzetin (T or *haute-contre*), chorus, orch (unspecified)

MS: *F-Pn* MS 17730 (3 ff., rectos only; in blue ink); tableau 1, Mezzetin's song (stanzas 1 and 3 from *Les uns et les autres*, sc. 1) 'Puisque tout n'est rien que fables' (see Ex. 56), extended sketch (2 ff.) with short score, dating from Jan 1914 or late Sept 1915. The third folio may be a setting for the masqueraders, also for the start of tableau 1, of *À la promenade* from *Fêtes galantes*; see Ex. 57

Debussy's score was never completed

*c*23 July 1912 – 25 Aug 1912 orchd 23 Aug 1912 – 2 Sept 1912 and 28 March 1913 – 24 April 1913 (12 June 1912 – 1917)

Jeux

ballet or 'poème dansé'

scenario: in 1 act probably by Sergei Diaghilev on an idea by Vaslav Nijinsky. The characters are as follows: première jeune fille, deuxième jeune fille, un jeune homme

music: scored for orch (2 pic, 2 fl, 3 ob, eng hn, 3 cl in A, b cl, 3 bn, sar, 4 hn in F, 4 tpt in C, 3 trbn, tuba, timp, tamb, tri, cymb, cel, xyl, 2 hp, str)

ded.: Mme Jacques Durand

MSS: 1 PLU, formerly in the private collection of

Robert Legouix: orch sketch, dated '23, 28, 29 Août – 1, 2 [Sept]'

2 *F-Pn* MS 1088 (24 pp., 22 pp. of music): pf red., showing the orig. ending (8 bars shorter) and reworking suggested by Diaghilev in Sept 1912 (see Ex. 43) and another slight revision to the end requested on 31 Oct 1912 (see Ex. 44)

3 *US-NYpm* Robert Owen Lehman deposit (31 ff.; in pencil): 'préparation orchestrale' without dynamic, expression or tempo markings, and with timp, percussion, fl and pic parts often missing; dated '28.3.13 midi ... 24.4.13, 6h.$\frac{1}{4}$' at the end

4 *F-Pn* MS 966 (79 pp.): full score

printed OS with autograph corrections: 1 *F-ASO*: OS with many corrections not incorporated into later Durand edns

2 *F-Plifar*: OS with perf. annotations by Diaghilev, Nijinsky and Debussy

pubn: R (Paris, Durand et Cie, 1912, 42 pp.) (bar 332 in OS (p. 56, bar 4) missing on p. 21) OS (Paris, Durand et Cie, 1914, 118 pp.)

prem.: stage perf.: Théâtre des Champs-Élysées, 15 May 1913, by the Ballets Russes. Tamara Karsavina (première jeune fille), Ludmilla Schollar (deuxième jeune fille), Vaslav Nijinsky (un jeune homme), cond. Pierre Monteux; scenery and costumes by Léon Bakst; choreography (based on the eurhythmic system of Jaques-Dalcroze) by Vaslav Nijinsky concert perf.: Concerts Colonne, 29 Feb 1914, cond. Gabriel Pierné

July – 30 Oct 1913 (Feb 1913 – Nov 1917) orch started ?April 1914; tableau 1, bars 38ff orchd by André Caplet, Oct – Nov 1919

La boîte à joujoux

'ballet pour enfants'

scenario: prelude ('Le sommeil de la boîte'), 4 (orig. 3) tableaux ('La magasin de jouets'; 'Le champ de bataille'; 'La bergerie à vendre'; 'Après fortune faite') and epilogue, by André Hellé, after his own illustrated children's story (Paris, A. Tolmer, 1926). The characters are as follows: la poupée, Polichinelle, Arlequin, le soldat anglais, la rose, with le marin, le policeman, le nègre, le pierrot, le capitaine, le tambour, le sergent de ville, le général des polichinelles, le berger, la bergère, and pantins, poupées, soldats, artilleurs, polichinelles

music: scored for orch (2 fl, 2 ob, eng hn, 2 cl in B flat, 2 bn, 2 hn in F, 2 tpt, timp, cymb, gr c, tamb militaire, tri, crisette, pf, cel, 2 hp, str)

MSS: 1 *F-Pmeyer*, sketchbook of 1913: unused themes for Arlequin and Polichinelle (listed in AND, p. 34, no. 182)

2 *F-Pn* MS 976 (45 ff.): R in 3 tableaux (21, 13,

11 ff.) with the third and fourth tableaux listed
above (under 'scenario') as tableau 3
  3 *F-Pn* MS 979 (114 pp.): full score in 4
tableaux; pp. 1-7 by Debussy, the rest by André
Caplet (see Fig. 19)
  4 PLU: set of second proofs of tableaux 1 and
2 with autograph corrections (36 pp.), Hellé's
manuscript scenario, and Hellé's designs for the
preliminary pages of the R (8 ff.) and the 12 colour
plates to be interspersed with the music (listed in
AND, p. 34, no. 181)
pubn: R (Paris, Durand et Cie, 1913, 52 pp.) with
scenario and colour illustrations by Andre Hellé
  OS, orchd André Caplet (Paris, Durand et Cie,
1920)
prem.: orig. version: Théâtre Lyrique du Vaudeville,
10 Dec 1919. Mlle Sakhy (la poupée), R. Quinault
(Polichinelle), Mlle J.-J. Moncey (Arlequin), Mlle
Gineva (le soldat anglais), Mlle Ricci (le pierrot),
cond. Désiré-Émile Inghelbrecht; produced by R.
Quinault; scenery and costumes by Andre Hellé;
choreography by R. Quinault
  marionette version: perf. with pf acc., ?Utrecht,
1962, with Hans Henkemans (pf); produced by
Feike Boschma, Peter Struycken

late Nov 1913   **Psyché**
(Oct – 1 Dec 1913)   text: dramatic poem in 3 acts by Gabriel Mourey
(Paris, Mercure de France, 1913)
music: incidental music; the project resulted in *La
flûte de Pan*, fl, to acc. Pan's mimed playing in his
dying moments
ded.: Louis Fleury
MS: PLU
pubn: as *Syrinx* (Paris, Jobert, Aug 1927) with bar-
lines apparently added by Marcel Moyse
prem.: *chez* Louis Mors, Paris, 1 Dec 1913, with Louis
Fleury (fl, played off stage)

Dec 1913 – early   *No-ja-li* (orig. *Le palais du silence*)
Jan 1914   ballet
(early Nov 1913 –   scenario: in 1 act with a prelude and 8 sc. by Georges
Oct 1914)   de Feure (pseudonym of Georges van Sluijters);
ballet intended for the Alhambra Theatre, London.
The characters are as follows: Hong-Lo, a dumb
Formosan prince; No-ja-li, a young captive princess;
Malang-Malang, the prince's Malayan jester; an old
man who carries No-ja-li's dolls; woman attendants
and dancers; guards enforcing the law of silence;

Malayan ballet troupe (sc. 8). MS: *F-Pdurand* (7 pp.): typed scenario by Feure, dated 2 Nov 1913

music: scored for orch (incl., in sc. 7 and 8, Malayan gamelan with bells, hps, deep-toned drums)

MSS: 1 *F-Pn* MS 17726, *No-ja-li* sketchbook: sketches for the prelude and start of sc. 1 appear on pp. 9 *v* − 20 *r* and possibly pp. 20 *v* − 22 *r* (though these may be for the Violin Sonata) (see Exx. 49-52)

2 *F-Pn* MS 17730 (8 pp.): two gatherings of sketches, probably for *No-ja-li* as one contains an idea also found in MS 17726, pp. 14 *r* − 17 *r* (see Chapter 8 and Ex. 53)

Debussy's score was never completed

1914	**Spring** ballet danced to *Printemps*, see p. 306
?1914	**Drame indien** project planned with Gabriele d'Annunzio d'Annunzio's lib and Debussy's score were never started
Feb 1914 − March 1916	**Tania** text: lib by unknown Russian author,? after Alexander Pushkin's verse novel *Yevgeny Onegin* (1831); a scenario (PLU) is known to have been written music: ?opera Debussy rejected the project
?1917	**Drame fantastique** project planned by Debussy, of which nothing survives
June − Nov 1917	**As you like it** text: comedy by Shakespeare, trans. Paul-Jean Toulet, intended for a production by Firmin Gémier; 7 extracts, probably for this production, pubd in Toulet, 1936, pp. 96-108 music: incidental music Debussy's score was never started

Select bibliography

The bibliography is in two sections. The first (arranged chronologically) consists of articles and reviews by, and interviews with Debussy relating to the theatre and to specific theatrical works; the items in this section are reprinted in LCr and elsewhere and translated in RLS as indicated. The second section (arranged alphabetically by author's name and then chronologically within each author entry) lists books, sections of books, theses and articles relating to Debussy and the theatre; I have included items cited in the text and items not listed in Claude Abravanel: *Claude Debussy: a bibliography*, Detroit studies in music bibliography, no. 29 (Detroit, Information Coordinators, 1974) (the latter category mainly includes published sources after 1970). For a fuller bibliography of theatrical source material, reviews etc. the reader is directed to Abravanel, pp. 106-23. In both sections the most important items are starred. A key to abbreviations may be found at the start of the book (pp. xv-xvii).

Articles, reviews and interviews by Debussy relating to the theatre
'Au Concert Lamoureux: ouverture pour *Le Roi Lear* d'A[lbert] Savard, première audition; le troisième acte de *Siegfried*', *ReB* (1 April 1901). LCr, pp. 24-5; RLS, pp. 14-15
'La chambre d'enfants de Moussorgsky', *ReB* (15 April 1901). LCr, pp. 28-30; RLS, pp. 20-1
'Vendredi Saint', *ReB* (1 May 1901). LCr, pp. 33-6; RLS, pp. 26-8
'Opéras' [Georges Hüe: *Le Roi de Paris*; Alfred Bruneau: *L'ouragan*], *ReB* (15 May 1901). LCr, pp. 38-42; RLS, pp. 33-7
'La musique en plein air', *ReB* (1 June 1901). LCr, pp. 45-6; RLS, pp. 40-2
'L'entretien avec M. Croche', *ReB* (1 July 1901). LCr, pp. 47-52; RLS, pp. 44-9
'Un opéra' [Saint-Saëns: *Les barbares*, cf *Gil Blas* (16 March 1903)], *ReB* (15 Nov 1901). LCr, pp. 56-7; RLS, pp. 54-5
'D'*Ève* à *Grisélidis*' [Massenet], *ReB* (1 Dec 1901). LCr, pp. 58-60; RLS, pp. 56-8
* 'Pourquoi j'ai écrit "Pelléas"' [note written in April 1902 for Georges Ricou, manager of the Opéra-Comique, pubd *Comoedia* (17 Oct 1920), repr. with introduction by Ricou and facs. *Comoedia* (18 Oct 1921)]. LCr, pp. 61-3; RLS, pp. 74-5

'À la veille de *Pelléas et Mélisande*' [interview with Louis Schneider, related in Schneider's own words], *Revue d'histoire et de critique musicale* (April 1902). LCr, pp. 265-8

'Weber and Debussy' [interview with Robert Godet after the dress-rehearsal of *Pelléas et Mélisande* on 28 April 1902, pubd in trans., *The Chesterian* (June 1926)]. RLS, pp. 105-8

'Critique des critiques: *Pelléas et Mélisande* [interview with Robert de Flers], *Le figaro* (16 May 1902). LCr, pp. 269-71; RLS, pp. 79-81

'L'orientation musicale' [reply to an enquiry by Charles Joly on the music of tomorrow], *Musica* (Oct 1902). LCr, pp. 66-7; RLS, pp. 84-5

'L'influence allemande sur la musique française', *Mercure de France* (Jan 1903). LCr, pp. 64-5; RLS, p. 83

'*L'étranger* de Vincent d'Indy. Théâtre Royal de la Monnaie [Brussels]', *Gil Blas* (12 Jan 1903). LCr, pp. 68-72; RLS, pp. 87-91

'Considération sur la musique en plein air. – Les concerts [Édouard Lalo: *Namouna*; Berlioz: *La damnation de Faust*; Vincent d'Indy: prelude to Act 2 of *L'étranger*]. – Le prince L[ouis]-F[erdinand] de Bavière [honorary president of the committee formed to erect a statue to Wagner in Berlin]', *Gil Blas* (19 Jan 1903). LCr, pp. 73-9; RLS, pp. 92-7

'À l'Opéra-Comique' [prem. of Georges Hüe: *Titania*], *Gil Blas* (21 Jan 1903). LCr, p. 80; RLS, p. 99

* 'Opéra-Comique. *Titania*, drame musical en trois actes, de Louis Gallet et M. André Corneau, musique de M. Georges Hüe', *Gil Blas* (26 Jan 1903). LCr, pp. 81-5; RLS, pp. 100-4

'À la Schola Cantorum [Acts 1 and 2 of Rameau's *Castor et Pollux*, cond. Vincent d'Indy]. – Deuils: Mme Augusta Holmès, Robert Planquette', *Gil Blas* (2 Feb 1903). LCr, pp. 87-92; RLS, pp. 110-14

'Reprise de *La traviata* à l'Opéra-Comique' [and Italian *verismo* opera in general], *Gil Blas* (16 Feb 1903). LCr, pp. 95-7; RLS, pp. 119-21

* 'Lettre ouverte à Monsieur le Chevalier C.W. Gluck', *Gil Blas* (23 Feb 1903). LCr, pp. 98-101; RLS, pp. 123-6

'Pour le peuple [*Opéra Populaire* etc.]. – M. Siegfried Wagner au Concert Lamoureux', *Gil Blas* (2 March 1903). LCr, pp. 105-10; RLS, pp. 129-33

'De l'Opéra et de ses rapports avec la musique', *Gil Blas* (9 March 1903). LCr, pp. 111-14; RLS, pp. 135-8

'Au Concert Colonne: MM. C. Saint-Saëns, Alfred Bachelet' [Saint-Saëns: *Les barbares*, cf *ReB* (15 Nov 1901); Bachelet: *L'amour des ondines*], *Gil Blas* (16 March 1903). LCr, pp. 118-23; RLS, pp. 142-6

'Théâtre National de l'Opéra-Comique' [prem. of Edmond Missa: *Muguette*], *Gil Blas* (19 March 1903). LCr, pp. 124-5; RLS, pp. 150-1

[untitled preview of plans for the spring season at the Opéra: the revival of Meyerbeer's *Les Huguenots*]. – À propos de *Muguette* [Missa]. – Au Concert Lamoureux [Alfred Bruneau: *Penthésilée*]', *Gil Blas* (23 March 1903). LCr, pp. 126-30; RLS, pp. 152-6

'Richard Strauss', *Gil Blas* (30 March 1903). LCr, pp. 133-6; RLS, pp. 159-61

'*Parsifal* et la Société des Grandes Auditions de France', *Gil Blas* (6 April 1903). LCr, pp. 137-40; RLS, pp. 164-7

'Concerts Spirituels' [Wagner: *Das Rheingold*, cond. Camille Chevillard], *Gil Blas* (13 April 1903). LCr, pp. 143-4; RLS, pp. 171-2

'Une renaissance de l'opéra bouffe [comparison of Offenbach's *La belle Hélène* and *Les contes d'Hoffmann* and Meyerbeer's *Les Huguenots* and

Robert le diable with Claude Terrasse's *Le sire de Vergy*]. – Reprise de *Werther* à l'Opéra-Comique', *Gil Blas* (27 April 1903). LCr, pp. 154-8; RLS, pp. 182-6

'Lettres de Londres' [29 and 30 April 1903, on Wagner's *Ring* at Covent Garden, cond. André Messager], *Gil Blas* (5 May 1903). LCr, pp. 159-63; RLS, pp. 187-91

'Berlioz et M. Gunsbourg' [who had adapted Berlioz's *La damnation de Faust* for the stage], *Gil Blas* (8 May 1903). LCr, pp. 164-7; RLS, pp. 192-5

'*Henry VIII* de Camille Saint-Saëns' [Opéra], *Gil Blas* (19 May 1903). LCr. pp. 168-9; RLS, pp. 196-7

*'Impressions sur la Tétralogie à Londres' [and on the Empire Music Hall, Leicester Square], *Gil Blas* (1 June 1903). LCr, pp. 175-9; RLS, pp. 203-7

'*La petite maison* de William Chaumet' [Opéra-Comique], *Gil Blas* (6 June 1903). LCr, pp. 180-2; RLS, pp. 208-10

*'Le bilan musical en 1903' [Opéra and Opéra-Comique], *Gil Blas* (28 June 1903). LCr, pp. 187-91; RLS, pp. 215-18

'L'état actuel de la musique française' [interview with Paul Landormy], *La revue bleue* (2 April 1904). LCr, pp. 272-3

'À propos de Charles Gounod', *Musica* (July 1906). LCr, pp. 192-4; RLS, pp. 223-5

*'Mary Garden', *Musica* (Jan 1908). LCr, pp. 195-6; RLS, pp. 226-7

'Wagner. Son influence après vingt-cinq ans de tombeau' [reply to an enquiry by Maurice Leclercq, intended for *L'éclair* (19-21 Feb 1908) but first pubd in C.F. Caillard and J. de Bérys: *Le cas Debussy* (Paris, Librairie Henri Falque, 1910), pp.1-6]. LCr, pp. 274-5

'À propos d'*Hippolyte et Aricie*', *Le figaro* (8 May 1908). LCr, pp. 197-200; RLS, pp. 228-31

*'Debussy talks of his music' [interview with Emily Frances Bauer, 6 Aug 1908], *Harper's weekly*, lii (29 Aug 1908), p. 32. RLS, pp. 232-4; French trans. by Marcel Dietschy, *Cahiers Debussy*, no. 2 (1975), pp. 3-5

'An interview with Debussy' [by George Delaquys], *The musical standard*, series 3, xxxv no. 891 (1909)

'La musique d'aujourd'hui et celle de demain' [interview with L. Borgex], *Comoedia* (4 Nov 1909). LCr, pp. 280-1

'Enquête sur la musique moderne italienne', *Comoedia* (31 Jan 1910). LCr, p. 282

'Une renaissance de l'idéal classique? Enquête', *Paris-journal* (20 May 1910). LCr, pp. 284-5

'Déclaration à un journaliste autrichien' [interview of Dec 1910 about Wagner, extract pubd by Léon Vallas as 'Debussy jugé par lui-même', *Revue musicale de Lyon* (8 Jan 1911)]. LCr, p. 289; RLS, p. 243

*[untitled interview with André Adorjan], *Azest/Le soir* (Budapest) (6 Dec 1910). *Cahiers Debussy*, no. 1 (1974), pp. 8-9 (research by François Lesure and Ivan Pethes); RLS, pp. 240-2

'Une escale à Gare-Saïd' [interview with Louis Vuillemin], *Comoedia* (17 Dec 1910). LCr, pp. 290-1

'La musique étrangère et les compositeurs français' [interview with Louis Schneider], *Le Gaulois* (10 Jan 1911). LCr, pp. 292-4

*'La pensée d'un grand musicien' [interview with Georges Delaquys], *Excelsior* (18 Jan 1911). LCr, pp. 295-7; RLS, pp. 244-6

'Pour la décentralisation musicale' [a comparison between Paris and French provincial cities as regards theatrical and performance standards; reply to an enquiry by G. Linor], *Comoedia* (26 Jan 1911). LCr, pp. 298-300

'Pour le mérite', *Paris-journal* (2 Feb 1911). LCr, pp. 16-17

* 'M. Claude Debussy et *Le martyre de Saint Sébastien*' [interview with Henry Malherbe], *Excelsior* (11 Feb 1911). LCr, pp. 301-3; RLS, pp. 247-9

'Sous la musique que faut-il mettre? De beaux vers, de mauvais, des vers libres, de la prose?' [reply to an enquiry by Fernand Divoire], *Musica* (March 1911). LCr, pp. 201-2; RLS, pp. 250-1

'La musique russe et les compositeurs français' [interview with Henry Malherbe], *Excelsior* (9 March 1911). LCr, p. 17

'Avant *Le martyre de Saint Sébastien*: M. Claude Debussy et la musique sacrée' [interview with René Bizet], *Comoedia* (18 May 1911). LCr, pp. 304-5

'Massenet n'est plus . . .', *Le matin* (14 Aug 1912). LCr, pp. 203-4; RLS, pp. 252-3

'Une intervioue [*sic*] de M. Claude Debussy' [by Paul-Jean Toulet], *Les marges* (Oct 1912). Toulet, 1926, pp. 123-31

'Jean-Philippe Rameau' [written Oct − 19 Nov 1912 for Caplet in America, pubd CAP, pp. 62-4]. LCr, pp. 205-7; RLS, pp. 254-5

'Du respect dans l'art', *Revue de la Société Internationale de Musique* (Dec 1912). LCr, pp. 212-13; RLS, pp. 268-9

'Fin d'année' [on Rameau, and the staging of Wagner's *Parsifal*], *Revue de la Société Internationale de Musique* (15 Jan 1913). LCr, pp. 218-19; RLS, pp. 273-4

* 'Du goût', *Revue de la Société Internationale de Musique* (15 Feb 1913). LCr, pp. 222-5; RLS, pp. 277-9

'Théâtre des Champs-Élysées', *Revue de la Société Internationale de Musique* (15 May 1913). LCr, pp. 234-5; RLS, p. 289

* '*Jeux*', *Le matin* (15 May 1913). LCr, pp. 236-7; pp. 291-2

'À propos du centenaire de Wagner', *Les annales politiques et littéraires* (25 May 1913). LCr, p. 238; RLS, p. 294

'L'Opéra de demain' [reply to an enquiry by Pierre Montamet], *Excelsior* (15 Sept 1913). LCr, p. 306

* [untitled article on the future of French symphonic and dramatic music and cinematographic techniques], *Revue de la Société Internationale de Musique* (1 Nov 1913). LCr, pp. 239-43; RLS, pp. 295-8

'Musique espagnole' [Albéniz: *Ibéria*], *Revue de la Société Internationale de Musique* (1 Dec 1913). LCr, pp. 244-8; RLS, pp. 300-3

'Sur deux chefs-d'oeuvre [Leonardo da Vinci's *Mona Lisa* and Wagner's *Parsifal*]. − Notes sur les concerts [Max d'Ollone: *L'étrangère*]', *Revue de la Société Internationale de Musique* (1 Feb 1914). LCr, pp. 251-4; RLS, pp. 307-10

* 'Claude Debussy nous dit ses projets de théâtre' [interview with Maurice Montabré on *La boîte à joujoux* and *Fêtes galantes*], *Comoedia* (1 Feb 1914). LCr, pp. 307-8; RLS, pp. 311-12

'An appreciation of contemporary music' [interview with Michel-Dimitri Calvocoressi], *The etude* (Philadelphia) (June 1914). RLS, pp. 317-20

'Enfin, seuls!', *L'intransigeant* (11 March 1915). LCr, pp. 259-60; RLS, pp. 322-3

'Lettre-préface [written Dec 1916], *Pour la musique française: douze cause-*

ries, ed. Paul Huvelin (Paris, Georges Crès, 1917). LCr, pp. 261-2; RLS, pp. 324-5

Books, theses and articles on Debussy's theatre music

* Abbate, Carolyn: 'Tonal design in *Pelléas et Mélisande*: Debussy's sketches and drafts for Act 4 scene 4' (unpubd senior thesis, Yale University, 1977)
* —— : '*Tristan* in the composition of *Pelléas*', *19th-century music*, v no. 2 (1981), pp. 117-41
Abraham, Marcel: 'Sous le signe de Pelléas', *Annales du Centre Universitaire Méditerranéen* (Nice), vii (1953-4), pp. 99-109
* Abravanel, Claude: *Claude Debussy: a bibliography*, Detroit studies in music bibliography, no. 29 (Detroit, Information Coordinators, 1974)
Ackere, Jules van: '*Pelléas et Mélisande*': ou la rencontre miraculeuse d'une poésie et d'une musique (Brussels, Les Éditions de la Librairie Encyclopédique, 1952)
Allan, Maud: *My life and dancing* (London, Everett, 1908)
* Allende-Blin, Juan: 'Eine Dokumentation'; '*La chute de la maison Usher*', *Claude Debussy*, Musik-Konzepte, ed. Heinz-Klaus Metzger and Rainer Riehm, nos. 1-2 (Munich, Die Reihe, 1977), pp. 3-9; 10-41
* —— : 'À la découverte de Debussy (à propos de la *Chute de la Maison Usher*)', *Musique en jeu*, no. 31 (1978), pp. 7-29
American Musicological Society (various authors): *Abstracts of papers read at the 44th annual meeting – Minneapolis, Minnesota, 19-22 October 1978* (typed booklet), pp. 114-19
André-Messager, Jean (ed.): Debussy's correspondence, see Debussy, 1938
* Andrieux, G.: catalogue of sale (1 Dec 1933) at Hôtel Drouot, Paris, incl. the collection of Emma Debussy (MSS, pp. 34-9)
Annunzio, Gabriele d': correspondence with Debussy, see Debussy, 1948
Ansermet, Ernest: *Écrits sur la musique* (Neuchâtel, La Baconnière, 1971)
Antoine, André: *Mes souvenirs sur le Théâtre Antoine et sur l'Odéon* [1894 – May 1906], (Paris, Grasset, 1928; repr. Paris, Plon, 1933)
—— : *Le théâtre* (Paris, Les Éditions de France, 1932)
Appeldorn, Mary Jeanne van: 'A stylistic study of Claude Debussy's opera *Pelléas et Mélisande*' (Ph.D. thesis, University of Rochester, Eastman School of Music, 1966)
Aprahamian, Felix: 'Pelléas et Mélisande', *Opera* (London), xx (1969), pp. 1008-16
Astre, Achille: *Souvenirs d'art et de littérature* (Paris, Éditions du Cygne, 1930)
Astruc, Gabriel: *Le pavillon des fantômes* (Paris, Grasset, 1929)
Austin, William: *Music in the twentieth century* (New York, W.W. Norton, 1966)
Baigent, Michael; Leigh, Richard; Lincoln, Henry: *The Holy Blood and The Holy Grail* (London, Jonathan Cape, 1982)
Bardac, Emma: correspondence with Debussy, see Debussy, 1957
Barraud, Henri: 'Commentaire littéraire et musical' [on *Pelléas*], *L'avant-scène*, no. 9 (March–April 1977), pp. 28-82
Beaver, Harold: 'Edgar Poe in France', *The listener*, c no. 2569 (20 July 1978), pp. 90-1

* Bellaigue, Camille: review of *Pelléas*, *Revue des deux mondes*, lxxii (15 May 1902), pp. 450-6

Benois, Alexandre (trans. Mary Britnieva): *Reminiscences of the Russian Ballet* (London, Putnam, 1941)

—— (trans. Moura Budberg): *Memoirs*, 2 vols. (London, Chatto and Windus, 1964)

Berman, Laurence: 'The evolution of tonal thinking in the works of Claude Debussy', 2 vols. (Ph. D. thesis, Harvard University, 1965)

* —— : *'Prelude to the afternoon of a faun* and *Jeux*: Debussy's summer rites', *19th-century music*, iii no. 3 (1980), pp. 225-38

Bidou, Henry: review of *Le martyre de Saint Sébastien*, *Journal des débats* (29 May 1911), pp. 1-2

Billy, André: *Stanislas de Guaita* (Paris, Mercure de France, 1971)

Blanche, Jacques-Émile (ed. and trans. Walter Clement): *Portraits of a lifetime*, vol. 2 (1870-1914) (London, Dent, 1937)

—— : *La pêche aux souvenirs* (Paris, Flammarion, 1949)

Bonheur, Raymond: 'Souvenirs et impressions d'un compagnon de jeunesse', *ReM*, vii no. 7 (1 May 1926), pp. 3-9

Borgeaud, Henri (ed.): Debussy's correspondence, see Debussy, 1945

Boucher, Maurice: *Claude Debussy* (Paris, Éditions Rieder, 1930)

Bret, Gustave: 'M. Debussy and the public', *The weekly critical review* (5 Nov 1903), p. 368

Briant, Théophile: *Saint-Pol-Roux*, Poètes d'aujourd'hui (Paris, Seghers, 1951; 3/1971)

Briscoe, James: 'The compositions of Claude Debussy's formative years (1879-87)' (Ph.D. thesis, University of North Carolina at Chapel Hill, 1979)

Brody, Elaine: 'La famille Mendès, a literary link between Wagner and Debussy', *MR*, xxxiii no. 3 (1972), pp. 177-89

Bruyr, José: *'Pelléas* et ses décors', *SMz*, cii no. 6 (1962), pp. 340-4

* Buckle, Richard: *Nijinsky* (London, Weidenfeld and Nicolson, 1971; repr. Harmondsworth, Penguin Books, 1975; rev. edn, 1980)

* —— : *Diaghilev* (London, Weidenfeld and Nicolson, 1979)

Bugeanu, Constantin: 'La forme musicale dans le *Pelléas* de Debussy', *Revue roumaine d'histoire de l'art* (Bucarest), vi (1969), pp. 243-60

Büsser, Henri: 'À propos du cinquantenaire de *Pelléas et Mélisande* de Claude Debussy: souvenirs', *Revue des deux mondes*, cxxii no. 7 (1 April 1952), pp. 534-40

* —— : *De 'Pelléas' aux Indes galantes* (Paris, Arthème Fayard, 1955)

—— : 'La création de *Pelléas et Mélisande*', *Revue des deux mondes*, cxxxvi no. 6 (15 March 1966), pp. 274-8.

Cadieu, Martine: *'Pelléas et Mélisande*: peinture visionnaire ou fait-divers?', *L'avant-scène*, no. 9 (March–April 1977), pp. 97-8

Cahn, Peter: 'Der Szenenaufbau in Debussys *Pelléas et Mélisande*', *Bericht über den Internationalen Musikwissenschaftlichen Kongress, Bonn, 1970* (Kassel, Bärenreiter, 1975), pp. 207-12

* Cain, Julien (ed.): *Claude Debussy. Bibliothèque Nationale. 1962* [exhibition catalogue] (Paris, Les Presses Artistiques, 1962)

Calvocoressi, Michel-Dimitri: review of *Pelléas*, *L'art moderne* (Brussels), xxii (15 May 1902), pp. 156-7

Caplet, André: correspondence with Debussy, see Debussy, 1957

Cardinne-Petit, Robert: *Pierre Louÿs, le solitaire du hameau* (Paris, Jean-Renard, 1942)

—— : *Pierre Louÿs, inconnu* (Paris, Éditions de l'Élan, 1948)

Cavendish, Richard (ed.): *Encyclopedia of the unexplored* (London, Routledge and Kegan Paul, 1974)

*Chailley, Jacques: 'Le symbolisme des thèmes dans *Pelléas et Mélisande*', *L'information musicale*, ii no. 64 (3 April 1942), pp. 889-90

Charpentier, Gustave: 'Hommage à Claude Debussy: sa jeunesse et sa mort', *Chantecler*, iii no. 100 (24 March 1928), p. 1

Chausson, Ernest: correspondence with Debussy, see Debussy, 1925, 1926, 1962

*Chimènes, Myriam: 'Les vicissitudes de *Khamma*', *Cahiers Debussy*, nouvelle série, no. 2 (1978), pp. 11-29

* —— : '*Khamma*. Ballet de Claude Debussy: histoire et analyse', 2 vols. (unpubd Ph.D. thesis, Université de Paris IV (Sorbonne), Ecole Pratique des Hautes Études, 1980)

Clément, Catherine: 'Mélisande à la question ou le secret des hommes', *L'avant-scène*, no. 9 (March–April 1977), pp. 15-19

Clive, Henry: *Pierre Louÿs (1870-1925). A biography* (Oxford, Oxford University Press, 1978)

*Cobb, Margaret G.: *Discographie de l'oeuvre de Claude Debussy (1902-50)* (Geneva, Éditions Minkoff, 1975)

—— : 'Debussy in Texas' [extracts from letters in the Lake collection at *US-AUS*], *Cahiers Debussy*, nouvelle série, no. 1 (1977), pp. 45-6

* —— : *The poetic Debussy: a collection of his song texts and selected letters* (Boston, Northeastern University Press, 1982)

Cocteau, Jean: 'Mme Ida Rubinstein dans *Saint Sébastien*', *Comoedia*, v no. 1340 (1 June 1911), p. 1

*Cohen, Gustave: 'Gabriele d'Annunzio et le *Martyre de Saint Sébastien*', *Mercure de France*, xci no. 336 (16 June 1911), pp. 688-709

—— : 'Gabriele d'Annunzio et le *Martyre de Saint Sébastien*: souvenirs', *Mercure de France*, xlix (1 June 1938), pp. 368-75

—— : 'Gabriele d'Annunzio et *Le martyre de Saint Sébastien*', *ReM*, no. 234 (1957), pp. 29-39

Cortot, Alfred: 'Un drame lyrique de Claude Debussy: *Rodrigue et Chimène*', *Inédits sur Claude Debussy* (Paris, Publications Techniques, 1942), pp. 12-16

Cossart, Michael de: *The food of love: Princesse Edmond de Polignac (1865-1943) and her salon* (London, Hamish Hamilton, 1978); trans. Jean-Claude Eger as *Une Américaine à Paris* (Paris, Plon, 1979)

Cox, David: *Debussy: orchestral music*, BBC music guides (London, British Broadcasting Corporation, 1974)

Crichton, Ronald: *Manuel de Falla: a descriptive catalogue* (London, Chester Music, 1976)

*Cuttoli, Raphaël: '*Le martyre de Saint Sébastien*: création et reprises', *ReM*, no. 234 (1957), pp. 9-28

*Debussy, Claude: 'Correspondance inédite de Claude Debussy et Ernest Chausson', *ReM*, vii no. 2 (1 Dec 1925), pp. 116-26

* —— : 'Deux lettres de Debussy à Ernest Chausson' [1894], *ReM*, vii no. 7 (1 May 1926), pp. 87-8

* —— (ed. Jacques Durand): *Lettres de Claude Debussy à son éditeur* (Paris, Durand, 1927)

*. —— (ed. Henri Martineau): *Correspondance de Claude Debussy et Paul-Jean Toulet* (Paris, Le Divan, 1929)

*. —— (ed. Gustave Doret): 'Neuf lettres et billets inédits de Claude Achille Debussy, commentées', *Lettres romandes* (Geneva), no. 1 (23 Nov 1934), pp. 7-8

*. —— (ed. Jean André-Messager): *L'enfance de Pelléas. Lettres de Claude Debussy à André Messager* (Paris, Dorbon-Ainé, 1938)

* —— (ed. Georges Jean-Aubry): *Lettres a deux amis. Soixante-dix-huit lettres inédites à Robert Godet et Georges Jean-Aubry* (Paris, Librairie José Corti, 1942)

* —— (ed. Henri Borgeaud): *Correspondance de Claude Debussy et Pierre Louÿs (1893-1904)* (Paris, Librairie José Corti, 1945)

* —— (ed. Guy Tosi): *Debussy et d'Annunzio. Correspondance inédite* (Paris, Denoël, 1948)

* —— (ed. Pasteur Vallery-Radot): *Lettres de Claude Debussy à sa femme Emma* (Paris, Flammarion, 1957)

* —— (ed. Edward Lockspeiser): *Lettres inédites à André Caplet (1908-14)* (Monaco, Éditions du Rocher, 1957)

* —— (ed. François Lesure): 'Cinq lettres de Robert Godet à Claude Debussy (1917-18)', *RdM*, xlviii no. 125 (July–Dec 1962), pp. 77-95

* —— (ed. François Lesure): 'Correspondance de Claude Debussy et de Louis Laloy (1902-14)', *RdM*, xlviii no. 125 (July–Dec 1962), pp. 3-40

* —— (ed. Edward Lockspeiser): 'Neuf lettres de Pierre Louÿs à Claude Debussy (1894-8)', *RdM*, xlviii no. 125 (July–Dec 1962), pp. 61-70

* ——: 'Textes et documents inédits' [10 letters from Chausson to Debussy, 1893-4], *RdM*, xlviii no. 125 (July–Dec 1962), pp. 49-60

* —— (ed. Jean Roy): 'Deux lettres à [Georges] Hartmann', *ReM*, no. 258 (1964), pp. 118-20

* —— (ed. Pasteur Vallery-Radot and James N.B. Hill): 'Lettres de Debussy à l'éditeur [Georges] Hartmann (pour servir à l'histoire des *Nocturnes*)', *ReM*, no. 258 (1964), pp. 111-15

* —— (ed. François Lesure): 'Lettres inédites de Claude Debussy à Pierre Louÿs', *RdM*, lvii no. 1 (1971), pp. 29-39

* —— (ed. François Lesure): *Monsieur Croche et autres écrits. Édition complète de son oeuvre critique* (Paris, Gallimard, 1971)

* —— (ed. and trans. Richard Langham Smith): *Debussy on music* (London, Secker and Warburg, 1977) [based on *Monsieur Croche et autres écrits*, ed. François Lesure, but with extra items by Debussy and additional introductions]

* ——: *Esquisses de 'Pelléas et Mélisande' (1893-1895)*, facs. with introduction by François Lesure (Geneva, Éditions Minkoff, 1977)

* —— (ed. François Lesure): *Lettres 1884-1918* (Paris, Hermann, 1980); trans. Roger Nichols (Cambridge, Cambridge University Press, forthcoming)

—— : correspondence with Dukas, see Dukas

—— : correspondence with Fauré, see Fauré

—— : correspondence with Lerolle, see Denis

—— : correspondence with Molinari, see Paoli

—— : correspondence with Peter, see Peter

—— : correspondence with Poniatowski, see Poniatowski
—— : correspondence with Toscanini, see Sachs
—— : correspondence with Varèse, see Lesure, 1965
—— : correspondence with Vasnier, see Prunières

*Denis, Maurice: *Henry Lerolle et ses amis, suivi de quelques lettres d'amis* (Paris, Duranton, 1932) (letters on *Pelléas*, pp. 29-33)

Desonay, Fernand: 'Le théâtre de Maeterlinck', *L'europe*, xl nos. 399-400 (July-Aug 1962), pp. 77-88

Destranges, Étienne: '*Pelléas et Mélisande*. Étude analytique et critique', *Revue musicale de Lyon*, viii no. 5 (13 Nov 1910), pp. 137-44; no. 6 (20 Nov 1910), pp. 176-81; no. 7 (27 Nov 1910), pp. 207-11; no. 8 (4 Dec 1910), pp. 240-4; no. 9 (11 Dec 1910), pp. 269-73; no. 10 (18 Dec 1910), pp. 302-6

Devriès, Anik: 'Les musiques d'Extrême-Orient à l'Exposition Universelle de 1889', *Cahiers Debussy*, nouvelle série, no. 1 (1977), pp. 24-37

Dickinson, A.E.F.: 'Symbolism triumphant?' [*Pelléas et Mélisande*], *MR*, xxxi no. 2 (1970), pp. 163-5

*Dietschy, Marcel: *La passion de Claude Debussy* (Neuchâtel, La Baconnière, 1962)

—— : 'Debussy, les femmes et la femme', *Revue musicale de Suisse Romande*, xxiv no. 2 (May-June 1971), pp. 3-5

* —— : 'À propos d'une interview inédite de Debussy' [1908], *Cahiers Debussy*, no. 2 (1975), pp. 1-6

Dinar, André: *Le croisade symboliste* (Paris, Mercure de France, 1943)

Doret, Gustave (ed.): Debussy's correspondence, see Debussy, 1934

Douglas, Alfred: *The Tarot. The origin, meaning and uses of the cards* (London, Victor Gollancz, 1972)

*Dubois, Jacques: 'La répétition dans *Pelléas et Mélisande*', *Revue des langues vivantes*, xxviii no. 6 (1962), pp. 483-9

Dukas, Paul (ed. Georges Favre): *Correspondance* (Paris, Durand, 1971)

Dunn, Margo: 'In praise of something loved: the dance of Maud Allan', *Makara* (Feb-March 1976)

*Durand, Jacques: *Quelques souvenirs d'un éditeur de musique*, vol. 1 (to 1909) (Paris, Durand, 1924); vol. 2 (1910-) (Paris, Durand, 1925)

—— : correspondence with Debussy, see Debussy, 1927

*Eimert, Herbert: 'Debussys *Jeux*', *Die Reihe*, no. 5 (1959), pp. 5-22; trans. Leo Black (Bryn Mawr, Theodore Presser, 1961), pp. 3-20

*Emmanuel, Maurice: '*Pelléas et Mélisande*'. *Étude historique et critique. Analyse musicale* (Paris, Mellottée, 1926)

*Estrade-Guerra, Oswald d': 'Les manuscrits de *Pelléas et Mélisande* de Debussy', *ReM*, no. 235 (1957), pp. 5-24

Fauré, Gabriel (ed. Jean-Michel Nectoux): *Correspondance* (Paris, Flammarion, 1980)

Favre, Georges (ed.): Dukas's correspondence, see Dukas

Ferneuil, T.: review of *Pelléas*, *Revue philomatique de Bordeaux* (1 Aug 1902), pp. 337-50

Flat, Paul: review of *Pelléas*, *La revue bleue*, xvii no. 19 (10 May 1902), pp. 590-3

Fogel, Susan Lee (trans. Béatrice Vierne): 'L'originalité de *Pelléas et Mélisande*: les inventions orchestrales', *L'avant-scène*, no. 9 (March–April 1977), pp. 84-9

Fontainas, André: *Mes souvenirs du symbolisme* (Paris, La Nouvelle Revue Critique, 4/1928)

Garden, Mary, and Biancolli, Louis: *Mary Garden's story* (London, Michael Joseph, 1952)

Garden, Mary: *Souvenirs de Mélisande*, Collection Brimborions, no. 98 (Liège, Éditions Dynamo, 1962)

Gatti-Casazza, Giulio: 'Gatti talks of *Pelléas* as sung in Milan and New York', *New York times* (15 March 1925), p. 6

* —— : *Memories of the opera* [La Scala, 1898-1909; Metropolitan, 1909-35] (New York, Charles Scribner, 1941; repr. London, John Calder, 1977)

Gervais, Françoise: *Étude comparée des langages harmoniques de Fauré et de Debussy*, *ReM*, nos. 272-3, 2 vols. (Paris, Richard Masse, 1971)

Gilman, Lawrence: *Debussy's 'Pelléas et Mélisande'. A guide to the opera* (New York, Schirmer, 1907)

* Godet, Robert: 'En marge de la marge', *ReM*, vii no. 7 (1 May 1926), pp. 51-86

—— : correspondence with Debussy, see Debussy 1942, 1962

Gold, Arthur, and Fizdale, Robert: *Misia* (New York, Knopf, 1980)

Goléa, Antoine: 'Genèse de l'oeuvre: la bataille de *Pelléas*', *L'avant-scène*, no. 9 (March-April 1977), pp. 20-3

Gourdet, G.: *Debussy* (Paris, Hachette, 1971)

* Grayson, David: 'The genesis of Debussy's *Pelléas et Mélisande*' (unpubd Ph.D. thesis, Harvard University)

Griffiths, Paul: *A concise history of modern music from Debussy to Boulez* (London, Thames and Hudson, 1978)

Grigoriev, S.L.: *The Diaghilev Ballet 1909-29* (London, Constable, 1953; repr. Harmondsworth, Penguin Books, 1960)

Gueullette, Alain: 'Une forêt, obscure et pourtant sans mystère', *Courrier musical de France*, xxiv (1968), pp. 229-32

Guichard, Léon: 'Debussy et les occultistes', *Cahiers Debussy*, no. 1 (1974), pp. 10-14; trans. in LO, 2, pp. 272-7

Handler, Louis: 'Avant *Le martyre de Saint Sébastien*: M. Gabriele d'Annunzio nous parle de son oeuvre française', *Comoedia*, v no. 1322 (14 May 1911), p. 1

Hardeck, Erwin: 'Debussys *Jeux*. Struktur-Stellung im Gesamtwerk', *Bericht über den Internationalen Musikwissenschaftlichen Kongress, Bonn, 1970* (Kassel, Bärenreiter, 1975), pp. 424-6

Hartmann, Georges: correspondence with Debussy, see Debussy, 1964

Hemmings, F.W.J.: *Culture and society in France 1848-98* (London, B.T. Batsford, 1971)

Hill, James N.B. (ed.): Debussy's correspondence, see Debussy, 1964

* Hirsbrunner, Theo: 'Debussys Ballett: *Khamma*', *AMw*, xxxvi no. 2 (1979), pp. 105-21

Hoérée, Arthur: 'Entretiens inédits d'Ernest Guiraud et de Claude Debussy' [1889-90], *Inédits sur Claude Debussy* (Paris, Publications Techniques, 1942), pp. 25-33

Hohlweg, P.: 'Debussy erinnert mich an ein Raubtier – ein Gespräch mit Pierre Boulez über Debussy, Wagner und *Pelléas et Mélisande*', *Opern Welt*, ii (1970), pp. 44-6

* Holloway, Robin: *Debussy and Wagner* (London, Eulenburg, 1979)

Howat, Roy: 'Debussy, Ravel and Bartók: towards some new concepts of form', *ML*, lviii no. 3 (1977), pp. 285-93
* —— : 'Proportional structure in the music of Debussy' (unpubd Ph.D. thesis, University of Cambridge, 1979)
* —— : *Debussy in proportion: a musical analysis* (Cambridge, Cambridge University Press, 1983)
* Indy, Vincent d': 'À propos de *Pelléas et Mélisande*: essai de psychologie du critique d'art', *L'occident* (Brussels) (June 1902), pp. 374-81
Inghelbrecht, Désiré-Émile and Germaine: *Claude Debussy* (Paris, Costard, 1953)
Jakobik, Albert: *Claude Debussy oder Die lautlose Revolution in der Musik. Analysen von 'Prélude à l'après-midi d'un faune', 'Les nocturnes', 'Pelléas' (1 Szene), 'La mer', 'Jeux'* (Würzburg, K. Triltsch, 1977)
Jankélévitch, Vladimir: *La vie et la mort dans la musique de Debussy* (Neuchâtel, La Baconnière, 1968)
—— : *Debussy et le mystère de l'instant* (Paris, Plon, 1976)
* Jardillier, Robert: *'Pelléas'* (Paris, Éditions Claude Aveline, 1927)
Jarocinski, Stefan (trans. Rollo Myers): *Debussy: Impressionism and Symbolism* (London, Eulenburg, 1976)
Jean-Aubry, Georges: 'Villiers de l'Isle-Adam et la musique', *Mercure de France*, xlix (15 Nov 1938), pp. 40-57
—— : 'Victor Segalen et Claude Debussy', *Cahiers du sud* (Marseilles), xxvii no. 288 (March–April 1948), pp. 263-5
—— : correspondence with Debussy, see Debussy, 1942
* Joly-Segalen, Annie, and Schaeffner, André (eds.): *Segalen et Debussy* (Monaco, Éditions du Rocher, 1962)
Jouffroy, Alain: *Les plus belles pages de Saint-Pol-Roux* (Paris, Mercure de France, 1966)
Jullian, Philippe: *D'Annunzio* (Paris, Arthème Fayard, 1971); trans. Stephen Hardman (London, Pall Mall Press, 1972), pp. 222-35
* Jullien, Adolphe: review of *Pelléas*, *Le théâtre*, no. 84 (June 1902), pp. 5-15
* Kasaba, Eiko: *'Le martyre de Saint Sébastien.* Approches historique et analytique' (unpubd Ph.D. thesis, Université de Paris IV (Sorbonne), École Pratique des Hautes Études, 1981)
* Kerman, Joseph: 'Music and play: *Pelléas et Mélisande', Opera news* (New York), xviii no. 8 (1953), pp. 13-15, 26
Kettle, Michael: *Salome's last veil. The libel case of the century* (London, Hart-Davis, MacGibbon, 1978)
Klein, John W.: 'Debussy as a musical dramatist', *MR*, xxiii no. 3 (1962), pp. 208-14
Knapp, Bettina: *Maurice Maeterlinck* (Boston, Twayne Publishers, 1975)
Knowles, Richard-E.: *Victor-Émile Michelet: poète ésotérique* (Paris, Librairie Philosophique J. Vrin, 1954)
Kochno, Boris (trans. Adrienne Foulke): *Diaghilev and the Ballets Russes* (New York, Harper and Row, 1970; London, Allen Lane/Penguin Press, 1971)
* Koechlin, Charles: *Debussy* (Paris, H. Laurens, 1941; repr. 1956)
Koelink, J.P.: 'Debussy en Pierre Louÿs', *Mens en melodie*, xxx (Aug 1975), pp. 247-59
* Laloy, Louis: 'Le drame musical moderne. IV: Claude Debussy', *Le mercure musical*, i no. 6 (1 Aug 1905), pp. 233-50

* —— : *Debussy* (Paris, Dorbon, 1909)

—— : 'La dernière oeuvre de Claude Debussy: l'*Ode à la France*', *Musique*, i no. 6 (15 March 1928), pp. 245-9

—— : 'Souvenirs sur le maître'. *Comoedia*, iii no. 91 (27 March 1943), pp. 1, 3

—— : correspondence with Debussy, see Debussy, 1962

Lastret, Louis: review of *Pelléas*, *Le théâtre*, no. 84 (June 1902), pp. 17-22

Leblanc, Georgette (trans. Janet Flanner): *Souvenirs. My life with Maeterlinck*, (New York, E.P. Dutton, 1932; repr. New York, Da Capo Press, 1976)

Leibowitz, René: '*Pelléas et Mélisande* ou le "no-man's land" de l'art lyrique', *Critique*, xiii (1957), pp. 22-32

Lenormand, Henri-René: *Confessions d'un auteur dramatique*, vol. 1 (Paris, Albin Michel, 1949)

Lerolle, Henry: correspondence with Debussy, see Denis

Lesure, François: 'Debussy et Edgard Varèse', *Debussy et l'évolution de la musique au XXe siècle*, ed. Edith Weber (Paris, Éditions du Centre National de la Recherche Scientifique, 1965), pp. 333-8 (incl. letters)

—— : 'Retour à *Khamma*', *RBM*, xx (1966), pp. 124-9

* —— : *Iconographie musicale* (Geneva, Éditions Minkoff, 1975)

—— : 'Debussy à travers le journal de Mme de Saint-Marceaux', *Cahiers Debussy*, no. 3 (1976), pp. 5-10

* —— : *Catalogue de l'oeuvre de Claude Debussy* (Geneva, Éditions Minkoff, 1977)

—— (ed.): Debussy's correspondence, see Debussy, 1962, 1971, 1980

—— (ed.): Debussy's sketches, see Debussy, 1977

—— (ed.): Debussy's writings, see Debussy, 1971

Lewinski, W.E. von: 'Die Rolle der Klangefarbe bei Strauss und Debussy', *SMz*, cx no. 6 (1970), pp. 357-61

Liebling, Leonard: 'Maud Allan here', *Musical courier* (New York), lxxiii (21 Sept 1916), p. 22 (cf [anon.] : 'Maud Allan to Europe', *Musical courier*, lxxii (27 April 1916), p. 10)

Lifar, Serge: *Serge Diaghilev: his life, his work, his legend* (New York, G.P. Putnam, 1940; repr. New York, Da Capo Press, 1976)

Linden, Albert van der: '*L'enfant prodigue* de Debussy au Théâtre Royal de la Monnaie en 1913', *RBM*, xvi (1962), pp. 97-106

Lobineau, Henri (pseudonym of Comte Henri de Lénoncourt): *Dossiers secrets* (Paris, Philippe Toscan du Plantier, 1967)

Locard, Paul: review of *Pelléas*, *Courrier musical*, v no. 11 (1 June 1902), pp. 167-8

Lockspeiser, Edward: 'Debussy and Shakespeare', *MT*, lxxvi no. 1112 (1935), pp. 887-8

—— : *Debussy*, Master musicians series (London, Dent, 1936; rev. edn, 1951)

* —— (ed.): *Debussy et Edgar Poe. Documents inédits* (Monaco, Éditions du Rocher, 1962)

* —— : *Debussy: his life and mind*, 2 vols. (London, Cassell, 1962, 1965; repr. Cambridge University Press, 1979)

—— : 'Quelques aspects de la psychologie de Debussy', *Debussy et l'évolution de la musique au XXe siècle*, ed. Edith Weber (Paris, Éditions du Centre National de la Recherche Scientifique, 1965), pp. 141-50

——— : 'Le martyre de Saint Sébastien', The listener, lxxv no. 1936 (5 May 1966), p. 662
——— : 'Portrait of Debussy. 11: Debussy in perspective', MT, cix no. 1508 (1968), pp. 904-6
* ——— : 'Debussy's dream house', Opera news (New York), xxxiv no. 21 (1970), pp. 8-12
* ——— : 'Frères en Art: pièce de théâtre inédite de Debussy', RdM, lvi no. 2 (1970), pp. 165-76
——— : Music and painting (London, Cassell, 1973)
——— (ed.): Debussy's correspondence, see Debussy, 1957, 1962
Lote, Georges; 'La poétique du symbolisme. IV: Poésie et musique', Revue des cours et conférences, xxxv no. 10 (30 April 1934), pp. 108-26
Louÿs, Pierre: correspondence with Debussy, see Debussy, 1945, 1962, 1971
Lugné-Poë, Aurélien: La parade, vol. 1: Le sot du tremplin: souvenirs et impressions de théâtre (Paris, Gallimard, 1930)
Lutaud, Christian: 'La musique de Pelléas, de Maeterlinck à Debussy', Fondation M. Maeterlinck. Annales, xxiii (1977), pp. 35-8
Luten, C.J.: 'Emerging from a shadow', Opera news (New York), xxxvi no. 10 (1972), pp. 24-5
* McDearmon, Lacy: 'Maud Allan: the public record', Dance chronicle (New York), ii no. 2 (1978), pp. 85-105
Macherey, Pierre: 'Debussy et Maeterlinck'; 'Proust et Pelléas', L'avant-scène, no. 9 (March-April 1977), pp. 4-12; pp. 94-5
* McKay, James: 'The Bréval manuscript: new interpretations', Cahiers Debussy, nouvelle série, no. 1 (1977), pp. 5-15
* ——— : 'Pelléas et Mélisande: the Bréval manuscript' (unpubd Ph.D. thesis, University of Chicago)
Maeterlinck, Maurice: Bulles bleues: souvenirs heureux (Monaco, Éditions du Rocher, 1948)
Mariel, Pierre: Dictionnaire des sociétés secrètes en occident (Paris, Culture, Art, Loisirs, 1971)
* Marnold, Jean: review of Pelléas, Mercure de France, xlii no. 150 (June 1902), pp. 801-10
* Martin, Auguste (ed.): Claude Debussy. Chronologie de sa vie et de ses oeuvres. Catalogue de l'exposition organisée du 2 au 17 Mai 1942 au foyer de l'Opéra-Comique (Paris, G. et R. Joly, 1942)
Martin, John: 'The dance: Maud Allan', New York times (8 Sept 1935)
Martineau, Henri: 'En suivant Shakespeare', La revue critique des idées et des livres (July 1922), pp. 403-7
——— (ed.): Debussy's correspondence, see Debussy, 1929
Maurer-Zenck, Claudia: 'Form und Farbenspiele: Debussys Jeux', AMw, xxxiii no. 1 (1976), pp. 28-47
* Merkling, Frank: 'The ultimate dim Thule', Opera news (New York), xviii no. 8 (1953), pp. 5-8, 30
* Messager, André: 'Les premières représentations de Pelléas', ReM, vii no. 7 (1 May 1926), pp. 110-14; repr. ReM, no. 258 (1964), pp. 57-60
——— : correspondence with Debussy, see Debussy, 1938
Metzger, Heinz-Klaus: 'Khamma', Claude Debussy, Musik-Konzepte, ed. Heinz-Klaus Metzger and Rainer Riehm, nos. 1-2 (Munich, Die Reihe, 1977), pp. 118-27
Michelet, Victor-Émile: Les compagnons de la hiérophanie: souvenirs du mouvement hermétiste à la fin du 19e siècle (Paris, Dorbon-Ainé, 1937)

Molinari, Bernardino: correspondence with Debussy, see Paoli

Moore, Doris Langley: 'The scapegoat' [review of Kettle, Michael, above], *Books and bookmen* (Feb 1978), pp. 14-15

Morrell, Lady Ottoline (ed. Robert Gathorne-Hardy): *Ottoline* (London, Faber, 1963)

Mourey, Gabriel: 'Memories of Claude Debussy', *Musical news and herald* (London) (11 June 1921), pp. 747-8

Myers, Rollo: *Claude Debussy: the story of his life and work* (London, Boosey and Hawkes, 1972)

* —— : 'The opera that never was: Debussy's collaboration with Victor Segalen in the preparation of *Orphée*', *MQ*, lxiv no. 4 (1978), pp. 495-506

Nattiez, Jean-Jacques, and Harbour-Paquette, Louise: 'Analyse musicale et sémiologie: à propos du prélude de *Pelléas*', *Musique en jeu*, no. 10 (1974), pp. 42-69

Nattiez, Jean-Jacques: '*Syrinx* de Claude Debussy', *Fondements d'une sémiologie de la musique* (Paris, Union Générale d'Éditions, 1975), pp. 330-54

Nectoux, Jean-Michel: 'Flaubert, Gallet, Fauré ou Le démon du théâtre', *Bulletin du bibliophile*, no. 1 (1976), pp. 33-47

—— : 'Maurice Ravel et sa bibliothèque musicale', *FAM*, xxiv no. 4 (1977), pp. 199-206

* —— : 'Debussy et Fauré', *Cahiers Debussy*, nouvelle série, no. 3 (1979), pp. 13-30

—— (ed.): Fauré's correspondence, see Fauré

* Nichols, Roger: *Debussy* (London, Oxford University Press, 1973)

* —— : 'Debussy, Claude', *The new Grove dictionary of music and musicians*, ed. Stanley Sadie, 20 vols. (London, Macmillan, 1980), vol. 5, pp. 292-314

Nijinsky, Romola (ed.): *The diary of Vaslav Nijinsky* (London, Victor Gollancz, 1937)

O'Connor, Garry: *The pursuit of perfection. A life of Maggie Teyte* (London, Victor Gollancz, 1979)

Orledge, Robert: 'Debussy's musical gifts to Emma Bardac', *MQ*, lx no. 4 (1974), pp. 544-56

* —— : 'Debussy's orchestral collaborations 1911-13. 1: *Le martyre de Saint Sébastien*'; '2: *Khamma*', *MT*, cxv no. 1582 (1974), pp. 1030-5; cxvi no. 1583 (1975), pp. 30-5

* —— : 'Debussy's *House of Usher* revisited', *MQ*, lxii no. 4 (1976), pp. 536-53

* —— : 'Another look inside Debussy's *Toybox*', *MT*, cxvii no. 1606 (1976), pp. 987-9

* —— : 'Debussy's second English ballet: *Le palais du silence* or *No-ja-li*', *CMc*, no. 22 (1976), pp. 73-87

—— : *Gabriel Fauré* (London, Eulenburg, 1979)

—— : 'Debussy's piano music: some second thoughts and sources of inspiration', *MT*, cxxii no. 1655 (1981), pp. 21-7

Paap, Wouter: '*La boîte à joujoux* van Debussy', *Mens en melodie*, xvii no. 11 (1962), pp. 347-9

Palmer, Christopher: *Impressionism in music* (London, Hutchinson, 1973)

Paoli, Rodolfo: *Debussy* (Florence, Sansoni, 1940; repr. 1952) (letters to Molinari, pp. 203-5)

Peter, René: 'Ce qui fut la "générale" de *Pelléas et Mélisande*', *Inédits sur*

Claude Debussy (Paris, Publications Techniques, 1942), pp. 3-11

*────── : *Claude Debussy. Vues prises de son intimité* (Paris, Gallimard, 1944); rev. and expanded (incl. letters) as *Claude Debussy* (Paris, Gallimard, 1952)

*Poniatowski, Prince André: *D'un siècle à l'autre* (Paris, Presses de la Cité, 1948) (letters (1892-3), pp. 305-10)

*Porter, Andrew: 'Fragments of the *House of Usher*', *New Yorker* (14 March 1977), pp. 130-6

Proust, Marcel: *Lettres à Robert de Montesquiou* (Paris, Plon, 1930), pp. 231-2

────── : *Lettres à Reynaldo Hahn* (Paris, Gallimard, 1956), pp. 202-6, 236-7

*Prunières, Henry: 'À la Villa Médicis', *ReM*, vii no. 7 (1 May 1926), pp. 23-42 (incl. letters from Debussy to Eugène-Henry Vasnier)

Pugh, Anthony: *Balzac's recurring characters* (London, Duckworth, 1975)

Raitt, Alan: *Villiers de l'Isle-Adam et le mouvement Symboliste* (Paris, Librairie José Corti, 1965)

────── : *The life of Villiers de l'Isle-Adam* (London, Oxford University Press, 1981)

Rauss, Denis-François: '"Ce terrible finale". Les sources manuscrites de la Sonate pour violon et piano de Claude Debussy et la genèse du troisième mouvement', *Cahiers Debussy*, nouvelle série, no. 2 (1978), pp. 30-62

Régnier, Henri de: *Portraits et souvenirs* (Paris, Mercure de France, 1913)

Reiche, J.P.: 'Die theoretischen Grundlagen javanischer Gamelan. Musik und ihre Bedeutung für Claude Debussy', *Zeitschrift für Musiktheorie* (Stuttgart), iii no. 1 (1972), pp. 5-15

Rey, Anne: *Erik Satie* (Paris, Éditions du Seuil, 1974), pp. 153-61

Ricci, Franco: *Claude Debussy* (Bari, Adriatica Editrice, 1975)

* Richardson, Philip: 'A chat with Maud Allan: the famous dancer talks about her art', *Dancing times*, vi no. 70 (July 1916), pp. 274-6

Rinaldi, Mario: '*Le martyre de Saint Sébastien* di Debussy su testo d'Annunzio', *Nuova antologia*, no. 2131 (July–Sept 1979), pp. 378-9

Robbins, Millie: 'Maud's sensational dance', *San Francisco chronicle* (13 August 1968)

* Robichez, Jacques: *Le symbolisme au théâtre: Lugné-Poë et les débuts de l'Oeuvre* (Paris, Éditions L'Arche, 1957)

Robinson, Bradford: 'Report from Berlin' [on the prem. of Juan Allende-Blin's version of *La chute de la Maison Usher*, 5 October 1979], *MT*, cxxi no. 1643 (1980), pp. 47-8

Rolland, Romain: *Richard Strauss et Romain Rolland. Correspondance et fragments du journal* (Paris, Albin Michel, 1951), pp. 159-62

Rorem, Ned: '*Pelléas* et Pierre', *Pure contraption. A composer's essays* (New York, Rinehart and Winston, 1974), pp. 51-5

Roy, Jean (ed.): Debussy's correspondence, see Debussy, 1964

Sachs, Harvey: *Toscanini* (London, Weidenfeld and Nicolson, 1978) (incl. letters)

* Sandre, Yves (ed.): *Saint-Pol-Roux 'La dame à la faulx' (version théâtrale inédite précédée de lettres à Jacques Rouché)* (Mortemart, near Limoges, Rougerie, 1979)

Schaeffner, André: 'Debussy et ses rapports avec la musique russe', *Musique russe*, ed. Pierre Souvtchinsky, vol. 1 (Paris, Presses Universitaires de France, 1953)

* —— : 'Claude Debussy et ses projets Shakespeariens', *Revue de la société d'histoire du théâtre*, xvi no. 4 (1964), pp. 446-53

Schelp, Arend: 'Debussys *Prélude à l'après-midi d'un faune* na 80 jaar', *Mens en melodie*, xxix (Dec 1974), pp. 367-70

Schwinger, W.: '*Melusine* und *Mélisande*', *Musica*, xxvii (1973), pp. 467-71

Scott, Cyril: *Music: its secret influence through the ages* (London, Rider, 1933)

Sède, Gérard de: *Signé: Rose+Croix. L'enigme de Rennes-le-Château* (Paris, Plon, 1977)

Sert, Misia: *Misia* (Paris, Gallimard, 1952)

Sherman, Robert: 'Debussy: première at Yale' [on the prem. of Carolyn Abbate's and Robert Kyr's version of *La chute de la Maison Usher*, 25 February 1977], *New York times* (20 Feb 1977)

* Smith, Richard Langham: 'Debussy and the art of the cinema', *ML*, liv no. 1 (1973), pp. 61-70

* —— : 'The parentage of *Pelléas*', *Music and musicians*, xxii no. 1 (1973), pp. 38-41

* —— : 'Debussy and the Pre-Raphaelites', *19th-century music*, v no. 2 (1981), pp. 95-109

—— (ed. and trans.): Debussy's writings, see Debussy, 1977

Souffrin-Le Breton, Eileen: 'Théodore de Banville et la musique', *French studies* (Oxford) (July 1955), pp. 238-45

* —— : 'Debussy lecteur de Banville', *RdM*, xlvi (Dec 1960), pp. 200-22

* Souris, André: 'Debussy et Stravinsky', *RBM*, xvi (1962), pp. 45-56

Spencer, Williametta: 'The relationship between André Caplet and Claude Debussy', *MQ*, lxvi no. 1 (1980), pp. 112-31

Spies, Markus: '*Jeux*', *Claude Debussy*, Musik-Konzepte, ed. Heinz-Klaus Metzger and Rainer Riehm, nos. 1-2 (Munich, Die Reihe, 1977), pp. 77-95

Spieth-Weissenbacher, Christine: 'La conduite vocale dans *Pelléas et Mélisande*' (unpubd Ph.D. thesis, Université de Strasbourg (3e cycle))

Staempfli, E.: '*Pelleas und Melisande*: eine Gegenüberstellung der Werke von Claude Debussy und Arnold Schönberg', *SMz*, cxii no. 2 (1972), pp. 65-72

Stravinsky, Igor: *Expositions and developments* (London, Faber and Faber, 1962)

Strobel, Heinrich: 'Boulez entdeckt *Pelléas* neu', *Melos*, xxxvii (1970), pp. 65-7

Terrasson, René: 'L'alchémie d'une oeuvre' [*Pelléas*], *L'avant-scène*, no. 9 (March-April 1977), pp. 100-3

Thompson, Oscar: *Debussy: man and artist* (New York, Dodd, Mead, 1937; repr. New York, Tudor Publishing, 1940)

Tinan, Mme Gaston de: 'Memories of Debussy and his circle', *Journal of the British Institute of Recorded Sound*, nos. 50-1 (April-July 1973), pp. 158-63

—— : 'Souvenirs de Claude Debussy', *SMz*, cxv no. 6 (1975), pp. 293-300

Toscanini, Arturo: correspondence with Debussy, see Sachs

Tosi, Guy (ed.): Debussy's correspondence, see Debussy, 1948

Toulet, Paul-Jean: *Lettres à Mme Bulteau* (Paris, Le Divan, 1924)

—— : *Notes de littérature* (Paris, Le Divan, 1926), pp. 123-34

—— : *Lettres à soi-même* (Paris, Le Divan, 1927)

—— : *Vers inédits* (Paris, Le Divan, 1936)

346   Select bibliography

—— : correspondence with Debussy, see Debussy, 1929
Umphrey, G.W. (ed.): *Las mocedadas de Cid por Guillén de Castro* (London, Henry Holt, 1939)
Valéry, Paul (ed. Jean Hytier): *Oeuvres de Paul Valéry* (Paris, Bibliothèque de la Pléiade, 1960)
*Vallas, Léon: *Claude Debussy et son temps* (Paris, Alcan, 1932; 2nd, rev., edn, Paris, Albin Michel, 1958)
—— (trans. Maire and Grace O'Brien): *Claude Debussy: his life and works* (London, Oxford University Press, 1933; repr. New York, Dover Publications, 1973)
*Vallery-Radot, Pasteur: *Tel était Claude Debussy* (Paris, René Julliard, 1958)
—— (ed.): Debussy's correspondence, see Debussy, 1957, 1964
Van Lerberghe, Charles: *'Pelléas et Mélisande': notes critiques*, Collection Brimborions, no. 97 (Liège, Éditions Dynamo, 1962)
Varèse, Edgard: correspondence with Debussy, see Lesure, 1965
Vasnier, Eugène-Henry: correspondence with Debussy, see Prunières
*Vuillermoz, Émile: 'Autour du *Martyre de Saint Sébastien*', *ReM*, i no. 2 (Dec 1920), pp. 155-8
*—— : 'La naissance du *Martyre de Saint Sébastien*', *ReM*, no. 234 (1957), pp. 59-63
Wacker, Hans: 'Boulez dirigiert *Pelleas und Melisande*', *Musica*, xxiv (1970), pp. 26-7
Walsh, Stephen: 'Debussy's operatic might-have-been' [*Usher*], *Observer review* (23 July 1978), p. 20
Warnke, Frank: 'Poet of the sung play', *Opera news* (New York), xxvii no. 8 (1962), pp. 26-7
Watson, William: *Guillén de Castro* (New York, Twayne Publishers, 1973)
Waxman, Samuel Montefiore: *Antoine and the Théâtre Libre* (Cambridge, Mass., Harvard University Press, 1926)
Weisberg, Gabriel: 'George de Feure's mysterious women', *Gazette des beaux arts*, lxxxii no. 1269 (1974), pp. 223-32
Wenk, Arthur: *Claude Debussy and the poets* (Berkeley, University of California Press, 1976)
Whittall, Arnold: 'Tonality and the whole-tone scale in the music of Debussy', *MR*, xxxvi no. 4 (1975), pp. 261-71
*Williams, Bernard: 'L'envers des destinées: remarks on Debussy's *Pelléas et Mélisande*', *University quarterly* (Cambridge) (Autumn 1975), pp. 389-97
Wocker, K.H.: '*Pelleas und Melisande*', *NZfM*, cxxxi (1970), pp. 65-8
Wolff, Stéphane: *Un demi-siècle d'Opéra-Comique (1900-50)* (Paris, Éditions André Bonne, 1953)
Ysaÿe, Antoine, and Ratcliffe, Bertram: *Ysaÿe: his life, work and influence* (London, Heinemann, 1947)
Ysaÿe, Antoine: 'Debussy et Ysaÿe', *L'ethnie* (15 July 1966); repr. in *Courrier musical de France*, xxiv (1968), p. 275

Notes

Chapter 1 Introduction

1 Statistics from Charles Beaumont Wicks: *The Parisian stage*, vol. 3 (1831-50), vol. 4 (1851-75), University of Alabama Studies, nos. 14 (1961) and 17 (1967).
2 Jarry's *Ubu Roi* (1896) proved a *succès de scandale* with the *avant-garde*.
3 Pseudonym of the Princess Meshcherskaya, a friend of Tchaikovsky and one of the first French translators of Swinburne.
4 According to Robichez, p. 163. This book is thoroughly recommended to anyone seeking to know more about the Symbolist theatre and the Théâtre de l'Oeuvre in particular.
5 Published by Enoch et Cie, Paris, 1898, as the third of three songs (*Trois musiques*) dedicated to Georgette Leblanc. Fabre set many other Maeterlinck texts after this, as well as Charles Cros's *L'archet* (Paris, Lemoine, 1894), which Debussy had set around 1883.
6 Robert Godet also says that Debussy knew the play from the printed edition 'since 1892' (p. 77).

Chapter 2 Before *Pelléas*: *Axël*, *Rodrigue et Chimène* and other early projects, including *Diane au bois*

1 According to Henri Roujon in *La revue bleue* (21 Sept 1889).
2 Edmond Bailly recalls a performance of *Lohengrin* in 'Poètes mélomanes', *L'ermitage* (15 Sept 1892). For the full extract see Raitt, 1965, pp. 121-2.
3 *Oeuvres complètes de Villiers de l'Isle-Adam*, 11 vols. (Paris, Mercure de France, 1922-31), vol. 4: *Axël* (1923), p. 247; and see Ex. 3 by Alexandre Georges. Villiers planned a fifth part to *Axël* titled 'Le monde astral' but did not live to complete it.
4 Page numbers from the complete works vol. 4; titles from Georges's piano reduction published by E. Baudoux et Cie (Paris, 1894, 57 pp.). An orchestral score of Georges's opening prelude was also published (27 pp.) using double woodwind, 2 hn, 1 tpt, 2 timp, hp and str.
5 2 vols. (Paris, Baillière, 1861).
6 According to Paul Chacornac: *Éliphas Lévi* (Paris, Éditions Chacornac, 1926), who also lists Balzac, Alexandre Dumas *fils*, Odilon Redon and Théophile Gautier among Lévi's admirers. This reference is cited in Pierre

Mariel's introduction (p. 23) to *Axël* (Paris, Éditions du Vieux Colombier, 1960), and I am grateful to Roy Howat for drawing it to my attention.

7   For instance Elaine Brody (p. 186); Lockspeiser (LO, 1, p. 98).

8   For further details see the introductions to Umphrey and Watson.

9   Opera in three acts with a libretto by the composer after Corneille. Its Wagnerian nature and the Wagnerian influence generally were as unsuited to Cornelius's lyrical talents as *Rodrigue et Chimène* was unsuitable for Debussy.

10 Opera in four acts, complete with 'Castellane' ballet, which was over-shadowed by the success of *Manon* the previous year. Its libretto was by Adolphe d'Ennery, Louis Gallet and Édouard Blau after Corneille. Mendès later collaborated with Massenet on the operas *Ariane* (1906) and *Bacchus* (1909).

11 The girls of Bivar, two by two and three by three, laughing, following and calling to each other with voices and signs, begin to appear on the hills at the rear of the stage . . . The men of Gormaz disappear for a moment, then enter the stage through the castle door, skirt the high walls noiselessly and arrive to position themselves to the back right of the theatre behind the trees, whilst the girls of Bivar fearlessly descend the rocky footpath, singing, cross the stage towards the left and reascend finally towards the right. (Act 1, f. 31)

Debussy, clearly working direct from Mendès' libretto, thought in terms of theatrical performance from the first. The stage directions, usually in red ink, occur in full throughout, in contrast to the often incomplete vocal text of the chorus itself.

12 As published by Paul de Musset, brother of Alfred, in 1859 with the title *Chanson* (Paris, Magasin de Librairie). Debussy's *Chanson espagnole* is a duet for equal voices beginning 'Nous venions de voir le taureau/Trois garçons, trois fillettes'. It became no. 7 of the Vasnier Songbook (it occupies ff. 20 *v*−25 *r*), which was sold at the Hôtel Drouot on 20 June 1977. The Vasnier Songbook (41 ff. music) is a collection of thirteen songs written between 1882 and 1884, in which the *Chanson espagnole* is preceded by five Verlaine settings (*Pantomime*; the first version of *En sourdine*; *Mandoline*; the first versions of *Clair de lune* and *Fantoches*) and a setting of Théophile Gautier's *Coquetterie posthume*. It is followed by six settings of poems by Paul Bourget (*Romance*; *Musique*; *Paysage sentimentale*; *Romance − Musique pour éventail*; *La romance d'Ariel*; and *Regret*). The symmetrical grouping suggests that the thirteen songs may have been intended for performance as a complete programme by their dedicatee Marie-Blanche Vasnier, with additional help in the central *Chanson espagnole*.

13 Prix de Rome *envoi* of 1885-6 (now lost), inspired by Georges Boyer's poetic adaptation of the central character in Heinrich Heine's *Almansor*. In the same letter Debussy told M. Vasnier: '*Zuleima* is dead and it will certainly not be me who resuscitates her . . . I am looking for something supple yet unpredictable enough to be adaptable to the lyrical feelings of the soul and to the caprices of the dream.' This he found six years later in *Pelléas et Mélisande*.

14 Letter quoted by kind permission of The Humanities Research Center, The University of Texas at Austin (*US-AUS*).

15 He apparently succeeded Victor Hugo (1844-85) and was himself succeeded by Jean Cocteau (1918-63): his illustrious predecessors included

Robert Fludd and Sir Isaac Newton. Debussy may have been recruited in Rome to this secret Masonic order dating back to the eleventh century and the Knights Templar. For further details on this fascinating subject see Michael Baigent, Richard Leigh and Henry Lincoln: *The Holy Blood and the Holy Grail* (London, Jonathan Cape, 1982).

16 For fuller details see LO, 2, pp. 272-7. The original (longer) version of the same article by Léon Guichard appears in French in *Cahiers Debussy*, no. 1 (1974), pp. 10-14.

Chapter 3 *Pelléas et Mélisande* (1893-5, 1901-2)

1 Which dissects it into 11, 630 beats and some 600 key areas.

2 Fromont edition, p. 169, bars 1-13, the passage leading into Durand VS, p. 188, bar 5 (OS, p. 249, bar 13). See Chapter 3, 'The manuscripts', list of cuts, no. 3. The first (fifteen-bar) cut in scene 4 consisted of Fromont VS, p. 164, bar 5 − p. 165, bar 7, which would be inserted between bars 3 and 4 on p. 184 of the Durand VS.

3 Letter kindly supplied by Madeleine Li-Koechlin.

4 The typescript (38 pp.), a copy of which was kindly given to me by Mme Li-Koechlin, is dated August 1949. It was written for Éditions Le Bon Plaisir but rejected for having too many (169) music examples!

5 Auguste Martin (p. 39) gives it as 4 May 1892.

6 See Appendix and compare Ex. 20b with Exx. 20e-g. The Lehman manuscript is clearly a complete draft from which six pages have been lost, although these pages could have been inserted into the Bréval manuscript as ff. 3-5 (LPm, pp. 99-109) as James McKay suggests (1977, p. 7). The 'June−July 1895' date at the end of the Meyer manuscript (LPm, p. 84) is probably the date when the manuscript was gathered together and given to Henry Lerolle rather than its date of overall composition, and this has led to confusion by such as Lockspeiser (LO, 1, p. 222), who attributes to the whole of this manuscript the date early summer of 1895. However, it is perfectly possible that different parts of this fascinating embryonic manuscript were written at different times, and whilst the sketches for Act 5 (LPm, pp. 63-84) may well date from 1895, the sketches for Act 4 scene 4 that the Meyer manuscript contains (LPm, pp. 53-8) represent the earliest draft of that scene (cf Durand VS, pp. 246-67), probably from September 1893. This, elaborated and revised, eventually became the Lehman manuscript, which was then recopied with some cuts and amendments as the Bréval manuscript (LPm, pp. 91-120). Later revisions, notably to the start of this scene, brought it closer in line with the published vocal score, which was attained by means of at least one other working stage, the Boston short score (now on deposit in *US-NYpm*).

7 See the first section of the Bibliography, and LCr, pp. 61-3 and 321 n. The manuscript is now in *US-AUS*.

8 All references to Debussy's correspondence are entered in the Bibliography under 'Debussy', where full citations of the many editions of his letters will be found.

9 Ff. 1-4 can be compared with the Durand VS, p. 232, bar 6 − end of p. 239; ff. 5 onwards with VS, p. 254, bar 3 − end of p. 267.

10 As in that of 23 October 1893 in which he says he wishes to 'see Chausson lose his preoccupation with the orchestral backcloth [in *Le Roi Arthus*]

. . . Too often we think about the framework before the individual scene, and sometimes the magnificence of this makes us forget about the poverty of the underlying idea.' (*ReM*, 1925, p. 122)

11 Letter to his brother Georges of 20 April, cited in LOU, p. 30 n. 1.

12 Whose refusal to hear *Pelléas et Mélisande*, in contrast to Dukas, upset Debussy.

13 Later Misia Sert. It is doubtful if Louÿs intended to invite Thadée's brother directors Alexandre and Louis-Alfred Natanson as suggested by Borgeaud (LOU, p. 32, n. 1).

14 He was rather given to self-pity in isolation and once told Ernest Bloch that Robert Godet was the 'only friend I ever had' (letter cited in Sotheby [César Franck] catalogue for the sale of manuscripts on 27 November 1980, p. 80, no. 216).

15 Here *poids* could refer to the relative importance, weight, or even the orchestral forces in a comparison between the *Pelléas* scores of Fauré and Debussy.

16 Auguste Martin, p. 43, no. 152. Debussy also held firm about not permitting extracts to be performed in concert after 1902, as his letter to the Royal Philharmonic Society in London of 24 September 1906 shows (see Lockspeiser, 1936, p. 287).

17 Camille Mauclair: 'Claude Debussy et les poètes', *Programme et livre d'or des souscripteurs*, programme for a festival of Debussy's works, comprising the *Nocturnes*, *Prélude à l'après-midi d'un faune*, *La mer* and extracts from *Le martyre de Saint Sébastien* and *Pelléas et Mélisande*, given at the Théâtre des Champs-Élysées on 17 June 1932. The meeting with Louÿs and Mauclair must have taken place after September 1898 when Debussy moved into his fifth-floor apartment at 58 rue Cardinet, Paris 17.

18 The alterations to the Bréval manuscript (LPm, p. 91, etc.) suggest that he may have used this as a basis.

19 Published on 14 April 1902, which claimed that 'the *Pelléas* in question is a work which has become foreign to me, almost an enemy. Stripped of all control of my work, I am reduced to hoping that its failure will be prompt and resounding.'

20 Albert Carré seems to have supported Debussy all along against Maeterlinck, and the composer victoriously told René Peter on 27 January 1902 that 'Maeterlinck is in the bag and Carré agrees with me that his case smacks of the pathological!' (LL, p. 113)

21 Büsser (1955, p. 112) says that Carré only requested the extended interludes after the rehearsals on 6 and 7 April. He claims (p. 119) that Debussy was still working on them on 26 June, the day of the last performance that season and that they were only introduced for Messager's revival of *Pelléas* on 30 October 1902 (p. 124).

22 Originally planned for 23 April, but postponed until the 25th, then the 27th, and then finally the 28th.

23 As with other aspects of this vast subject, fuller accounts are readily available and the interested reader is directed to Messager; Büsser, 1952, 1955, 1966; Dietschy, 1962, Chapter 14; LO, 1, Chapter 18; and *L'avant-scène*, no. 9 (March–April 1977) – a special *Pelléas* edition.

24 It was reintroduced on 30 October 1902 when Yniold was sung by Suzanne Dumesnil. Carré complained in *Le figaro littéraire* (23 Sept 1950) that the scene slowed up the dramatic action as well as providing the opportunity for Yniold to become the principal 'target for sarcasm', but there is no evidence to suggest that Debussy agreed with him in the long

term. In addition the whole Noël Gallon saga may well be another instance of Büsser's unreliability, as Blondin was apparently rehearsing with the rest of the cast as early as 5 March. (I am grateful to David Grayson for supplying me with this and much other valuable information on *Pelléas et Mélisande*.)

25 Bibliothèque de l'Association des Régisseurs de Théâtre (P.4.1, 105 pp.) – cf *mise-en-scène*, pp. 52-3 and p. 73, with the Durand VS, pp. 156-7 and pp. 218-19. (The library is at 24 rue Pavée, Paris 4.)

26 See the list in Abravanel, p. 111, no. 1196; extracts in Dietschy, 1962, pp. 150-9; Vallas, 1958, pp. 238-42. For Debussy's response to some of his critics in *Le figaro* and extracts from the reviews in question, see RLS, pp. 79-82.

27 This shows how far *Pelléas et Mélisande* was from the world of Wagner's *Tristan und Isolde*, whose plots and themes of love, jealousy and vengeance have often been compared.

28 All extracts from unpublished Durand letters are quoted by kind permission of Durand et Cie, Paris, and I am grateful to Guy Kaufmann for allowing me access to their archives.

29 The furthest he went was to doubt to his friend Raymond Geiger on 13 July 1915 that she really had appendicitis when a performance of *Pelléas* had to be cancelled as a result. 'Alas', he lamented, 'it is still the theatre of war which does the best box-office business' (letter in the Lake collection in *US-AUS*).

30 *US-NYcobb*, quoted by kind permission.

31 See *L'avant-scène*, no. 9 (March–April 1977), pp. 112-25; Auguste Martin, pp. 60-3; Emmanuel, pp. 73-4; Abravanel, pp. 112-13; Wolff, pp. 138-9, etc.

32 See Brunet's review of *Pelléas et Mélisande* in *Le guide musical* (Brussels), liii no. 2 (13 Jan 1907), p. 29.

33 Letter of 23 May 1909, *GB-Lbm* Fr. Egerton 3304, f. 134. This assistance must have included translation, for Debussy spoke little or no English.

34 It was also mentioned in condolences sent by Gheusi to Emma Debussy on 27 March 1918 (private collection of Robert Orledge).

35 It was also only after Debussy's death that Maeterlinck finally consented to see his opera – in America on 27 December 1920. Two days later he told Mary Garden (1952, p. 111): 'For the first time I have entirely understood my own play, and because of you.'

36 American Musicological Society (various authors), *Abstracts*, p. 118, and see her thesis cited in the Bibliography.

37 Mélisande is often associated with F sharp, both as a key and a pitch, and the first part of the scene is based on the progression C sharp to F sharp, balanced by C natural to F natural towards the end (VS, p. 258, bar 12 – p. 267), though with F sharp still making its presence felt.

38 This letter was probably written to Adolphe Jullien, whose favourable review in the *Journal des débats* (16 May 1902) expressed surprise that a composer of Debussy's high principles had made concessions to public taste in permitting the suppression of certain sentences and the shortening of the scene between Yniold and Golaud after the dress-rehearsal. The text of the letter, dated 'Lundi' (? 19 May 1902) was kindly communicated to me by Margaret G. Cobb. I am grateful to David Grayson for the above suggestion.

39 This would be inserted at the end of VS, p. 85. This and all subsequent VS references in Chapter 3 are to the Durand 1907 edition.

40 Through which Roy Howat has opened wide the field of formal analysis of Debussy in his recent study (see Bibliography). For compositions like *La mer* and *L'isle joyeuse* the golden section can precisely explain events and relationships which were previously thought to be purely intuitive.

41 For further details see RLS, pp. 24-5, n. 1, and Schaeffner (1953).

42 From his article '*La chambre d'enfants* de Moussorgsky', *ReB* (15 April 1901; LCr, p. 29).

43 Maurice Emmanuel (pp. 135, pp. 145-203) lists thirteen and is the most reliable guide. Jules van Ackere (pp. 31ff) lists twenty, of which several are variants of each other (cf nos. 13 and 15; 2 and 16).

44 The example Kerman gives for Act 1 scene 3 incidentally comes from the start of Act 5 (VS, p. 268, bars 1-2), though this is probably just a printer's error in the placing of the examples.

45 'Elle est de couleurs et de temps rythmés' (*F-Pn* W.54 (1), p. 3). The date 1907 is suggested as the observation comes with sketches for *Ibéria* and was repeated in fuller form in the letter to Durand of 3 September 1907 (DUR, p. 55). Colour and rhythm were central to Debussy's aesthetic and were the elements he admired in Hungarian gipsy violinists (see his letter to M. Barczy of 19 December 1910; LL, p. 202).

46 Louis Laloy (1905, p. 246) comes close to suggesting this and makes the excellent point (p. 244) that the perpetual modification of the motif 'imitates the instability of our own reactions' which are never quite the same twice over. He also observes (p. 243) that VS, p. 85, bars 5-6 (which Chailley (p. 890) refers to as a transformation of the 'warning' theme first heard at VS, p. 62, bar 3), is in fact simply another aspect of the Pelléas motif (Ex. 22d). This would also help to explain its omission from Maurice Emmanuel's list of themes, which Chailley makes so much of.

47 This chord was to recur at strategic moments in Stravinsky's *The rite of spring*, Janáček's *Kátya Kabanová*, Berg's *Wozzeck* and Orff's *Carmina burana*, as William Austin has demonstrated (AMS *Abstracts*, 1978, pp. 118-19; see n. 36 above).

48 Such as Bartók's *Bluebeard's castle* and Poulenc's *La voix humaine*. Dukas's *Ariane et Barbe-bleue* is, in my view, wrongly seen as a successor, as its symphonic development in the orchestra is of a more solid and Germanic nature.

49 'Le florilège de Claude Debussy', *Programme et livre d'or des souscripteurs*, for the Debussy Festival at the Théâtre des Champs-Élysées on 17 June 1932 (see n. 17 above).

Chapter 4   After *Pelléas*: the Poe operas (*Le diable dans le beffroi, La chute de la Maison Usher*)

1 From an equally suicidal letter, written to an unnamed solicitor on the same day (*US-AUS*), it appears that Debussy's first wife was then suing for maintenance. The Maeterlinck reference to 'événements' is to Arkel's speech at the start of Act 4 scene 2 of *Pelléas* (VS, p. 201, bars 9-10).

2 Debussy's incomplete copy, mysteriously marked 'D.L.M.' by him on the brown paper cover, survives as *F-Pn* Rés. Vmd. 41. Only *Berenicë, Usher* and part of *The pit and the pendulum* remain. Twenty-four short passages in *Usher* are singled out in pencil (pp. 90-110) and there are three marginal comments in black ink, though the latter are not directly linked to any

of Debussy's librettos. Indeed the other selected passages are of little help to a study of the genesis of the opera and Lady Madeline's song *Le palais hanté* is unmarked.

3 Cited in Merkling, p. 8.

4 Robert Godet (GOD, p. 34) remarks on Debussy's 'sort of obsession' with the mere names of these Poe heroines.

5 *Cahiers Romain Rolland*, v (1954), p. 206.

6 Clues to Debussy's reading and current interests can often be found in the numerous literary allusions and quotations in his letters, a fascinating angle which Margaret Cobb explores in her book *The poetic Debussy: a collection of his song texts and selected letters*.

7 He may also have had in mind Roderick Usher's 'wild improvisations on his speaking guitar'; one of his 'fantastic' improvisations is *The haunted palace*, which symbolically mirrors his own interior state of mind with its reference in the third stanza to the 'lute's well-tunèd law'.

8 *US-STu*, n.d. (1 p.), reproduced as 'Esquisses inédites', I, in POE. This was to have been a cycle for baritone and orchestra and was never intended for the theatre. The motif in bars 3-5 of the sketch, however, shows distinct rhythmic similarities with the main motif of *Usher* (Ex. 34a), and in bars 10-15, Debussy seems to be foreshadowing the *Première rapsodie* for clarinet (also started in 1909) in both melody and triplet accompaniment (cf Durand OS, p. 3, fig. 1, and p. 33, fig. 9). The complete text of *La saulaie* as copied out by Debussy can be found as *F-Pn* Rés. Vmb. MS 19 and is printed in LOU, pp. 190-1. The Poe similarities, and thus the appeal to Debussy, are obvious in such phrases as 'fantômes de nos jours de silence' and 'roses . . . encor rouges de sang'. The words of the last two lines of the extract from *La saulaie* given here were omitted by Debussy, but they fit perfectly the untexted vocal line in the *US-STu* manuscript.

9 *F-Pn* Rés. Vm. Dos. 13 (1-2).

10 *F-Pn* Rés. Vm. Dos. 13 (3).

11 On the same day both Maeterlinck and Debussy signed a contract to this effect (Cain, p. 46, no. 155) which suggests that they were back on speaking terms for a few hours at least.

12 Plus 10,000 francs on delivery of the score.

13 Debussy's piece is no. 6 on p. 9 of the January 1905 issue. The results were published in April (p. 65). See Appendix.

14 Typed letter of 27 March 1918, private collection of Robert Orledge.

15 An advertisement (*New York times*) for the New York première of *La chute* at the Alice Tully Hall on 18 April 1978 mentions that this was the '75th Anniversary of the Commission by the Metropolitan Opera'. This would imply that Debussy started thinking seriously about *both* his Poe operas during the summer of 1903, and that Gatti-Casazza had a very good reason to try to secure some positive results from the composer in July 1908. Further details about the various librettos of *Usher* can be found in the Appendix.

16 Title of Stephen Walsh's article in *The observer* (23 July 1978).

17 The recovered single pages given away by Emma Debussy have still not brought the manuscript beyond half-completion and rumours of a substantial cache amongst the Busoni estate papers seem to have proved groundless.

18 That of Graf Mouen at Yale University (25 February 1977, Abbate/Kyr

version) has Roderick and Madeline sharing a bed-sitter and brought early-morning tea by the doctor. Madeline laments the death of her pet budgie as she sings *Le palais hanté* and chases her brother round the room in her death agonies (see Porter, pp. 134-5, for further details).

The production by Nikolaus Lehnhoff in Berlin *à la* Patrice Chéreau (5 October 1979, Allende-Blin version) has Roderick's friend 'dressed as a dude cowboy in Stetson hat, [who] enters by live pony against a Marlboro sunset to confront the doctor, villainously costumed in black to resemble Poe's Raven, and is invited to sit on one of the Thonet bentwoods strewn about the otherwise empty stage to observe his friend Usher, barechested and pigtailed, deliver his monologue from an unmade bed' (Robinson, p. 48). The musical 'merits' of the two versions (whose orchestral conceptions are very different from each other) will be discussed later.

19 Another unpublished letter to Durand on 8 June shows that Debussy did not expect to get this. Perhaps through last-minute nerves he was unusually scathing about his favourite producer, adding on 9 June, 'for once, let us hire Albert Carré out'!

20 *F-Pn* MS 14520. After revision and concentration this became the prelude in the 1916 score (*F-Pn* MS 9885).

21 For the years before his marriages. Debussy looked back on the time when he composed *Pelléas* as the happiest of his life: had he and Gaby Dupont stayed together, events might have taken a very different course.

22 Hereafter Lady Madeline Usher, as she is titled by Baudelaire and thus by Debussy.

23 *F-Pn* MS 17727, extra unnumbered page not included in Allende-Blin's vocal score (Jobert, 1979; hereafter VS).

24 See VS, pp. 36-41, comprising *GB-Lbm* Add. MS 47860 (3), f. 25 (pp. 36-8); *F-Pn* MS 17727, p. 1 (pp. 39-40); *F-Pdavid* (p. 41, lines 1-2, which should, I feel, come earlier in scene 2); *F-Pn* MS 9885, p. 21 (p. 41, line 3 – end, which was intended for the end of the opera, but which has Roderick screaming: 'Ah! damné! tu me l'as volée', a line not found in any other source). The spectacular demise of the House of Usher, complete with symbolic 'blood-red moon' (shades of *Salome*), and its envelopment by the 'deep and stagnant tarn', takes place in less than six bars of apparently fast-moving music!

25 Debussy was perhaps confused by the line before Ex. 31: 'J'avais tant besoin de vous voir' (cf bar 8). This is definitely a 1916 setting of libretto C as the lines set in Ex. 31 are missing in A and B (p. 7). Neither was skipping lines or setting a different word from that in the text unique, as Chapter 9 demonstrates (see Ex. 56).

26 More detailed textual comparisons of the three librettos, with excerpts, can be found in Orledge, *MQ*, 1976, pp. 536-47.

27 The rearrangement of B was made in early 'October 1915. Pourville' according to Auguste Martin (p. 83, no. 448), though the alteration of the 'II' of 'Scène II' to 'I' in the manuscript (p. 4) may date from as early as 1910. Debussy told Godet he had nearly finished C on 4 January 1916 (GOD, p. 147), adding 'je souffre comme un damné' (cf n. 24). He informed Durand on 4 September (DUR, p. 168) that the libretto was 'at your disposal', though he did not give him a copy until autumn 1917.

28 Hôtel Drouot catalogue, 20 June 1977, no. 107. Perhaps written after

Dukas received the letter cited at the start of this chapter.

29 Composed 1908-15 but not performed at the Paris Opéra until 9 June 1920. The libretto was by d'Indy himself, based on the medieval religious story *La légende dorée* by Jacques de Voragine.

30 My italics. Dukas is referring to Debussy's complete edition of Chopin's piano music (12 vols.) for Durand (late 1914 – March 1915, with the proof-reading extending to August 1915 at least). If this letter dates from 1917, it may also refer to the six violin and three cello sonatas of J.S. Bach edited that April for Durand.

31 See Bibliography, first section.

32 See *Pélleas*, Act 5, bars 34-5 (VS, p. 270), where Golaud sings: 'Est-ce que ce n'est pas à faire pleurer les pierres?'

33 Ex. 34b shows its origins in the cyclic motif of the String Quartet, as it occurs at the start of the Scherzo.

34 See Orledge, 1975, pp. 33-5. The published short score of *Khamma* was, curiously, described as a 'partition pour le piano, réduite par l'auteur', even though, at the time, no full score existed from which it could be 'reduced'.

35 Because he wanted to use them later in scene 2 (VS, pp. 22-3, bars 199-203).

36 *F-Pn* Rés. Vmd. 41, where there are no 'cymbal and tympani' indicated but rather a 'léger coup de cymb[ale]', and where the violas do not play 'on the bridge' (*sul ponticello*) but in 's[ons] h[armoniques]' (see interview with Robert Sherman, *New York times* (20 Feb 1977), and Porter, p. 136). Similarly, these indications do not come with the words 'LA PEUR!' on p. 94 (in Debussy's copy of *Usher*), as Miss Abbate suggests, but on p.109 as the brass shield falls heavily upon the silver floor at the crucial moment in the story of the *Mad trist* when Lady Madeline's struggles are first discerned in the vaults below.

37 The correct point in Debussy's score for this cymbal and viola effect would be VS, p. 40, bar 380 (*F-Pn* MS 17727, end of first numbered page), though this final section was only spoken in the Abbate version, apparently in a mixture of English and French! (Porter, p. 135)

38 This may help to account for the unexpected closeness of their friendship, and we know that Satie maintained his connections with Joséphin Péladan and his circle to the end of his life (see his letter to Victor-Émile Michelet of 23 November 1924 in Nigel Wilkins: 'Erik Satie's letters to Milhaud and others', *MQ*, lxvi no. 3 (1980), p. 417).

39 Guaita founded the Ordre Kabbalistique de la Rose-Croix with Joséphin Péladan and Dr Gérard Encausse (better known as Papus) in 1888, to which Henri de Régnier, Michelet and probably Debussy belonged. The schism with Péladan, who then founded the Ordre de la Rose-Croix Catholique (for which Satie was official composer), came in 1890.

40 (Paris, Albert Méricaut, 1910), Chapter 11, p. 135. Jean Lorrain was a pseudonym for Paul Alexandre Martin Duval.

41 As at the start of Act 1 no. 2 of *Le martyre*, where Saint Sebastian speaks emotively of the arm-guards of the imperial archers on which were 'engraved the zodiacal figure of Sagittarius surrounded by stars'. See also the end of Henry Bidou's review of *Le martyre* in the *Feuilleton du journal des débats* (29 May 1911).

42 Cited in Lesure, 1975, p. 160.

43 See Act 3 scene 1: 'Je vois une rose dans les ténèbres' (VS, pp. 123-4).

44 Scorpio and Sagittarius also played a substantial part in the initiation rites for novices in certain occult sects, as Pierre Mariel describes (p. 397): 'The neophyte who follows the path of initiation finds first Scorpio agitated by the passions of Mars, which will then be consumed by the eagle of Jupiter, guardian of Sagittarius, to allow him to arrive at Capricorn, the "gateway to the Gods".' Traditionally, the scorpion committed suicide when surrounded by a circle of fire and this symbolised the death of the novice as he or she left the material world to be spiritually reborn. The Prieuré de Sion, to which Debussy is supposed to have belonged, also had an extra sign *between* Scorpio and Sagittarius, called Ophiuchus (The Serpent Holder), but I have been unable to ascertain the significance of this. My thanks go to Roy Howat for pointing this out to me; and see Baigent, Leigh and Lincoln, pp. 72 and 425 n. 31 for further details. One further coincidence is that Poe's own life was ruled by the dark planets Jupiter and Mars (associated with Scorpio and Sagittarius), according to John Matthews, to whom I am grateful for this information.

Chapter 5 *Khamma* (1911-13)

1 Perhaps with *Khamma* in mind, he wrote on 27 July 1916: 'I am too old to begin the battle of yesteryear with *Pelléas* all over again. The masterpiece written in poverty is an old, old story.' (Letter in *US-NYpm*, Mary Flagler Cary collection, addressee unknown.)

2 He left his 25 million francs to the Pasteur Institute to show his disapproval of his niece's conduct (see Dietschy, 1975, p. 6).

3 The undated contract (*F-Pn* Rés. Vm. Dos. 13 (20)) was probably drawn up late in September 1910 as a letter from Maud Allan to Debussy of 30 September, questioning some of its clauses, is preserved as Rés. Vm. Dos. 13 (21).

4 Debussy cannot have seen her dance in 1908 as he was no longer in London by the time her season opened. In February and May 1909, when Debussy was again in London, Maud was stunning St Petersburg and Moscow.

5 She dropped the outer names after her elder brother, Tom Durrant, was hanged for the murder and rape after death of two young girls in San Francisco, where she grew up. Her expensive education (which far from perfected her written English) was rumoured to have been financed by an ex-Mayor of San Francisco, Adolph Sutro, who may have been her true father. She kept her private life secret, especially after her case against Noel Pemberton-Billing in 1918 (see p. 137), though some further biographical details can be found in Allan, Kettle, McDearmon and Moore.

6 The *New York sun* (21 Jan 1910) reported that during her first American performance at the Carnegie Hall on the previous night 'three times in the musical interludes a squad of four ushers rushed frantically down the aisle bearing an enormous pot of orchids . . . After the performance it was announced that the orchids were a little tribute of appreciation to Miss Allan from Miss Hoffman.' (cited in McDearmon, p. 91) Rumours that Maud was a lesbian were, however, unfounded.

7 Letter of 1 June 1978.

8 It was seeing Botticelli's *Primavera* in the Uffizi Gallery in Florence in 1900 that inspired her whole career of 'alternative' dancing (Allan, p. 63).

9   Maud Allan would have had to use the revised and expanded third French edition (Paris, E. Guilmoto, 1905), as Mrs C.H.W. Johns' English translation of the fourth edition did not appear till 1915 (London, H. Grevel); the story she used occurs on pp. 159-67 of the 1905 edition and pp. 172-9 of the 1915 edition.

10 I am grateful to Patrick Buckland, Reader in Modern History at Liverpool University, for help with this etymology.

11 *F-Pn* Rés. Vm. Dos. 13 (23), p. 2.

12 More extensive quotations from the numerous contracts and letters relating to *Khamma* can be found in Chimènes (1978, pp. 11-29, and 1980).

13 Vallas, 1973, p. 217. *Le palais du silence* was intended for the Alhambra music hall (see Chapter 8) and Debussy did not consider this to be any sort of drawback.

14 This was hardly the right description as no full score existed, see Chapter 4, n. 34.

15 Koechlin began work from the piano reduction (R), p. 7, bar 9 onwards. Debussy orchestrated 78 of the 458 bars, pp. 1-10 of the 80-page orchestral MS score (see Appendix). For further details of this collaboration, in which Debussy carefully supervised and even adjusted Koechlin's orchestration (carried out directly from R), see Orledge, 1975, pp. 30-5.

16 The proposal for Koechlin as collaborator was made by Durand who knew of his skill from his orchestration of 'Saint-Saëns' scenic trifle entitled *Lola*' in 1901 (Durand, 1925, p. 28). As Fauré had suggested Koechlin for this first commission, it is indirectly to him that we owe the bulk of the orchestration of *Khamma*.

17 All otherwise unacknowledged letters by Debussy, Ernest Bloch and Maud Allan quoted in this chapter come from the Paris archives of Durand et Cie and are quoted by kind permission. The forty minutes dropped to thirty-five on 6 August 1912 (see *F-Pn* Rés. Vm. Dos. 13 (24)).

18 *F-Pn* Rés. Vm. Dos 13 (23).

19 Now with the Maud Allan Company and the Maud Allan Orchestra, conducted by Ernest Bloch. She opened on 16 October at the 44th Street Theater, moving to B.F. Keith's Palace Theater on 27 November; her first performance here was advertised as the 'most important début in the history of vaudeville' (McDearmon, p. 98). Coincidentally, Debussy was also planning an American tour about this time.

20 *Nair, the slave: a love tragedy of the orient*, with music by Enrico Belpassi and a scenario by Pietro Boldini, which she performed in New York with a cast of six principals. Predictably, it told the story of a dancing slave who kills her master when she fears for her lover's life (see McDearmon, p. 98). The cynical might have called it a rewrite of the Ballet Russes' successful *Schéhérazade* (1910) with Maud Allan in Nijinsky's famous role of the golden slave.

21 5-5-3-4-3, making a total of 39 players. Bloch even told Durand on 21 July that 'Maud Allan declared to me that Debussy was engaged in making a reduction for small orchestra himself.'

22 This letter did not arrive till 1923! It belongs to Mme Suzanne Bloch and was kindly communicated to me by Margaret G. Cobb.

23 *GB-Lbm* Fr. Egerton 3304, no. 14.

24 This was curiously similar to Debussy refusing Ysaÿe permission for *Pelléas* to be given in concert form in 1896 (see Chapter 3).

25 *Voyages; film dansé* which was found to be too difficult for performance at the Opéra-Comique and was eventually replaced by *L'âme heureuse*, first performed at the Opéra-Comique on 20 February 1948.

26 Letter kindly supplied by Madeleine Li-Koechlin.

27 *Étude sur Charles Koechlin par lui-même* (1939, revised 1947), published in *ReM*, nos. 340-1 (1981), p. 65.

28 There is a notable similarity between Ex. 37 A and the bass theme at the start of the magic chamber prelude in *Le martyre de Saint Sébastien* (Act 2 no. 1, VS, pp. 30-1).

29 Only one page of sketches for *Khamma* has survived (*F-Pn* MS 17728), for instance, though appropriately they show the genesis of the Khamma theme (D) itself.

30 The reference is to the third of Ravel's *Trois poèmes de Stéphane Mallarmé* (1913), the only one not also set by Debussy in the same year.

31 *The firebird* at the Paris Opéra on 25 June 1910 (after which, backstage, he first met Stravinsky), and *Petrushka* at the Théâtre du Châtelet on 13 June 1911.

32 It is to these introductory trumpet-calls that Heinz-Klaus Metzger refers (p. 124) when he praises *Khamma* as a precursor of Honegger's *Pacific 231*.

Chapter 6 Nijinsky and Diaghilev's Ballets Russes (1909-13): *Masques et bergamasques, L'après-midi d'un faune* and *Jeux*

1 For the fullest available picture of Diaghilev's life and career see Richard Buckle's excellent *Diaghilev* (1979).

2 See Michel-Dimitri Calvocoressi: *Musicians gallery* (London, Faber, 1933), p. 136.

3 See Nectoux, 1979, pp. 20-1. As he says, Debussy's incidental music to accompany readings of Pierre Louÿs' *Chansons de Bilitis* in 1901 belongs to the same *tableau vivant* tradition, a mixture of dance, mime, poetry reading, song and choral items extremely popular in Parisian salons at the turn of the century.

4 The masque being a predominantly English courtly entertainment of the sixteenth and seventeenth centuries, and the bergamasque (*bergamasca*) a contemporary Italian dance using variations with a simple recurring harmonic scheme.

5 As well as calling him a 'contorted Chinaman', according to Mme de Tinan (interview on 1 April 1979). Laloy was, however, as French as Debussy.

6 A letter to André Caplet (CAP, p. 37) on 24 July contains 'a two-day interruption during which I wrote the book for a ballet for Claude Debussy and for the next Russian season'.

7 Nothing came of this project, needless to say.

8 Perhaps the 'ballet persan' that Toulet refers to later in a card to Debussy on 20 February 1912, or even a revival of plans for *As you like it* (see Chapter 12).

9 Nijinsky not Fokine. As Buckle points out (1980, p. 124), this shows that Diaghilev intended Nijinsky to be a choreographer 'as early as the first Saison Russe'. He may thus have intended to entrust all Debussy's ballets to Nijinsky's tender care.

10 The third tableau of Laloy's scenario for *Fêtes galantes* of 1913 hinges on a similar unmasking (see Chapter 9).

11 Cain (p. 54, no. 193) lists a water-colour sketch by an unidentified artist,

from Jean-Aubry's collection, marked '1909. Masques. Debussy', which suggests that some progress was made in the direction of a performance.

12 See his books on *Diaghilev* (pp. 185-6, 219, 223-9) and *Nijinsky* (pp. 279-89) for a fuller account of the genesis, performance and criticisms of this ballet.

13 The first performance was given on 20 February 1910, conducted by Gabriel Pierné, at the Concerts Colonne. *Ibéria* lasts about eighteen minutes altogether, and with Diaghilev's desire for novelty and its more suitable length, would seem to me to be a more likely proposition.

14 'Debussy au Théâtre des Champs-Élysées', *Programme et livre d'or des souscripteurs* for the Debussy Festival there on 17 June 1932.

15 See letter no. 3 by Emma Debussy in *F-Pn*, undated but probably 1916 or 1917. Debussy is described as suffering from 'flu, fever and shingles'!

16 *F-Pn* Rés. Vm. Dos. 13 (7). Diaghilev probably signed with Durand's London representative as Debussy's signature is missing from the document.

17 If the incident as Blanche describes it did take place it must have been between 12 and 17 June, for the company only crossed the channel on the 11th and the contract was signed on the 18th.

18 The legendary aeroplane in *Jeux* has taken a long time to ground. The first Diaghilev ballet to include an aeroplane (off stage) was *Romeo and Juliet* in 1926 (Buckle, 1980, p. 307). By coincidence Mary Garden claimed (1952, p. 87) that Debussy promised to write her a *Romeo and Juliet* opera after *Pelléas*, though there are no other signs of this.

19 Russian pronunciation of 'Nana' (Nyanya).

20 An interesting sidelight on this is that Diaghilev had visited Maeterlinck at the Abbey of St Wandrille on 4 October, perhaps to discuss a ballet version of his popular *L'oiseau bleu*, first performed in 1909 (see Buckle, 1979, p. 237). Was Debussy in mind for this project too? (Any suggestions as to the identity of the 'diminutive lady as biting as a mosquito' would be most welcome.)

21 With only minor differences in that bars 3-4 are an exact repeat of bars 1-2 in R (cf R, p. 42, bars 14-17, with Ex. 44, bars 1-4).

22 Letter cited by kind permission of *US-A US*.

23 These extra classes proved unpopular and she was nicknamed 'Rithmit-chka' by the company in jest (Buckle, 1979, p. 247).

24 viii no. 6, p. 72, signed 'Swift'; cited in Ornella Volta (ed.): *Erik Satie: écrits* (Paris, Éditions Champ Libre, 1977), pp. 134-5.

25 See Whittall, pp. 269-71 for a study of tonality in *Jeux*, and Eimert for a detailed analysis which shows the impossibility of applying 'traditional formal schemes' to the ballet, as Debussy had pointed out.

26 Letter to Pierné of 4 February 1914 (Cain, p. 67, no. 286).

27 See Holloway, pp. 167-79.

28 For instance, he makes oboes 1 and 2 and the cor anglais play continuously between figs. 46 and 47, and adds them to the melody line more extensively between figs. 68 and 69.

29 LO, 2, p. 182; and see pp. 178-88, and Souris for a fuller discussion of the relations between Debussy and Stravinsky.

30 BAR, pp. 109-10. The news of Nijinsky's marriage on 10 September to Romola de Pulszky and its disastrous effect on his relationship with Diaghilev were by then common knowledge.

31 Filed with the correspondence of Jacques Rouché, director of the Paris Opéra, in *F-Pan* AJ[13] 1206 (I). I am grateful to Roger Nichols for bringing this affair to my attention.
32 Whom Debussy knew well. She had invited him to her box at the Opéra on 24 May 1914 to see the Ballets Russes in *Petrushka* and *Le coq d'or* (ANN, p. 95), and was high up in Diaghilev's inner circle because of her lavish financial patronage.
33 Letter in the private collection of Robert Orledge.
34 Letter of 27 October 1920, kindly sent to me by Madeleine Li-Koechlin.
35 In *Messiaen* (Berkeley and Los Angeles, University of California Press, 1975), p. 102.

Chapter 7 *La boîte à joujoux* (1913)

Parts of this chapter first appeared in *MT*, cxvii no. 1606 (1976), pp. 987-9.

1 There was no fourth tableau ('Après fortune faite') in the original conception such as occurs in the Durand piano score, pp. 45-7. The third tableau ran from p. 37 into the epilogue (p. 48) but was subdivided.
2 *Comoedia* (1 Feb 1914; LCr, pp. 307-8). A translation of Hellé's version of the scenario can be found in Vallas, 1973, p. 239.
3 So did Mme de Saint-Marceaux in her journal after the 1912 première (see *Cahiers Debussy*, no. 3 (1976), p. 10).
4 *F-Pan* AJ[13] 1207 (C) (4 pp.). Undated letter written some time during the summer of 1919.
5 See Paap, p. 349, though his article does not make clear exactly when or where (perhaps Utrecht) the 'second première' was given; the production was by Feike Boschma and Peter Struycken.
6 *F-Pn* MS 14521, for two tenors, piano and trumpets, 'sans prétensions pour remplacer la "Christmas-Card" '. It also contains quotations from the *Marseillaise*, like *Feux d'artifice*.

Chapter 8 The Alhambra Theatre: *No-ja-li* or *Le palais du silence* and *Printemps* (1913-14)

Parts of this chapter first appeared in *CMc*, no. 22 (1976), pp. 73-87, and are reprinted with permission of The Trustees of Columbia University in the City of New York.

1 Opened 11 June 1913. 8d. a mile was the current fare for a long tour by taxi-cab; the fashionable haunts that might be visited on such a trip provided the tenuous link between the various items in the revue.
2 As in Theodore Kosloff's Assyrian ballet *Asiduena*, which closed the first act of *Keep smiling* (18 October 1913) and which used arrangements of Glazunov, Rimsky-Korsakov, Borodin and Ravel (conducted by Landon Ronald), perhaps in imitation of Diaghilev's Russian Ballet successes.
3 See Nectoux, 1977, p. 203. These two commissions to Ravel may have arisen as a result of Feure seeing Nijinsky's ballet troupe (formed after his break with Diaghilev) in *Carnaval*, which opened at the Palace Theatre, London, on 2 March 1914, and for which Ravel orchestrated four items from Schumann's piano suite.
4 'Du goût', *Revue de la Société Internationale de Musique* (15 Feb 1913; LCr, pp. 222-5). For fuller details and descriptions of, and pictures from the 1889 Exhibition, see Devriès.

5 Debussy probably chose to ignore Victor Segalen's letter of 30 January 1912 (SEG, p. 131) as irrelevant to this project. Segalen described the 'boring theatre music' in Tientsin (near Peking) thus: 'Once a year there is a Confucian hymn like those Laloy took down, and that is all'!

6 *F-Pn* Rés. Vm. Dos. 13 (9) (3 pp.) in French and signed in Paris by Debussy, Charlot and another director of the Alhambra Co. Ltd., M. Lavenais.

7 Manuscript in *US-R* (4 pp.), dated 17 January 1914 and described as a 'transcription pour piano et Hartmann'.

8 Nicholas Rauch sale catalogue, Geneva, 24 November 1958, p. 25, no. 95.

9 Letter cited by kind permission of *US-AUS* (Lake collection). The concert was probably that of 15 March which included the première of Koechlin's *Études antiques* (Op. 46, nos. 2-4) at the Théâtre du Châtelet, though no review by Debussy appeared.

10 Extract from his diaries (now in the possession of Madeleine Li-Koechlin), which mentions that Debussy had influenza. Koechlin wrote to Debussy on 16 April, perhaps to make a final refusal.

11 *F-Pn* Rés. Vm. Dos. 13 (11).

12 *F-Pn* Rés. Vm. Dos. 13 (10) (3pp.); unsigned and dated '1914'. M. Guy Kaufmann, director of Durand et Cie, says that this codicil was signed by Debussy and Charlot on 17 April 1914.

13 As the first performance of *Printemps* was on 4 May 1914, this would have meant notice by 4 June and delivery by 4 July at the latest. By common consent, this was postponed till 1 September 1914 on 17 April.

14 Probably early in April between reading and agreeing to the new contract. The 'Jeudi' on the otherwise undated letter in *F-Pdurand* could be 2, 9 or 16 April.

15 At the Théâtre des Champs-Élysées with Nellie Melba as Desdemona. Debussy also arranged to meet d'Annunzio in 'première loge 9' (ANN, p. 94).

16 *F-Pan* AJ 1208 (F). Letter of c10 June 1923, signed George [*sic*] de Feure.

17 In the Theatre Museum of the Victoria and Albert Museum to whom I am most grateful for permission to reproduce material relating to the Palace and Alhambra Theatres.

18 Letter of 30 September 1965 amongst the Lockspeiser papers in the University of Lancaster. This was kindly brought to my attention by Richard Langham Smith.

19 Not *No-ya-ti* as is often maintained (e.g. LO, 2, p. 207). There is no connection either between this ballet and Louis Laloy, as Dietschy says (1962, pp. 223, 276-7).

20 See Rauss for a full discussion of the genesis of this complex work and its several finales, with which much of the rest of the *No-ja-li* sketchbook is concerned.

Chapter 9 *Crimen amoris*, later *Fêtes galantes* (1912-15)

1 *F-Pn* Rés. Vm. Dos. 13 (5).

2 The poem was written in Brussels in July 1873 although the original version (*Crimen amoris – mystère*) did not appear in print until 9 January 1926 in *Le figaro* (ed. Maurice Monda). The revised edition was first published in *La libre revue* (1-15 May 1884) and was included in *Jadis et naguère* (Paris, Léon Vanier, 1884) which was put on sale on 3 January

1885. It also appeared in *Le chat noir* (28 November 1885) and a further revised version appeared in the 1891 edition of *Jadis et naguère* (Paris, Léon Vanier). For more information on *Crimen amoris* see Octave Nidal's study of Verlaine (Paris, Mercure de France, 1961), pp. 72-5.

3 The coincidence arises from the similar titles of *Crimen amoris* and *Amour*. The latter, which contains the poem *À Charles Morice*, was a collection of elegies written by Verlaine between 1873 and 1888 and published by Léon Vanier in Paris in March 1888.

4 *F-Pn* Rés. Vm. Dos. 13 (6). The new title is given as *Fête galante*, in the singular.

5 Their authorisation was secured only through the intervention of Ravel, according to a letter from Ravel to Ida Godebska on 27 August 1913 (see LCat, p. 136).

6 See Roy Howat's article on this 'thirteenth *Étude*' in *Cahiers Debussy*, nouvelle série no. 1 (1977), pp. 16-23. His convincing completion of the 'Étude retrouvée' was published by the Theodore Presser Co. (Bryn Mawr, Pennsylvania) in 1980.

7 See Laloy, 1928, pp. 245-9, and *F-Pn* MS 17673 (15 pp.), which shows that Marius-François Gaillard only had to complete the orchestration, some of which was suggested by Debussy in detail. The first (concert) performance took place at the new Salle Pleyel on 2 April 1928.

Chapter 10 *Le martyre de Saint Sébastien* (1911)

1 In *Memoirs of a ballet master*, trans. Vitale Fokine (London, Constable, 1961), p. 155 (cited in Buckle, 1980, pp. 159-60).

2 This article in *Mercure de France* gives a full account of the action, concepts and sources of *Le martyre*.

3 Something akin to being buried alive (cf *Axël*, Lady Madeline Usher and *La grande bretèche*), though in this case the result is not fatal. This decadent practice was more typical of the Emperor Heliogabalus (204-22) than of Diocletian (245-303).

4 D'Annunzio persuaded Astruc to add it to the plan on the following day, though both had reservations about its staging. Whilst *Le martyre* was published as a 'mystery in five acts', the première was in only four, with the appended paradise scene as the climax to the fourth act (see Cohen, 1911, p. 701).

5 *Conférencia* (20 Sept 1927), p. 325 (cited in ANN, p. 20).

6 *Cahiers de la quinzaine* (19 Sept 1911), p. 132. His attack on d'Annunzio's *Saint Sébastien* can be found in LO, 2, p. 166.

7 Roger-Ducasse's letters of refusal in November 1910 due to pressure of other work can be found in ANN, p. 114. Philippe Jullian records (p. 227) that Henry Février was approached, and as a precaution Ida Rubinstein also obtained an acceptance in principle from Florent Schmitt!

8 Debussy is referring to Maud Allan and Ida Rubinstein.

9 *F-Pn* Rés. Vm. Dos. 13 (4). This is the 'great news' that d'Annunzio refers to in his telegram to Debussy on 10 December (ANN, p. 54), for a copy was dispatched to him on the day of signing.

10 *Music catalogue 106* (Tunbridge Wells, Richard Macnutt, 1975), p. 12, no. 27. Perhaps written to Caplet in Boston around 10 December 1910.

11 Undated letter (probably 12 January 1911), quoted in Nicholas Rauch sale catalogue, Geneva, 24 November 1958, p. 17, no. 62.

12 ANN, p. 60. Probably the *Madrigal* that became the *Chorus séraphicus* (VS, pp. 24-6). This must have been sent in advance, for the complete first act did not arrive till 13 February.

13 In Charles Perrault's celebrated fairy story, which was the inspiration behind the second movement of Ravel's suite for piano duet *Ma mère l'oye*, which Durand had published in 1910.

14 Which d'Annunzio had decided on 7 February should be in French verse as opposed to liturgical Latin.

15 Caplet was conductor of the Boston Symphony Orchestra between 1910 and 1914. For a picture of Caplet and Debussy together around 1910, see Fig. 32.

16 See Appendix, and Orledge, 1974, for full details of this orchestral collaboration.

17 Nicholas Rauch sale catalogue, Geneva, 24 November 1958, p. 18, no. 64, letter, n. d. (4 pp.). Louis Ganne, an exact contemporary of Debussy and a pupil of Dubois and Franck, composed over 200 works aimed at the lighter end of the classical market. His operettas, like *Hans, le joueur de flûte* (1906), were popular in Paris and Monte Carlo, where for years Ganne was the musical director at the casino.

18 Letter, *F-Pdurand*, cited by kind permission. The start of Debussy's *Excelsior* interview had praised the art and passion of Palestrina and sixteenth-century liturgical music (RLS, p. 247).

19 This impossibly quick change in Act 5 was still a problem in June 1922 when *Le martyre* was revived (see Cuttoli, p. 20), and Debussy never wrote extra music to cover this technical difficulty, as he had done in the case of the *Pelléas* interludes.

20 Pubd in *Cahiers Debussy*, no. 3 (1976), p. 10.

21 See Cohen, 1957, pp. 37-8.

22 An American, Vidal-Hunt, who had been introduced to Ida Rubinstein by Georgette Leblanc, was interested in filming *Le martyre* in December 1913. Nothing came of this, however, and Debussy seems not to have been involved. I am grateful to Michael de Cossart for this information and for help with n. 26 below.

23 For further details on Debussy and the cinema see Richard Langham Smith, 1973, pp. 61-70.

24 Although after seeing d'Annunzio's *La pisanelle* in the theatre Debussy told him critically on 12 June 1913 (ANN, p. 86): 'you make use of material that is too beautiful . . . both for the mouths of actors and for the ears of a public whom the multi-coloured confusion of the staging has once more bewildered'.

25 BBC Radio 3 interview on *Music weekly* in January 1979.

26 Mr Harcourt-Smith says Diaghilev, but this is most unlikely. He also talks of a leopard, rather than the panther Ida is known to have kept, and the whole seems rather like garbled version of a story told by Léon Bakst. Mr Harcourt-Smith's father was then head of the Victoria and Albert Museum and was a friend of Debussy.

27 *Le martyre* was also revived on the stage by the Opéra in June 1923 and February 1924; by the Théâtre de la Monnaie, Brussels, in May 1924; and by Ida Rubinstein at La Scala, Milan, in March 1926, when the conductor was Toscanini. The merits of the subsequent versions in their various forms are evaluated by Raphaël Cuttoli (pp. 19-28).

Chapter 11 The remaining incidental music (1899-1913) and the plays written in collaboration with René Peter

1 On p. 77 Peter says that Debussy gave him 'two theatre lessons a week' for four years, but this is most unlikely considering the number of letters Debussy needed to write to him about the various plays.

2 (58 pp.) The selection committee included the editor Alfred Vallette, Henri de Régnier, André-Ferdinand Hérold, Louis Dumur and Rémy de Gourmont. According to a letter from Louÿs to Debussy (wrongly dated December 1897 in LOU, p. 106), only the last was likely to oppose the play. That *La tragédie de la mort* was published in 1898 is unlikely: in a letter to Louÿs (*RdM*, 1962, p. 34) Debussy claims to be sending him a 'new edition' of the work on ?27 January 1899, yet he also asks his permission for it to be edited by the Société du Mercure de France! See also PET, pp. 215-18 for more details regarding the preface.

3 From the *département* of Poitou in Western France which borders on the Bay of Biscay. It is possible that the berceuse uses a genuine folk melody, despite what Peter says. The contrived prosody of Ex. 62 lends substance to this argument.

4 See Mme Gérard de Romilly: 'Debussy professeur, par une de ses élèves (1898-1908)', *Cahiers Debussy*, nouvelle série no. 2 (1978), pp. 3-10.

5 Donnay began as a writer of comic sketches for Le Chat Noir and later became known for his elegant comedies of Parisian life, such as *Amants* (1895) and *L'affranchie* (1898). Donnay and Messager were Debussy's two sponsors for membership of the Société des Auteurs in 1902.

6 See Lenormand, p. 45, Michelet's *Théâtre*, vol. 1 (Paris, Éditions Pythagore, 1932), pp. 5-67, gives the text of this two-act historical tragedy set in fourteenth-century Brittany, which includes a British invasion that sets sail *from* Hastings!

7 The manuscript, in Debussy's hand (see Appendix), describes it as a 'comédie en trois tableaux'. See PET, pp. 78-88, and Lockspeiser, *RdM*, 1970, for further details. I am grateful to Richard Langham Smith for providing me with a copy of *Les 'Frères en Art'* from the Lockspeiser collection at the University of Lancaster. The three tableaux contain 7, 6 and 7 scenes respectively.

8 Maltravers and Raland, the sculptor, are described in scene 5 of the first tableau as being 'almost anarchists'.

9 A worldly, practical woman (then separated from René's brother Michel), Alice may have been the real reason behind Debussy's theatrical collaborations. Their affair lasted as long as she could contrive, and may have been the cause of the break with Gaby Dupont, who found a certain letter in Debussy's pocket early in February 1897 (LOU, p. 87). Debussy often expressed his true opinions about the Peter collaborations to women connected with René, in the sure (and cowardly) knowledge that they would be passed on.

10 A play by Gerhart Hauptmann, performed at the Théâtre Antoine on 29 May 1893 (just twelve days after *Pelléas*) and published in the same year (see LL, p. 87, n. 3). It had a familiar Communist theme about the proletarian masses and their struggle against Capitalism.

11 A notable year for theatrical plans, scenarios, and writings about the new techniques of the cinema.

12 Letter, probably dating from very late 1898 or early 1899, cited in PET, p. 220.

13 Written in collaboration with Robert Danceny and published by the Société d'Éditions Littéraires et Artistiques in 1905.

14 See LOU, pp. 156-9, for further details and pp. 195-6 for a full report of the première on 7 February 1901.

15 LOU, p. 158. Letters to Hartmann (14 July 1898), Godet (13 June 1902; GOD, p. 105) and Messager (18 June 1902; MES, p. 25) make identical Shakespearean allusions. Debussy saw Forbes-Robertson's *Hamlet* at the Lyric Theatre, London, on 15 July 1902 and was gripped 'like a child in a trance' according to Mary Garden (1952, p. 76).

16 The numbers come from the original parts (*F-Pn* MS 16280) and the omission of items could well be due to an oversight by *Le journal*. Most of MS 16280 is the work of a copyist and the lost celesta part was recreated by Pierre Boulez in 1954. The different realisation in the Jobert score (1971) is by Arthur Hoérée. It is unlikely that Debussy improvised this at the première as Vallas suggests (1958, p. 196): first because it goes against Debussy's principle of planning his theatre music down to the last detail in order to make it the best possible; and second, because cues for the celesta part occur at the starts of *Les courtisanes Égyptiennes* (no. 8) and *La pluie au matin* (no. 12). *Le souvenir de Mnasidica* (no. 11) has the most material copied by Debussy (flutes 1 and 2, harp 1); during the development of the project the number of *Chansons* was referred to as eleven, and *Le souvenir* may thus have been the one added at the last minute, making the total twelve.

17 Itself a return of the flute theme of no. 7 in augmentation.

18 Peter claims that this was in 1902 and that Antoine has the date wrong (p. 156, n.). See PET, pp. 154-61, for his full account of the affair. Antoine's production was scheduled for 1904 and the Shakespeare trans. he used was by Pierre Loti and Émile Vedel.

19 See Debussy's review of his pleasing but superficial comic opera *Muguette* in *Gil Blas* (19 March 1903; LCr, pp. 124-5; RLS, pp. 150-1) in which his literary style beautifully matches that of the music. Asked to expand on this in the issue of 23 March (LCr, pp. 127-8; RLS, pp. 153-4), Debussy added that whilst 'Missa is a kind and devoted friend of mine . . . the fault I find in him is his persistent plagiarism of tired old ideas, although he is by no means alone in this . . . I am only sorry that he does not put his undeniable facility and light touch to better use.'

20 Act 1 scene 1, line 89.

21 A retelling of fragments of a twelfth-century romance about Tristan and Brittany by the Anglo-Norman poet Thomas, published by Firmin-Didot, Paris (1902-5).

22 See Debussy's letter to Gabriel Mourey of 29 March 1909 in Marc Pincherle: *Musiciens peints par eux-mêmes* (Paris, Cornuau, 1939), p. 227.

23 Debussy's library contained a copy of Mourey's *Aventures merveilleuses de Huon de Bordeaux et de la belle Esclaramonde*. 'Les promesses et faitz du noble Huon de Bordeauz', one of the *chansons de geste* in the thirteenth-century cycle known as *Le geste du roi* was, through Wieland, a major source for Planché's libretto for Weber's *Oberon*. Perhaps this link with one of his favourite operas (in which Huon was the hero) was another reason why Debussy did not dwell long on Mourey's suggestion.

24 An allusion to Clemenceau's attitude as Minister of the Interior to the strike of 'postiers' (see LL, p. 174, n. 3).

25 Debussy also told Toulet in a mock interview in October 1912 that the project was 'extremely fresh' in his mind, rather than being in a 'very advanced state' (Toulet, 1926, p. 130).

26 In three acts with a prologue and eight tableaux. The text was published in *La petite illustration*, no. 434 (15 June 1929). Frank Martin also wrote an oratorio based on three chapters of Bédier's text in 1938-41, entitled *Le vin herbé*.

27 (Paris, Mercure de France, 1913). By coincidence, Louÿs also suggested *Psyché* ('the most dramatic and charming tale there is') to Debussy for a possible opera in April 1895 (LOU, p. 52).

28 Nicholas Rauch sale catalogue, Geneva, 24 November 1958, p. 25, no. 93.

29 Letter cited by kind permission of *US-AUS*.

30 Letter cited by kind permission of *US-AUS*.

31 There were apparently none in the manuscript although this has now disappeared. I am grateful to Roy Howat for this information.

Chapter 12 *As you like it*; Louÿs, Segalen and the projects from *Pelléas* onwards (1895-1917)

1 See the rest of this article for a fuller discussion of Debussy's links with Shakespeare. See LO, 2, pp. 246-53 (Appendix A) for more information on *As you like it*.

2 As expressed in *Gil Blas* (19 Jan 1903; LCr, pp. 73-5; RLS, pp. 92-4) and elsewhere.

3 This libretto, with the words Debussy wanted changed underlined in pencil, still exists somewhere. Its whereabouts since it was sold on the death of Mme Cahen Martineau are unknown.

4 Ambroise Thomas's *Hamlet*, complete with onstage alto saxophone solo, was first performed at the Paris Opéra on 9 March 1868. According to Schaeffner (1964, p. 451), Shakespeare gradually supplanted Ibsen on the *avant-garde* Parisian stage at the turn of the century, and Debussy's letters are peppered with Shakespearean allusions, as we have seen.

5 The two had first met in 1899 and shared an interest in Dickens and Stendhal in particular (see LO, 2, p. 247).

6 A prestigious Parisian choir whose championship of Palestrina and Victoria Debussy admired. He told Prince André Poniatowski in February 1893 that 'when you hear this music, you ask yourself why such a beautiful art branched off in directions where it would meet with nothing but disaster. For it is its very essence which was transformed, and it comes as a great shock that it managed to culminate in the [Paris] Opéra!' (Poniatowski, p. 309; and see RLS, p. 31, n. 2).

7 Apart from odd references in letters (to Durand, 11 Sept 1905, DUR, p. 33; to Walter Rummel, 5 Sept 1916, *US-NYcobb*) which refer to the English title.

8 Adapted for the Société Shakespeare into six tableaux by Lucien Népoty. Alfred Mortier in *Le courrier musical* (June 1917, p. 251) found the production marvellous, but complained that Gémier's so-called innovations at the Théâtre Antoine (players entering through the audience etc.) originated with Max Reinhardt in Berlin. Gémier had also caused the text to be modified considerably and new characters added, to which end Népoty even had Shylock return in the final scene to allow Gémier to be on stage when the curtain fell! (In Shakespeare he disappears humiliated in Act 4 scene 1.)

9 Seven extracts in *Vers inédits*, pp. 96-108, which included Toulet's versions of the main songs and various alternating choruses for huntsmen and foresters.

10 Cited by kind permission of *US-AUS*. Also quoted in Paul Valéry: *Lettres à quelques-uns* (Paris, Gallimard, 1952), pp. 62-3.

11 Published in Valéry (ed. Hytier), p. 1281. See Lockspeiser, 1973, pp. 95-6 for more information on the *Orphée/Amphion* projects.

12 *Cendrillon*, based on a French folk-tale, is a different story from the one performed as the pantomime *Cinderella* in Britain.

13 With Geneviève (or Psyché), la reine des aulnes, and Cendrelune on the side of the 'baddies'.

14 Originally published in *Scènes de la vie privée*, vol. 3 (Paris, Mame, 1832). It is retold twice in *La comédie humaine* by Bianchon: first with two other vengeance stories in *La muse du département* (1843), and second at the end of *Autre étude de femme* (1845), set in the Parisian salon of Mme d'Espard.

15 Later director of the Théâtre du Gymnase (see *L'utile aventure* in Chapter 11).

16 Which became known as La Bodinière after its founder M. Bodinier.

17 An Englishman who became a naturalised German and married Eva Wagner, the composer's daughter.

18 Louÿs gives the address as 20 rue Chaptal, Paris 9, though this did not become the Théâtre du Grand-Guignol until 1897.

19 See LOU, pp. 122-3, letter dated 'December 1898' by the editor.

20 *Aphrodite. Moeurs antiques* (Paris, Société du Mercure de France, 28 March 1896). Debussy refers to it as *Chrysis* and the confusion arises because *Chrysis ou la cérémonie matinale*, published as a *plaquette* by Bailly's Librairie de l'Art Indépendant in 1893, became the opening chapter of *Aphrodite*. See his letter of 10 April 1896 (LOU, p. 74) for Debussy's full appraisal. *Aphrodite* was a *succès de scandale* and made Louÿs' fortune: its fiftieth edition was sold out within seven months!

21 There had also been a plan to turn *Aphrodite* into an operetta for the music-hall star Yvette Guilbert (who wanted to play the role of Chrysis) in late October 1896. Maurice Donnay and Saint-Saëns accepted the project as librettist and composer and it was only abandoned because Louÿs insisted that his name should not be mentioned in connecton with the operetta, which proved unacceptable to its co-authors (see Clive, pp. 135-6).

22 LOU, pp. 122-3, n. 2. Limited rights were granted to Albéniz, Leoncavallo, Ernest Moret, Henri Rabaud, André Pollonais, Arturo Luzzati and Arturo Berutti. Berutti's four-act opera *Khrysé* was the first to be performed, at the Teatro Politeama Argentino in Buenos Aires in 1902 (see Clive, p. 186). Puccini also considered the subject in his search for a successor to *Tosca* in 1899, but rejected it in favour of Belasco's *Madame Butterfly* (see Mosco Carner: *Puccini: a critical biography* (London, 1958), p. 114).

23 This production was enormously successful and reached its 100th performance by November 1913, no doubt to Debussy's chagrin. The libretto was by Louis de Gramont.

24 See Fauré (ed. Nectoux), pp. 157, 160, 169.

25 Letter cited by kind permission of *US-AUS*.

26 Subtitled *Acta Rosae Crucis Templi* (Paris, E. Dentu, 1892). I am grateful to Roy Howat for bringing this to my attention, as well as Debussy's use

of proportional structures employing the principle of the golden section.

27 It was completed one episode at a time in conditions of forced labour and later published complete in 1901 (Paris, Bibliothèque Charpentier), subdivided into four sections or books. The inspiration probably came from a sketch Louÿs saw at the Moulin Rouge in February 1896 depicting the visit to Paris of several kings. These included le roi d'Yvetot, king of a small medieval principality which owed no allegiance to the French crown (see Clive, p. 133).

28 Which does not begin until Chapter 4 of Book 2 and only covers a distance of 7 kilometres.

29 In the archives of the Société Baudelaire, Rencontres Internationales des Arts et Lettres, which are quoted here by kind permission of Richard Isée Knowles. Extracts from these letters (wrongly dated) appear in Richard-E. Knowles' book on Michelet (p. 231), which states that the five instruments the Odéon had at its disposal included a harpsichord. I am grateful to Roy Howat for bringing this source to my attention.

30 Debussy used the same imagery when he was trying to persuade Antoine to engage thirty musicians to play his incidental music for Le Roi Lear (see p. 250).

31 Debussy was later greatly impressed by Hungarian gipsy violinists in Budapest and spoke to the impresario Barczy (who had arranged his visit) of the violinist Radics, who 'made one forget one's surroundings . . . You breathe the scent of forests; you hear the trickle of streams. His playing also tells the melancholy secrets of a heart which suffers and laughs almost simultaneously.' (letter of 19 Dec 1910; LL, p. 202)

32 c1930-5, PET, p. 194, n. 1. The date of 1903 comes from Dietschy (1962, p. 268, no. 112).

33 See SEG, pp. 52-3, 64-8, 93, 111, for fuller details on Siddartha.

34 The title is cut away in the manuscript (F-Pn MS 1005, p. 4) and may well have been altered by Debussy when he came to publish the Images.

35 See Appendix, and Myers, 1978, for fuller details. The facsimile extracts from the manuscript libretto in SEG, pp. 269, 287, show how Segalen noted down Debussy's suggestions in the margins, appending Debussy's monogram to each. Copious footnotes throughout the text (SEG, pp. 219-341) demonstrate the full extent of Debussy's amendments during the two earlier stages of Orphée-roi.

36 The article appeared on 1 November (LCr, pp. 239-43; RLS, pp. 295-8) and includes a long discussion of music and Nature, music in France, the need for clarity and simplicity, and the case for a revival of interest in symphonic music.

37 J'avais appelé la montagne, et la montagne avait frémi, sous ma voix!
J'avais aimé le fleuve, et il descendait avec des ruissellements sonores!
J'avais interpellé les hommes!
This came from the start of Act 3 in the first version of early 1908. In the final version, Segalen did take Debussy's advice for once and shortened the above to: 'J'ai nommé la montagne. J'évoquais le fleuve coulant.' (SEG, pp. 287-8)

38 See letters to Jean-Aubry (29 Sept 1908; US-AUS); Stravinsky (18 Aug 1913; Souris, p. 47; and cf the cantata Le roi des étoiles, dedicated to Debussy); and Godet (4 Jan 1916; GOD, p. 147). See also LO, 2, p. 177, n. 2.

39 LCr, p. 296. A revival of this one-act ballet, first performed on 27 August 1748, had been announced in *Le ménestrel* on 31 December 1910 (no. 52bis, p. 420).

40 See Debussy's article in *Le figaro* (8 May 1908; LCr, pp. 197-200; RLS, pp. 228-31).

41 Edited by Saint-Saëns and Charles Malherbe (later Maurice Emmanuel and Martial Teneo) and published by Durand between 1895 and 1924 (repr. 1968).

42 I am indebted to Brian Merrikin Hill, the devoted and unselfish translator of the writings of Saint-Pol-Roux, for bringing this proposed collaboration to my attention and for providing me with much relevant information about it.

43 Briant's excellent study, as well as those of Alain Jouffroy and Yves Sandre (pp. 7-57), should be consulted for further background information about *La dame à la faulx* and for a fuller poetic evaluation of the unworldly Saint-Pol-Roux.

44 This resulted in the 'version théâtrale', edited by Yves Sandre (1979). The description of the modifications comes from a letter of 23 November 1911 (Sandre, p. 47) to Gilda Darthy, whom Saint-Pol-Roux hoped to have for the role of ELLE.

45 Saint-Pol-Roux's Rosicrucian side can be seen most clearly in the three collected volumes *Les reposoirs de la procession* (Paris, Mercure de France, 1893-1907), of which the first (*La rose et les épines du chemin*) is a baroque prose poem (which Brian Merrikin Hill has translated but which unfortunately remains unpublished), dedicated to Gustave Charpentier, for whom Saint-Pol-Roux supplied (clandestinely) much of the libretto for *Louise* in the 1890s. See Briant, pp. 13-15, for more details on Saint-Pol-Roux's links with Sar Péladan and La Rose-Croix Esthétique.

46 1878-1914. Dupont was a pupil of Gédalge, Massenet and Widor at the Paris Conservatoire and achieved his first success with an opera *La cabrèra* in Milan in 1904, which won the competition organised by the Milanese publisher Sonzogno. His later four-act opera *La glu* was performed in Nice in 1910.

47 Tanya is the affectionate Russian form of Tatyana. Besides Tchaikovsky's opera of 1877-8, Prokofiev also wrote a score for *Eugene Onegin* in 1936 for the Pushkin centenary celebrations, but this was withdrawn after production difficulties. It was rediscovered in 1978 and completed by Edward Downes.

48 Letters on *Tania* are cited by kind permission of *US-AUS*.

Chapter 13 Debussy in and about the theatre: some observations and conclusions

1 *Les annales politiques et littéraires* (25 May 1913; LCr, p. 238). This analogy is first made *à propos* the third act of *Siegfried* in *La revue blanche* (1 April 1901), where Debussy speaks of 'la Tétralogie . . . Bottin musical' (LCr, p. 25).

2 See Gabriel Fauré: *Opinions musicales* (Paris, Éditions Rieder, 1930), p. 18 (repr. from *Le figaro*, 9 May 1903; and cf his reviews of performances of Berlioz's music in *Le figaro*, 14 and 28 Dec 1903, and 21 Nov 1904).

3 Director of the Opéra de Monte Carlo from 1890. His staged version of *Faust* was first performed there on 18 February 1893 and then brought to Paris. Fauré was later to suffer in his theatrical hands with the Monte Carlo première of *Pénélope* in March 1913.

4 *The etude* (Philadelphia), xxxii no. 6 (June 1914), pp. 407-8, cited in RLS, pp. 319-20.

5 In the *Revue de la Société Internationale de Musique* (15 Jan 1913; LCr, pp. 218-9; RLS, pp. 273-4).

6 In his preface in the form of a letter to *Pour la musique française: douze causeries*, ed. Paul Huvelin (Paris, G. Crès, 1917). The full text of this is given in LCr, pp. 261-2; RLS, pp. 324-5, and the extract cited is translated from LCr, p. 262. The lyric drama Chabrier died in pursuit of was *Briséïs*.

7 See *Opinions musicales* (1930), p. 125 (repr. from *Le figaro*, 23 May 1908); cf Debussy's enthusiastic response to the première of Rimsky-Korsakov's *Schéhérazade* in *My apprenticeships* by Colette, as quoted in RLS, pp. 148-9, n. 3.

8 *La revue blanche* (15 May 1901; LCr, p. 39; RLS, p. 34); *Gil Blas* (19 Jan 1903; LCr, p. 76; RLS, p. 94; 2 Feb 1903; LCr, p. 91; RLS, p. 114).

9 Probably some time during its initial run of only fifteen performances (due to otherwise hostile reactions) beginning on 6 March 1882. Debussy's father regularly took him to the theatre during his youth, though mainly to more popular *opéras comiques* like Donizetti's *La fille du régiment* (PET, p. 99).

10 Later renamed *Louise* (completed in 1896), which introduced Mary Garden to the Parisian public (and Debussy) when she took over the title role from Marthe Rioton at the Opéra-Comique in Carré's 1900 production. *La vie du poète*, a symphonic drama in three acts, was first performed at the Opéra on 17 June 1892 and was a sort of latter-day equivalent of Berlioz's *Lélio*. The bulk of Charpentier's later output borrowed from or reworked these early Bohemian autobiográphical essays. See also Chapter 12, n. 45.

11 Completed in 1896. See *Gil Blas* (6 April 1903; LCr, p. 142; RLS, p. 168) and *Revue de la Société Internationale de Musique* (1 Nov 1912; LCr, p. 211; RLS, p. 267).

12 See RLS, pp. 147-8 n., for fuller details.

13 He cites Leoncavallo's imported *Pagliacci* as an example of a work whose success was out of proportion to its artistic merits.

14 This was based on his 1902 experiences when he visited London at Messager's invitation; see RLS, p. 140, n. 1.

15 LL, p. 89. The other replies (minus that of Debussy) were published in Jules Huret's book *Loges et coulisses* (Paris, Éditions de *La revue blanche*, 1901).

16 Compare this passage with Valéry's similar views on *Amphion* in Chapter 12.

17 *Comoedia* (26 Jan 1911; LCr, pp. 298-300).

18 Letter to *Le temps* (8 Oct 1909; LL, p. 186) in answer to an enquiry 'Sur les théâtres de musique et de la disposition de l'orchestre' by the theatrical editor. Debussy's letter was published in the issue for 13 October together with the replies of Saint-Saëns, Massenet and Widor.

19 *ReM*, 1964, p. 118. The Salle Favart was destroyed by fire on 25 May 1887, after which the company moved to the Théâtre Lyrique (place du

Châtelet). In 1898 they moved to the Théâtre du Château d'Eau before the new Salle Favart was inaugurated on 7 December that year.

20 Jusseaume worked for the Opéra-Comique between 1898 and 1924 and Ronsin began there under Carvalho in 1895. Ronsin was responsible for the sets of *Pelléas* for Act 1 scenes 2 and 3; Act 2 scene 3 (see Fig. 8); Act 3 scenes 1 (see Fig. 31) and 3; and Act 4 scene 2. Jusseaume designed the rest including the deaths of Mélisande and Pelléas (see Figs. 6 and 7).

21 See Orledge, 1981, for further details.

22 That of 12 October is wrongly dated 16 October in DUR, p. 169. See also LCat, p. 143, no. 135.

23 See Chapter 12, p. 268.

24 The war can only be considered as an excuse for Debussy's abandoning *No-ja-li* (see Chapter 8). Debussy's cancer was diagnosed and treated only during the winter of 1915-16, and Paul Dukas told Édouard Dujardin on 12 August 1917 that he had dined with Debussy, before he left for St Jean-de-Luz and had found him 'in very good spirits. Durand told me that Debussy was in fine form and his wife had told a mutual friend that he was in better shape than he had even been!' (Dukas, p. 114).

25 *F-Pn* Rés. Vm. Dos. 13 (19), entries for 20 and 25 January 1908.

26 P. 32 of the typescript (38 pp.), a copy of which was kindly given to me by Madeleine Li-Koechlin.

Index of Debussy's works

General index

DATE DUE

JUL 1 2 1984		
MAR 2 7 1986		